Learning to Love

THE JOURNALS OF THOMAS MERTON / Volume 6: 1966–1967 / Patrick Hart, O.C.S.O. General Editor

Thomas Merton

Learning to Love

Exploring Solitude and Freedom

EDITED BY CHRISTINE M. BOCHEN

HarperSanFrancisco
A Division of HarperCollins*Publishers*

Grateful acknowledgment is made to the following for permission
to reprint previously published material: Poetry by Thomas Merton
from *Eighteen Poems*. Copyright © 1977, 1985 by The Trustees of the
Merton Legacy Trust, © 1968 by The Abbey of Gethsemani.
Reprinted by permission of New Directions Publishing Corp. Lines
from *The Bones of the Cuttlefish* by Eugenio Montale, translated by
Antonio Mazza, Mosaic Press, 1252 Speers Road, Units 1 & 2,
Oakville, Ontario L6L 5N9; copyright translation, 1983. "Motet XX"
by Eugenio Montale translation copyright 1990 by Dana Gioia.
Reprinted from *Mottetti: Poems of Love* with the permission of
Graywolf Press, Saint Paul, Minnesota.

HarperCollins Web Site: http://www.harpercollins.com
HarperCollins®, 📖®, and HarperSanFrancisco™ are trademarks of
HarperCollins Publishers, Inc.

Book design by David Bullen

FIRST HARPERCOLLINS PAPERBACK EDITION PUBLISHED IN 1998

Library of Congress Cataloging-in-Publication Data
Merton, Thomas, 1915–1968.
    Learning to love : exploring solitude and freedom /
Thomas Merton; edited by Christine M. Bochen. — 1st ed.
      p. cm. — (The journals of Thomas Merton; v. 6)
    ISBN 0–06–065484–8 (cloth)
    ISBN 0–06–065485–6 (pbk.)
    1. Merton, Thomas, 1915–1968—Diaries. 2. Trappists—United
States—Diaries. 3. Catholic Church—United States—Clergy—
Diaries. 4. Spiritual life—Catholic Church. I. Bochen, Christine M.
II. Title. III. Series: Merton, Thomas, 1915–1968. Journals of
Thomas Merton; v. 6.
BX4705.M542A3 1997
271'.12502—dc21
[B]   97–19840

99 00 01 02 ❖ RRDH 10 9 8 7 6 5 4 3 2

One thing has suddenly hit me—that nothing counts except love and that a solitude that is not simply the wide-openness of love and freedom is nothing. Love and solitude are the one ground of true maturity and freedom. . . . True solitude embraces everything, for it is the fullness of love that rejects nothing and no one, is open to All in All.

April 14, 1966

Contents

Acknowledgments

Editing this journal has made me mindful that work like this is never done by an individual alone. I have enjoyed the company and assistance of many to whom I gladly express thanks.

First I wish to thank Robert Giroux, James Laughlin, and Tommie O'Callaghan III, trustees of the Merton Legacy Trust, for appointing me editor of this volume. Together with Anne McCormick, secretary of the Trust, and Abbot Timothy Kelly of the Abbey of Gethsemani, they have offered wise counsel. I also wish to thank Brother Patrick Hart, O.C.S.O., general editor of the Merton Journals, for his confidence and support during every phase of my work. I especially appreciate his patience and his help in deciphering Merton's sometimes inscrutable handwriting and in decoding Merton's more obscure references. I am grateful to the editors of Volumes I–V – Brother Patrick, Jonathan Montaldo, Lawrence S. Cunningham, Victor A. Kramer, and Robert E. Daggy – for the fine example of their work and their readiness to share with me their editorial experience.

Special thanks are due to all those who helped me prepare this volume for publication: to Beverly Evans of the State University of New York at Geneseo, Marion Hoctor, SSJ of Nazareth College of Rochester, William H. Shannon and Francis Cecilia English, SSJ of Rochester for assisting in the translation of foreign language passages found in the journal; to Jonathan Montaldo and to Erasmo Levia-Merikakis for their careful transcription and translation of "Notebook 17." To the staff of the Lorette Wilmot Library of Nazareth College of Rochester, especially to Richard Matzek, Sheila A. Smyth, and Jennifer Burr for making available to me their expertise and the library's resources; to the staff of the George Arents Research Library, Syracuse University and to Robert E. Daggy of the Thomas Merton Studies Center at Bellarmine College for making archival materials available to me; to Jillian Brown for the enthusiasm and determination with which she tracked down countless citations; to Diane Curley and Anne

Wolcott for their skillful typing; to Linda Loree for giving so generously of her time and computer skill in the final stages of manuscript preparation; and to John Loudon, Karen Levine, and Terri Leonard of Harper San Francisco for the care and skill with which they transformed the manuscript into a book.

Members of the Nazareth College community continue to be supportive in numerous ways. I am grateful to Rose Marie Beston, president, and Dennis Silva, vice president for academic affairs, for their generous support of my work; to my colleagues in the Religious Studies Department and other faculty colleagues, especially those in Carroll Hall, for their day-to-day collegiality and good cheer; and to my students for their curiosity, interest, and insight, which energize my work.

I am especially grateful to my family and friends who listen, ask just the right questions, share wisdom and, sometimes, advice, and support me, in so many loving ways, in my work and my life. For them, I am more thankful than I can say.

I dedicate this volume to three individuals who have worked with indefatigable energy to make the Merton corpus available to readers: Robert E. Daggy, as director of the Thomas Merton Studies Center; Brother Patrick Hart, as general editor of Merton's journals; and William H. Shannon, as general editor of Merton's letters. Each, through his work as editor, writer, and mentor, has promoted knowledge and understanding of the life and work of Thomas Merton. Each, in his person, has embodied something of Merton's expansive spirit. For what they have done and for who they are, I and so many others are deeply grateful.

Introduction

For most of his life Thomas Merton kept a journal. To date five volumes of his journals have been published; this is the sixth; a seventh, written in his final years, will appear shortly. Together these journals tell a story that spans more than thirty years in the life of this remarkable monk and writer. "Journals take for granted that every day in our life there is something new and different," the young Merton wrote in 1940; a few days later he observed that "Every day is different, but also every day is the same." Certainly when he entered the monastery in December 1941, he was able to confirm his intuition of each day's sameness and difference. Each monastic day was intentionally meant to be the same as the next – structured according to a time-tried schedule of prayer, work, and study that created a framework designed to encourage persistence and fidelity in the monastic vocation even as it discouraged individuality. To that measure of monastic sameness Merton brought a poet's eye and a mystic's spirit as he looked around and within to notice and record what was different, what set that day apart from the ones that had preceded it – in the monastery, on the Kentucky landscape, in the world, and within his heart. Merton attended closely to the ordinariness of life and in doing so opened himself to its unexpected surprises. Compelling descriptions of the commonplace mix with astute, even profound, reflections of one who regularly penetrated below the surface of life to explore its inner depths. Glimpses of the realities of day-to-day life at Gethsemani are interspersed with visions of what monastic life could be. Acknowledgments of his own shortcomings and sinfulness appear alongside prophetic pronouncements against assaults on human dignity around in the world: against war, racism, totalitarianism, and inhumanity.

This volume, which covers the period from January 2, 1966, to October 8, 1967, contains a mix of the expected and the astounding. What makes this journal strikingly different from the other journals is the story it tells of the well-known monk and writer, enjoying a life of solitude in a hermitage on the grounds of the monastery, who suddenly falls in love and enters upon a tumultuous and unsettling period unlike anything he had ever experienced before. In his journal, Merton writes, with remarkable candidness, of his relationship with M. – how they fell in love, what their relationship meant to him, and how their love challenged, threatened, and eventually deepened his experience of solitude. This journal falls into four parts:

January–March 1966: a period of relative tranquillity during which his entries capture the ordinariness of his daily life in the hermitage;

April–September 1966: a time of emotional intensity during which Merton experiences himself as "a monk in love"; he is initially swept away by his love for M. and her love for him, is then soon disturbed by the contradiction it implies, and finally struggles to reconcile this newly found love with his life of solitude;

September–December 1966: a time of recommitment to the life he first chose when he entered the monastery, and now chose again as he reaffirmed his monastic vocation and rededicated himself to a life of solitude – aware that his love for M. was as much a "fact" in his life as was his vocation; and

January–October 1967: a time during which Merton settled once again into the routine of life as a hermit and writer.

Also included in the appendices to this volume are "A Midsummer Diary for M.," which Merton wrote in June 1966, and a substantial portion of "Notebook 17," written in January–March 1966.

A Journal: January 2, 1966–October 8, 1967

When Merton took out a new ledger and began this new journal, he was almost fifty-one years old and had been, for almost a quarter century, a monk of the Abbey of Gethsemani. During those years he had been away from the monastery only a few times. Yet he wrote of the issues facing people in his day with uncanny insight and counted among his friends people all over the world – making contacts and maintaining friendships through correspondence. A selection of his letters published in five volumes spans more than two thousand pages. He wrote many books, too numerous to name, though special mention must be made of his best-selling autobiography, *The Seven Storey Mountain*, published in 1948. During the 1950s and early 1960s, he wrote extensively on contemplation and prayer. Also in the late 1950s and early 1960s, much to the dismay of some of the very readers who had acclaimed his writings on spiritual topics, he began to address the social issues of his day: war, peace, violence, racism, and the abuses of technology. His stand was controversial in the Catholic church of his day, and for a time he was forbidden to publish on the subject of war and peace. Through his writings and example he demonstrated an openness to the wisdom of the world's religious traditions and readiness to dialogue with individuals whose vision of life and of the holy differed from his own. He had withdrawn from the world to embrace a life of silence and longed for even deeper solitude, yet he was deeply concerned about the world in which he lived. He had chosen a life of solitude, yet he was a warm, affable person – one who enjoyed human contact and companionship. When, in 1965, he was given permission to live alone on the monastery grounds, his dream of being a hermit was finally realized. But he was no ordinary hermit, as this journal and the others show. He continued to write letters, receive visitors (only somewhat reluctantly), and write and publish widely: in 1966, *Raids on the Unspeakable* and *Conjectures of a Guilty Bystander*; in 1967, *Mystics and Zen Masters*. During this period, he also wrote a myriad of articles, prefaces, reviews, and poems, while his earlier work was being read in translation in Latin America, Europe, and the Far East.

The entries of January – March 1996 show Merton learning how to *be* in the place for which he had longed during his life as a monk: a place of solitude that was his own. He was settling into the hermitage and enjoying the simple routines of daily life punctuated with prayer, reading, writing, walking, housekeeping, and just being. He was attentive to the ordinary, taking particular delight in his natural environment: observing the stars and constellations in the night sky, watching the ripples of water in his favorite creek, noting the antics of critters (birds, deer, woodchuck) with whom he shared the woods, and celebrating nature's springtime awakening. Living close to nature nourished him spiritually. Though he seemed genuinely content in many ways, he was troubled in others. The escalation of the war in Vietnam grieved him; the abbot's narrowness irked him and plans for a new monastic foundation tempted him; concerns about his health and the thought of impending surgery disturbed him. Even his newly found solitude weighed heavily on him at times. There were moments when he felt alone, days when he was frustrated, times when he was keenly aware of his own hostility, desperation, and meanness. But he was deeply grateful for the hermitage and the elemental life it made possible: "To go out to walk silently in this wood – this is a more important and significant means to understanding . . . than a lot of analysis and a lot of reporting on the things 'of the spirit'" (March 2, 1966). In the solitude of the hermitage, he was able to see himself more clearly, to realize how muddled and distracted he was, to admit how he was not free. Solitude invited him to let go of all that stood in the way of freedom – of involvements, of projects, "of all that seems to suggest going somewhere, being someone, having a name and a voice" (January 29, 1966). But that was not to be accomplished easily or quickly; he realized that he needed to embrace solitude, again and again. "What matters," Merton wrote on January 29, 1966, just two days before his fifty-first birthday, "is to love, to be in one place in silence." Read in retrospect those lines seem to auger what lay ahead: an invitation to learn about love, freedom, and solitude in ways he could not possibly have imagined.

Merton left the hermitage to go to the hospital for back surgery on March 23. A week later he met M., a student nurse assigned to care for him, and they fell in love. In the weeks and months that followed, as spring turned to summer, they exchanged letters, talked on the phone when Merton was able to call, and spent some time together at Gethsemani and in Louisville. Their visits were few, hours alone fewer still. But, almost from the beginning, their love blossomed and, almost from the beginning, Merton knew that the relationship could not endure. He was, after all, a monk.

Journal entries Merton wrote between April and September 1966 reflect his amazement and gratitude as well as his ambivalence and anxiety. That he should at this point in his life experience love in this way – with all of its passion and mystery – astonished and frightened him and, as one might expect, the experience also bewildered him. Recognizing in himself the "deep emotional need for feminine companionship and love," Merton was discovering, apparently for the first time, what it felt like not only to love but to be loved by another.

I have never seen so much simple, spontaneous, total love. And I realize that the deepest capacities for human love in me have never even been tapped, that I too can love with an awful completeness. Responding to her has opened up the depths of my life in ways I can't begin to understand and analyze now. (May 9, 1966)

Some years before, in his book *The New Man*, Merton had observed that the "vocation to charity is a call not only to love but to be loved," insisting that "we cannot love unless we also consent to be loved in return." What Merton had earlier realized intellectually he now knew experientially. And he recognized that the experience had the potential to transform him: "I feel I must fully surrender to it because it will change and heal my life in a way that I fear, but I think it is necessary – in a way that will force me first of all to receive an enormous amount of love (which to tell the truth I have often feared)" (June 3, 1966).

He was "scared by so much love" and withdrew when he thought "it can't possibly be real, there must be a catch in it somewhere." There were other reasons to be fearful: he saw the contradiction, the risk, the duplicity, the potential for delusion, the possibility of it all getting out of hand. And though his spirit soared, he was also full of anguish and torment – for himself and for M. He thought of her pain and suffering and feared hurting her; he realized that it might be "in some ways worse for her" than for him.

Between April and October 1966, Merton wrote a series of poems inspired by his love for M. Five of the poems that he copied into his journal are included in this volume. While Merton was critical of the view of his love for M. presented in his journal, noting on September 6 that what he wrote was "a bit distorted by self-questioning, anxiety and guilt . . . too much of a tendency to question," he felt that the poems came closest to expressing what was in his heart. He shared these poems with M. and apparently could not help sharing them with others too. In April, he read "With the World in My Bloodstream" to the novices and later considered reading other poems on tape. When he told his friends Victor and Carolyn Hammer about the poems, they wanted to print them. A "very elegantly printed, strictly limited edition: a real work of art" might be a possibility, Merton thought, provided the identity of the poet was concealed. "Few people will have had such a memorial to their living love," he remarked in "A Midsummer Diary." Merton entrusted copies of the poems to his friend Jay Laughlin for safekeeping and eventual publication; in 1985, Laughlin oversaw the printing of *Eighteen Poems* in a limited edition of 250 copies by New Directions.

The summer was something of a roller coaster for Merton (as it must have been for M.) – with intense highs and acute bouts of fear and anxiety. He was alternately amazed and appalled, elated and distraught. By September he seemed to see things more clearly ("Though I have admitted this verbally, today I could see in my 'right mind' that if I had been really aware of the meaning of my vows and my commitment I would not have let my love for her develop as it did at the beginning") and he took responsibility:

The wrong steps began with my first love letter, and the phone call on April 13 arranging to see her in town on the 26th.

Yet even as I say this and admit it, there is a sense in which I see it was almost inevitable. I had fallen so deeply in love with her already that it was difficult to do otherwise – yet I suppose I could have made another choice. And yet too – I am glad I didn't. . . . I can admit it was out of place, yet I cannot altogether repudiate everything about it. Least of all can I in any way repudiate, or seem to repudiate *her.* (September 4, 1966)

Later in the day as he reread the journal to see if he "could make any sense out of it" he remembered more: how lonely he was for M. when he left the hospital, his "anxiety to hear from her" and the impact of her first letter, his distress at the passion that talking with her aroused in him, his "obscure sense that she was somehow supposed to enter deeply" into his life, their unrealism, imprudence, and carelessness, "the moments of miserable confusion." He summed it up this way:

The overall impression: awareness of my own fantastic instability, complexity, frailty, and the nearness to disaster in May and early June. . . . And in the end: respect for M. and for our love, gratitude for it, sense of the underlying reality and seriousness of it, sense of immense responsibility to her, desire for her happiness, realization also that in spite of all my hectic confusion (and her seductiveness), I owe a great deal to her love and this is a lasting reality that cannot be denied – and we *do* belong to each other. In a way for keeps! (September 4, 1966)

Note the caveat: "In a way." The next day Merton reflected further on "the really overwhelming experience of the summer," admitting that it was an experience in which he did not fully recognize himself: "Sitting up and reading tonight through all this was, however, a kind of shattering experience in its own way – seeing the whole thing all at once in all its frank and pitiable confusion yet also in its goodness and joy – and above all in it danger, so much greater than I realized. . . ." It was a humbling experience:

What I see is this: that while I imagine I was functioning fairly successfully, I was living a sort of patched up, crazy existence, a series of rather hopeless improvisations, a life of unreality in many ways. Always underlain by a certain solid silence and presence, a faith, a clinging to the invisible God – and this clinging (perhaps rather His holding on to me) has been in the end the only thing that made sense. The rest has been absurdity. . . . I will probably go on like this for the rest of my life. There is "I" – this patchwork, this bundle of questions and doubts and obsessions, this gravitation to silence and to the woods and to love. This incoherence!! (September 5, 1966)

On September 8 he made a commitment in writing, witnessed by his abbot, "to live in solitude for the rest of my life" (September 10, 1966). Then, just days later, he called M., enjoyed talking with her, and soon felt guilty about the call, which involved "a certain duplicity." Clearly the break was not complete, nor would it be final in the months that followed. They continued to have sporadic contact. Still the emotional intensity of the summer months was behind him, and in the months that followed his life gradually returned to "normal" as he set about the task of reclaiming his solitude. Though the romance ebbed, Merton's affection for M. endured. In October, when Merton was again a patient at St. Anthony's Hospital and M. visited him a few times, he admitted that he did not see her as much as he wanted to, but also that "really for the first time since April," he could see "that the affair is no longer so intense" and he felt "much freer." He began to see the relationship with M. as "an attempt to escape the demands" of his vocation: "Not conscious, certainly. But a substitution of human love (and erotic love after all) for a special covenant of loneliness and solitude which is the very heart of my vocation." At the same time he was struggling to reconcile the two – his love for M. and his vocation to live love in solitude – as this passage, written in late November 1966, shows:

Somehow in the depths of my being I know that love for her can exist with my solitude, but everything depends on my fidelity to a vocation that there is no use trying too much to rationalize. It is there. It is a root-fact of my existence.

The last day of 1966 was a "dark, rough, depressed day but after a lot of anguish it ended in hope and comfort" and Merton began the new year with the resolve "to get back in right order" and to achieve an "inner detachment." He was determined to recover what he had termed "a life without care" in his last address to the novitiate on August 20, 1965, just before he moved into the hermitage. Merton saw the phrase as descriptive of monastic life and indeed of Christian life, but most especially as expressive of the meaning of the hermit life. A life without care is synonymous with a life of inner freedom in which anxiety and concern about all things – work, prayer, relationships – are cast upon the Lord. A life without care is not a life characterized by disinterest, lack of involvement, or refusal to act responsibly. It is life lived "in right order." For Merton, a life without care meant a life consistent with his commitment to solitude. Where M. was concerned, Merton succeeded more or less in getting his life back in "right order." Certainly there were fewer calls and letters. Yet he continued to think of M. and remember their times together. It was apparent that as the new year dawned and unfolded he looked back with a little regret and much relief.

Though Merton's love for M. is a prominent motif, the journal documents other aspects of his life and thought as well. The journal is a record of what Merton was reading and writing, the reading often leading to writing.

Immersion in the writings of Albert Camus resulted in a series of essays. A fascination with William Faulkner led first to informal talks to the monks and then several essays. Early in 1967, he came across the story of Ishi and wrote a review of Theodora Kroeber's *Ishi in Two Worlds* (1964) for *The Catholic Worker* (March 1967), then a handful of essays (which were collected and published posthumously in 1976 under the title *Ishi Means Man*). Merton's interest in indigenous peoples led him to study the Cargo Cults and to read anthropology. Though Merton lived in the relative isolation of the hermitage, he was hardly alone. His companions included a host of writers he read with interest, enthusiasm, and pleasure – writers such as René Char, Edwin Muir, Rainer Maria Rilke, Eugenio Montale, Jean-Paul Sartre, T. S. Eliot, John Milton, and Louis Zukofsky. He corresponded with old friends and developed new contacts, including feminist theologian Rosemary Radford Ruether, whom Merton described as "the most fiercely anti-monastic person" he knew. She sent him the manuscript of *The Church Against Itself* and challenged him to rethink and defend his monastic vocation. The struggles of the 1960s – the war in Vietnam, racial conflicts, changes in the church, monastic reform – all captured Merton's attention. He was increasingly disturbed by what he saw happening in America: as he wrote in September 10, 1967, "A feeling of great violence is in the air everywhere."

As this journal ends in October 1967, we leave Merton reflecting on his "lifelong homelessness, rootlessness." Merton was feeling an urge to travel. Of course, the abbot would not approve of Merton's participation in the meetings and conferences to which he was receiving invitations; Merton vacillated between frustration and a sense that it was for the best. Plans for a new monastic foundation in Chile were under way and once again he was tempted to go to Latin America and live there as a hermit. Dom James refused permission. Merton acquiesced, seemingly content "to live here and meditate and take advantage of the silence of the woods."

Reading Gaston Bachelard's philosophical reflection on space, Merton thought about places in his life: Gethsemani, where he felt like "an alien" despite being so identified with "this strange place"; the hermitage, which Merton felt was "OK"; and a new place toward which he felt some ambivalence – the Merton Room at Bellarmine College in Louisville (which became the Thomas Merton Studies Center), which struck Merton as a place "Where my papers live. Where my papers are more than I am." The Merton Room, he remarked, was an image of his lifelong homelessness: "A place . . . in which a paper-self builds its nest to be visited by strangers in a strange land of unreal intimacy." Meanwhile he was hard at work on a long poem, *Geography of Lograire*, in which he was locating himself in a larger world, hoping that it would be his "final liberation from all diaries." "Maybe that is my one remaining task," he mused.

"A Midsummer Diary for M."

"A Midsummer Diary for M.," one of two additional accounts Merton wrote during the summer of 1966 about his relationship with M., appears as an appendix in this volume. Merton entrusted to his friend, James Laughlin, the second account, written in July 1966 and entitled "Retrospect." "Retrospect" was not made available for publication. Merton shared both accounts with M. He started "A Midsummer Diary" on June 17 and wrote feverishly for a week, producing thirty-two pages of single-spaced typed text – some twenty-three thousand words. When he began, he was still reeling from two experiences that shook him deeply: an intense visit with M. on June 12 and a confrontation with the abbot on June 14. The visit with M. scared him. To make matters worse, one of the monks had overheard a call to M. and reported Merton to the abbot. Merton went to Dom James and owned up "to the phone calls." Though the abbot was "kind and tried to be understanding to some extent," he called for "a complete break." "A Midsummer Diary" shows Merton struggling with the inevitable separation.

"A Midsummer Diary" is part journal, part love letter. It presents a picture of Merton as M.'s *lover:* passionate, tender, vulnerable, melancholy, full of longing, lonely, confused, and anguished. The diary also reveals Merton as the *hermit monk* struggling to make sense of this passionate love and searching for ways to reconcile love and solitude, turning his loneliness for M. into a dimension of "a general loneliness" that is his "ordinary climate" and insisting that "love and solitude must test each other" in one who seeks solitude. Solitude is an act, Merton writes, not something one undergoes "like standing in a cold shower," and it is the act of a person in all his or her needfulness. "The only solitude is the solitude of the frail, mortal, limited, distressed, rebellious human person, made of his loves and fears, facing his own true present" and opening himself to others and to God. At the heart of solitude is mystery and the solitary is called to "return to the heart of life and oneness, losing himself not in the massive illusion but simply in the root reality . . . plunging through the center of his own nothingness and coming out into the All which is the Void and which is . . . the Love of God."

Recognizing the conflict between his love for M. and his commitment to solitude, he appears convinced that, in some mysterious way, the two realities can be reconciled:

If I could have both solitude and M. (it might be theoretically possible), then I would certainly take both. But as in concrete fact the issue becomes a choice: then I choose both in another form. She will be my love but in this absurd and special way.

An evasion of the hard reality? A profound insight into solitude transformed by love? Probably both. Perhaps Merton comes closest to the heart of the matter when he consigns what he is experiencing to the realm of mystery, admitting that "I will never really understand on earth what relation this love has to my solitude. I cannot help placing it at the very heart of my aloneness, and not just on the periphery somewhere."

Some Personal Notes ("Notebook 17"): The Beginning of 1966

Merton was in the habit of keeping working notebooks into which he copied notes from his reading, reflected on what he found there, jotted down ideas for what he was writing, drafted poems, made lists of work done and planned, and occasionally recorded more personal reflections in journal-like entries. "Notebook 17" (October 1965–early March 1966) is unusual among his notebooks in that it *is* actually a journal. The first section of "Notebook 17" (October–December 1965) was published as an appendix in the preceding volume of Thomas Merton's journals, *Dancing in the Water of Life*, edited by Robert E. Daggy. The remainder of "Notebook 17" appears in this volume. The themes that Merton takes up "Notebook 17" – hermit life, solitude, and freedom – weave their way in and out of his primary journal.

This volume ends with "A Postscript," a selection from another notebook Merton kept between March and July 1966.

Editor's Reflection

Though this volume chronicles a relationship, it tells but one side of the story: Merton's. He was clear about his own desire to tell his story:

I have no intention of keeping the M. business entirely out of sight. I have always wanted to be completely open, both about my mistakes and about my effort to make sense out of my life. The affair with M. is an important part of it - and shows my limitations as well as a side of me that is – well, it needs to be known too, for it is a part of me. My need for love, my loneliness, my inner di-

vision, the struggle in which solitude is at once a problem and a "solution."
(May 11, 1967)

Merton's openness – in this journal as in others – is admirable. But his personal candidness intrudes on the privacy of people in his life. This is especially true of M. because of the nature of their relationship. It seems important to acknowledge that the account that we read here is Merton's: it reflects *his* recollection and is shaped by the meaning *he* finds in and gives to this relationship. Merton shapes the narrative. M. has no voice of her own here. She remains an anonymous figure in this volume, deliberately identified by the editor as M. (though Merton used her name), not to diminish her but to acknowledge the privacy that is her due.

This journal, like the others, deserves to be read as a chapter in Merton's life story, its significance neither discounted nor permitted to dominate the Merton story. Thomas Merton was a complex and paradoxical figure – monk, spiritual master, social critic, and an ordinary human being. This journal shows him as he was: capable of profundity and pettiness, sensitivity and self-absorption, insight and illusion, focus and distraction. What sets him apart is the expansiveness of his spirit and his candor. Perhaps by telling his story, he invites us to reflect on our own stories. In learning to love, Merton was made to explore the very depths of solitude and freedom, and, perhaps, by sharing his exploration with us, he invites us to do the same.

Editor's Note: Editorial intrusions have been kept to a minimum. Merton's journal, "A Midsummer Diary," and "Notebook 17" appear as written with two exceptions: the use of initials for certain names and a few deletions, made to protect the privacy of the individuals involved. Deletions are duly noted in the text with "[. . .]." All other ellipses are Merton's own. Identifications and brief explanatory notes appear in brackets as do translations of foreign language passages. Longer explanatory notes appear in footnotes; these have been used sparingly. Merton had the practice of dating each journal entry and indicating that he was beginning a new entry with a symbol of a cross (+). Though this symbol is not reproduced in this volume, spacing between entries reflects Merton's own divisions. Except for "A Midsummer Diary," the content of this volume has been transcribed from Merton's own hand. In the few instances in which it has been impossible to decipher Merton's script, the missing word is noted as "[indecipherable]."

Merton took the epigraph for this journal from a poem entitled *"E Alma que Sufrio de Ser su Cuerpo"* ["The Soul That Suffered from Being Its Body"].

See César Vallejo, *Poemas Humanos Human Poems* (trans. Clayton Eshleman [New York: Grove Press, 1968]; Spanish ed., Paris, 1939).

General Editor's Note: For the sole purpose of protecting the privacy of persons still living, the members of the Merton Legacy Trust and the Abbot of Gethsemani have asked Christine Bochen, the editor of this volume of the journals, to delete a very few brief passages involving the invasion of other persons' privacy, and to indicate the deletion ellipses within editorial brackets.

– Patrick Hart, O.C.S.O.

Tu pobre hombre vives, no lo niegues
Si mueres, no lo niegues
Si mueres de tu edad! ay! y de tu epoca.

You poor man, you live; don't deny it,
if you die; don't deny it,
if you die from your age, ay! and from your times.

César Vallejo

PART I

Being in One Place

January 1966–March 1966

The one thing for which I am most grateful: this hermitage. . . . I am just beginning to really get grounded in solitude.

March 23, 1966

January 2, 1966. Feast of Holy Name of Jesus

It has been raining steadily for almost 36 hours. This morning toward the end of my meditation the rain was pouring down on the roof of the hermitage with great force and the woods resounded with tons of water falling out of the sky. It was great! A good beginning for a New Year. Yesterday in a lull I was looking across the valley at black wet hills, sharply outlined against the woods, and white patches of water everywhere in the bottoms: a landscape well etched by serious weather.

Working on an essay for Hildegard Goss-Mayr ([for] *Der Christ in der Welt*). Reading E. A. Burtt's book, sent by him from Cornell – and galleys of a good book on the Church trans[lated] from Dutch [*The Grave of God: Has the Church a Future?* New York, 1967]. The author is an Augustinian, R. Adolfs. Still have Endo Mason's excellent book on [Rainer Maria] Rilke and England. Reading Romans in *lectio* and finding it difficult (chs. 5–6). Finished a curious journalistic book on the liberation of Paris – a symbolic event! Hitler was set on annihilating the city and his military evaded the order. De Gaulle and the communists, etc. One cannot help admiring de Gaulle, even though he is a stubborn ass. There is something providential about his character. He was just reelected President of France in December. I like him better than Churchill, anyway!

January 3, 1966

The weather cleared up a bit. Tonight the half moon is shining. Last month I had an attack of what was practically dysentery. I decided it was no use even thinking of going to Nicaragua (to help [Ernesto] Cardenal at Solentiname), but today a letter came urging me to come anyway. I decided I would maintain my consent and trust completely in God. In any case it is such a fantastic proposition – they must go directly to the Pope to try to get me there (because of Dom James [Fox's] impossible and absurd attitude on all such things). Rome may or may not say "yes." God alone knows what will happen. In any event, my only job is to make my own decision and it is "yes" to the project as far as I am concerned. I will go if I am sent. I consent to it gladly if it is God's will, in so far as this will be a chance to leave everything and give myself to God in such a way as to live for others, and bring the contemplative life to Central America, and so on. As for my health, though, I will certainly have to be *extremely* careful of dysentery. I will simply have to pray to God and trust Him entirely. I made all this the intention of my mass, said mass as attentively and fervently as I could, asking nothing but the grace to do God's will and offering myself with Christ to the Father. Was especially moved at the words *"et sacrificium Patriarchae nostri Abrahae* [the sacrifice of our Patriarch Abraham]" – it was my desire to make this inner consent a sacrifice of faith like that of Abraham. And I resolved not to play around with my imagining of Solentiname – good or bad – but simply to pray that I may do God's will whatever it is. Certainly I am not taking any special joy there. It would be a real sacrifice to leave this hermitage and the real security I have here. And a real risk with my back as it is and my guts as they are.

January 5, 1966. Vigil of Epiphany

Steady rain all day. It is still pouring down on the roof, emphasizing the silence in the hermitage, reinforcing the solitude. I like it. Did a little work on the book about Abbé Monchanin – which I am supposed to review (have been dragging my feet because this review is supposed to be in French). In a way his Indian venture was a failure. Nothing came of the ashram. Yet one cannot judge. Certainly he was a great liberator and had the right idea about Christianity in Asia.

I read an account by Hervé Chaigne of the (communist-sponsored) peace conference in Helsinki last summer. Peace conference! The general idea was that all the Third World should take up arms against American imperialists. This would promote "peace"!! I don't mind them calling for world revolution if they want to call it by its right name – but to call this a peace movement! . . . No nonsense about non-violence and conscientious objection either.

The thing that depresses me is that H. Chaigne, hitherto a Gandhian, didn't say a word about non-violence. He approved the whole thing and seems to have bought the Chinese Marxist line all the way.

What can be the meaning of a genuine peace movement in the middle of all these people who make war in the name of peace (for the nine-millionth time!)?

January 8, 1966

Full moon obscured by clouds but visible from time to time and winds and flakes of snow on my face in the dark. It is about 25. Reading the [Robert] Schinzinger book of [Kitaro] Nishida's, [*Intelligibility and the*] *Philosophy of Nothingness* (almost unobtainable. Fr. [William] Johnston finally got a copy from Schinzinger himself) and a good study on Rilke and death by W[illia]m Ross.

Ed Rice came yesterday, got up to hermitage in the late afternoon. We had supper together in the hermitage and a good talk.

Bob Gerdy died of a heart attack on the street outside his apartment a few days ago (end of December some time). He had been an editor of *The New Yorker* for a long time. I think back to the summer of 1940 when Rice and I and Gerdy and Knight hitchhiked together from Olean to Cleveland and stayed with some relative of Gerdy's.

January 10, 1966

Feast of St. Paul the First Hermit – he has dropped out of our calendar, but I commemorated him in the office anyway and will say his Mass.

Saturday was v[ery] cold all day. Drove out with Rice to Edelin's Hollow and saw the sunny silence and stillness of the place, still very attractive to me. (It has been given to the monastery by Edelin now. Was surveyed in the summer. Do not know what the plans for it are!) Rice took pictures. We came back and had supper in the hermitage. It was a cold night. Yesterday, Sunday, it warmed up again. Rice left in the afternoon.

When he drove the Scout he drove mostly down the middle of the road and pulled over brusquely if some other car appeared. Is having trouble with his wife. *Jubilee* has been doing good things but I rarely receive it (it does not get through the Abbot's hands to me). R. very encouraging about Nicaragua. My idea is, however, perhaps to wait before letting E.C. take decisive action in Rome. Perhaps 1967. See what this year brings, and plan accordingly. Perhaps by summer it will be clear what action should be taken this year – or perhaps next. One thing is sure, once any action is taken, all communication with C. will be stopped by the Abbot. That is the problem.

What a stupid way to exist! I wonder if he has any comprehension of the Council Decree on Religious ["Decree on the Appropriate Renewal of the Religious Life, 1965"].

January 12, 1966

Great experience – reading Nishida's *The Intelligible World*. How like Evagrius, and yet better. Splendid view of the real (trans-conscious) meaning of Zen and its relation to the conscious and the world.

Monday – an illegal visit of W[illia]m Grimes, ex–Br. Alcuin. It is a pity I am where people know where I am and can get at me (parking car by lake off Bardstown Road, cutting across St. Theresa's field and through the pine woods, climbing the fence where the hunters come in!). I don't know what to do – but be patient and I was glad to see him. He is working with Little Brothers of the Poor in Chicago and their work (with the aged and sick poor) is most moving and good.

There has been a "peace offensive" over Vietnam which many think is only a prelude to hotter war when, because of its inevitable contradictions, the effort fails.

The badly printed postulants' guide (an incredible mess!) is to be done over again by the printers.

January 13, 1966

Nishida throws much light on Rilke. He makes clear and explicit what R. was reaching for in the *Duino Elegies:* the *pure event.* This must become a dimension in my own life – it is what the present transcends. (If I could see Nicaragua as "pure event" there would be no further question about it. But really it seems like more – and more useless – "flowering.")

January 15, 1966

St. Paul the Hermit has not vanished from the ordo – he is *today*. I don't know why he was moved from the 10th.

Yesterday was grey and cold and I thought there would be snow (there has been none this year), but sun came out in the afternoon. I sent off the commentary on the Council Constitution on the Church and the World ["Pastoral Constitution on the Church in Modern World," 1965] to Burns Oates.

A Rule for Recluses edited by Olgin in *Antonianum* came on interlibrary loan from St. Bona's [St. Bonaventure University]. Though it is rather pedestrian yet it means a great deal. (English Rule of 13th century, or later.)

There is no question that documents like this really speak to me and move me. I am completely attuned to them and to that time (Isaac of Stella, for instance). Lately with all the emphasis on being "contemporary" I have perhaps felt a little guilt about my love for the Middle Ages. This a foolish and rather servile feeling, really! "You have been bought with a great price – do not become the slaves of men!" (I Cor. 7:23) Where is my independence? That is the meaning of solitude, to be free from the compulsion of fashion, dead custom etc., and to be really open to the Holy Spirit. I see, once again, how muddled and distracted I am. Not free!

It is worthwhile, studying Rilke, to remind myself of what I am *not* and never will be, a poet in this sense. Yet there is so much in him that is valid for me. His thoughts on death, "pure event" etc. (After Mass yesterday that was clarified a bit. Suppose I go to Nicaragua purely to "be available" and hoping nothing for myself, seeking no "ideal"? etc. . . .)

"Nihil est (se incluso) majus necessarium quam Deum adorare vivientem [nothing (including myself) is more necessary than to adore the living God]" (says the *Rule for Recluses*). It seems a platitude – really it is a deep mysterious, unfathomable living need – an imperative for one's whole life, a demand that is often forgotten and never met. I am in solitude precisely to confront *this* demand and others like it (in Zen terms, for example). I recognize I do not cope with others really. Yet I must keep on with it, however much I fumble around. No one else can tell me what to do now, I have to try to find out for myself (of course people will come at the right time with the right word – books too – but I have no one to *rely on*). This is my life and I don't pretend to understand it. Only the mere playing of a role would be intolerable and mere living is also not enough, though at times it seems to resolve itself into that. There is living and living.

January 16, 1966
Finished Nishida's *Intelligible World*.

As to the *Sonnets to Orpheus* – German text that came yesterday from the U.K. I think the best way to read it is this: each day take *one* sonnet in the German, without English, and try to translate it straight on through as on an examination, not fearing to write nonsense, however. In this way, to stop holding back from the German, simply plunging into it. I really know more German than I think, maybe, and am enough attuned to Rilke to be right in first guesses now. My own guesses will be better for me than the translation

(J.B.L. [Leishman]) which sometimes distorts in order to rhyme. Then I can find out my mistakes from the translation.

January 18, 1966

Guess who comes today to preach the retreat: Bishop [Fulton J.] Sheen! But I am not expected to come to conferences. Arranged yesterday with Rev. Father: I will see the Bishop and perhaps take him for a walk to the hermitage (Rev. Fr.'s suggestion). Actually I like Bishop S. He is a pleasant person.

[W. H.] Auden's "Letter to a Wound" – a Rilkian experience, but with sanity, irony, detachment. Rilke was not capable of this. Too narcissistic to risk standing back for a moment. Could only plunge deeper into the pool. That is the trouble with all introverts: not that they look within but that they are obsessed with "looking within" and afraid to do anything else. Afraid that if they stop looking they will disintegrate. Hence the "Letter to a Wound" is *not* Rilkian. It is a parody of Rilkian experience.

Read a little of [Allen] Ginsberg before retreat – sending off the books to Ludovico Silva, in Caracas. G. is a good poet and what he writes of is America all right (the America I don't know, the half of it that completes the other half that I don't know either). All very clear, this America (fine poem on the movement going on on a college campus), intent, convinced, getting around. He does not judge.

Ginsberg is important, one of those people who causes a whole country to judge itself or come under judgment. Everybody has to say one way or the other what he thinks of Ginsberg and what Ginsberg is trying to say. Maybe I should write a poem about this. His nakedness is perhaps the significant – extraordinary – thing. But I am beyond the point of worrying about someone being naked, narcissistic, etc. No diagnosis: I think you have to see Ginsberg *without* reaching at once to the medicine chest, or without "deciding" his case with a handyword: fairy, schiz etc. This is the elementary sense of charity demanded by the situation: that here is Allen Ginsberg and he remains an identity which one refuses to evade. And then suddenly you see that the whole country is full of people exactly like that in a way. All the earnestness, sincerity, pity, pointlessness, might, of the U.S. is there, even the space-men. Yet one still has to account also for the Pentagon's view of itself. What a phenomenon this country is. (I like Ginsberg better than [Theodore] Roethke, simply because he is more explicit. He is warmer and more personal than William Carlos Williams.)

Evening. Beginning of retreat. Since it is the Night of Destiny (27 Ramadan) I stayed up late. Like Christmas. The Night of D. is perhaps a Moslem "Christmas" – heaven open to earth – the angels and "The Spirit" come down, all the prayers of the faithful are answered. Night of joy and peace! I shared the joy of Moslems and prayed for them and for my own needs, and for peace.

Saw Bishop Sheen after dinner. We had a good conversation. No matter how people may disparage all his TV work and so on, he is an extraordinary person and has done immense good and also is very intelligent, widely read, articulate. I suppose people dismiss him with a shrug just because he is popular and effective (a lot of them probably do the same for me!). But that is childish. One has to respect him. He is very vigorous and alert, just as he was sixteen years ago when he was last here. The community is being a bit supercilious about the fact that he's retreat master. That is not so much because of him as because of the abbot, who is trying to create an effect, of course failing. Those tapes in the guesthouse certainly have got people tired of Bishop Sheen too!

Light snow most of the day first time this winter.

January 20, 1966

Yesterday there were small deer tracks in the snow of the path as I went down to say Mass in the morning. Some of the light snow melted in open spaces, but the ground is still covered in the shady patches and the temperature did not get much above 35. It was 20 when I got up and is going down now towards 15 or lower perhaps.

Dan Walsh picked up a fine drip coffee maker in an auction for $1.25 and I have been using it. It makes fine coffee – which adds to these mornings. But Ernesto [Cardenal] also sent over instant coffee from Nicaragua, which I have not tried yet.

Working on [Pablo] Neruda, Rilke and now Octavio Paz (fine book on poetry). Have got to overcome a certain laziness with Spanish writers (i.e. not reading only superficially and not staying only with the obvious and easy – e.g. have to really get into [César] Vallejo's *Espana* for example).

January 22, 1966

It was not too cold when I got up (about 32). At 6 or 6:15 in the dark I went out to find it was snowing. Now (nearly 8) dim blue grey light and snow falling. I put crumbs out on the porch for birds. Will not cut wood (it is good I got mine into the woodshed yesterday. I did not expect snow and thought I was wasting time). Nishida on contradiction: that is the value of life: one must work with and against the elements in a state of productive contradiction ("action – intuition"). The point of contradiction is also the real – where the personal self expresses the world *now*. In community, everything theoretically arranges so that one is "free" to think and pray (all material needs taken care of). In fact two things happen. (1) Thought becomes abstract, (2) one *creates* problems and conflicts in desperation. They are unreal contradictions. Hence the sense of futility.

(Evening.) Heavy snow all day. Traffic of birds on the porch; juncos first, the cardinals, a mocking bird, titmice, myrtle warblers, etc. Also at least 3 whitefooted mice (pretty with their brown face and big ears) came out of the wood piles – mice more interested than birds in the crumbs. Birds like the shelter and drink from the pools of melted snow.

Had a hard time keeping on schedule. Tried to answer a tiresome query from Doubleday about quotations from Auden, Eckhart etc. and could not trace them. Had splinters in my hand and had to go down to get them out. Did not say Tierce and Sext until the mid-afternoon (after trying to find copies of some of my own poems). By mid-afternoon was tired and distracted but psalms and tea and the silence of snow re-ordered everything.

January 23, 1966. III Sunday after Epiphany
Deep snow. A marvelous morning (early in the night hours) in which among other things, I suddenly wrote a French poem. Had a good breakfast and the coffee turned out wonderfully this time: better than anything I have had for years except in the hospital, or perhaps here and there in Louisville. (Breakfast coffee in the hospital; always something I like, if I am well enough to enjoy it!)

Curious dimension of time: in four hours (besides writing this poem, getting breakfast and cleaning up) reread a few pages of Burtt's book and perhaps twenty pages of Nishida. That was all. But the time was most fruitful in depth and awareness and I did not know what happened to all these hours.

Later I would see by the deer tracks that sometime in the dark before the dawn a couple of deer jumped the fence right out in the front of the hermitage – but I did not notice them. (Too dark, and with my desk light in front of me I do not see out when it is dark.)

Cold going down to monastery: then the heavy heat of the buildings. At concelebration I was soaked in sweat, and there is flu everywhere in the community (my neighbor Fr. Herbert had it, or a bad cold). So I wonder if I will concelebrate in weather like this.

As regards prayer – in the hermitage. To be snowed in is to be reminded that this is a place apart, from which praise goes up to God, and that my honor and responsibility are that praise. This is my joy, my only "importance." For it *is* important! To be chosen for this! And then the realization that the Spirit is given to me, the veil is removed from my heart, that I reflect "with open face" the glory of Christ (II Cor. 3, end [v. 12–18]). It would be easy to remain with one's heart veiled (as Rilke did in some sense) and it is not by any wisdom of my own but by God's gift that it *is* unveiled.

January 24, 1966

Dark. Cold. Thermometer crawling down to zero. Finished Burtt and Nishida (*Unity of Opposites*). N. is certainly the one philosopher to whom I respond the most.

Kranth in *Monumenta Nipponica* suggests comparison between Nishida and the generation of 1898 in Spain. [Miguel de] Unamuno and Ortega [y Gasset]. Don't know Unamuno but have him here. Try him maybe!

Steel grey dawn. Hard frozen hills. A curious low hanging cloud over the field. The tops of the trees disappear into it. Below, everything sharply outlined. The birds are there on the porch, frantically picking up crackercrumbs. The first pages of Unamuno's *Agonia* look promising. Now to sweep, wash, type.

(Evening.) This has been the coldest day, this winter so far. Down to five below, they said at the monastery (though my porch thermometer did *not* go down to zero finally) and it did not get above 25 all day. Snow still deep. I took a short walk in the hollow behind the hermitage after dinner, then wrote a draft for a preface for Ernesto Cardenal Meditations (*La Vida en El Amor*), which are excellent. Some of them written when he was novice here.

I realized today after Mass what a desperate, despairing childhood I had. Around the age of 7–9–10, when Mother was dead and Father was in

France and Algeria. How much it meant when he came to take me to France. It really saved me.

In the afternoon–evening: realized that the *one thing* that is of any worth whatever in me, the one thing of value, and this is infinitely valuable, is the light to know God, the gift of faith that makes Him present in my heart. He who called forth light from darkness has shone in my heart! (II Cor. 4:6).

For this I love II Corinthians, which is my reading now and strikes me very deeply – especially all that is said about suffering (4:7–18). It is becoming one of my favorite epistles (especially 3:12–18).

Yesterday apparently Jim Morrissey's article about me was in the *Courier Journal* (Sunday Magazine). I suppose everyone in Kentucky has seen it but me (and the other monks). No matter. Dan Walsh will probably bring a copy along eventually. And I don't anticipate being thrilled, only embarrassed and wearied.

January 28, 1966

Still much snow. Only yesterday did the thermometer go above freezing in the afternoon. Not much melted. Cold again at night.

I still read a lot of Rilke and Unamuno – with questions and reservations. They are often unsatisfactory in much the same way. Sometimes their intuitions are brilliant, at others merely irresponsible. Both are utter individualists. This is their weakness and their strength.

For Rilke: I have no questions about the value of the *Neue Gedichte*, or the real beauty of the *Elegies* and some of the *Orpheus Sonnets*. But I still do not know about the spiritual world of the Sonnets. For a Christian there is always a natural tendency to read such things in implicitly Christian terms and to ensure, therefore, that he understands. But this is lazy. And where the question is once raised – I wonder if I get anything that he says, really! Except that he praises poetry, in poetry, for being poetry. Which is OK. But if this implies a view of life itself . . . it raises many questions.

Yet Unamuno's *Agonia* is a fascinating, though sometimes unsatisfactory book. Many excellent points – and above all he has a fine sense of the insufficiency of Christian rationalism, activism etc. "Power Christianity." Is he truly Pauline? Was he unacceptable in Spain because he had *protestant* insights? Indeed in many ways he is like [Karl] Barth.

January 29, 1966

Yesterday the thermometer barely went above 20. Now it is down around
10 (6 a.m.) and light, tiny flashes of ice are falling, a kind of mist of ice, that
will be slippery: only a thin coat over the hard frozen snow of the other day.
It has been falling for at least three or four hours and the footprints are still
visible.

Today I feel I must do some summing up: *agonia* (and peace!).

With the snow all around it, the hermitage is particularly peaceful. And
so am I. Though solicited by various troubles and "agonies," which are in
fact of no account whatever. And the more they are multiplied the more
they are seen to be senseless.

First of all – it is obvious that I do not need to be taking this or that "position" and making statements (unless in some exceptional case I am obviously required to) in public. I will stick to my decision not to comment on
events, and I will even keep quiet about what is going on in the Church.

For example, here are only a few of the "options" that have presented
themselves in four or five days – three days rather – since the end of retreat.

a. Liturgy – asked to help in the translation of the liturgical books
(missal) by the official commission in Washington. To be exact – to submit sample translation of collects. NO.

Asked on the other hand by a disturbed and somewhat fanatical representative of the conservative thinking to come out *against* new liturgy.
Obviously no.

(This reaction against the liturgical change is pretty neurotic in the form
it takes, though objectively I can see reasons for some of the criticisms.)

b. Poetry etc. Letter from [Clayton] Eshleman upbraiding me (not without reason) for my crack in *Harper's* about Ginsberg in South America.
Yet the letter was full of other implications – seemed to be centered on a
demand to live life with a kind of poetic orthodoxy, to declare myself
"with" the new poetry written in America. [Charles] Olson, [Robert]
Duncan, [Robert] Kelly, Ginsberg etc. I like what I have read of it (not
much) and I know I have made impossible and sweeping statements about
it. E. (obviously homesick in Peru and probably getting a rough time because of the U.S. in Vietnam) criticizes me for identifying with South
American poets against U.S. poets in this "black" hour for our country
etc. In a word, demand to conform to poetic and patriotic orthodoxy of
some sort. Nuts.

c. There is always the question of race: besides the obvious choice of being for civil rights – there are the unlimited esoteric options and the whole neurotic business of identifying with the Negro, who now is absolutely not permitting himself to be identified with – yet enjoying the courtship. (I am involved in more of this – saw a report of some congress or other of writers in which the whole theme was "No matter how hard you try you can't identify with us, Charlie, you don't know how we feel.") Nuts. No courtship.

d. War and peace: Again – I am on record as having made the obvious option – *against* the war in V[iet] N[am]. But then the issue is *immensely* complicated. Johnson is trying to get out of it now – some say sincerely, others no. China obviously wants the war to continue, to bleed and humiliate America. The Pentagon wants to continue it so as to beat up North V.N. and get at China. And so on. There are a hundred possibilities for saying "yes" and "no." I have no obligation to come out with these ambiguities and will not. I do not know the ins and outs of it well enough. Who does? (Yet I do think the situation remains terribly serious, precisely because it is so complicated and ambiguous.)

e. Monasticism. Dom James is first going to Rome for a meeting of abbots. Interminable petty questions about details of observance (radio or no radio!). The whole thing gets to be more and more trivial. I am not concelebrating even on Sundays because last Sunday evening coming in from the snow to the overheated Church I spent the whole mass in a sweat. I have no part in the business of change in the order. Certainly this is important. But things being what they are I have no way of getting into it in any way that makes sense. Also I do not think that the order in America is going or can go in any direction that leads anywhere except to mediocrity and bourgeois comfort – and superficiality. Yet there are such good young monks here and some good possibilities. Maybe I am too pessimistic, since Dom James blocks the whole view.

f. Literature in general – all this about people like Rilke, Unamuno etc. Superficial and unimportant. Same with the new theology people – the Bonhoefferites et al. None of my business – though since I have started on Rilke I will keep after this study until I am satisfied or get enough of it and can stand no more of him.

g. "Mysticism." The rather absurd discussion of mysticism and regression being carried on by the people at McGill. And all the literature about questions of drugs, psychiatry etc. I may give an opinion if asked – and certainly I am ready to help L.P. [Linda Parsons] personally if I can.[1] Don't expect to do much.

h. Zen – this will probably get sticky and unfortunate soon. Zen itself will keep me from "Zen" as a movement. All the other Oriental stuff – the same.

i. [William] Du Bay and his priests' union!!! He has asked the Center at Santa Barbara for advice. [W. H. Ping] Ferry asked me. This is part of a movement that is going to be very active and cause an enormous amount of stir and upheaval. I am rather dubious about it and have already said I want no part in any of it. But of course will give an opinion on various points if asked.

j. Health etc. It is true my back is bad and my hand is not in good shape. I write with difficulty and it is painful. My stomach is as usual. Probably I will have to go to see [Dr. William C.] Mitchell about the back, but will put it off as long as I can and try to avoid an operation. Skin of my hands all broken up again with dermatitis.

Reviewing all this: it seems to be my life and is not. It offers itself, suggests itself, asks to be taken seriously. I see that I am called to be free of it and to deal with it all in freedom, seeking only isolated occasions to help others here and there, not getting involved in any program.

The other thing is that with my hands in bad shape, and with the fantastic trouble I now have with my typewriter, writing will be slowed down and that is good too!

In all these things I see one central option for me: to let go of all that seems to suggest getting somewhere, being someone, having a name and a voice, following a policy and directing people in "my" ways. What matters is to *love*, to be in one place in silence, if necessary in suffering, sickness, tribulation, and not try to be anybody outwardly. Not try to have a public identity. And this, just at the time when papers all over the place have picked up the story that was about me in the *Courier Journal*.

Life is very funny! *Vive la neige!* [Long live the snow!]

Monday is my 51st birthday. Hence the summing up.

---

[1] Linda Parsons [Sabbath] wrote to Thomas Merton in April 1965 after reading *The Ascent to Truth*. In their letters, they explored a host of common interests, such as religious experience, mysticism, Zen Buddhism and its relationship to Christianity. For Merton's letters to Linda Parsons Sabbath, see *The Hidden Ground of Love*, edited by William H. Shannon (New York: Farrar, Straus, & Giroux, 1985), 516–33.

It would be fine if I really think the *CJ* story was my way of saying "Good-bye" and getting out for keeps. I know I cannot avoid still writing (do not want to avoid it) and occasionally blasting out about something – but surely now it can take on a whole new direction.

Certainly I am going to write a lot of letters saying "No!"

January 31, 1966

Yesterday was bitterly cold. About 10 below in the early morning (14 below on the unprotected thermometer at the monastery, 16 below at the cow-barn). It hardly got above 15 at the warmest time of the day and there was a biting wind. Had a couple of fine walks in the snow – stayed on my own hill-side, which more and more is enough for me.

Today, my 51st birthday. Gratitude and a kind of astonishment that I should be so old. A good day. Reading more of Isaac of Stella, finishing his sermons.

A bit perplexed by the stupid picture book job that has dragged on and on. After we had paid Peter Geist a good sum to do some rather interesting layouts, Bro. Pius, entirely on his own initiative, has taken the book over, changed many of the pictures and some of the pages and the result is a banal and confused mess. I worried a bit about whether I should put up a fight over it and decided not to. It is not worth the trouble. Nobody gives a damn anyway whether the book is really interesting or not. It is simply something for tourists. So I decided to forget it, write my text when I can get up the courage to do so, and that will be that. I hope.[2]

February 3, 1966

Purple landscape coming into view, still full of snow. Dom James leaves today for a committee of Abbots in Rome and probably a visit to Norway. I have not talked with him about it and I have no idea what is coming up except of course they are implementing the council decree. Our decree from the congregation on "unifying" the communities really was quite general.

Yesterday was a fine feast for me. Did not go down to the candle-blessing, procession and concelebration but said mass privately as usual, and thought deeply about Our Lady afterwards, prayed much to her, saw her immense importance in my life, "gave" myself as completely as I could. I have a great

[2] This book was published as *Gethsemani: A Life of Praise* (Trappist, KY: Abbey of Gethsemani, 1966).

need to "belong" to her. All this is not easily explained and easily becomes confusing if put into words. It is something to be lived in secret. It is the way for me to learn the purity of love and trust. A love that should be completely non-sentimental and even in a certain sense non-objective, "through" her entirely to the invisible, yet not possible in that purity without her – and it is aware of her, yes and no, and of the void too. Impossible to explain and I don't need to.

My (desk) typewriter has been impossible. Yesterday Br. Clement gave me an almost new portable, a Hermes.

February 7, 1966. F[east] of St. Romuald

I don't know what happens to *time* in the hermitage. Three and four hours in the pre-dawn go by like half an hour. Reading, meditation, a few notes, some coffee and toast – there is not much to show for it, but it is probably the most fruitful part of the day.

Today I have spent all this time on a discovery. "John the Solitary," a Syrian, whose *Dialogue on the Soul and Passions* was published by Hauscherr (in French) in 1939. It has remained practically unknown. Yet is extremely interesting. Can use a bit of it in the article I am writing now on Spiritual Direction in the Desert Fathers (for Hermits).

Yesterday, Septuagesima, it finally began to thaw (before that there were some wonderful zero nights with full moon on the hard, sparkling snow). Last night I could have my window open again and melting snow ran off the roof into the buckets all night.

Yesterday was a full day – some good ideas in the morning, and the realization that I am on my right way, that I am at grips with a critical problem – which is also a reason why Rilke holds my interest: what is lacking in him? There is perhaps in him a central neurotic falsity which I probably have to negotiate in myself also, and for me a poetic solution, however brilliant, will not do. It has to be coped with in grace, in true solitude, in authentic love, not bypassed. I realize though that I cannot plan on perfect success. Have to have a sober estimate!! But what matters is that I sincerely face it and do what I can and not tamper with the truth.

Then this Orpheus idea – this is important (as a kind of *theoria*) and attractive. Much to be done here. An entirely different question.

In the afternoon, musing on the *Prajna paramita Sutra*, out at the top of the hay field, really *saw* it (instead of simply understanding that there was something in it to see). And really laughed! It means exactly what it says, and yet one does not break through. To break through *everything!* With whom does emptiness shake hands when it shakes hands with itself?

After that two deer started off in the red brush on the east side of the hill, only fifty or a hundred feet from where I was walking, and ran away without haste in long, slow, curving leaps, with their huge white tails up like flags.

Talked on Rilke in Chapter Room and read 3 poems from the *Book of Hours* – their merits and deficiencies.

February 10, 1966

All week, warm days, like spring. Then today, rain all day. This evening the storm is breaking up. Long low blue-black clouds came trailing up over the black ridge out of Tennessee, low and fast, streaming to the North. I stood and watched them in my evening meditation. Perfect silence, but for a dog barking far down the valley somewhere, towards Newton's.

Today I finished a first draft of an article for *Katallagete* which was difficult to write. They insist on my writing something and I do not really know the South. So it is general! Walker Percy had a very smart piece in their last issue. They are just starting – it is one of the only really articulate voices in the South and so deserves support.

Yesterday I heard from Cardenal. He has started his project on Solentiname, though very unofficially, with full approval of his bishop.

Ammon Hennacy writes that he is coming to Kentucky and wants to visit, but I don't think it will be possible.

After three weeks of snow it is good to see the green!

February 13, 1966

I have had almost all I can take of Rilke – turn now with relief to people like [Paul] Celan, [Heinz] Piontek, [Karl] Krolow. Need to finish more of this. This is what I have not well enough known, what has been going on while I have been fighting here with the phantoms in Gethsemani.

February 17, 1966

Today was *the* prophetic day, the first of the real shining spring: not that there was not warm weather last week, not that the there will not be cold weather again. But this was the day of the year when spring became truly *credible*. Freezing night, but cold bright morning, and a brave, bright shining of sun that is new, and an awakening in all the land, as if the earth were aware of its capacities!

I saw that the woodchuck had opened up his den and had come out, after three months or so of sleep, and at that early hour when it was still freezing. I thought he had gone crazy. But the day proved him right and me wrong.

The morning got more and more brilliant and I could feel the brilliancy of it getting into my own blood. Living so close to the cold, you feel the spring. And this is man's mission! The earth cannot *feel* all this. We must. But living away from the earth and the trees we fail them. We are absent from the wedding feast.

There are moments of great loneliness and lostness in this solitude, but often then come other deeper moments of hope and understanding, and I realize that these would *not be possible*, in their purity, their simple secret directions, anywhere but in solitude. I hope to be worthy of them!

After dinner when I came back to the hermitage the whole hillside was so bright and new I wanted to cry out, and I got tears in my eyes from it!

With the new, comes also memory: as if that which was once so fresh in the past (days of discovery when I was 19 or 20) were very close again, and as if one were beginning to live again from the beginning: one must experience spring like that. A whole new chance! A complete renewal!

February 20, 1966. Quinquagesima

Cold clear night. It was 25 this morning early and now at sunrise is nearly down to 20 with a keen wind.

The other night in the clear sky about 3:30 suddenly saw in the South the great sign of Scorpio rising. It is awesome to see the T-shaped head climb into the sky and the twisting body slowly follow it up out of Tennessee, with red Antares in its heart!

Seeing this I got out and looked at other constellations with a star map for July (which does not quite fit Feb. at 3:30 but July at 8 or 9 is close). In the west my view is hindered by the tall pine but the sickle and Leo are high and I see them. In the East the beautiful Swan, and the Eagle. Today I went out in the open and could see the Cassiopeia upside down over Boones' in the North.

Condemnation of [Andrei] Sinyavsky and [Yuli] Daniel, the writers, is treason. Sickening pharisaism of the Soviet establishment! How can anyone be taken in by these people? It is possible *only* if one wants to submit to a secure, stupid, self-righteous, "orthodox" system. From which God preserve us! Two more condemned for trying to talk as if they were alive!

February 21, 1966

Rilke again.

Rereading the II Elegy and [Romano] Guardini about it. It seems to me that Guardini, while right in many judgments about R., takes too seriously R's own "passionate" rejections of Christianity in letters etc. For passionately one should understand emotionally. For subjective reasons beyond his control (his mother) R. simply could not be at peace with conventional Christian language and even with the idea of Christ as Mediator. I do not minimize this – objectively a failure of faith. Yet G. does not see that R. was also struggling with a false religious problem imposed on him by 19th-century Christianity. The problem of finding *wholeness* (ultimate truth etc.) in God by *denying and excluding the world.* The holy is the non-secular. Feeling himself called upon to *deny* and exclude what he saw to be in reality necessary for "wholeness," "holiness," "openness," he finally refused this denial, and chose his "open world." In a sense he does come up with a cosmology that seems a parody of Christianity – but *is it* really as G. thinks, a "secularization" in the sense of a degradation? Is he not really reaching for the kind of Pleroma revealed in Colossians? Yes, his choice of angels is in a sense a failure, acc[ording] to Paul – yet was it entirely his fault? Was it forced on him by a manichean type of Christianity?

I cannot agree with all Rilke says – but I do not think he himself would have expected, still less demanded, an act of theological faith in the content of the *Duino Elegies!!*

But on the other hand this pharisaic shunning of it, this cutting him dead in public etc. – analogous to the condemnation of Sinyavski and Daniel, no?

February 23, 1966. Ash Wednesday

The curse is in the skin of my hands again – all broken up. Also I will need X-rays of that vertebra again soon, my hands easily get numb, and even hurt.

Last night I stood out in the cold late trying to see Canopus in the south sky, but there was haze along the hills and horizon. There was a star trying to look through the haze which might have been it. Going down to monastery in the dark at 5 for ashes and concelebration, the sky was bright – Corvus up in the west over the monastery and Castor and Pollux down in the northwest.

————

Another discovery: this time the Sufi tales of Nasruddin. Where can I get the whole collection? I know I have much to learn in them. They are fascinating and very funny: but point in all directions at once!

February 25, 1966

Lent is getting into full swing.

The Abbot returned from Rome and Oslo Wednesday night. Saw him yesterday. No information about Norway except that there was a lot of snow and "too much snow for skiing." He excels in giving irrelevant information. Tried to find out something about the *Collectanea [Cisterciensia]*, but again nothing precise. Fr. Charles had come to see him. The English edition would be mailed out from Gethsemani. He would not, however, admit that there was an English edition. I came away exasperated with him and his politics.

His letters from Rome have caused a lot of laughter and some commotion in the community (especially his way of getting around higher authority – which he was for once embarrassingly *clear* about!!). The impression one gets is that – he is going to enforce his own ideas and those of a few members of the community against the vocal opposition of others (the senior or sub-senior brothers like Colman, Clement etc.) and with the indifference of the majority.

This disturbs me and I have to negotiate it. I have no confidence in the man, and am convinced his motives are much more "natural" than he realizes, indeed perhaps somewhat neurotic. I have no respect for his ideas of monasticism, based on *no* real acquaintance with tradition, or with the real meaning of the life – and indeed full of bad theology.

To be a prisoner of such a man and helpless to do anything about it is a real problem to me, and can hardly see what to do but accept it; but I have to accept it reasonably and naturally, not masochistically. The demonic thing about the situation is the real power of the sado-masochism that he injects into everything he says and does. It is really a terrible, defeating force. Life-defeating, depressing, hopeless – no wonder so many leave.

Fr. Flavian wants to go now and join Dom [Jacques] Winandy. I really can't blame him, though it would be sad to lose one of the best monks in the monastery and one who really knows what a monk is!

February 27, 1966. 1st Sunday in Lent

I sing parts of Lauds and Vespers, and the Salve, and Antiphons of Our Lady. Great love for the Lenten hymns and antiphons – and for the old

Lenten masses now gone. (Of course they can be said privately, but new masses are sung in the community – Sundays and weekdays too.)

Dom James, having said nothing of Norway, is to announce his plans (as ambiguously as he usually does) this morning in chapter. Some, including Fr. Callistus, who is slated to head the Foundation, think it may be put off and will not be this spring. No one knows anything definite yet.

March 1, 1966

As I vaguely suspected, the Norway foundation has been put off, more than that abandoned altogether. (Is there no possibility? I don't know.) An experimental "new" type foundation was quietly and smoothly made in Denmark by one of the most progressive abbots in the order, Dom André Louf. Evidently he did not think this represented any kind of threat to Dom James (only six monks, small flexible foundation with new perspectives), but Dom J. took it as a betrayal and has been somewhat tragic about it. In fact it represents a big defeat for his conservative and rigidly institutional conception of monasticism, and at this I must admit I feel a certain satisfaction – though I am sorry the Norway foundation is off, as there were still certain hopes and possibilities, since young and alert monks were going on it and Bishop John [Gran] has broader views than Dom J.

Dom James may now attempt a foundation in Latin America and this in my opinion would be *disastrous!* There above all a new formula is needed and the "old" rigid, feudal, opulent type establishment is totally useless. Moreover the whole of Latin America is about to flame up in guerrilla wars. The U.S. was never more hated. Monks out in the country, with no awareness of the local mentality and problems, would be in the worst possible situation.

An ironic thought occurred to me: a sure way to make Dom J. take back any possible intention of a Latin American foundation – would be for me to show enthusiasm over it and ask to be sent there!

March 2, 1966

There is no question that the solitary life is fraught with problems and "dangers," but on the other hand I see that it is necessary for me to meet these precisely as they come to me in solitude. They would take a different and perhaps, for me, non-negotiable form in community. At any rate things were never so clear. I see that it is to face what I cannot face that I am in solitude, and everything in my life is affected by the change – my ordinary anxieties, my writing, my attitude toward the world, my attitude toward myself, my work toward my spiritual goal – my life in Christ. Whereas in the community all this was still to a great extent separate, dissipated and confused, here I can see it all in one ferment of change, at times frightening, basically hopeful and alive – sometimes exciting!!

Writing for instance: for the first time I can see how this can be reduced to a "normal" and non-obsessive role in my life! And I face the prospect with relief and joy. In community, this was only a "worry," abstract and non-negotiable. I was somehow condemned to an evasion which I now see to be futile and self-defeating. Here I think it can become once again fruitful – my work I mean, not the "obsession."

Yesterday – more truly spring; and this is a spring dawn today, cold, but with birds singing. First time I have heard the whistling of the Towhee this year. And the cardinals up in the woods to the west. The promise grows more and more definite. I look up at the morning star: in all this God takes His joy, and in me also, since I am His creation and His son, His redeemed, and member of His Christ – sorrow at the fabulous confusion and violence of this world that does not understand His love – yet I am called not to interpret or condemn the misunderstanding, only to return the love which is the final and ultimate truth of everything and seeks all men's awakening and response. Basically I need to grow in this faith and this realization, not only for myself but for all men.

To go out to walk slowly in this wood – this is a more important and significant means to understanding, at the moment, than a lot of analysis and a lot of reporting on the things "of the spirit."

March 3, 1966

Yesterday was completely beautiful – especially the bright cool morning walk in the woods, cleaning up a fallen dead pine. The afternoon – quiet, did no writing work, only replied to Hervé Chaigne about my book in France *Foi et Violence*. (Additions made to it. The Simone Weil article, Schema 13[3] etc. I also sent "Blessed Are the Meek.")

Today, warm, grey, went down early for Mass, took a hot bath in the infirmary and got into secular clothes to go to town for back X-rays. (Hand

[3] Merton's *Faith and Violence* (Notre Dame, IN: University of Notre Dame Press, 1968) was published in French, translated by Marie Tadié, in 1969. The articles he refers to are "Pacifism and Resistance in Simone Weil" and "Schema 13: An Open Letter to the American Hierarchy."

has been numb for some time.) At the U[niversity] of L[ouisville] library was really moved by parts of Rilke's *Letters to a Young Poet* (they certainly complete and deepen some of the things said about love – and criticized – in the *Duino Elegies*).

Got to the Medical Arts Building, and the X-rays showed up a real mess. A back operation is unavoidable, unfortunately.

Jim Wygal I found very depressed and even a bit maudlin. He has a real problem with all the patients he gets that are priests, religious, etc. A discouraging example of Catholic spirit!

Got home, back to the hermitage. Rain broke. I am up late. Rain poured, on the roof. I let the idea of the operation sink in, and I adjust to it.

March 5, 1966

Evening. Snowing hard. This morning I decided to try to clean up a little and leave the ground around the hermitage in relatively good shape – as I probably won't be able to do very much work for a couple of months after the back operation! Burned some bush, and there were flurries of snow falling into the flames.

Going over the copy edited ms. of *Conjectures [of a Guilty Bystander]* for Doubleday. Am bored with it. When I read proof I am slightly more interested. I have seen enough of the ms.

The snow has stopped again. The full moon has risen in the blue, cold, evening sky. The snow all day, coming and going, falling and melting, has been March snow with dark scudding clouds and moments of brightness, and biting wind, and all the trees bending, and a fire in the fireplace.

A fine book on *Creativity and Tao* by Chang Chung-Yuan from McGill. (Took so long to get here it is already due back!)

My arm is painful. I can see the operation is needed (saw it in the X-rays!).

Tomorrow is already the II Sunday of Lent!

Dom J. is thinking of taking over the Spencer foundation in Chile. That is at least more reasonable than starting a new one, for instance in Columbia. I perfunctorily mentioned he might need someone who knew Spanish (myself). He was profuse in denying that he wanted me to go! Oh no, no, no, no!! And he said "The old hermit idea would come back again." Come back? It has not left, and I hope it won't! What else is there?

March 6, 1966. Second Sunday of Lent

Cold again. I took a good walk in the woods, watching the patterns of water in my quiet, favorite creek. Then walked up and down in the sheltered place where we used to go for Christmas trees, thinking about life and death – and how impossible it is to grasp the idea that one must die. And what to do to be ready for it! When it comes to setting my house in order I seem to have no ideas at all.

In the evening, stood for about 15 minutes on the porch watching deer etc. through field glasses. The deer – five of them, were out by the brush piles beyond my fence, barely a hundred yards – less perhaps – from the hermitage. Hence I would see them very clearly and watch all their beautiful movements – from time to time they tried to figure me out, and would spread out their ears at me, and stand still, looking, and there I would be gazing right into those big brown eyes and those black noses. And one, the most suspicious, would lift a foot and set it down again quietly, as if to stomp – but in doubt about whether there was a good reason. This one also had a stylish, high-stepping trot routine which the others did not seem to have. But what form! I was entranced by their perfection!

March 7, 1966

Though the feast vanished from our Ordo I said the Mass of St. Thomas Aquinas, and wrote to [Jacques] Maritain.

Cold, sunny March day. Finished a very summary reading of the edited ms. of *Conjectures*. It seems to be a fine book – at least partly representing my right mind.

In the evening, saying the Hymn for Vigils, I was struck by the line:

Spes una mundi perditi. [Sole hope of the lost world.]

Whatever people may do or say, this seems to me fairly central in our Christian faith! The world is "lost" and has no hope but in Christ. Today they are turning it around, as if the world were the sole hope of the Church!

And Christ before Pilate. John 18:36: My kingdom is *not of this world.*

Certainly we must do what we can to live reasonably and decently and to provide for others the means of a truly human existence. Does "the world" suffice for this? Or is Christ the hope even of a *human* existence? On one hand we say the whole world must become "affluent" and on the other we find that the production of affluent society has become humanly meaningless.

I'll stick to the *Spes una mundi perditi*.

March 8, 1966

The solitary life itself reduces itself to a simple need – to make the choices which constantly imply preference for solitude fully understood (better "properly" understood in relation to one's capacity at the moment). I find myself confronted with these choices repeatedly – they present themselves in their own way, and what they add up to these days is the question of emotional dependence on other people, simply, collectively – the community, friends, readers, other poets etc. Over and over again I have to make small decisions here and there, in regard to one or other. Distractions and obsessions are resolved in this way. What the resolution amounts to, in the end: letting go of the imaginary and the absent and returning to the present, the real, what is in front of my nose. Each time I do this I am more present, more alone, more detached, more clear, better able to pray. Failure to do it means confusions, weakness, hesitation, fear – and all the way through to anguish and nightmares. It is not purely up to me to "succeed" each time. I cannot calculate the force of unidentified emotion that will well out of my unconscious. There are days of obscurity, frustrations and crises when *nothing* is straight. However, I know my aim and I try at least to meditate. Discovering how hostile I have been, how desperate, how mean and unjust. (For instance, today again it comes back to me that I had been unjust, suspicious and ungrateful to [Frank C.] Doherty, the Headmaster at Oakham, who had really been kind to me and concerned with my best interests. I could not believe him.)

So, when it comes to "preparing for death" – in my case it means simply this reiterated decision for solitude as the reality called for me by God, as my penance and cleansing, as my paying off debts, as my return to my right mind, and as my place of worship and prayer.

It was cold this morning – about 20 at sunrise, but warmed up to become a good, bright, spring day. I thinned out our young trees in the woods to the north of the hermitage – enjoyable work while I can still swing a brush-hook! Then in the afternoon Bro. Benedict, the orchard man, came up with a couple of walnut trees which we planted in the field. There are 5 pecan trees coming too. Proper for a hermitage, though I myself can't eat many nuts on account of my stomach. Some other hermit in future years may perhaps profit by them. In the evening, at supper, read the little booklet on Ford Abbey that Etta Gullick sent.

March 10, 1966

I was going to finish cutting brush this morning, but it looks like rain. I'll see. My back hurts anyway. I am to go into the hospital on the 23rd and apparently the operation is the next day. In a way I have *not* adjusted to the idea, and cannot fully do so. I distrust the mania for surgery in this country, though Dr. Mitchell is certainly a reasonable and prudent man and no fanatic. Also, I can see that the condition of my back is such that if he does not operate now, I will hardly be able to work with my arms and hands in a little while. (My hand gets numb fast holding a pen and writing a few lines.)

Still, having to undergo surgery is a kind of defeat, an admission that I have not lived right, that I have in fact been too much a prisoner of a very unreasonable culture. Honestly I think it is too late for me to escape the consequences, altogether. But I hope I can salvage something. My life in the hermitage is much saner and better balanced than it was in the monastery, my health is much better, I sleep well, have a good appetite, no colds, stomach a bit better. I suppose my eating is wrong.

When the operation is over, perhaps I can start afresh and really try to get everything in order. I hope so! But meanwhile I do not expect much help from doctors and their damned pills.

March 15, 1966

The Norway foundation is going to be made after all. Bishop John and the Bishop of Copenhagen decided that if there has to be a choice, the "experimental" foundations must go and the Gethsemani "establishment" style foundation must be made. A victory for Dom James' conservatism and Americanism. But I still think there was no real need to regard Dom André Louf as a rival and force him out. The whole event is typical. But I do not criticize Dom James – his nature is what it is, and he must see things as he does. And he is the Abbot God has willed for me. Certainly in many ways he is "right" – he is at any event a success. He keeps order, and the abbey is prosperous, though many are unhappy and restless, and others still leave. But the crisis is universal and in the end we seem to be weathering it better than most. Suppose the next abbot is liberal and understanding toward modern problems – he may wreck the place or let it wreck itself by letting it go this way and that. Dom J.'s narrowness has some points, but in the end I think this community represents the past rather than the future. One always ends by realizing how many good people there are in it, how much honesty, how much sincerity, how much real desire for truth. With these signs of God's blessing, one cannot render firm negative judgments on the place!

Then, in the end, I am grateful for being here, and accept the mystery of my vocation with all that disconcerts me about it, and hope to be faithful to it. And humble about it! For I know I will never have things exactly as I wish they ought to be – and as I would take pride in them.

If the community has failings, they correspond to my own failings and the limitations of the Abbot were chosen in view of my faults, sins, and limitations. I suppose that is why I am so sensitive to them!

After all, he has been patient with me, and kind in his own (political) way, and I do at least owe to him the fact of being here in a hermitage, which is amazing enough!

The Palomares incident makes me very sad. Two planes (SAC) crashed over this poor Spanish village, 4 H-bombs were lost, 3 were recovered. Of these 3, one or two had practically gone off (i.e. the conventional triggers had exploded) and there was radiation material all about. The crops and fish have been ruined. The whole place is being scoured and cleaned up. Dirt shipped to America. Some of the people contaminated. The village itself is economically ruined. Gets news about itself mostly from foreign radio. A typical incident, paradigm of an age, its gigantic and stupid anti-Communism.

In spite of myself, and with many hesitations, finished yesterday first draft of an article "Apologies to an Unbeliever" which I plan to send to *Harper's* before going to the hospital. Why did I write it? I don't know. Compassion for Victor Hammer, who is after all a very believing "unbeliever" and for so many others who have to be alone and confused, penalized for the sincerity which prohibits facile options! Perhaps it was well that I wrote this. I must now go over it again.[4]

The danger of a nuclear attack by this country on Red China is very real. Of course there is a great deal of opposition to it. The majority of the people are humane enough to see the error and insanity of it – as well as its total uselessness, and the awful irresponsibility that would endanger people who

---

[4] "How It Is: Apologies to an Unbeliever" was eventually published in *Harper's* magazine in November 1966.

are supposed to be our allies (Japan for example). Yet the opposition of the people is always a half-hearted thing, a question of feeling rather than of principle. Certainly this will not seriously hold anyone back if the Pentagon finally determines that the attack must be made. This criminal act of moral blindness is altogether possible. I do not know if it is *likely* at the moment, but any significant change can make it likely. And this calls for thought and decision on my part. An ordinary verbal protest means little or nothing. "Political" action on the scale possible to us these days is trivial. At best it salves one's own conscience. Once again, I think of simply renouncing American citizenship etc. But that raises the problems of my being fixed at Gethsemani and so long as I am here it makes very little difference what country I am a "citizen" of. The situation has to be brought in the religious sphere, where it is less easily explained and where grace offers concrete suggestions. This remains a matter for myself and God, and He alone knows what will come of it.

Evening – mild. Fluffy cumulus clouds. A few small flocks of migrating birds go over, heading north. Buds are reddening on my maple saplings.

I finished, quickly, a preface for the Japanese translation of *Thoughts in Solitude*[5] and certainly wrote it with more satisfaction than the article yesterday – and less trouble. Spanish translation of my existentialist piece, for *Sur*, came in. I will correct and return it. Ernesto Cardenal wrote that he is now on Solentiname, is clearing brush, and that there are plenty of mosquitos after all!

March 16, 1966

The latest in Religion:

Los Angeles, *"A Genuine New Revival" "Astronauts and Cosmonauts of Youth"*

Why, spaceships and spacemen from Mars and other worlds have landed on earth! Miss Velma will descend from high out of the skies in a spaceship wearing a gold space suit and space helmet and preach her entire sermon from a spaceship surrounded by spacemen! Positive proof that spacemen from Mars and other worlds have landed on earth!

(Miss Velma is shown emerging from a Flying Saucer with a space helmet in one hand and a Bible in the other.)

---

[5] Merton later revises this preface for publication in English – see his entry for April 14, 1966.

Closer to home – Kentucky. A Protestant group at the U[niversity] of K[entucky] is invited to see a magician "prove" the Resurrection. He puts a picture of Jesus in a box. Closes the box. When he opens the box the picture is gone.

Catholic Aggiornamento. A priest is amazed that some of his people continue to say the Rosary at Mass. He announces a "special service." Sunday Evening all are to bring Rosaries and candles. They light the candles and walk in procession to a spot outside the Church where they find a hole has been dug. They are told to throw their rosaries in the hole. The rosaries are then buried. Spirit of liberty of Vatican II.

March 19, 1966. St. Joseph

A marvelous, clear, clean spring morning: after some warm days and rain yesterday afternoon, the sky is washed of any trace of clouds. The hills in the south stand out sharp against the immaculate morning. Soon the sun will rise. In the most pure silence a pileated woodpecker drums on a loud tree and the solemn sound goes out through the clear halls of the forest.

After five, I looked at the stars, and discerned my zodiacal sign rising in the East, Aquarius, and Venus glittering in Capricorn.

Read some Angela of Foligno (I love her admirable, passionate fervor and honesty) and St. Thomas on the light of glory – also some Milarepa which I must return to Linda Parsons today. Sending off the preface to Japanese translation of *Thoughts in Solitude* and, tentatively, to *Harper's*, "Apologies to an Unbeliever," though I do not like the tone of it and will have to make changes – if they want it.

In the last few days – two different visitors, total strangers came up here with questions. This is a sign that the place can after all be easily found and it is a bad sign. Something that will have to be met with when I return from the hospital. (Probably in part a result of the *Jubilee* article.)

March 20, 1966. Laetare Sunday

Yesterday was perfect. Went for a walk in the warm sun and strong, cool wind down to one of my corners, a little spot at the edge of the wood by St. Edmund's field, and there walked up and down with simple hesychastic resolutions taking deeper shape in me. "When I get back . . ." etc. Momentarily bothered by the fact that I sent off "Apologies to an Unbeliever," but it can be changed and must be. It's the tone that is bad above all. And really I have no more need to be making pronouncements.

The sun was very good!

Came back and boiled three eggs for supper, as it was a feast, and drank green tea.

Then as it got dark I saw that the hills across the valley were at one place covered with a wide warm circle of biting and rapidly advancing red flame in a big sweep half a mile across or more. This morning the fire was there but the perimeter was broken and there was a flame wandering jaggedly eastward. Before dawn even that was gone. Either men fought it all night, or else the dew got so heavy that everything was too wet.

Prepared a formal conference on Rilke's *Letters to a Young Poet* for the group today. There seems to be something to his ideas on love – at any rate they complete some of the rather mystifying notions in the *Elegies*.

Yesterday I sent the ms. of [Robert] Lax's (unnamed) Journal to New Directions. He has been keeping it on his Greek Island, Kalymnos, and there is a lot of good stuff in it, especially about the sponge-fishers. Forty or thirty years ago we went to France to live in the [indecipherable]. Now that would be too crowded I imagine, and Greece would still be possible. More exactly South America.

March 21, 1966. St. Benedict

Song of robins and cardinals in pre-dawn dark. I am trying to clear the porch of wood before going to the hospital, so though it is only 45 or so I had a fire, a bright one that flamed high and lit up all the ikons. Then drank my coffee with honey in it (to use up the honey – and am no longer using sugar) and read Angela of Foligno, who is great: intense purity, sincerity, penance, like the warm clear light of the Florentine primitive painters, and those of Siena. Began the book on [Abu'l Qāsim] Junayd which Abdul Aziz sent – perhaps will take this to the hospital, but don't know how much I will be able to read.

[Justus George] Lawler sent Notes of R. Garaudy's (Marxist) view of Marxist Catholic dialogue. Clear-cut division between us. God simply "is not" and *any* view that is based on the idea of a divine presence *in* and *to* the world, and a divine will ruling all for His ends, is excluded by Marxism.

Marx on the contrary is master, responsible to no one but himself, and he must learn to rule all for *his* ends. This is at once a comic and apocalyptic myth, and the results are already evident in our world. We are doing a magnificent job of ruining things!!

The "acceptable" point of contact seems to be Teilhardian, in which God is accepted and man, as God's servant, makes himself and makes a world that will be an eschatological manifestation of God's love. His view is emotionally active and activistic – and in its own way "mystical" too.

On both sides, Marxist and Teilhardian, there is agreement in rejecting the contemplative life as "static" – because it accepts God simply as infinite, transcendent-immanent presence and truth in its wish for the dynamism of salvation history to work out. The contemplative is "with" this dynamism not by virtue of some elaborate project and historic plan, but in Zen-like, mysterious fluidity in here and now *immediate* and existential every-day-ness.

The danger I see is this: in "getting with" Marxism one consents *in* fact

1. to trust God as "absent" and as a presence to be "realized" in the future classless society

2. to substitute the dynamism of Marxist-Communist *theory* for "salvation history" or rather to identify the two

3. so that in fact the "will of God" is "secularized" in the name of faith and becomes simply the party line.

This means nothing more than a transition from the rigidity of curial-control to the political rigidity of party control. I can imagine nothing more futile! All in the name of freedom of the sons of God. My task is to preserve that freedom.

March 23, 1966

The bell tolls slowly in the dark for the preface of the conventual Mass and I listen to it with the wind swaying the heavy pines in the night. The icebox is already turned off. I have a little oleo to return to the infirmary kitchen when I go down. Mass at 9:30, then to the eye-doctor, then to the hospital for the back operation. One other thing: a small tumor in my stomach (can be felt on the surface) has been growing a little in these last weeks and had better be investigated. Fr. Eudes thinks offhand it is not a malignancy.

Anyway, if I can be serious, I suppose I am so now. And yet not terribly, not alarmed or concerned. Yet I know I have to die sometime and may this not all be the beginning of it? I don't know, but if it is I accept it in full freedom and gladness. My life stands offered with that of Christ my brother.

And if I am to start now on this way, I start on it gladly. Curious that the operation will coincide with the big protest against the Vietnam war. It is my way of being involved.

Bell for Consecration at the monastery!

The high mass on the Feast of St. Benedict was very fine. Certainly the spirit of the community is excellent and the place is blessed. There are some very good men there. It is a sincere and excellent community. Fr. Chrysogonus is writing fine new melodies which are very authentic, probably as good as any Church music being written now. In fact may turn out to be the best. This is an extraordinary mass. Fr. Flavian may soon be a hermit, and he has impressed many with the seriousness of his life of prayer. Fr. Eudes is doing an excellent job. Fr. Callistus is a good person and will be head of the Norway foundation. And so on. Dom James himself, with all his limitations and idiosyncrasies, has done immense good to this community by stubbornly holding everything together. He too is an extraordinary man, many sided, baffling, often irritating, a man of enormous will, but who honestly and in his own way really seeks to be an instrument of God. And in the end that is what he has turned out to be. I am grateful to him. Am part of all this *non meis meritis* [not on my own merits].

The one thing for which I am most grateful: this hermitage. The ability to spend at least half a day (the afternoon) here frequently, sometimes daily, since December 1960. Then sleeping here and having also the pre-dawn hours here since October 1964. Finally being here all day and all night (except for Mass and dinner) since August 1965. This last was the best and I am just beginning to really get grounded in solitude (getting rid of the writer of many articles and books), so that if my life were to be on the way to ending now this would be my one regret. Loss of the years of solitude that might still be possible. Nothing else. But there are greater gifts even than this and God knows best what is for my good – and for the good of the whole world. The best is what He wills.

PART II

Daring to Love

April 1966–September 1966

Now I see more and more that there is only one realistic answer: Love. I have got to dare to love, and to bear the anxiety of self-questioning that love arouses in me, until "perfect love casts out fear."

April 25, 1966

April 10, 1966. Easter Sunday

Back in the hermitage sooner than I expected (sleeping in the infirmary). The operation was much more smooth and effective than I expected, and apparently went beautifully. Had a hard time the first walk and am still troubled by the leg from which they took the bone graft, but on the whole have had less trouble than I anticipated. The worst was just the strain of the abnormal mechanized routinized life of the hospital, poked and pushed and stuck and cut and fed and stuffed with pills, juices etc. Got home yesterday and came up to the hermitage as soon as I could, silly with exultation. I suppose it is all a bit childish really.

[On] the 23rd left with Bernard [Fox] on time, rain started pouring down in sheets. It rained all the way in and I was glad, because of the fires I had seen in the woods at night. The eye-doctor did not find anything specially wrong with my eye. The tumor was not malignant and not even something to bother with at all. The one thing that bothered me most was the myelogram and that went well enough, though I found it hateful to be looking in a screen and seeing fluid running up and down my spine and seeing the needle sticking in me.

As to the operation, it was on the 25th, the Annunciation (I was glad of this), the Friday before Passion Week. I went up and semiremember the anesthesiologist introducing himself as Dr. St. Pierre and Dr. Marshall appearing in the green suit. That was the last I clearly knew of anything until I found a lot of people milling around my bed in my room and I asked what time it was, and was told it was eleven o'clock at night. For some reason (half-aware of being there for some time) I had imagined that a day had gone by and I had missed communion. I was surprised to find I could lie on my back without pain.

I remember being fed by a nurse at my first meal, then trying to eat one myself and picking a small piece of veal off a plate with my fingers and sticking it in my mouth. That was all I could take. The first day was hard and when after four or five days I still could not sit up and read without pain, I began to get scared and thought it would be a long haul. Then I also had a fever and apparently some pneumonia. They gave me an antibiotic which made me sick; and then when I finally got off that everything began to improve rapidly.

One week after the operation Friday in Passion Week, I was able to get up and go out to walk a while on the grass, and this made an enormous difference and also did the fact that I got a very friendly and devoted student nurse[1] working on my compresses etc. and this livened things up considerably. In fact we were getting perhaps too friendly by the time she went off on her Easter vacation, but her affection – undisguised and frank – was an *enormous* help in bringing me back to life fast. In fact all the nurses were very interested and friendly and warm. Being surrounded with all this care and esteem was a great indulgence! A huge luxury. And I realized that though I am pretty indifferent to the society of my fellow monks (can live without being lonely for the community *at all*, and it is a work of will to go down and participate in the essentials, not an emotional need), I do feel a deep emotional need for feminine companionship and love, and seeing that I must irrevocably live without it ended by tearing me up more than the operation itself.

The best thing of all was lying reading Eckhart, or sitting up, when I finally could, copying sentences from the sermons that I can use if I write on him. It was this that saved me, and when I got back to the hermitage last evening to say the Easter offices everything else drained off and Eckhart remained as real. The rest was like something I had imagined.

The doctors were fine. Had some amusing visits with another patient with a lumbar disc, Dr. Handelinan, and visited Mother Peter, the Carmelite prioress, who also has, apparently, a lumbar disc.

Began saying Mass on Laetare Sunday. Concelebrated with numb sweat on Holy Thursday with the two chaplains – and again here this morning. The Mass here was beautiful, but I found myself wondering if I would be able to get down three sanctuary steps without falling on my head, and got Fr. Matthew to help me as we left.

Spent the afternoon at the hermitage. Warm sun. Eckhart – Toward the end of the afternoon Bro. Eric came walking by and I made some signs to him. He wants to come up and talk some time so I said sure. (Permissions are given for this.)

---

[1] Parenthetically in the margin, Merton identified the student nurse as M.

April 12, 1966. Easter Tuesday

Yesterday, cold rain all day, thanks to which I stayed in the infirmary and rested. I needed it. Easter day had tired me more than I realized. Came up to the hermitage only to pick up a notebook and write addresses of the nurses to whom I had promised autographed books. The infirmary is depressing and I found it hard to sleep in the overheated room (where I cannot turn the heat entirely off). Then there are so many snide or deranged people around (Dom Vital seems to be gone in senile dementia now, poor man), though some, like Bro. Jerome, are wonders. Bro. Jerome seems almost blind now but he gets around and seems happy I am a hermit, for he greets me with much liveliness once he recognizes me.

Last night as I lay awake in the hot room, seriously considered disobeying all orders and coming up here. Did not. Came up after dinner today – warm rain, gentle, spring rain, and my redbuds are bursting out for real. Easter I was here in a kind of daze. Today I made my regular hour's meditation and began to get myself together again.

The community has moved out of the Church (yesterday) to a temporary chapel on the third floor. Already, there is a lot of banging in the Church, getting ready to tear everything out and remodel the interior. I have not seen much of the community, have no taste for meals in the infirmary refectory, and found the reading today very tedious (a speech of Pope Paul on Catholic Action, praising the aspect of organization etc. etc.). The best moments have been at Mass, back in the library chapel! Psalms and office getting back their old savor. Capitulum of II Noct[urn], Christ died for all that we *might no longer live for ourselves but for him who died for us and rose again.* This is the heart of Eckhart, and remains that in spite of all confusions. At least that is the way I understand him, though he does speak of the Godhead, and living *"in"* the Godhead rather than "for Christ."

Again the old men in the infirmary: it is disconcerting when they are *walled off* in blackness and you can do nothing to cheer or help them. I suppose prayer is all, and the ordinary physical services.

Beginning to think a little of work again – I mean writing. But I do not feel I can type yet and do not intend to try. Have no really serious ideas either. Yet I can feel them coming back again. I am more myself.

April 14, 1966. Easter Thursday

I dreamt that I was talking to Dom Vital and that he made sense; and today he was better, was up – fully dressed, not looking blank, walking around with his cane, and sitting in prayer before the Bl[essed] Sacrament.

For my part I too am becoming once more myself, deeper and deeper. It is shocking to realize that you sometimes have to fight to get yourself back when some great trauma has broken in on you. The hip incision is improving. I sleep better, sweat less and less. Yesterday I wrote a longish poem about the hospital experience[2] and I think it is a good poem too. Better than the others I have done so far this year. Today revised the notes on solitude written as preface for the Japanese *Thoughts in Sol[itude]*[3] and I think deepened and improved it. One thing has suddenly hit me – that nothing counts except love and that a solitude that is not simply the wide-openness of love and freedom is nothing. Love and solitude are the one ground of true maturity and freedom. Solitude that is just solitude and nothing else (i.e. *excludes* everything else but solitude) is worthless. True solitude embraces everything, for it is the fullness of love that rejects nothing and no one, is open to All in All.

After several days of rain the sky is clearing. Afternoons at the hermitage become once again possible. I walked a bit in the woods, under the pines, and again plan work, study, ideas, not to affirm myself but to *give* to others. Anything I have that is good is worth sharing. What is not worth sharing is not worth bothering about. What is "mine" can be tolerated only in so far as I am willing to share it with everybody.

I see this is ambiguous though. It needs qualification.

One worry remains – numbness in the right leg. Is there another problem? Will it someday mean another operation? I have got to be faithful, detached, obedient, concerned not only for my own life as I want to live it, but for God's will that remains to be realized in and through me. That is all.

Dom James has, I think, been badly treated, tricked and dealt with rather shamefully and stupidly by the people making the "experimental" founda-

---

2   "With the World in My Bloodstream," is published in *The Collected Poems of Thomas Merton* (New York: New Directions, 1977), 615–18.

3   See Thomas Merton, *"Honorable Reader," Reflections on My Work*, edited by Robert E. Daggy (New York: Crossroad, 1989), 107–18. Merton revised, enlarged, and published this preface as "Love and Solitude" in *Critic* (November 1966); this final version also appears in Thomas Merton, *Love and Living*, edited by Naomi Burton Stone and Brother Patrick Hart (New York: Farrar, Straus & Giroux, 1979; New York: Harcourt Brace Jovanovich, 1985), 15–24.

tions in Denmark. Of course I have not heard both sides and Dom J.'s position sounds a little rigid to me, but still, they have not dealt with him freely or even maturely. It puts the *avant-garde* of the order in a rather different light. I have had reservations about this experiment since it began, and I still have them. I wonder if these people are simply monastic agitators. They do not strike me as having much to offer. But again, I do not know the whole story. For my part I don't want to get involved in debates about it – one of this set, in Kenya, wrote me recently trying to engage me in a silly "action vs. contemplation" argument – obviously using me to draw attention to himself and his friends. It is a bit silly and I told him I would have no part of it. Anyway, the Gethsemani foundation in Norway seems to be definitely off. They will go to Chile instead – or rather take over Spencer's Chilean foundation, which is certainly an economy!!

April 16, 1966. Saturday in Albis

Dom Columban is here for the visitation and surprised me by a visit to my infirmary room, where I was resting after dinner. Last evening a group of the "infirm" sat around the loudspeaker in the common room to listen to his halting English speech for the opening of the Visitation. Fr. John Baptist, Bro. Jerome, and the novice Bro. Columban, whom I will talk to this evening. Has had flu for two weeks!

Dom C. told me that the Viet Cong had blown up a huge supply of gasoline and a lot of planes at an American base, as this fantastic, tragic, absurd war goes on. More and more I am convinced that the real problem is the delusory character of American thinking about life, reality, what the world is all about. Men with incredible technical skill and no sense of human realities in Asia – lost in abstractions, sentimentalities, myths, delusions, Narcissism and the Great Mania fixation of America! This can lead to nothing but disaster on an enormous scale if the more realistic minds cannot get something across! The Viet Nam venture is a pure absurdity.

April 19, 1966

Warm wind swaying the very leafed out branches of the rose hedge. The grass was cut yesterday for the first time (and smelled sweetly). The dogwood blossoms are just beginning to open. Bro. Benedict finished planting those pecan trees yesterday.

And a letter came from M. I was glad to hear from her. Have to think – my way around the problem of this tenderness – but anyway, I will do the only thing possible, and risk loving with Christ's love when there is so obvious a need for it. And not fear!

Harper's (Catherine Meyer) wrote they would take "Apologies to an Unbeliever" if I would cut it and "jimmy it down." Which I did today.

The question of love: I have to face the fact that I have simply sidestepped it. Now it must be faced squarely. I cannot live without giving love back to a world that has given me so much. And of course it has to be the love of a man dedicated to God – and selfless, detached, free, completely open love. And I have not attained to such a level, hence the risk. But facing the risk – not after all great since I am out here in the woods!! – I will learn. And God deliver me from selfishness.

April 20, 1966

I can hear the demolishers shouting from the top of the steeple. They are now stripping it. A momentous change: the steeple has been so much a sign of the place – the thing one looks for when one is getting close – the expression of the abbey's identity – the sign that it is *there!* I was disquieted by the steeple's going. The Church is raided and ruined inside (Sunday I concelebrated on the third floor and it was already hot, but I like the simplicity of the long room and the beams). Fr. Idesbald has been turned out of his nook[4] (*"Abbates in Pace"* ["Abbots in Peace"]). Warm afternoon. Dom Columban came up to the hermitage on his tour.

April 21, 1966

Dark day, colder. Andy Boone's buzz saw is going and it sounds like winter again. But the grass is very green, the redbuds show well against the green pines and the brush bursting into leaf, small wildflowers everywhere and the May apples opening their shiny new umbrellas. St. Anselm's day. It has been a day of struggle and prayer for me – the need for inner freedom, the urgency of constant work, and the difficulty of getting back into solitude after the hospital. In fact there is now a real doubt in my mind about the value of the whole hermit experiment as it is here. Certainly it means more to me than the artificialities of the community, but this is artificial and arbitrary in its own way. I would organize it otherwise if I could – more open, less rigid. But I have no way of doing so, and really perhaps it is best to have to take it, as I do, on someone else's terms, especially if that other is an Abbot with whose views I in no way agree. But there *is* the question of char-

---

4 The "nook" was the burial place for the abbots.

ity, of being open to others. Of course I am really bothered and worried. M. wants to see me and I – want to see her. I tell myself it is because I want to help her. And so on. Yet the bother is that one has to *calculate* how it might possibly be done. And then the letters . . . will they be stopped, or interfered with etc. Things should not have to be this way. In the hospital, where I could confront everything directly and frankly, there were no such Byzantine problems of tactics and justifications.

However, I must admit that I can do her little or no good as long as I am emotionally attached to her. I must try to be more free and more sure of what I mean by love in Christ – and not kid myself.

April 22, 1966

More shouting on the steeple. Slowly the plates of lead come off and the old brown lumber appears. Warm afternoon. For a while I sat in the sun surrounded by lovemaking bumblebees. The other day I saw the feathers of a cardinal which a hawk had killed, and was sad, thinking a pair had been broken up. Today I saw this male sitting beautifully on a fencepost singing joyfully – but at first no female. Then I saw her flying in and out of a big rose bush in the hedge, where the new nest is, and was happy.

Cannot eat much, do not feel like work (writing). Am delaying work on the bits for Ned O'Gorman's book[5] (plenty of time anyway I found out). Nothing terribly pressing to be done, and I don't yet feel much like typing. But walking around, my neck feels fine (today is exactly 4 weeks since the operation). The left leg is still a bit numb, and the incision still bleeds. Otherwise everything is fine.

April 24, 1966. II Sun[day] after Easter

One warm grey day after another, continued struggle in my own heart. I am losing weight (five more pounds in the last week). Repugnance for food. Perhaps this is something to do with the antibiotic that made me sick in the hospital. It will be better for me when I can work again. Yesterday, the whole day revolved around a long (illegal) phone conversation with M. I got in the cellarer's office when everyone was at dinner (with his approval – he went off and left me locked in), reached her in the hospital cafeteria (cry of joy when she found out who it was!). We had a good long talk, and it was in many respects necessary, cleared up a lot of confusion in my own mind (from

---

5 "Seven Words" published in *Prophetic Voices: Ideas and Words of Revolution*, edited by Ned O'Gorman (New York: Random House, 1969).

sheer lack of information and communication). Yet on the other hand one thing led to another and this is another link in an uncomfortable kind of karmic chain. In my heart I know it would really have been better if I had followed my original intuition and been content with a couple of letters and nothing more. But we want to see each other etc. etc. Still we both know there is no future to it and there is no sense making much of it. Sooner or later it will all end, anyway, and it would be better to end it before it gets more complicated than it is. And now I fear that a chain of events has started that cannot be stopped – only slowed down, directed, guided (I hope!).

Today – back to meditation on the *Dhammapada* – something sound to support me when everything else is quicksand.

April 25, 1966. F[east] of St. Mark

Yesterday I went down to begin my conferences again, having thought of reading my hospital poem – yet doubting and hesitating. I read it, and at the end, though I am sure that most of them did not understand much of it, they all seemed very attentive and moved – some (whom I would not have expected to be so,) quite visibly. I think to begin with that they were first of all happy that I should share a poem with them (of my own – which I never do. Perhaps read one twelve years ago in the scholasticate). Also, they were obviously glad to have the conferences start again. In a word, in spite of all my anxieties and doubts about myself and my hesitations about the community, I am someone they (at least those who come to the conferences, and others too) appreciate, to whom they look for something that seems to them alive and valuable. Usually it disturbs me to admit this, since it starts a conflict between narcissism on one hand and self-doubt on the other. And my usual reaction is flight.

Now I see more and more that there is only one realistic answer: Love. I have got to dare to love, and to bear the anxiety of self-questioning that love arouses in me, until "perfect love casts out fear."

Same with M. (but with no nonsense!). The basic fact is that she does love me – she does need from me a certain kind of love that will support her and help her believe in herself and get free from some destructive patterns and attachments that are likely to wreck her. Her love arouses in me at once an overwhelming gratitude and the impulse to fling my whole self into her arms, and also panic, doubt, fear of being deceived and hurt (as I lay awake half the night tormented by the thought of the guy she is probably sleeping with!).

After several days of this conflict and anxiety, last night I took a sleeping pill and Bro. Camillus, the infirmarian, gave me some old bourbon that had been tucked away in a closet since Dom Edmund's days (marvelous too!). I slept nearly 9 hours (sweated up and changed 3 times) and awoke with the deep realization that my response of love to M. was *right*. It might have nothing to do with the rule books or with any other system, it might be open to all kinds of delusions and error, but in fact so far by and large I have been acting right. I have been in the Truth, not through any virtue of my own, nor through any superior intuition, but because I have let love take hold of me in spite of all my fear and I have obeyed love, and have honestly tried to see her truly as she is and love her exactly as she is, to value her uniquely and share with her this deep faith in her. And I know that the result has been a deep, clear, strong, indubitable resonance between us. Our hearts really are in tune. Our depths really communicate. And this is all. It is the real root and ground of everything and of this sexual love can only at best be a sign. Certainly it would be marvelous if we could communicate the whole thing in this sign, but I see no way of doing this without falling away completely from truth. Hence I will never touch her, and will make sure that this is perfectly clear – without being sanctimonious about it, and she is very aware of the problem too!

Then too of course, I have to continue my work of eliminating all craving, all passionate attachment, all self-seeking from this. And it is work. Evasion is no answer, and I am not sure I have a real answer or know just what to do. I have only in the end to trust God in this as in all my other perplexities and He will bring me through it all right.

April 27, 1966

There is no question that I am in deep. Tuesday (yesterday) M. met me at the doctor's. Appeared in the hall, small, shy, almost defiant, with her long black hair, her grey eyes, her white trench coat. (She kept saying she was scared.) [Dr. James] Wygal[6] (on whom I depended for transportation and lunch) was along, and kept peppering everything with a kind of earthy crudeness that annoyed me, but it was a good thing I guess. His house just burned down and he was upset, drank too much, left me and M. alone for a half hour in our booth at Cunningham's. It was a wonderful lunch, so good to be with her, and more than ever I saw how much and how instantly and how delicately we respond to each other on every level. Also I can see why she is scared. I am too. There is a sense of awful, awesome rather, sexual

---

[6] Merton had begun to see a psychologist, Dr. James Wygal, in 1960 and they soon became friends.

affinity – and of course there can be no hesitations about my position here. I have vows and I must be faithful to them. And I told myself that I can and will be, but I have moments of being scared too. Apart from that, though, we had a very good talk and once again it was clearer than ever that we are terribly in love, and it is the kind of love that can virtually tear you apart. She would literally tremble with it. But also it exists on other levels, and really so, and I tried to make this clear, and the meaning of it, trying desperately. I do so much want to love her as we began, spiritually – I do believe such spiritual love is not only possible but does exist between us, deeply, purely, strongly, and the rest can be controlled. Yet she is right to be scared. We can simply wreck each other. I am determined not to give in to this, not to yield to fear and despair, to keep it on the level where it belongs, but I can see I really don't know how to handle this if it ever breaks loose. I have been imprudent. Wygal added to it afterward with his warnings, prophecies of doom and gloomy insinuations. The man has an appalling death wish, and sado-masochism gets more and more into his friendship, and that is really depressing. Yet there were some peaceful moments sitting at the airport in the rain, drinking brandy and soda and watching the planes. Yet it was unreal. I do hope that my fondness for M. will not turn into an ugly, bloody conflagration. It would be so good to be able to help her, to have real sweet, tender, good friendship. I am going to fight for it, against all odds because I *do* believe in this kind of love (look at Jacques and Raïssa Maritain) and in fact I do have plenty of friends on this basis (Mother Angela for instance). It is just that M. is terribly inflammable, and beautiful, and is no nun, and so tragically full of passion and so wide open. My response has been too total and too forthright, we have admitted too much, communicated all the fire to each other and now we are caught. I am not as smart or as stable as I imagined.

But such good things – her response to the poems, her words about her love, her fears, her hopes . . .

April 28, 1966

Last evening I called M. again from the Cellarer's Office. Another imprudence. Several people saw me hanging around waiting to get her on the phone (she was at supper) and I had to spend 3/4 hour there reading Dag Hammarskjøld and waiting. Then I talked for about 1/2 hour and seven or eight people were in and out. This can't go on forever, it is not safe.

However, it was once again a wonderful call. She was perfectly happy and at peace, with a blissful, childlike kind of happiness about our meeting

Tuesday: a total certitude about our love, all fear gone, a perfect confidence in our affection and in the greater worth of a love in which we are determined in advance to stay pure, according to our obligations. I respond so much to her now, to the inflections of her voice, her laughter, everything, that I was flooded with peace and happiness and wanted just to talk to her forever. There is in her a wonderful sweet little-girl quality of simplicity and openness and I suppose this is closest to being her true self. It is with this self that she told me "I will love you *always*." She was up until 1 o'clock writing me a letter after our meeting Tuesday (an "epic"). She laughed about her striding into the Medical Arts Building fighting her fears ("Joan of Arc with her banner"). All I know is that I love her so much I can hardly think of anything but her. Also I know that in itself this love is a thing of enormous value (never has anyone given herself to me so completely, so openly, so frankly, and never have I responded so completely!). Yet it is in absolute conflict with every social canon, feeling, predetermination etc. And *everyone*, the pious and the feisty, will use it for one thing only – to crush and discredit us.

I suppose that is the next thing to face. If I believe in love and in M., am I willing to face all the consequences frankly and despise the ridicule, the criticism and the injury without in any way cheaply giving in? The worst is that inevitably we will be cut off from each other with brutality and self-righteous refinements of official cruelty. In the solitude of my heart I will have to struggle to be ready for this, for here again we are both vulnerable and can so easily be destroyed. I keep thinking if only we could really go through it all *together*, supporting one another by our love and closeness, it would be bearable. I see how badly I need her love to complete me with its warmth and understanding and how utterly alone I am without her now. Some talk for a hermit! But it is true and I may as well admit it.

Then the other temptation – when I see how rough this can all become, I instinctively go back to the old routine of drawing into my shell and putting up the defenses – *not* letting it go any further, anticipating the break to make it easier for myself, etc. etc. That would be a betrayal. I want to share as much as I can of my heart and life with her in the next couple of months so that we are as much as possible "transformed" in each other and that no matter what happens we will always love each other and be filled with each other no matter what people do to us. It seems like a contradiction of all I have been striving for and writing about . . . and living for. Somehow I know it isn't. Yet I have no way of rationalizing that one! I will just have to leave it as it is – vulnerable and ridiculous.

———

Of course too I have kissed her and in the chastity and tenderness of it (as I *knew* it would be) felt this deep, total, vibrant resonance and response of a whole warm little being, totally surrendered. This much, surely, has to be said with the senses! I know she also received me as totally, blindly, rashly but deliberately given.

Groping for support and strength – where else but in God's word?

"Dear children you belong to God and you have conquered (all who are opposed to love and to Christ) for *He who is within you is greater than he who is in the world . . .*"

"Beloved, let us love one another, for love belongs to God and everyone who loves is born of God and knows God: he who does not love does not know God, for God is love."

"God is love and he who remains in love remains in God and God remains in him. Love is complete within us when we have absolute confidence about the day of judgment, since in this world we are living as He lives. Love has no dread in it; no, love in its fullness drives all death away . . ." *1 Jn. 4.*

How does all this fit the standards of "the cell"? How does "the cell" judge it? There seems to be no problem. Solitude has not become distasteful to me, or changed its meaning. It is true! I am not ready to go back to sleeping up here – medicinally and perhaps psychologically. That it is the only place where I feel at home and feel I can be myself. And I think, if the truth be told, what I am looking for is not to "be a hermit" but just to be myself, the person God made me to be – and also incidentally the person loved by M.

(She was looking at the pictures in *Jubilee* – which embarrass me – and said she was just doing this "because it was you." And the hospital librarian came along and said what a miserable life I must be leading etc. etc.)

April 30, 1966

Heavy rain, breaking up in the warm afternoon.

Every day I have to resist the temptation to call her again. We are waiting for the Abbot to leave (Monday) so that we can get letters through more easily (I hope!). Insecurity is bad for me, and I begin to seethe with physical desire, then become restless, disturbed, distressed, and fearful for the future. Always a possibility of disaster! But a good deep effort at prayer (this afternoon for example) is a help. Work also is a help (yesterday – wrote an article *Commonweal* asked for, about "The World").[7] Reading too. Just walking around trying to collect my thoughts is not much help. They all tend to be about her and I become desperately lonely.

There is *no other way* but deep prayer, renunciation of all surreptitious desires for self-satisfaction and consolation, and a firm determination to love her only in God. I can see I have not really made this act of renunciation deep down, and have to keep renewing and deepening it. It means renouncing also the desire to continue calls and visits beyond a certain necessary point. All very complex and difficult. My solitude in the hermitage (at least part of each day) is one of the biggest helps after all. After an afternoon here I am at peace and relatively sane again though I was terrified to the point of physical pain and trembling earlier this p.m.

If in all this I can also truly and unselfishly love *her* (and not just my own love or my "being loved by" her), there will be much gained. But being away from her makes it so easy just to fall back into imagining and longing and remembering, and this is not love. All I can think of is to pray for her as earnestly and honestly as possible and leave the rest to God.

May 2, 1966

Continuous pounding rain all day yesterday (Sunday. F[east] of St. Joseph the Worker) and in addition the time changed and this afternoon was an hour longer. I got into a rain coat and went out for a walk, and the desolate yet beautifully green rain-soaked fields were a joy to be in. I went out toward the south skirting St. Joseph hill where the sweep of fields is very wide. Emptiness, nothing but rain, no cars, no people, just rain and larks rising out of the green barley or whatever it is. In the vast emptiness and desolation of it I was at peace – without thought and without much preoccupation. Not lonely *for* M. but in some strange way lonely *with* her, as if she had somehow peacefully become part of my loneliness and of my life that tries to be in God, tries to dwell at the point where life and grace well up out of the unknown.

The afternoon was comforting, for this is what I have been grasping for and it is the only thing that makes relative sense: i.e. her love in this way (only) can become a harmonious part of my vocation. And I believe that in this way it can also be very fruitful – but it also presupposes the Cross, always!

7 "Is the World a Problem? Ambiguities in the Secular," *Commonweal* 84 (3 June 1966): 305–9.

It is in this, strangely, that I seem to really love her, as if in this emptiness my love really reached out to her own heart, for I know she is lonely for and perhaps "with" me and that in her heart is the same struggle and that I must do what I can to sustain her and comfort her – my own struggle to find peace is not just for myself but for her, since I will share it with her as best I can – in a letter and when I see her and my prayer. This too makes sense. But the difficulty of communication is my worst suffering.

What is most frustrating about being so blocked in something that seems so human and real, is to confront the low level of communication within the community. Heard on the loudspeaker some remarks of Dom James in evening chapter about notes which had been handed to him concerning the new church plans. One had the sense that it was all a childlike game – the notes were well meant and often tried to make good points, but in every case he read each note in such a way as to make it sound idiotic, and in each case the community accepted this distortion. In this way the community – most of whose representative members wrote this – consented to its own degradation and humiliation. The final impression was that they were all childish idiots whose views were absurd and would never be seriously considered, and yet each one was happy that this note had actually "been read" to the community. What a burlesque of "family life" and of community! When this kind of indignity is systematically substituted for real communication, then there is something basically wrong. And there is nothing to be done about it (for instance how could one ever have explained such a thing to Dom Columban last week? To him it would be perfectly understandable that a monastic community should be treated as a collection of infants without judgment).

No wonder there is trouble everywhere, in seminaries, in religious houses etc.

May 4, 1966

Brilliant May days after the rain. Have walked out twice into the deep woods behind Dom F[rederic]'s lake. M. is supposed to be coming out for a picnic this Saturday. More letters, another phone call (this time legal). She has settled down to a sweet little girl happiness that completely disarms and ravishes me. I just don't know what to do with my life, finding myself so much loved, and loving so much, when according to all standards it is all wrong, absurd, insane. Yet here it is. And I can't help coming back again and again to the realization that somehow it is not crazy – it makes sense. Here is someone who, because I exist, has been made much happier and who has made me happier, and revealed to me something I never thought to see so intimately again – the beauty of a girl's heart and of her gift of herself. But this is one of the great, deep realities, like the spring itself and this blue day and the green hills and the light of the sun – much more real and perfect than all these, because conscious, aware and free.

So though it can all be perplexing or even frightening (what will happen when inevitably we are separated?) I see one thing only: to go on hesitantly perhaps, but trustingly trying to answer the demands of this deep personal commitment to her in love, to really, deeply return her love, to make her happy, to give her joy and support and help, to make her life more beautiful.

Of course I would be more peaceful, secure and safe just minding my own business in the hermitage and trying to forget her – but thank God for this blessed disturbance, for this love that sometimes upsets me, which, at a certain cost to me, makes another person happier. And which opens up in her such a revelation of love and goodness.

If I seem a bit disoriented by it, that is good. More reason to trust in God and hope to come out where I could not have come without her help. I so much want her life to be happy and fulfilled, in God, humanly, every way – and that brings up other problems.

J[ames] Laughlin and Nicanor Parra are arriving here this evening.

May 7, 1966

The brilliant weather has continued all week and now it seems to be the most brilliant day of them all. M. should be leaving Louisville about now with Jack Ford and his wife (and M. is scared that they will be scandalized at us – which is quite possible. How are the two of us going to sit politely at a picnic lunch without giving away the obvious fact that we are in love?). M. and I will have trouble providing safe small talk that will not let all the cats out of all the bags, because Thursday with J. and Nicanor I ended up in Louisville taking her out to supper at the airport. First I was only going to call her from Bardstown. Then I thought we could go to Bernheim Forest and call from there. But there were no public phones there. So we went out to the big restaurant and motel on the turnpike beyond the toll gate and by the time I got there I decided that, since we were practically in Louisville, we might as well go all the way. So I called M. to expect us in twenty minutes and soon there we were outside Lourdes Hall, and she came out looking more lovely than ever. I had on only my Trappist overalls but anyhow we got into the Luau Room at the airport. Lots of rich people were arriving for the Derby (which is today) and the place was full of brass and money and there I sat having a marvelous time, looking like a convict, unable to turn my head to see all the swanky jets landing behind me, satisfied to look at M. I could hardly eat anything – not unusual as it has been that way since the operation.

After supper M. and I had a little while alone and went off by ourselves and found a quiet corner, sat on the grass out of sight and loved each other to ecstasy. It was beautiful, awesomely so, to love so much and to be loved, and to be able to say it all completely without fear and without observation (not that we sexually consummated it).[8]

Came home dazed, long after dark (highly illegal!) and wrote a poem before going to bed. I think Nicanor Parra was highly edified. He was saying something about how one must "follow the ecstasy" – by which he meant evidently right out of the monastery and over the hill. This of course I cannot do.

The poem is of course unpublishable. So it will be for M. only, and I'll try to read it to her today in the woods without choking with emotion.

LOUISVILLE AIRPORT, MAY 5, 1966

Here on the foolish grass
where the rich in small jets
land with their own hopes
And their own kind

We with the gentle liturgy
of shy children have permitted God
To make again that first world
Here on the foolish grass
After the spring rain has dried
And all the loneliness

Is for a moment lost in that simple
liturgy of children permitting God
To make again that love which is His alone

His alone and terribly obscure and rare
Love walks gently as a deer

---

[8] Merton appears to have added the parenthetical note later.

to where we sit on the green grass
In the marvel of this day's going down
Celebrated only
By all the poets since the world began

This is God's own love He makes in us
As all the foolish rich fly down
on to the paradise of grass
where the world first began
where God began
To make His love in man and woman
For the first time
Here on the sky's shore
Where the eternal sun goes down
and all the millionaires in small jets
land with their own hopes
and their own kind.

We with the tender liturgy
And tears
of the newborn
celebrate the first creation
of solemn love
Now for the first time forever
Made by God in these
Four wet eyes and cool lips
And worshipping hands
when the one voiceless beginning
of a splendid fire
Rises out of the heart
And all the evening is one flame
which all the prophets
accurately foresaw
Would make life plain
And created the world
over again

There is only the one love
which is now our world
our foolish grass

Celebrated by all
The poets since the first beginning
of any song.

May 9, 1966

M. and the Fords and Fr. John [Loftus] came Saturday – arriving late (an hour of waiting and I made desperate acts of patience) – the woods were beautiful. It was a brilliant cool day, something like my ordination day, lovely May weather. A good picnic with a bottle of St. Emilion. Then M. and I went off for a couple of hours together (Gladys Ford gave us some funny looks when we came back and I think Fr. John was worried). But M. and I sat on the moss by the little creek in one of my favorite places, and talked and loved and opened our hearts to each other. It was the longest, greatest time we had had together, not as ecstatic as the evening at the airport, but sweet and deep. There are in us both deep capacities for love, especially in her. I have never seen so much simple, spontaneous, total love. And I realize that the deepest capacities for human love in me have never even been tapped, that I too can love with an awful completeness. Responding to her has opened up the depths of my life in ways I can't begin to understand or analyze now. And of course there could be all kinds of "danger." But what danger? Where does the danger really lie? I am struck by the fact that the social rules of thumb for handling such situations offer no real structure, no authentic answer, and one cannot begin to make sense of norms!

I can't spell it all out here. But all kinds of questions have obviously arisen.

1) M. has decided that after graduation in August she will get a job in Louisville instead of going home to Cincinnati. She will get a car and will come out regularly to see me, like once a week, and we will go on with this as long as we can. Obviously this means meeting her without permission – phone calls without permission. The danger of a conscience correspondence[9] that Dom James may decide to open and investigate etc. It is practical for our present need, but is no solution. And I am still determined to stick to my vows. Hence it is really no solution at all. How can we hope to go on for the rest of our lives like that? Especially how can I ask her to live such a life, instead of marrying and having a home. She refuses even to think of marrying anyone else etc. etc.

[9] Letters designated "conscience matter" generally were not subject to the customary review of correspondence by the abbot or someone designated by him.

2) The question has obviously arisen: whether we should not just go off and live together "married." But the problems are appalling. Excommunication, *fuga cum muliere* [flight with a woman], apostasy, and all the hounds after me perpetually from Dom James to the Roman Curia! Yet strangely enough now I can see where this could be for some people the only answer. There comes a time when all this legal machinery for fulmination simply does not convince. It claims to be the voice of God, it pretends to damn in His name and by His authority . . . Does it really? Is it a mark of faith to accept this in timid fear, so that one closes his mind in desperation to all other more intimate and more personal values? These are questions that can and should be seriously asked in this time after Vatican II! Obviously the question is not whether contumacy becomes a virtue. And one would always try to work it out with the Church, not *against* it. Yet with someone like Dom J. there are no possible solutions, no chances of reasonable communication. Especially where women are involved everything has been long settled in advance and there are no questions even to be raised.

3) It is, however, now, to me, a really serious option: that if in the near future the way *does* open for a married clergy, I should take it.

I don't know if the above makes sense. At times I am so carried away by M. that I can't think of anything but of finding some way to spend the rest of my life with her. I have no compunction about this, for I do not feel it is in any way an infidelity to God, since I think our love comes from Him. But *practically*, in the framework of social obligations I have, it is a pure impossibility and even thinking about it can perhaps become ruinous.

Her beautiful letters keep coming. Cries of love out of the late night when she sits up writing to me in the silence. Today, one she wrote Thursday, after we had met at the airport.

". . . I want to be with you, to never be without you. . . . I want to live with you darling! I want to share everything in your existence, I can't bear separation. To love you, to walk hand in hand with you straight to God . . ." She breaks my heart. How can we possibly be together unless I leave this place and how can I possibly get out of here? I really would if it were possible. How can we go on just seeing each other occasionally for a few hours? How can she build her life on that? This is all crazy. Perhaps after all the only thing is to be tough about it, and simply say that what is impossible is impossible, and not let our hopes get built up. But when we are together it seems so sane and obvious that we belong together.

She summed it all up, *"To be ourselves."*
The crux of the matter is: this is not allowed.

Poem I wrote yesterday (Sunday) –

I ALWAYS OBEY MY NURSE

> I always obey my nurse
> I always care
> For wound and fracture
> Because I am always broken
> I obey my nurse
>
> And God did not make death
> He did not make harm
> But the little blind fire
> That escapes from one wound into the other
> Knitting the broken bones
> And fixing scars so that they can be forgotten.
>
> I will obey my nurse who keeps this fire
> Deep in her wounded breast
> For God did not make death.
> He did not make pain
> or the arrogant incision
> under the official bandage
>
> Because I am always broken I obey my nurse
> who in her grey eyes and her mortal breast
> Holds an immortal love the wise have fractured
> Because we have both been broken we can tell
> that God did not make death
>
> I will obey the little spark
> That flies from fracture to fracture
> And the explosion
> where God did not make death
> But only vision
>
> I always obey my nurse's broken heart
> Where all fires come from
> And the abyss of flame

Knitting pain to pain
And the abyss of light
Made of pardoned sins
For God did not make death

I always obey the spark that smacks like lightning
In the giant night
I obey without question
The outlaw reasons, cries in the abyss
From this world's body that the wise have fractured
For God did not make death
He did not make prisons

The stalking canonical raven
The dirt in the incision
I will obey my nurse
I always take care
of my fractured religion

And God did not make death.

A voice says in me – love: do trust love! Do not fear it, do not avoid it, do not take mere half-measures with it, but *love*, believe in it, without any special program, without rebelling against the whole structure of the church, without ignoring or neglecting (or idolizing) concrete obligations which you may have, but *love* within the actual framework where you are and see what comes of it. This must mean a great freedom of spirit in regard to a lot of things and even a certain flexibility with regard to some monastic rules. (But my own suspicion says: where can it ever get you?) Never mind, you will never let go of your image of yourself in order to love another. You will have sacrificed your own profession in trying to make another happy. (But can it make her happy, in the long run?) Do not worry about the results: only do what you do: *love*.

Pray to learn how!!

May 10, 1966

Frost this morning. Bright sun now. Birds singing loudly. Wrens hopping about on the wood on the porch.

Whatever else I do, reading and meditation remain important, to keep in perfect touch with reality, to avoid the divisions created by yearning and

speculation. One thing is evident – no use building my life on mere possibilities, whether an ideal self as a perfectly solitary hermit or a fulfilled and
human self living with M. somewhere on an island. I *am* myself. I do not
make myself, or bring myself into conformity with some nonsensical ideal.
One of the good sane things about this love is seeing myself as loved by M.
True, she idealizes me impossibly, yet at the same time unavoidably I am
known to her *as I am*, and many of the things she loves in me are things I
find humiliating and impossible. But she loves them because they are con-
cretely mine, and I love her in the same way. This surely is a very good
thing!!

May 12, 1966

There is no question that this love is a hard thing to bear – and to live with,
precisely because it is so much *better* than the ordinary routines of my life
before it. And yet inevitably it is a difficult good to cope with, just because
there is so much that is excellent, and fine, and desirable, and wonderful in
it. Hence the only thing to do is to take all of it with a good heart and joy
and not fear the pain that must come with it.

Her last three letters have been to me almost unbearably beautiful. Her
love and her heart are a revelation of a most perfectly tuned and fashioned
personality, a lovely womanly nature, and an almost unbounded affection,
all of which she has given me. I can only regard this as a kind of miracle
in my life – that is the first thing necessary if I am to understand it at all. Her
reactions to our moments together simplify and perpetuate the joy and
deepen my own memory and experience of them – and this love keeps
growing, both in her heart and in mine. She seems to have a limitless capacity to love more and more. And yet I with my ingrained pessimism keep
thinking of the time when we must stop – for it cannot go on like this. I have
only a limited time to see her – when I stop going to the doctor's I will not
be able to meet her – at least legally – in Louisville, and if she comes out
here it will be without permission and we may well get caught and stopped,
with a lot of hullabaloo. Well, we can go on until they stop us, at least that!
We are certainly not doing anything wrong, and loving each other most
purely and innocently. And this, too, is very beautiful – for when we kiss
each other our lips say everything – without any effort or any of the smokey
wisdom of passion. And so it goes – I ask myself how I will live without her,
and forget what a wonderful thing it is that *we have had so much* (last Thursday and Saturday!) – such incomparable meetings as I never dared imagine

or expect. There will be more – and then I know that when she says she will always love me, and never stop loving me, whatever happens, she really means it. And I do too. This is merely something to live for and to rejoice in, even though we may have to be lonely and separate for long periods at a time. And God who has given us so much will, if we trust Him, continue to deepen and to fulfill our love.

Clearly this love is not a contradiction of my solitude but a mysterious part of it. It fits strangely and without conflict into my inner life of meditation and prayer – as it does much more obviously in her, since for her all articulate and affective love is most spontaneous. But it fits also into my own way of emptiness and unknowing, and indeed my moments of inner silence are my main source of strength, light and love – along with my Mass which is most ardent these days and in which I feel most closely united with her in Christ.

May 13, 1966

Last night as I was about to go to bed I got the urge to call M. and so wandered in the dark over to the Steel Building, found the cellarer's office open and went in and called – it was the third call this week! She was delighted, was in fact in the middle of writing me a letter on my "emptiness and nothingness" stuff which I really should not have written her, she does not need it. Her whole inner life is centered on love and on the other as person and is very realistic – I distressed her a little with this other approach but she understood it I think anyway. We talked of seeing each other Saturday, of her coming out next Thursday, etc. She is having exams for which she has not studied enough. She was out walking by the grotto etc. Before I was through Bro. Clement, who had been working late, came in and looked angry, but seeing it was only I he was mollified. Normally he would be furious at finding someone using his phone at that – or any other – hour. I hope he stays on my side!!

This morning I wrote another (love) poem for her, an aubade, just at the time she would be waking up (7 a.m.). That's three in a week.

AUBADE ON A CLOUDY MORNING

Today no sun shines
Yet it is another morning
When in a distant room
Which I have never entered

No one sees your eyes first open
Only the dim light
which is now perhaps at this moment changed
Into the light you look at
And the day that is known to you
Knows the moment of your return
From the rivers of night
From that nowhere
That ocean of sightless quiet
Inviolate unknowing where your heart
Slept for me
For me restored itself to life and to the love
By which alone I stay alive
For whose essential and direct messages
I am waiting now pacing up and down
In this messy, lonely place
Waiting once again to live
And at war with my own heart
Because I cannot be there
To see your eyes reveal you
Opening not only to the light of my day
But to my own eyes and waiting heart
So that I might declare
As the one who knows best
That you are truly present again
That your identity
Has really been restored to the world
And your presence
The very necessary presence
And even the person of love
Has been thank God granted us again
For another day in which I can
Again breathe, work a little
Write something
(If I write for you
I can write something)
Try to exist
(If I am yours

I can exist)
Even though I am at war with my own heart
Because I am never by your side
When those eyes first open
To recognize the new day

But if this is at least a day
That is known to you
And now seen by your eyes
Though without a sun
Its dim light is enough
I am satisfied with it
I look for no other.

May 16, 1966

Saturday I went to see Dr. Mitchell. It turned out I had bursitis in the left
elbow and for this he gave me a (painful) shot, which was especially painful
after I got home in the evening. Meanwhile I had lunch alone with M. at
Cunningham's and we had a very good time, though getting too much in
love and talking too freely about what we would like to do – vague unrealistic possibilities, and too much along the lines of the above Aubade, which
does not rest lightly on my conscience!! Not exactly fitting for a monk! But
it was a lovely quiet grey afternoon and I enjoyed it – a pleasure I was really
not entitled to at all. When I got home I woke up in the night and began to
worry, and from then on it has been anxiety and unrest. In the middle of
Sunday afternoon, out in the woods, I saw clearly that it can't go on like
this. I simply have no business being [in] love and playing around with a
girl, however innocently. It is true I do sincerely love her and I know she
loves me too, and we do owe each other something – but all in all it is simply a game, a fascinating, pleasurable exciting game that she plays perfectly
and I have enjoyed it almost to ecstasy (Saturday again). What a beautiful
thing it is! But after all I am supposed to be a monk with a vow of chastity
and though I have kept my vow – I wonder If I can keep it indefinitely and
still play this gorgeous game!

[Merton scratched out the first four lines of this paragraph, rendering
them indecipherable.] It is certainly as deep or deeper than anything I can
remember and we have had beautiful moments together – but I can see it
has to end sooner or later, and probably soon. I called her today again, and
I am afraid she sensed the difference and was hurt (and this has added to my

self-reproach). I can't get my mind on anything else this afternoon though I intend to do some writing, if I can.

But the main thing is this. It may be painful to end it, but it will be better. Not to solemnly declare everything finished, but we cannot possibly plan to go on seeing each other regularly. Perhaps we can exchange a letter or two once in a while, and I would miss her badly if I never saw her at all, but we can't plan anything sanely and it would only lead to a great deal of trouble. So we just have to face it. Thursday will probably decide it all. But what a sweet person she is and how bad I feel about having to let this end. I hope really we can keep in contact and go on really loving each other in our hearts as we have promised, because in a way it will be simply impossible for me to stop loving her. It is out of the question. I think I will love her as long as I live.

May 17, 1966

The trouble is that with M. and me it is not a game. What I wrote yesterday was in large part a shameful evasion, since somehow on Sunday I had suddenly convinced myself I had to find a way out – and there is no easy way out of love. The suffering is great but there is no getting around it. It is true the very nature of things will make it necessary for us to see each other less. And that in itself is no real solution. In real anguish I called her twice yesterday, and of course this disturbed her a little. She was also terribly lonely and depressed at the beginning of last week I learn. Today I called her again and it was a fine call, happy and sane and got things back to normal – i.e. not so much anguish and depression.

Humanly speaking the situation is impossible. We are terribly in love, and it goes very deep, perhaps more even with her than with me, for her capacity to love seems inexhaustible. It is *not* a game. That was a wicked thing for me to say, especially after Saturday. If anyone ought to know it, I ought. She loves me totally and beautifully and I am so in love with her it is almost impossible to do anything but think of her. It is an obsession and that is bad. But it is love. I have never loved anyone so much, never wanted to give myself so much to anyone, and it is totally impossible. We both want our love to go on in spite of all the obstacles, at least in our hearts (and there is no way around that!!), but the pain of separation is awful in just three or four days and what will it be for weeks at a time? We will get used to it I suppose! And even that sounds callous and mean. But there is no human solution. We have talked over everything, even apostasy, which is of course impossible. But we considered every theoretical possibility. There just is nothing. There is no real hope of a married clergy and the last priest to be able to get a dispensation would be I. If we continue as we are we might possibly manage to see each other surreptitiously once in a while with a lot of trouble – but how long can I keep up those phone calls from the Cellarer's office? He did not look too happy about it today.

We are planning to spend the day together Thursday (Ascension).

We are determined that our love must stay spiritual and chaste – I think there is no other way!! But the longing for her is frightful – and of course so is the conflict that goes with it. I know how much she wants me too, and I also know that a crude botched-up affair in the woods would be worse than nothing. There are moments when I simply die to go away with her and live with her and surrender to our love and forget everything else, but it is obviously *impossible*. All through everything I come back to the one word impossible.

Above all what affects me most is M. herself. She is the sweetest person I have ever known. Her love is the tenderest, simplest, sincerest thing that has ever come into my life. It is utterly beautiful and I take back nothing I have ever said to her in any letter or poem or anything else. She has a lovely heart, entirely full of love and sweetness, and she has given it completely to me – and I have accepted her gift and given myself in return. Now we face the frightful ordeal of being in love without being able to be together and talk to each other, see each other, kiss each other . . . But we are not the only ones in the world!

This morning we were awake thinking of each other at 1:30 (she likes this and so do I), but after I went back to sleep I woke again at 3:30 in a splendid and terrible crisis of love.

I had been dreaming of some beautiful day and a voice said "of course it is beautiful, it is Derby Day and Derby Day is always beautiful" (that was the 7th – the day she came out with the Fords). Then I woke up with a sense of eternal reality and validity of our love and became flooded with really ecstatic love and tears in which I could see her heart, so to speak, in all its preciousness before God, all its beauty and lovableness, the enormously valuable gift of her love to me! I wept for half an hour, shaken with sobs, still not completely awake, absorbed in the deep reality of this vision and this hope. God knows I have little else left that I live for! We are doggedly hoping for one thing – that we will be united at last forever in heaven! But the way there will be terrible, with the anguish and longing we feel for each other.

May 20, 1966

On Wednesday (the 18th) I woke again in the same way but this time with M. as mysteriously present in my heart and saying "Dear, it is a beautiful day!" and again I was flooded and swept with this sense of a "day" that eternally belongs to us. This is not and cannot be on any calendar, the day of our love which is forever full of light and joy; the "day" that shines on us when we are together in the solemn, unending, leisurely rite and play of our love that just goes on and on (I see how truly this is a kind of contemplation and understand the place of sexual love in Hinduism). Though in fact the 18th was an awful day of continual rain, I kept hearing M. say "Dear, it is a beautiful day" and within me it was a beautiful day. I felt like it could not possibly rain Thursday – Ascension Day – when she was to come out. In fact it did not. It was a beautiful day!

Poem written Wednesday:

CERTAIN PROVERBS ARISE OUT OF DREAMS

Certain proverbs arise out of dreams that are not known to the analyst, when a sleeper wakes with the cry that he has seen everything. But before this cry is silent he has already forgotten all that he saw.

What he saw was too good to remember. It showed that only the impossible can be trusted. To most men happiness is impossible. They would rather put their confidence in a small prize.

Certain dreams reveal a day which is not in the calendar. On this day no harm can come to lovers. They can do each other no wrong. Only those who have dreamed it can live without harming those they love. The cruel do not come upon this day which is incredible. If they discovered it they might be forgiven. They could never bear it.

Nevertheless even cruel lovers dream what is contrary to their cruelty.

We have always known we were winners but we did not know what we had won, and when you told me I did not believe it.

There is something better than winning all; it is the enormous need for another. There is one dream more solemn than judgment day, in which the dreamer knows that without his Beloved he is lost, so lost that no trace of him will ever be found even in hell. My need for you is my judgment.

Who would have guessed this? No harm ever comes to one who loses himself entirely in the love of another. A few sleepers recognize this proverb.

In my sleep I know that without you I am lost and in your sleep you know that without me you can no longer exist. In blackest misfortune this comfort comes to the very sorrowful whose pillow is wet with tears.

My sin was this: I wanted to understand my own problem. In punishment for which I was instantly given a problem to understand. All understanding then became impossible until in my sleep I turned again to you.

Who can trust? Only one who has dreamed. There is no assurance in daylight that has not been prepared by the dark. In the night when nothing can be seen I turn to my Beloved and her voice is my security.

When there is no time for my problem but only for you, I turn to you and see I have no problem. The winner is he who needs no problem. To him there can come no harm. He will never be cruel. The cruel lover needs a problem to excuse his cruelty.

In dreams there is only one great day to be celebrated. Its only reason is the other. You and I together make one holiday. Together we create the light of this day for each other. This is love's Genesis, always beginning and never ending. We are at all times in the first day of creation.

I will no longer burn your wounded body. We do not need to weary ourselves grasping anything, even love: still less the bloody jewel of desire.

Why has God created you to be the center of my being? You are utterly holy and to me you have become a focus of inaccessible light. Suns explode from the light you spread through my guts and torn with love for you my cry becomes a hemorrhage of wild and cool stars. I wake with the knowledge of my whole meaning which is you. Our luck is irreversible. We are the chosen winners of sleep whose secret light is now clear to us after five or six explorations.

———

So yesterday, Ascension Day, was beautiful. She came out driven by another nurse in a light blue Ford, who came back to pick her up in the late afternoon.

We walked off into the woods at the foot of Vineyard Knobs, carrying things for a picnic, she with a bag of food dripping from the ice that was cooling the sauterne. Because of the dripping ice we could not go far – not to the place I had thought of, but just went off into the bushes and probably it was just as well because we were completely hidden – there was no special beauty to it and no one was likely to come there! It was good that we were hidden and totally alone!

We ate herring and ham (not very much eating!) and drank our wine and read poems and talked of ourselves and mostly made love and love and love for five hours. And though we had over and over reassured ourselves and agreed that our love would have to continue always chaste and this sacrifice was essential, yet in the end we were getting rather sexy – yet really instead of being all wrong it seemed eminently right. We now love with our whole bodies anyway and I have the complete feel of her being (except her sex) as completely me. Yet it seemed right because we do really belong to each other in our love (bad argument – it could justify anything!). Of course the grave thing is – this solemn and beautiful thing – that we are doing what lovers perhaps rarely do today – we are moving slowly toward a complete physical ripening of love, a leisurely preparation of our whole being, like the maturing of apples in the sun – and I suddenly realized I had never permitted this before – had always in my youth been in a hurry, and thought about it too much and tried to precipitate everything before its time. No wonder I was unhappy.

Now yesterday was this slow, gradual new stage of ripening, and the grip of this deep warm sexual love disturbing me and flooding through me, shaking my whole being from the heart (not just genital excitation) – and it was as yet only a little! But this is awfully serious, because here in spite of all we were wanting and saying, nature placidly and inexorably said something more profound and perhaps irreversible.

Yet I refuse to be disturbed by it. I am flooded with peace (whereas last Sunday the mere idea that this might happen tore me with anguish and panic). I have surrendered again to a kind of inimical womanly wisdom in M. which instinctively seeks out the wound in me that most needs her sweetness, and lavishes all her love upon me there. Instead of feeling impure I feel purified (which is in fact what I myself wrote the other day in the

"Seven Words" for Ned O'Gorman).[10] I feel that somehow my sexuality has been made real and decent again after years of rather frantic suppression (for though I thought I had it all truly controlled, this was an illusion). I feel less sick, I feel human, I am grateful for her love which is so totally mine. All the beauty of it comes from this that we are *not* just playing, we belong totally to each other's love (except for the vow that prevents the last complete surrender).

And always in the end there is this enormous, unthinkable problem of my vow and my dedication which really come first and make the whole thing absurdly impossible. Yet she insists that she is totally mine and will never love anyone else. I have stopped trying to argue her out of this. And I know we will have to suffer terribly. But now I just don't think of it. I cannot. There is all the reality and peace and beauty of yesterday. And I find that if my love for her is in a way *less* ideal, more incarnate, it is also more ideal. To have body and earth more in it is to have a better grip on what supports the true ideal (as in the poem "Proverbs Arise out of Dreams").

Anyway, I love her more deeply than ever, and just can't think about the future. It will have to take care of itself. God will take care of it.

Afternoon. Nevertheless, as always, I end up impatient of sex, backing away from domination by it, suspicious of its tyranny, and this afternoon I am turning with all my being toward freedom. I love her but do not want to think of her. I want to get to work, to write my conference for Sunday, to read, to meditate, to get the heaviness of passion off my mind. Once again too I want to *eat*, I have an appetite for the first time in two months – though I don't expect it will get very far. Try some herring left over from yesterday perhaps, later!

May 21, 1966

Yesterday as time went on I saw more and more how foolish we had been and what a dangerous game we were playing and that it had to stop. The great wave of that love subsided slowly and left a rather stark expanse of mud-flats!!

In the evening to get away from it, began reading Walker Percy's new novel *[The Last Gentleman]* and then finally called her from the Cellarer's office after 8 when everyone was in bed.

[10] See "Purity," reprinted in Thomas Merton's *Love and Living.*

She was writing me a letter, had been disturbed and was worrying herself and was badly wanting me to call. I was glad I did, because it was a long healing conversation in which we agreed that it had not been "bad" in itself but was clear[ly] contrary to what we are supposed to be doing and to what our love is all about. Both of us see clearly that to yield to sex would just wreck our love – we would *have* to break it up! There is no alternative. So we comforted one another. I saw she was afraid. She saw how grim I had become. But we renewed our love and joy. The only solution to our problems is to turn to each other and find strength [in] our love and start on our way again. But it is *hard* to love in this way, with all the gruesome, untidy contradictions with my monastic life and all the immense possibilities of all kind of trouble. Yet we are completely connected to each other; I reread M.'s last letter (17th) and it is heart rending in its beauty, its total gift of herself to me in God's love, her sense that our two destinies are *completely* intertwined. This is an awful trust and it *cannot help radically changing my whole life* and outlook even though I remain here a hermit, even if we were never to see each other again.

I am not yet ready to face all the implications of this. They stagger me. Once again *this is no game.* This is deadly serious and we are playing for keeps, life and death are at stake, our salvation itself is involved, and immense suffering may come to be part of it.

It is in this way at last that God has finally cornered me into an inexorable gift of myself and I see once again that I want to evade it – or half evade it. I will certainly never take back my interior commitment to her. The problem is – the conflict between my monastic rules and my gift to her. This is agonizing already and we have to face it too. As yet, I simply cannot. But I have to get ready to do it – with honesty and the capacity to seek original solutions – but not just perpetual improvisation.

May 23, 1966. Monday

Called her again Sunday morning, but Sunday night moved up to the hermitage to sleep and the wonderful night made me feel more myself. The birds falling silent, then fireflies, then Scorpio coming up over the trees – deep silence. Today, the long early morning hours, reading, a little manual work (though my back hurt). There is no question at all that this is *right* for me. I am a solitary and that's that. Sure, I love M. but can never interfere with my main purpose in life – and that is that. God knows! This aloneness, this freedom, this being without care, unconnected, with nothing to gain and nothing to lose! Nothing to explain.

Tonight finally some pictures of her that I had taken on May 5th and 7th came. They were charming but I did not spend much time looking at them. Our love is on a certain level serious . . . but there is something more serious yet, and that is this freedom from all special danger, all particular project. I called her in the evening, plans for her coming on May 30th seem to be falling through and I said, "Well, let's skip it!" She said "What do you *mean?*" True it would be a whole day, but – so many complications and yet I do love her.

May 24, 1966

Lay awake a long time last night: what was that other call? She left the phone very hurriedly for something – evidently another call she had been expecting. That was a jolt and a liberation, and I was glad of it, though it was painful. And yet she is obviously sincere in saying she loves me more than anyone else, etc. etc.

Truth of the matter is that *she needs me to need her.* And that is exactly the last thing in the world I need: to be here in solitude with a "need" for someone else!! From the beginning I have been telling myself I wanted to help her with my love and I really do – on the other hand there is this involved and complex machinery of love one has to get into, with all its wheels within wheels, this leading to that and that implying this, etc. A wearying, delightful, endless involvement that spurs on and on and onwards itself and puts out threads that become inextricably tangled. What do I want with such a snarled up ball of string! All because of *need.* I suppose I want her to need me too. And I do want to help her if I can, not hurt her. If I drop her (and I suppose in a way I must – at least eventually), it must be gently and lovingly and not with pride (not seeking any kind of revenge!) and not flatly and forever. We will always be friends, and will always, I know, have a certain special love for each other, in our hearts. But all this business of phone calls, letters, visits, especially illegal visits and long periods dangerously alone in the woods – all this has to stop. Last night I thought: I could ask her to come Saturday instead of Monday, but will not.

The thing is that we do *not* meet completely in our love: it is partial, not whole. There are aspects of ourselves, sides of ourselves that come together, are in harmony, respond deeply. But there are other sides which do not. And where we *do* meet we try to pull ourselves wholly together and fail – each tries to envelop the whole self of the other – and this is where my own ambiguities come into play. My deepest self evades this and is jealous of absolute freedom and solitude. Hers too has its reservations – the freedom to love others and perhaps this is why we both protest so much about our love, the wholeness of it, the totality of it. Have any two people ever sworn to each other such total and unending love? I guess all lovers do. But do we really mean it? Are we in a position to mean it? I think we are desperately trying to persuade ourselves and failing. Why do we think it necessary to persuade ourselves in the first place?

May 27, 1966

All week I have been struggling with myself over M. The fuss Monday night turned out to be absurd. The long distance call was from her mother. And I was really looking for a *pretext* to get loose, which is very bad of me and not honest. I was ashamed of my tantrum, and we cleared it all up. Yet there is no question that I have got myself in a much more difficult situation than I realize. We got ourselves quite aroused sexually last Thursday and since then I have suffered a great deal of confusion, anguish, indecision, and nerves. There is no question that I *cannot* let this become a sexual affair, it would be disastrous for us both. It simply must not happen. Also she is too curious about all that – and too passionate for me (her body to tell the truth was wonderful the other day, ready for the most magnificent love). In calls and letters since we have agreed again that our love has to be chaste, and I know she means it and wants it, so do I, but we are not safe with each other, and I am disturbed about our meeting alone out here. We should not do it. Fortunately several occasions have fallen through and I cannot see her again until the 4th in Louisville. We will be safe enough there. I think, however, I cannot even be so free about kissing her etc. It is all lovely and healthy, yet it is not for me. I am a priest, twenty-five years a monk. I have given up this kind of joy, and now I see that I have been wrong to let this get as far as it has.

Yet the truth is we do love each other deeply, but that is no real excuse or justification. And there is still plenty of chance for illusion. I have to face it. She is a lovely, sweet person and in the depths of my heart I love her true self, for I think I know her well now, and she is a most precious person, to whom I am attached with all the power of my heart. But precisely because our love is so deep we can ruin each other, if not by sex, then just by nerves and anguish and sorrow at being torn apart, etc. I can see it is going to be a terrible cross for us both, and the only thing is to face it all honestly if I can. I am very aware of the temptation of easy, abrupt, dishonest solutions now.

If authorities step in brutally and cut it all short that may be merciful in the long run, but I want to spare her suffering if I can and try to do this easily and lovingly – but sooner or later we will have to cut it down to a few letters, calls and visits if any very rare!

But at this moment we are deeply, terribly attached and in love and very concerned with each other. I doubt if I have ever loved any one so deeply or ever been loved with so much passion. The poems and letters I have written have only intensified all this.

I can see that it is going to go on like this now with questioning, anguish, moments of passion, joy, then more anguish. Better settle down wisely and peacefully to a long struggle in which we sweat out our passion and (if possible) simmer down to a peaceful, loving, lasting friendship that will sustain our affection for years to come. That is what we both want. I must really pray for wisdom and guidance. But I *do* love her deeply!

Actually , as I wrote her today, the only answer is *sacrifice*.

If we are willing to love each other in a spirit of true sacrifice, our love will endure and deepen and will be consecrated to God. If we fail, our love will soon be lying in ruins and we will both be very hurt, frustrated and ashamed. My objective now should be *to prevent this happening* at all costs!

May 28, 1966. Vigil of Pentecost

A bright, beautiful morning. Bro. Frederic is cutting grass in the next field with the whirlybird. They are going to build a hermitage for Fr. Flavian at the far end of the hill.

Today M. was going to come out and spend the day (illegally) alone with me in the woods but she did not get transportation, so went home to Cincinnati instead and I cannot help thinking it is very good she did not come. It would have been disruptive and would have led to more anguish. Too much stirring up of sex. What strikes me most of all is the wastefulness of spiritual energy that all this gets me into. I believe deeply in our love and I know that the spiritual upheaval is basically good and healthy, but I get all kinds of warning signals. I know not only full sexual consummation would be wrong and harmful, but also even the more or less "licit" lovemaking we have indulged in. It leads to an upheaval and a wasteful division of spiritual energy and ultimately to false and deceptive spiritual experiences (at the highest level), not to mention the plain *nerves* and anguish one has to go through physically. I must give everything I have to my real task. Love for M. is not incompatible with that task but it has to be left on a certain level.

One on which both of us are helped, taught, grow, deepen, and do not merely squander ourselves absurdly, as we tend to do.

If our love can teach us this, then we will certainly gain by it immensely!

(Evening.) Spent a long afternoon alone out on the edge of St. Edmund's field in the sun and for the first time since going to the hospital felt that some of the old peace and freedom – the sense of having no worries in the world and nothing to take too seriously because I don't have to take myself seriously. Clearly M. is an occasion of taking myself seriously as well as her. But today I thought that if I *really* loved her as a totally full man, I would take neither one of us too seriously. Certainly not with all the silly anguished seriousness of the past few days, which is in reality no seriousness at all!! But I know again that I can be free, that freedom is right there if only I want it, and believe me, I want it! And to want it without too much crazy need is to realize you have it, and that the things you worry about are pure illusions.

Today I see I have been a very great damn fool even more than usual. This is not M.'s fault – she just loves me, but that is a significant reason for me to be a damn fool, I suppose. But I should never have got in love in the first place. That too is the statement of an idiot, because this love had to be, and because I do not handle it right, I have to be foolish about it. To love with complete simplicity and freedom and not worry about consequences (trivial ones at least) would be much more sane. No, I have to worry and see all the problems. And I suppose they are not entirely illusory either! But they could be simpler if I were simpler.

This evening – John Heidbrink is bringing a Buddhist from Vietnam [Thich Nhat Hanh]. I go down to supper with them now.

Saturday night.

One thing I have *got* to realize. The extraordinary character of this love between myself and M. We really seem to be psychic, or to respond to each other in fantastic ways at a distance. Today she was in Cincinnati worried and lonely and feeling she had to some extent "lost" me, as I felt about last Tuesday. It turns out that Tuesday she was indeed very upset because a certain person was there, and he upsets her (past incidents). This communicated itself to me in some way and that was what I sensed, but I responded wrongly! In fact cruelly. She needed me and I started to reason out ways of delivering myself from this. She did not need me to need her. She desperately needed my love. And today too. When I start trying to free myself *she feels it*. I have got to realize that. I can't trifle with this – we are too deeply involved in each other. It is a love too great for my pettiness and yet I have to measure up to it. A most poignant, distressed, loving phone call and I am *so glad I made it*, in violation of everything – also I am so glad of all that I have gone through this week even though I have been wrong.

May 31, 1966

A lonely weekend with M. away – except for my surreptitious call to her from the Steel Building at 9:30 p.m. after I had left Heidbrink, [Thich] Nhat Hanh, and A. Gould (we had a fine talk, made a tape for Dan Berrigan etc. More of this later).

M. was terribly lonely and upset, being away "where there are no associations with you" and feeling the undertones of my own tantrums (my urge to "escape" and "be free"). At times I felt she was ready to cry. But we had a good talk, I came back later, happy, to the hermitage and sat up until 11:30 writing her a letter. Concelebrated the next day, often close to tears thinking of her and of our love. Nhat Hanh lost his voice, and got no sleep (just worn out), so they canceled an engagement in Nashville and stayed until the evening of Pentecost Sunday. So in the afternoon we drove around, to Lincoln's Knob Creek house, to Bardstown, and back and then I gave my talk Sunday evening.

Monday was a desolate sort of day, though very bright and beautiful. I was hoping M. would be back in Louisville and went to call her – did not realize I could have got her at her mother's in Cincinnati but would have tried anyway, only I no longer had the number on me. This piece of foolishness spoiled the day for me. I went over to the tobacco farm with Bro. Alban and took off by myself up at the top of the long fields, sat and lay in the sun, watched the clouds sail by over the knobs – it was like the old days at Oakham when Whitmonday was always a holiday and I would get a bike and go to Uppingham. Came back walking along the road and got picked up by a car with a Confederate license plate, driven by Gerald Boone it turned out. Slept badly at night and woke with a somewhat frightening dream about M. which I interpreted as a warning against my *own* cruelty. Several times now, with my own sensitivity and withdrawal I have been unjust to her, and I hope by now I have learned!!

Today I begged God to forgive me and not to take away the gift of love He gave us. Then I went down and offered Mass for "us" again – but this time before it I was moved to offer God my life for her, as a complete acknowledgment of the wonderful gift she has been, and as a total expression of love, in response to the total generosity of *her* love! Perhaps that is part of the trouble. She is so total, so overwhelming, so admiring, so unable to see any wrong in me that I sometimes imagine she *must* be kidding! But no, she means every word of it and her sincerity moves me to tears. She is simply a beautifully warmly loving person who loves completely and totally and has found in me a hope of an adequate response to her immense capacity to love. I am scared by so much love, and withdraw when I think it can't possibly be real, there must be a catch in it somewhere.

Every time I am the one who has turned out wrong. There is no *catch*. She is a perfectly, wonderfully honest and sincere person who says she is totally in love with me and *is*. And though I am totally in love with her a lot of the time, yet I have my moments of doubt and of them I am ashamed. Very ashamed when I see how perfectly and how simply she just lavishes her love on me. It is the most beautiful thing that has ever happened, and yet it breaks my heart – how can we go on like this without ending up in the most terrible disappointment? Nothing else is possible. Yet she is willing to take the risk, provided we can at least communicate and see each other somewhere once in a while.

I called her at dinner time (had a hard time getting the "safe" phone and made part of the call in the Gatehouse, which is terribly risky); we had a wonderful warm talk. She is happy again. So am I. And I think I never loved her as much as now.

In fact this afternoon (a beautiful and sunny day) I took off and went for a walk around the place where we had been together. Two spots where we sat alone on Derby Day and the place of our marvelous long Ascension picnic, that day of marvelous love! I was deeply moved in all those places and thanked Our Lady for the pure gratuitousness of this love and the expression we have been permitted to give to it in this way. It has been a terribly beautiful, unexpected, miraculous month that I cannot begin to understand. All I know is that I *must* love. She is the most beautiful thing that has ever happened to me and her love is a gift from heaven, it is so pure and clear and total. I want to do all I have said in my letters and really love her perfectly, completely – (within the limits of my vows) and do all I can to make her relatively happy. And any expression of my love seems to make her terribly happy. Her love is as precious to me as life itself.

I wrote another poem Sunday, in the evening, about Saturday night's call.[11] But I simply cannot copy all the poems here. They will probably never be published, though I am sending J. Laughlin copies to keep on file.

June 2, 1966

Since Tuesday, when M. came back, I have had some good phone calls, the best of which was today. We get deeper and deeper in love. She challenged me on a point about "detachment" (I suppose I must have said something about that as she was so terribly lonely on the phone Saturday). But of course to talk about detachment when you are in love is just nonsense. Yet it came as a mild shock. Of course I am not detached and neither is she. We are profoundly and firmly attached to each other. I am more aware of it all the time because my nature at times rebels against being "held" like this. So today on the phone I made a frank commitment on this point. I *am* attached and I know it and my life is profoundly changed – in a most serious way – by the fact. It is no joke at all. This love of ours – very joyous today, very sure of itself, triumphantly articulate – is still an immense reservoir of anguish, especially for me. But I don't care. Now I can accept the anguish, the risk, the awful insecurity, even the guilt (though we are doing nothing radically wrong, i.e. not sinning). I hope I am not lying to myself anywhere. Certainly I am not just loving now for the joy of it. I am loving because of our commitment to each other, our bond to each other, what we mean to each other. We are far beyond the point where I used to get off the bus in all my old love affairs. I am in much deeper than I ever was before. (In the light of M.'s love I realize for the first time how deeply I was loved back in those days by girls whose names I have even forgotten.)

Anyway, I am seeing M. Saturday again in Louisville.

Finished [Idries] Shah on Sufism [*The Sufis* (New York, 1964)] the other day. Parts of its are good. Reading Laura [Anagarika Brahmacari] Govinda on *[Foundations of] Tibetan Mysticism* [New York, 1960]. Article in the *Commonweal* is probably coming out tomorrow. A Buddhist nun burned herself to death in Vietnam. The Abbot's off to Chile tomorrow to see about taking over the Monastery of Las Condes.

---

[11] The poem, "Evening: Long Distance Call," was published in *Eighteen Poems* (New York: New Directions, 1985).

The visit of J. Heidbrink, A. Gould and Thich Nhat Hanh last Saturday–Sunday was very impressive. Nhat Hanh is first of all a true monk; very quiet, gentle, modest, humble, and you can see his Zen has worked. Very good on Buddhist philosophy and a good poet. Like Camus, is a Buddhist existentialist. I read an article of his in *Frères du monde* a year or two ago and thought of writing to him about it. He left a couple of his books. We had several meals with Fr. Abbot who got very interested in Nhat (mostly I suppose because he looks like such a kid and is yet so smart) and tried out a lot of Christian arguments on him etc. When Nhat was ill Sunday morning I had a long talk with John Heidbrink.

Getting back to M.: this love *cannot* be a matter of playing around. I wrote in a way that it could. It's altogether serious. It scares me at times. She has given up saying we should live together and fully accepts my vows, etc. But love demands contact and much communication and this remains a constant problem here. My phone calls are illegal and so too are some of our meetings. This does not make for peace, but it meets the demands of love and I think in conscience – and in love – I must meet them. The sincerity and depths of all this will probably be tested, and God knows I will need help!! There's something in me that wants freedom at any price and can claim all sorts of religious justification. More or less clear sightedly, at least now, I am going in the opposite direction. I am taking a course that can be harmful to me as a monk, a contemplative and a writer. And I am doing it for love. Not out of passion and enthusiasm, but out of simple love for M. However, I think it is understood that when a show down with the vows comes, I have to stick by the vows. (I take back what I said about it being harmful to me as a writer. Have written some of my best poems about all this.)

It is the question of regularity – observance – discipline, etc.

These are to some extent shot on account of her. I keep a pretty good day in the hermitage, reading better now – meditating a little, not well. Thinking a lot about her. Tonight I will be up a little late doing that . . . and asking myself a lot of questions.

So many other priests are doing the same tonight – everywhere! It is a strange crisis in the whole Church.

June 3, 1966

The heart of the matter is this. M. is a person with an enormous need to give love. She felt herself providentially drawn to me in the hospital and began to give me love immediately the first day she cared for me. I knew before I left the hospital that she loved me. It was confirmed even in the first letter she wrote me. I responded very positively because I already loved her. Since then we have continued to discover more and more the true dimensions of our love. It is not simply a passion, a bodily need (though the physical reactions are profound!); it is a deep love of our heart. I feel I must fully surrender to it because it will change and heal my life in a way that I fear, but I think it is necessary – in a way that will force me first of all to *receive an enormous amount of love* (which to tell the truth I have often feared). To be loved by this infinitely, totally inexhaustively loving girl who wants to pour out all her affection on me. And to love her in return with a deep spontaneous strong love that will support and help her in life. (She says that my love has completely changed her life, brought her peace, a sense of direction, liberation from sin etc.) The realities of this love cannot be ignored. They demand, however, disconcerting sacrifices from us – including that of the ideal image of myself as solitary, detached, remote, "pure," out of this world. In place of this – my reality and actuality seen in its limitations and utterly *unsatisfying* – humiliating – to me, balanced by the view her love takes which, while being impossibly exaggerated, is different from my view and must have *some* objective value (she is nobody's fool!).

This love is a disconcerting, risky, hard-to-handle reality. But it is *real*. It does not fully interfere with or invalidate my solitude (gives it a strange new perspective all right!).

Danger of "platonic love" – concentration on the "essence of love" or on the "essence of woman" – whereas what love demands is to find *the actuality of love and of woman* in this concrete, existing woman who gives herself to me as she is; to love *her* womanliness and be conquered by it in order to give to her what she asks out of her deepest heart. But M. does not ask sex: she asks a love that fully respects her in her wholeness as person (this does *not* exclude sex by any means, but in our case circumstances do – what is important is the union of which sex is only a sign). I have to stop making sex a problem in this (torment, wanting it so badly and knowing it has to remain impossible, fear of going into it in some messy dishonest way!).

There is a real danger of my cracking up under the pressures and contradictions of love in my absurd situation. OK, I accept it. I will not evade the obligations of love just to protect a little ego held together with bits of string. But I won't crack up. Quite the contrary, letting the strings be pulled apart and thrown away, refusing any longer to hold together this small and vulnerable "self" with its illusions of autonomy, I will find new depths and a new consciousness higher than my own and my anxieties will be healed in love and transcendence – *in which there are no ideals* – only the reality of what is greater than any "I" and incomprehensible to it. M.'s love, which looks superficially like an enslavement, is actually part of a great insurmountable way of liberation that goes far beyond our affection and its expression.

Returning to learn from Camus – to prefer happiness, or the taste for it, even though absurd, to a taste for Apocalypse: "*à force de médiocrité on revient aux Apocalypses* [by force of mediocrity one returns to the Apocalypses]!" Precisely – my "tragedies" turn out to be evidence of inner disposition to mediocrity disguised as a religious ideal.

June 4, 1966
Seriousness of love. Judgment and crisis where the ideal image is called into question. My great danger is that in such crisis I become so disturbed that I refuse love. This is I think the basic and very urgent problem. Whatever may be right or wrong about my love for M., this is what is being shown me: the true relationship is not between her and my ideal self, but between her and my real, actual self – and that I must be glad if the ideal self is from time to time discredited – by my own stupidity and selfishness, not by her – she is too sweet and *too* eager to see good in everything. But this too causes insensitivity – expectations to which I must measure up constantly (and which of course I can't). All foolish. I must manfully face this judgment and find my center not in an ideal self which just *is* (fully realized), but in an actual self which does all it can to be honest and to love truly, though it still may fail.

June 5, 1966
Two important days.
Yesterday went in town and had a long time with M. at Cunningham's – in a room together. It was perfect from beginning to end. She came out looking lovely and joyous in a light dress, long hair flying in the wind, face literally shining with love. From that moment (11:45) until I left her (about 4:10) it was simply perfect. We talked and loved and scarcely ate anything, but drank Chianti and read poems and loved and loved. The thing that was most clear was the simple perfection of our love, the total "givenness" of it

and our complete surrender to its delights and perfection, its peace, its freedom, with no care and no afterthought. Nothing was ever so clear as the fact that we really, truly, completely love each other. She brought up some of her "problems" (uncertainty about which has been disturbing me) and they were much less than I thought. Mostly fears. Good to have it all straight now! Also it is terribly clear to me that she really depends on my love for her. It is terribly important that I continue faithfully to love her, and not be misled by doubts. It is not that she needs me to "need" her, but that she needs to give her love to me and to have me respond to her warmly and totally.

Today called her at 7 and had a long talk with her sweet sleepy voice, confirming everything and getting it all more clear, and deeper and deeper into her love and confidence. My own love grows. Beauty of the chaste freedom of yesterday's love. Yet it has terribly deep repercussions. Haunted and comforted by her womanliness, her sweetness, her hair, cheeks, neck, lips, her lovely look of love and surrender. Her inexhaustible capacity to give love, to pour it out more and more, and all on me.

Slept badly, though. I know I can still be stirred by deep anxieties.

June 9, 1966. Corpus Christi

Concelebration early. I stood there among all the others, soberly aware of myself as a priest who has a woman. True, we have done nothing drastically wrong – though in the eyes of many our lovemaking is still wrong even though it stops short of complete sex. Before God I think we have been conscientious and have kept our love good. Yet is it reasonable for me to be writing her love poems – even a song?

True as our love may be, we have to be perfectly realistic about it. Today especially I was thinking we must be realistic in our expectations for the future. There just is no real future for our love as a real *love* affair. In heaven maybe we will be one. It is perhaps true that she loves me more than she ever loved anyone and that she wants to give herself totally to me for life. But we cannot do anything about it. I see clearly that we are both torn by contradictions. She cannot go on indefinitely without full sexual expression of our love, though she thinks she can (and fears she cannot. We discussed all this frankly). She knows she is attracted to others and to opportunities of passion in spite of love for me and I know I have no right to hold her and do not want to: in the sense that I think she ought to marry. [. . .] The only solution for us is to envisage a future of warm and lasting friendship, love in that pure sense – and much less contact than we have now. I am not pushing for drastic change, but things will just change themselves gradually and it must be done so no one gets hurt. I do not see any alternatives but I am simply letting things go the way they obviously will go. Yet at the same time our love really deepens and it is terribly real and beautiful – and exciting. But I see my own way clear. She needs support, love, encouragement, sacrifice, and all these I will gladly give because I love her deeply – but no upheavals, and no wild attempts at solution. We are certainly getting no cooperation from anyone else in things, like transportation for her to come out to see me. In all this, I see that I have to really *love her* and not just love love or love her body. It is a training in realism and in love of *the person* she is (a person inexhaustibly beautiful and lovable to me).

At noon – angst about the telephone system. The direct phone to Louisville has been cut off in the Cellarer's office and I worried that it might be on account of me. Did not understand Bro. Kilian's reply to my questions, the night he was being evasive. Only after our afternoon of Zen emptiness did it occur to me that perhaps he was only telling the straight truth and that the Louisville calls could now be made on the other phones OK. I will see tonight when I try to call M. on the way to night adoration!

Every time I come out of one these struggles about love I realize I am being selfish, and unfair to M's love. And refusing to be loved, since to me being loved means anxiety over loss, possible loss, and I have always been so negative and despairing that I have preferred to forego love rather than run the risk of loss. Now if there is one reason to go on it is this: to *give* love and not worry about loss. I really want to try to give her a little joy, peace, light, security. But the problem is the illusion that goes with it: the awful illusions that our love has a wild earthly future! Can't have one? Only by miracle! Because some kind of loss is almost inevitable. Not the loss of love (I am sure we will always love each other in our hearts), but just the impossibility of contact. It is a grim prospect, but I know I must not despair, for her sake and for my own, and go ahead hopefully no matter what! I can see I am too ready to see trouble and give up! The old story. This is not authentic solitude! My hermit tendencies today have been suspicious. But the Zen afternoon was good, for walking in the dry dirt at the margins of St. Edmund's mowed field I forgot the flies and thought "What do you lack?" In fact I lack nothing! Or rather what is "lack"?

———

Evening – read some poems of Piontek in German, with difficulty but satisfaction on the relatively cool porch.

June 10, 1966

I can be wrong and wrong and wrong. She is right and true in asking me to stop analyzing and figuring and running the risk of misunderstanding her. She tells me over and over that she loves me totally with a love she has never known before for anyone and a love that she could not possibly give to anyone else, and in my right mind I know she means it and that I feel the same towards her. Scruples about my vocation and worries about preserving my old identity are the two things that get in the way, for this love will eventually change me completely and is changing me already, and unconsciously with great anguish sometimes, I resent it. Yet last night before the Bl[essed] Sacrament I was realizing the thing to be is without care and without too many preconceived notions and completely open to risk. Her love is not just "another question" and "another problem" – it is right at the center of all my questions and problems and right at the center of my hermit life.

June 12, 1966

I wonder what all my reasonings and resolutions amount to!

Yesterday I had to go to Louisville for a bursitis shot in the elbow. M. and I had arranged with Jim Wygal that we would borrow his office and get together there, which we did with a bottle of champagne. [. . .] When I got home I called her and we were talking again, foolishly of possibilities, living together, my leaving here, "marrying" her etc. But it is all preposterous. Society has no place for us and I haven't the gall it takes to fight the whole world particularly when I don't really want married life anyway; I want the life I have vowed.

This morning I woke up (after a night of light and fitful sleep) without self-hate or undue guilt but with the realization that something has to be done. We can't go on like this. I can't leave her. I have to try to live the life I have chosen. Yet I love her. [. . .]

I can't face the business of a complete break (which in the circumstances would be very bad for her though much easier in the long run for me). I love her completely, as I have never loved anyone in my life. Yet I know this love means only suffering for us. The only thing to grasp hold of in it all is that it is at least a common human reality and not just something in the head.

June 14, 1966

Yesterday the abbot came home. Last night I went down to the Steel building to call M. Bro. Clement was there and said Bro. G. in the gatehouse had listened in on one of my many calls to M. (Thursday Night? Sunday morning – the worst!!) and had reported the matter to Dom James. I don't know how much he knows but I know he is mad and is waiting to give me the devil about it, which is only natural. I have to face the fact that I have been wrong and foolish in all this. Much as I loved M., I should never have let myself be carried away to become so utterly imprudent. But I suppose I knew that – my time was limited and she loved me so much I wanted to respond all I could... Well, it is clearly over now. I called her once more (she was desolate and so was I). She said, "I had the most terrible feeling something was wrong when I was waiting for you to call. . . . Will we ever see each other again?. . . What will I do without you? . . . How unfair it is, even inhuman. . . ." But we have both anticipated this. However, the results may be very bad if they reported some of our frankest conversations!! God knows what the abbot knows! I will soon find out I imagine!

In any case, from what I have been through since Saturday, I certainly realize the real spiritual danger I have got into. Things have really got close to going wrong and it is providential that everything has been blocked at the moment. Perhaps it is saving me from a real wreck. Jim Wygal on the phone Saturday was saying "Be careful you don't destroy yourself!" He is perhaps more right than I thought at the time. Hope I can see him about it.

Decided the best thing was to own up and face Dom James (about the phone calls *only!*)[12] before he summoned me in. So I did. He was kind and tried to be understanding to some extent – his only solution was of course "a complete break." Wanted to write to M. himself but I refused – that would be disastrous – and he does not know who she is and I don't think he needs to know. He was hinting around about how lonely I have been in the hermitage, how I ought to come down and sleep in the infirmary etc. But I refused. The only concrete solution we arrived at was that I should go back to ecumenical work in the retreat house – as a cure for loneliness!! – but I suppose some constructive contacts with others would be a good thing. Obviously though he thinks the hermitage has been too much for me and has

---

[12] Merton inserted this parenthetical remark later – perhaps on rereading the entry.

made me too vulnerable. He did, however, welcome the idea of talking to the ecumenical groups, Protestants, Buddhists etc.

It is a beautiful afternoon. I said Vespers and walked in the silent grass looking at the clouds and all the essence of my love for M. was there ("Every beautiful day is our invention").[13] I know her loneliness, but I also trust she will have the grace to have this same sense of acceptance and peace and deep union now that the *inevitability* of separation is clear. I think we will continue to love each other on a very full free and spontaneous level in our heart. If it had gone on as it was going there would have been nothing but turmoil and confusion, I think. Now we have to be detached and freed from our compulsions, and yet we can surely love more perfectly and more peacefully.

Later afternoon – I went for a walk out to St. Edmund's field after work (study of an old book on Dervishes on 2-week loan from the Library of Congress) and looked at the tall woods and thought of M., perhaps out walking by the grotto after work, thinking of me thinking of her lonely. How miserably life can treat people. The great bronze carpet of the wheatfield. The flies. The wind. Our love. The abbot would not give me the thick letter he recognized to be hers even though he could not open it ("conscience matter" – yet he might anyway if I know *him!*). I think of her again tonight, after reading a poem of Heinz Piontek of a parting on a snowy night, and the wind leaning against the girl's tears!

Lately borrowed from Fr. Chrysogonus records of Joan Baez (especially "Silver Dagger"!!) and Bob Dylan, which I liked a lot ("Tombstone Blues" and "There is something happening here and you don't know what it i-i-s, Do you, Mister Jones?"). Very pointed and articulate.

It is good enough for me not to resist my solitude – it is like normal. But she does not know how. How can she accept solitude? Especially if she thinks *I* am accepting it? Yet shall I resist uselessly when my solitude is really closer to her than my resistance? I drink iced Xtian [Christian] Brothers brandy out of an old marmalade jar: Where is my love? My dear love to whom I cannot even write now! Damn the abbot's compassion for my "powerful

[13] The first part of Merton's poem, "Six Night Letters," opens with the words "Every beautiful day / Is invention. . . ." See *Eighteen Poems* (New York: New Directions, 1985).

emotions"! He enjoyed not giving me the letter. Yet nonetheless I am better and freer in solitude, total and accepted, including loneliness and sorrow for M. – I am much more separated from everyone else, alien to the community. Very alone in the field. Invisible. "Like a rolling stone." M., my darling, where are you? The abbot's secretary averts his eyes in embarrassment when we meet. The gatehouse brothers smile much too politely. I am known as a monk in love with a woman.

I am going to write maybe a new book now, in a new way, in a new language too. What have I to do with all that has died, all that belonged to a false life? What I remember most is me and M. hugging each other close for hours in long kisses and saying, "Thank God this at least is real!"

June 15, 1966
"In order to untie a knot you must first find out how the knot was tied" (Buddha). This morning for the first time, really since going to the hospital, I have real inner freedom and solitude – I love M. but in a different way, peacefully and without disturbances or inner tension. I feel that once again I am *all here*. I have finally returned to my place and to my work, and am beginning once again to be what I am. It has been a time of gruesome yet beautiful alienation. Had a hard restless night, kept waking up thinking of her, of what she might be feeling and suffering (I am worried, knowing her intensity) and then realizing my complete aloneness – and the solitude of the woods all around me, but realizing it as *right*.

"The self is the relationship to oneself," Kierkegaard. But not prescinding to relationship to the other seen as oneself. I need badly to hear from her and know how she feels – I can guess. It is inhumane to forbid even letters.

A good morning, cool and free. I can at least read again. Finished [Robert C.] Tucker's excellent book *Philosophy and Myth in K[arl] Marx* [London, 1964] – material for conferences. Trouble with arm still makes typing hard but I will get at these notes.

My mind is coming back to life. Ambiguity and illusion in the love M. and I have for each other. Deep down it is a true, simple, excellent love – a material passion that is valid and profoundly reciprocated. But our compulsions have made it much more complex and ambiguous. For instance now – in our separation, I know it is a matter almost of life and death for her to want me to be *not* liberated, to need her in anguish. Hitherto I think I have made things worse for myself and her by dutifully complying with this when I did not really mean it in that way. It is much better to love freely and be able to do something else – and in fact she has had plenty to do with her work, her social life, her company with the other nurses etc. I have hurt myself by needing her so much and so impractically in this solitude, instead of loving her more simply. She has I think grossly exaggerated her "need" and love for me as a kind of perfect being. Yet I know too she sees me clearly. But she has been very possessive – naturally. So have I. The fact remains that this separation is cruel for both of us, but *in different ways*, not in exactly the same way. And we have different defenses. For me solitude is not a problem but a vocation. For her it tends to be *the* problem. And she knows that for me it is a solution. Added cruelty! Yet by it I can perhaps bring her some hidden spiritual help. At any rate I want to.

Jubilant evening – Jim Wygal came out unexpectedly and we had a good afternoon talking about "the problem" which was worrying him. But in the end we went over to New Haven and from a liquor store called M. at the hospital (after failing to get her on the phone). M. was jubilant – said she had been terribly lonely, loved me more than ever, wanted to see me, etc. It was a short call but jubilant and good and I was delighted to hear the life and joy in her voice and to hear her say over and over "I love you." She got my letters today and I was able to give some practical information (about the uselessness of writing me here etc.).

On the way home, in the brilliant evening and the sunlit knobs Jim said, "You are on a collision course," but I did not care. Still he is right, I must be careful. And this does *not* fit in with my life! But as I said it is a question of tapering off, gradually.

June 16, 1966
"*Il n'était pas mon père, il était avec les autres* [He was not my father, he was with the others]," says Meursault in Camus' *L'Étranger [The Stranger]*, speaking of the prison chaplain.

June 17, 1966. F[east] of the Sacred Heart
A magnificent day, bright yet cool, you can walk in the sun without getting up a sweat (as I just did, saying office and looking out over the brilliant valley).

Went down to concelebrate early, then came back and spent the whole morning on a slow reading of *The Myth of Sisyphus* (Camus) which I shied away from before. Now it is just right, just what I need, suits me perfectly for I see my vocation to be an absurd man if ever there was one! Or at least to *try* to think in some such honest terms.

Yesterday I was forbidden absolutely to try to call M., write her a letter or any contact like that. I am glad I got in that last call the evening before. I wonder what she thinks and feels – I can guess. But it is terrible not to hear the sound of her voice at all or to read a letter of hers. This is bad enough when I have already had *two* calls this week, three including Sunday. What will it be when there are no calls for days – no calls or letters ever?

June 19, 1966. III Sunday after Pentecost

Again cool, almost cold. The Hammers came yesterday. Last night could not sleep, thinking of M. But things are better. And got up, went out, looked at the stars, called on the Name – sense of presence, totality, peace. What is there to look for or to yearn for but *all* reality here and now in whatever I am?

"Who is like unto God?" The secret of knowing that there is none like Him and of disposing my whole thoughts and being in accordance with this secret. The long labor of getting back to this center. Helped by a return to [Shaikh Ahmad al'] Alawi – contact also with F.S. [Frithjof Schuon]. (Letter from [Marco] Pallis yesterday.) My solitude has to mean what it really means! It has to become once again totally sincere – or if it has never been so, it must become so now.

"To live without appeal" says Camus: i.e. *without* resorting to calling on God. And yet it is less a contradiction than it seems. To invoke Him only is to invoke *No-thing* and to have no visible, definable, limited appeal. To call upon everything – reality itself, such as, in some sense indecipherable.

The great and deliberate flaw in Camus – a flaw on which he insists – is the "ethic of quantity." Certainly this is decisive for our time – perhaps the only way of not being quixotic (the repetition of the absurd in complete lucidity – Don Juan – is non-quixotic). This I cannot accept. I'd rather fight windmills. But am I fighting them? Or does it come back to the same thing – and to the fact that "knowing oneself to be mortal" is in fact a disguised return to *quality!* That is the ambiguity in Camus and *La Peste [The Plague]* proves it. (*Sisyphus* is by no means final!)

The desert landscape in Camus – the hidden Islamism.

Finished *Sisyphus* in a rush, finally bored by it.

June 22, 1966

Hot. Tired. Valley full of heat and evening mist. A loud pump chattering by itself. I realize wearily how wrong I have been. How mistaken. Not that I regret loving M. – it has been beautiful, even though mixed up – but I still see I never should have become involved in such a thing in the first place. The whole seriousness of my own life is in question – I suppose I should not be surprised at that! To realize how much of a phoney I am. But I might as well face it and try to mend matters. We have been straight with each other and I think we have not hurt each other, though we have had our compulsions. Very understandable ones. I see her very clearly and love her as she is, love her more because of her frailties. I hope she is not hurt and suffering now. Have no idea how she is reacting, as I cannot contact her. Very tempted to try and phone her again, but it would be disastrous, and what's the use? The whole thing has to be given up. Only I don't want her to hurt necessarily.

June 25, 1966

Dream – "another" girl. I am supposed to date her soon but now she is in the hospital. I am talking to her mother (a heavy mother – battle-axe type), not interested in any of them much. But then someone suggests we go and see this girl in the hospital and I feel an inner awakening of interest and love, and know that briefly seeing her will awaken in us both a deeper rapport. I then wake up thinking – but this is *another*, not M., and go back to thinking consciously of M. with a little guilt. Is it another? Imagery later – after difficulty in starting –

I see a tangle of dark briars and light roses. My attention singles out one beautiful pink rose, which becomes luminous, and I am much aware of the silky texture of the petals. My Mother's face appears behind the roses, which vanish!

Also in there somewhere a student nurse who came to see me briefly in hospital one day when I was preparing to go out for a walk. I was short and rude with her.

Today I go in for X-rays. Exactly 3 months since the operation. Am not supposed to see M., but I think she may come and meet me at the doctor's office, in which case I will give her "Midsummer Diary" (practically a book, I wrote it for her this last week).[14]

---

[14] The text of "A Midsummer Diary" appears as the first appendix in this volume.

And then it will have to be clear that we can't see each other any more, at least now. And that I can't write or call. (Though I still think before God that in a real emergency, if charity *really* demands it, I should simply ignore the prohibitions. But it is a delicate question to know when it is really necessary.) After communion and Mass yesterday it was as if I were told firmly "Do what you think right and trust in me!" Temptation? I still have to be extremely careful. I am in bad shape due to all this affair and have to get back, with difficulty and struggle, to what I ought to be as far as discipline goes. Prayer etc.

Began the gospel of Mark. Very moved by the first 10 or 15 lines – up to "repent and believe the good news!" So I begin again.

I realize that what is most wrong in my relationship with M. now is that I no longer trust her fully, and this may gravely affect my attitude – it may even make me unconsciously try to defend myself by insincerity and evasion. God help me and prevent me from this!

Came upon [Eugenio] Montale's magnificent poem on the sea of ancient wisdom, which sums up exactly my task. (*Antico, sono ubriacato dalla voce* [Ancient one, I am intoxicated by the voice] . . .)

> . . . *Tu m'hai detto primo*
> *che il piccino fermento*
> *del mio cuore non era che un momento*
> *del tuo;* che mi era in fondo
> la tua legge rischiosa: esser vasto e diverso
> e insieme fisso;
> *e svuotarmi cosi d'ogni lordura*
> *come tu fai che sbatti sulle sponde*
> *tra sugheri: alghe asterie*
> *le inutili macerie del tuo abismo.*

> [. . . You were first to tell me
> that the tiny ferment
> of my heart was but a moment
> of your own; *that deep inside my being*
> *was your perilous law: to be immense and diversified*
> *and at once constant;*
> and thus empty myself of all foulness
> as you do who beat yourself against the shores

among corks seaweeds starfish
the futile rubble of your abyss.][15]

June 26, 1966

Got my X-rays quickly – the back has healed OK. I have another deterio-
rated disc but it poses no problem as yet.

Came out of the office looking for M. – she was on the first floor just
about to get on the elevator I was getting out of. Went back up to the 4th
floor and sat alone in the hall by the window, talking, deeply moved, torn
with sorrow. She had called Jim W. in desperation and he had told her, apparently rather coldly, to leave me alone. She was trembling like a leaf in the
elevator. But as soon as we sat down (and I gave her the ms.) all our love
came out again and deeper and more complete than ever. We just sat looking into each other's eyes and saying what we had in our hearts and what we
needed to know, and I realized once again not only that our love was the
deepest thing in our lives, but was growing deeper.

She said she had sent in her application for a job at the _____ Hospital. ("Everything reminds me of you at St. Joe's – it would be too much!")
Obviously Wygal's attitude and that of the abbot had a lot to do with this.
Then on top of everything her fiancé is missing in action over North Vietnam. (She heard the night before, from his mother.)

She thought S. knew of our love from having read one of my letters (!)

I insisted that she come to lunch with me and W. at Cunningham's,
though he was very peeved about that and was quite hostile towards her.
Nevertheless we had a good lunch, and she and I anyway laughed and
talked, and enjoyed being together – played some of our favorite records,
like Nancy Wilson singing "Together Again" etc. Then finally Jim left us
alone for a little while and we fell on each other in desperation and love,
kissing each other over and over, swept with love and loss. In it, knowing it
would probably never be like that again. Then we took her to St. Joe's, and
she vanished into the shadows through the glass doors – will I ever see her
again? I don't know! But I think we will meet again.

We went out to Anchorage then, and she called me out there, sounding as
if she were almost in tears. She was just about to go to work on the 3–11
shift.

[15] Eugenio Montale, *Ossi di Seppia* (Milan: Arnoldo Mondadori Editore, 1948). The English
translation is from *The Bones of Cuttlefish*, translated by Antonio Mazza (Ontario: Mosaic Press,
1983).

What is the use of saying over and over that we love each other? It is the most obvious thing in the world. We are completely possessed by love for each other, fully reciprocated, the kind of thing that grows with every little bit of fuel – and everything is fuel for it! I know if we saw each other more often it would become a raging furnace. It could very well destroy us. But in spite of all the suffering and loneliness, it even grows when we are not together.

I am helpless to say more about it. Slept very little last night. From 11 to 1 (when she was off work and probably reading the Diary) I was walking up and down the porch. Slept fitfully from one to five. Got up and said Lauds, made some strong black tea and ate some rye bread. She is right at the center of my life and my solitude. I know I must now make a determined effort to be what I am supposed to be, and it means not seeing her, and obeying the commands that have been given me. Yet there will be slight exceptions perhaps, when necessary. However, in so far as regularly seeing her goes, in so far as continuing our affair, it is all over. And that is how it has to be.

I forgot the most moving thing of all – she just mentioned it in passing and the full impact only struck me this morning. She signed up for work with special hard cases – I forgot the term, it distracted me from the meaning of what she was saying – and that she would offer all this up for me. How deep and beautiful her love is. The others have not realized this – they see in it only what they want to see.

June 28, 1966

After a hard weekend I think I am finally turning the corner and getting back on my true road. Wrote what is I hope my last letter to M. (normally anyway, in this "intense" series – not excluding some future friendly note from time to time). Had a great struggle over it and what I felt was a real mess. The struggle was to keep out anything suggesting a commitment to meet her any special time in Louisville between now and the time she leaves in August. This I finally accomplished – I mean after tearing up page after page I finally got a letter that just said I loved her but not that we would meet on such and such a day. Thus I am left free, and there is actually no need to worry about future meetings: they can be avoided. It is better that way, though terribly difficult. The sacrifice is I think demanded.

Ping Ferry came and we drove all over the place – Hodgenville, Campbellsville, Lebanon, Bardstown, ate some hamburgers on the tobacco farms. Then when he left I got back to the hermitage – very hot indeed, about 100 on the porch – and felt that M. and I had at last reached the point where we were able to get along without hanging madly on to each other's necks – I hope so anyway. But one can never be sure. The letter I sent was too sentimental and may start everything up again.

There is an immense amount of work to be done to get back to being solitary. How much I have lost in a way! How weak and confused I have become! The state I am in is in some way quite appalling. As if I had lost everything. And yet I trust in God's grace – and feel that though I have proved once again that I am totally absurd and helpless when left to myself, He nevertheless has secretly remained with me and is supporting me.

June 29, 1966

A good night's sleep for a change – was able to get up on time, make a halfway decent meditation. There was a thunderstorm about 4:30 (still going on); dirty rain frothed off the roof into the baskets like beer. Eating breakfast, read Ernesto Cardenal's first circular letter from Solentiname. It sounds fine! A letter from him yesterday (with charming photographs of the island) says one has already left.

Difference in my inner climate: this morning I am no longer singing "Silver Dagger" but "*Sur le Pont d'Avignon*" – my music is getting out of the M. syndrome.

I don't read German well enough to read Von Balthasar in the original, and in French he is fogged and confusing (one can't come to grips with it easily). Yet if something looks interesting in French and you go to the original you are likely to get a real flash of light. See the correctness of this: "*Der Glaubensakt wesentlich existenzial ist, das heisst die ganze Wirklichkeit des Glaubenders als Gehorsamsopfer einfordert* [The act of believing is essentially existential, that is to say, the entire reality of the believer is put forward as a sacrifice of obedience]."

Much more real than French, "*le don de tout son être* [the gift of all his being]" etc.

June 30, 1966

Gehorsamsopfer –

To offer oneself to God as a sacrifice of obedience in faith. This is the crucial point. Too much emphasis on one's *own* truth, one's own authentic freedom, and one forgets the limitations and restrictions of this "my own." Tendency to take "my own" truth and freedom as unlimited, ultimate, "in my own case." This is a total loss. Paradox that only God's truth is ultimately my truth (there is not one truth for me, another for my neighbor, another for God) and only God's will is my freedom. When they appear to be opposed, am I acting freely?

Linda Parsons was here yesterday. We had a good long talk.

"Blessed are the pure in heart who leave everything to God now as they did before they ever existed." Eckhart. This is what I have to get back to. It is coming to the surface again. As Eckhart was my life-raft in the hospital, so now also he seems the best link to restore continuity: my obedience to God begetting His love in me (which has never stopped!).

July 8, 1966

Last week and its excesses. Drank with L.P. [Linda Parsons] at the lake, then in the evening called M. and she was coming out Saturday, changed it to this Saturday and then I called it off. And regained some perspective. Instructive to see how easily I am shaken and thrown off balance. I am going to have to do a lot of work to get really steady again. Reading book on Zen: not the best, but good things in it.

I have been writing more notes for M. going back over the story of our love, but this too is probably useless. Still I will finish.[16] Last night when sleepless I at least resisted the temptation to write to her!

"Silver Dagger" is back and I know all the words.

I can see how much I was deluded – and how much in fact I really wanted to be deluded and went out to welcome it. Because there is such a great good in human love – and I needed this good, or thought I did. Well I did. But I needed to know that I was called to something else, and the fact that I risked my other and special calling now frightens me! Have I perhaps gone too far? Will they now take the whole thing away from me? Have I started on a chain of inexorable mistakes? I certainly hope not! There is *nothing* I want but to make sense of this seemingly absurd solitary life which is nevertheless such a wonderful gift and has such enormous possibilities. I have not measured up at all and have not been worthy of it at all, but I beg God to let me continue with it and to give me the grace to do better.

[16] This is a reference to "Retrospect," which Merton wrote between June 30 and July 8, 1966.

I wonder how much M. and I have really been totally frank with each other. I think we have been more than ordinarily sincere, but still I think there has also been a slight duplicity and calculation: what was necessary for us to *hold on* to each other with one hand while looking around for some other support with the other. I in my solitude, she doubtless with another man. Not that I have been ambiguous about solitude – but still I have made it appear that I am more *desolately* lonely than I am. I am alone and I love her, but the choice between her and solitude presented itself and I chose solitude. (Though I don't think it was that real a choice – was there any way in which I could have *effectively* chosen her?) As for her – I don't hear from her now and don't know what she is doing. I know she loves me and is lonely for me, but certainly do not expect to remain a kind of exclusive love-object for her!

Walked over to Fr. Flavian's new hermitage, which is being built now in the woods beyond the creek and to the East. At the top of a little hollow looking directly toward my own place, but with nothing but woods in view. It will be hot in the afternoon – no protection from all day sun. One enters as though by a rabbit hole – small road plunging into thick brush and low trees. Smaller, more compact than my house, it will be more modern, better "appointed" – inside john etc.

July 10, 1966

Yesterday was very hot. I was glad M. did not come out, though of course I missed her. It would have been a fatal mistake in many ways and probably would have been pretty ghastly too. [. . .] And that would really have messed up everything, besides the sheer folly of risking loss of the hermitage merely by seeing her out here in the woods. Glad I called it off! I can see that I am better off without any alcohol. At least in this kind of situation. Drank some heavy, dull California sherry Dan gave me and it put me in a stupor. Only made the heat harder to bear and meditation impossible.

Borrowed a record player, played Joan Baez over again – and now really know "Silver Dagger" (before I had the melody confused with "East Virginia"). One record I like more and more is Bob Dylan's "Highway 61." Fr. Augustine sent me some Asian (Folkways) records but at the moment they are too subtle and I can stand only so much music. In a word, what I really need is the simple reality of my own solitary life in its nakedness, absurdity, or whatever you want to call it (I must be careful of imposing arbitrary words on it).

For instance – this early Friday morning is great. A big woodpecker out there drums on a hollow tree. A fly buzzes on the porch. It will be a hot day. I have read a little, emptily, thoughtfully or rather receptively, and that is that. There is little to be said except that I have been too involved in what is alien and irrelevant to this. And am not quite sure I know what *is* relevant. It is as if I had to start learning – I don't say over again – I have the impression of never having learned and of never having begun.

July 12, 1966

Before dawn, in the dim light, I sat on the porch and looked out at the peaceful valley. I realized that no matter how much I may love M. and be attached to her, there has never for a moment really been any choice. If it is a question of leaving Gethsemani and trying to live with her, and staying here in solitude and doing whatever it is I am supposed to do, then the answer is easy. There is not even a credible question. Even when she was talking so earnestly about my coming to live with her "in the world," it simply never was a realistic option for me. I don't think I was ever able for a moment to consider it. When Ping Ferry said I could have a job at the Center in Santa Barbara – it did not even click for a second. It is just inconceivable. (I remember us driving somewhere around Campbellsville and my trying to explain how impossible it would be.) Life "in the world" has become for me quite inconceivable. I cannot imagine myself living it, except as a fireguard in a distant forest or something like that. I am wildly surprised that someone like M., who seems to understand me in so many ways, could find my leaving believable.

Yet there is no question I love her deeply, and am drawn to her with an almost agonizing desire sometimes. I keep remembering her body, her nakedness, the day at Wygal's, and it haunts me. At moments it gets so bad I feel a kind of utter despair at my frustration. I suppose really what my nature, in its hunger, really secretly planned was to have her as a kind of mistress while I continued to live as a hermit. Could anything be more dishonest? I must say I never really accepted the idea, although I really think she would have. I am convinced that if she had come Saturday, it would have been a kind of showdown in which, perhaps, I could have been enslaved to the need for her body after all. It is a good thing I called it off.

The main thing is to get back to reading, study, meditation, more depth. Curious book on LSD – informative. Something one has to know about.

Charles Luk a bit unsatisfactory. Yet a lot of information comes through between the lines.

July 14, 1966

Yesterday was one of the hottest days I can remember – and it seems today will be another. Officially 101 in Louisville, said to have been 104 at the monastery; the hermitage was stifling because what little breeze there was was blocked off by the rise to the SW. Jim Wygal came out to get some books, and we spent the day together, driving around and drinking beer, which was not much help and in the end I was hotter, heavier, stupider than ever. Was sweating like a pig all day.

We got some hamburgers at Riley's in Bardstown and went to eat them on the new farm, where Jim told me his opinion of M. – very negative. (He says she is narcissistic, selfish, is not capable of really loving me etc.) He is much too hard on her, and does not see her as I do, the real sweetness and sincerity of her heart, and the real love she has given me. [...] But I see the real core of excellence that is in the depths of her being and that he does not see, and I love her and want to help her be true to that inmost center. In the late afternoon I wanted to call her and Jim would not cooperate at all – which I thought was a bit self-righteous of him.

We went to Loretto in the afternoon – very hot – Sister [Mary] Luke [Tobin] was not there. Sat in a room with a bunch of very warm nuns and talked for an hour or so – about Zen mostly. One of them played some Gershwin and Debussy very well on the piano. I enjoyed it, but felt uneasy about talking so much and so glibly.

Noted: general dispersion and distractedness all yesterday, obviously, and all night. Only recovered a real awake "mindfulness" after about 3 hours reading etc. this morning. The other state was of an anxious, disoriented consciousness, not properly centered, and making erratic and desperate acts, calling on God, trying to recover orientation, thinking of M., questioning self, fearing consequences of imprudence etc.

July 15, 1966

Blazing hot yesterday afternoon – I found a good breeze at one of my favorite spots, the N.E. corner of St. Edmund's field where the road (track) plunges into the woods. Read on Buddhist meditation [*The Heart of Buddhist Meditation* (London, 1962)] ([Bikkhu] Nyanaponika Thera – excellent) – on "bare attention"! Then Alan Watts on LSD (poor). Later came back and read some, *The Idiot*. It is too hot to work in the hermitage. I am not writing anything. Also hard to get a typist who will copy my stuff these days. Bro. A. is a bit temperamental, and others are not available.

Naomi Burton [Stone] having vanished into Maine seems to have lost interest in publishing and I don't hear from her – a word indirectly through the Abbot now in California.

This morning – after a hot night – some rain. It is cooler. I am moved by Luther's distinction between God's "alien work" (in which by suffering and humiliation He reveals to us what we are) and His "own work," in which He lifts up and heals us with His love. Certainly in all this business of M. I have seen a lot of both – and she has too. I think of her with just as deep a love and need as ever. Yet soon she will be gone – one month and she returns to Cincinnati to work after graduation. I have to face the fact of living without her and of being without much contact. Perhaps I will even have to finally let go and be without all contact whatever, which I still find impossible to accept, yet I have to accept it I guess.

July 16, 1966

Went to see Dr. Mitchell about my ankle (sprained it the other day) and M. came to meet me in a taxi – we went on to Cherokee Park and had a quiet picnic together and it was marvelous. One of the most lovely days we have spent together – to begin with the weather was bright and cool again and then something deep and purifying seems to have happened to both of us in the days of separation and loneliness in which we have been unable to communicate. Our love seemed to have been greatly deepened, was more peaceful and more concerned but above all even more intensely serious than ever. I felt how completely we really had come to belong to each other. We loved and kissed each other with passion. She looked tired and serious, and clung to me with such warmth and love!

Her graduation is getting near and she will have to go to Cincinnati, which I will understand. She has not been back since Pentecost (and what a pain that 3-day separation was!). Her mother called with a lot of silly prescriptions for graduation (who and who not to invite) – this made M. almost an hour late at the MA building.

I can understand her dislike of Wygal (I still think he might have let me call her the other afternoon!).

She told me with deep conviction that I am the "only truly kind and gentle person" she has ever known. Whether she is right or not it means a lot to me to know that, what my love means to her – that it is to her gentle, kind, warm, tender. I want to give her infinite tenderness and healing warmth and gentle care. She has said several times that this is the real love and no one accepts this kind of love. I have instinctively known that this, in any case, is what she loves in me, what is truest and most personal in me, whatever it is – something that no one else has ever fully accepted or believed in.

Today, when I had become all but convinced that our love had reached a kind of plateau – a level it would keep more or less statically – it suddenly grew more than it ever has before. And here I am loving her more completely, more rooted in her love, than ever. Because once again I am astounded by the reality of it. We drank a bottle of Sauterne, the big trees cast their shade over us, we were disturbed by no one but some kids from a Baptist picnic, who ran by now and again.

Her indignation at the disapproval of me expressed by someone in the monastery. Her agreement that I need my complete freedom. Her ideas of our living together are more complex than they seem (not just the "vine-covered cottage" as her note said). The fact that we both stubbornly refuse to give up our love and our hope of continuing.

But I was too passionate and in a way that was I think unfair (I don't think either of us are *obliged* to confess anything – but it was dangerous) and at one point she was getting worked up and so was I. This was wrong, really, and I am sorry. Her notes about us told me enough about the very high ideal of me she had when we met and still has though she knows me. She is really convinced that I "love God" – I wish I did as truly as she believes I do.

She says she thinks of me all the time (as I do of her) and her only fear is that being apart and not having news of each other, we may gradually cease to believe that we are loved, that the other's love for us goes on and is real.

As I kissed her she kept saying, "I am happy, I am at peace now!"

And so was I.

July 20, 1966

Cooler. A fine morning.

Difficult to work (at writing) and difficult to get anyone to do my typing since Bro. Dunstan Foretich left. Yesterday, though it was very hot in the hermitage, forced myself to begin the long delayed introduction to John Wu's book.[17] But I still don't feel I am ready yet.

[17] Merton's introduction to John Wu's *The Golden Age of Zen* appeared as "A Christian Looks at Zen" in *Zen and the Birds of Appetite* (New York: New Directions, 1968), 33–58.

Ed Rice wrote – he wants [a] second chance on the notes on "Buddhism and the Modern World" if they are rejected by *Cross Currents*.[18] A good letter from Cid Corman with whom I have begun corresponding (about *Origin* etc.). I like him and I think it is very worth while to write to him. Must read all of [Louis] Zukofsky as he suggested. But how to get it?

Ed Rice is anxious to have me do a piece on Bobby Dylan. Will send records if I ask. D.'s autobiography (!!) is appearing this summer. How old is he? 28? Not that.

Reading Dostoievsky's *The Idiot*, a marvelous and fascinating book. What a world! And how he structures it, with what ease – from the very first chapter.

Also [G. J.] Warnock on *English Philosophy Since 1900* [London, 1963], a new area for me – I always assumed these people were complete squares. Need to know Wittgenstein. The book is well written.

Finally also Nyanaponika Thera's excellent treatise on Buddhist meditation – the basic elements – so easily despised, but very practical indeed. There is a healthy empiricism in Buddhist ascesis!

July 21, 1966

Revising some notes on monastic life – read through the Council Decree *Perfectae Caritatis* ["Of perfect charity," "Decree on the Appropriate Renewal of the Religious Life"]. Deeply impressed by these lines:

Through the profession of obedience, religious offer to God a total dedication of their own wills as a sacrifice of themselves; they thereby unite themselves with greater steadiness and security to the saving will of God.

Very clear and helpful – and I have been evading this. I need to hear and take it to heart. No doubt my love for M. entails certain obligations to her, but I have been too willing to disobey in order to contact and console her. But I have been ordered to break off contact and sooner or later this will have to be final. I have to take it more seriously perhaps than I have. I am still committed to see her once more before she leaves, but really that should end it. Extremely difficult! I wonder if I can really do it! Hence I should not be too upset about the possibility of Dom J. clamping down again – as if I ought to resist. If he does, I must certainly see in it God's will and accept it. How I will do it I don't know – must keep praying for the grace – with the conviction that this "union with the saving will of God"

[18] "Buddhism and the Modern World" was published by *Cross Currents* (Fall 1966). Reprinted in *Mystics and Zen Masters* (New York: Farrar, Straus & Giroux, 1967), 281–88.

will benefit her even more than myself perhaps. (Is this after all one of the real purposes of our love?)

July 22, 1966. F[east] of St. Mary Magdalen

Though the feast has been reduced in rank, I said the whole 12 lesson office of Vigils with much joy and consolation – especially the lessons from the Canticle and the antiphons and responsories about the "precious pearl." It struck me all of a sudden that pearl = [. . .] = M. and I thought of God's love for her and mine. I can see absolutely no reason why my love for her and for Christ should necessarily be separated and opposed, provided I do not go loving her in some way opposed to His will. But if I love her purely and un-selfishly – as I surely do here in solitude – then my love for her is part of my love for Him, part of my offering of myself to God. On the other hand I have to be careful to truly obey. And yet are there exceptions? Same old question, same old risk. The real change is that even when we become very erotic I do not *feel* guilt because I love her so much and we are both totally committed to each other. This is of course a great danger and it shows how essential it is for us to keep out of trouble's way – and for her too. She loves this feast and Mass, and I have thought much about her yesterday and today (both "beautiful days" not only in reality but in our secret and mystical sense).

Finished the first draft for my preface to John Wu's book on Zen. It is a great relief to get this out of the way. Writing of articles etc. becomes harder and harder. Much more inclined to spontaneous notes, poems etc. Letters are also an enormous chore which I go at with infinite repugnance.

Am to see more "ecumenical" visitors this year – some seem worth while: and it is certainly providential. Four Buddhists have been recommended one way or another in the last week or two. It does really seem that my Buddhist relationships will turn out to be fruitful and important. And I can anticipate enjoying such visits. Donald Allchin also, who wrote *from* Oxford that he will be here early next year. Now in the summer there are the routine birds of passage, monks of the order stopping off on their way to Rome. (At this precise point Fr. Timothy from Vina came in to worry for an hour about the future of the Order – he is probably going to resign his job as Master of Students in Rome because so many have left Vina that he is needed there. He speaks of people leaving the Order everywhere – of the large house at Monte Cistello being more than half empty – 31 students in a house built for 100 – It is mostly the Roman students who cause trouble and leave etc. etc.)

July 23, 1966

In a good article on "Suffering in Greek Thought and in the Bible" (*Recherches de Science Religieuse*, 1955) the author has this to say of Oedipus at Colonus. The old king has learned from suffering to be *fully content*. [indecipherable Greek word]

"*[Il a] appris à chérir ce monde qu'il ne voit plus, à faire bon accueil aux imprévus journaliers de sa vie errante*. La solitude orgueilleuse du tyran s'est muée en sympathie universelle. *Ce chemin qui l'a conduit de Thèbes à Colone, où les dieux vont le ravir auprès d'eux, ce fut une montée incessante où la souffrance a joué, nous dit-il, le premier rôle.*" ["(He has) learned to cherish this world which he no longer sees, to accept well the unforeseen everyday events of his errant life. *The proud solitude of the tyrant is transformed into universal sympathy*. The road which led him from Thebes to Colonus, where the gods came to ravish him in their presence, was a ceaseless rise where suffering played the main role."] *p. 495*

It is *perfect* solitude and perfect compassion. The union and fusion of these two opposites is effected only by suffering. I don't know why I am reading this article now and why I am so impressed. Obviously there is a special meaning (perhaps the sacrifice – M. has opened me to it at last) – but anyway I am reading it. Found the reference in Von Balthasar.

The same article goes on very wisely to discuss the fact that Israel "learned nothing" definitive from the chastisements of Yahweh. That it was not important to have a treasure of wisdom for – or rather *against* – the future. "*Il vit entre la prise de conscience de sa faute et celle du pardon de Dieu, ce n'est pas lui qui mène sa vie. Quand il veut résumer son histoire, il la voit comme une dialectique incessante du péché à la grâce, dialectique dont le moment central est le cri, issu de la souffrance, de la misère coupable de l'homme et pourtant, déjà, expression la plus authentique de la Foi.*" ["Between the awareness of his fault and that of God's pardon, he sees it is not he who leads his own life. When he wants to summarize his story, he sees it as an incessant dialectic from sin to grace, a dialectic the central moment of which is the cry, rising from suffering, of the culpable misery of the man, and yet, already, the most authentic expression of faith."] *p. 503*

Job in the same article: this sums up the real meaning of the B[ook] of Job.

"*[La] confrontation puissante [qu'il realise] entre une souffrance, censée porter en elle même un sens objectif susceptible de la rendre supportable*, et un épreuve pour qui cette même souffrance n'acquiert de signification qu'à l'intérieur de son propre dialogue avec Dieu." ["The powerful confrontation (that he realizes) between a suffering, thought to carry within it an objective sense capable of making it bearable, *and a test, for which this same suffering acquires a meaning only within its own proper dialogue with God.*"] *p. 503*

It is in fact the Eckhartian "spark" that momentarily wails and cries on in the real depths of suffering accepted and understood – momentarily transcending life and death. The spark is that in the soul which is truly free and truly of God.

July 25, 1966

Yesterday my chapter talk was on [Josef Luk] Hromadka's *Gospel for Atheists* [Geneva, 1965] and today I read an article on [Gabriel] Vahanian which deepened and perfected the same ideas (by Rosemary [Radford] Ruether in the Spring *Continuum*). Clear admission of a demonic element in the Church institution that is unfaithful to the Gospel (how can an institution be faithful completely to the Gospel) – and yet one must be nevertheless loyal to the church as the center where the word is proclaimed. Yet there seems to be "another eschatological" anti-group group . . . all apparently ambiguous but underneath it I can hear the authentic voice of this time, in spite of the confusions. A remarkable – and dangerous !! – article. Its implications will work in me for a long time. First time I have seen the real point of this "God-is-dead" theology.

Am going back to Camus' *L'Homme révolté* – and as with *Sisyphus* I now find I am ready for it.

July 27, 1966

Trouble with bursitis and obviously another disc, also cervical. I wonder if the operation did not simply set this one up for trouble. Anyway I had a lot of pain yesterday – had to make an appointment for Friday (not Saturday, as the Hammers may be coming over). Since I go Friday I will not be able to see M. Mixed feelings about this – in a way I am glad (can keep to my agreement and resolutions etc.) and also I am sorry, for I still miss her terribly. On the other hand the whole thing is obviously over, as far as the meetings

and lovemaking are concerned and we both know it and have "accepted it"
I imagine. But as for my love – of this there is no question, in it there is no
change.

Am reading Sartre's *Les Mots*, a curious, brilliant book, one of his best. An
anti-autobiography – the variety of self-iconoclasm. But there is a certain
pathos in it.

Profoundly struck by the eschatology of the God-is-dead theologians
([Thomas] Altizer) – this is very serious indeed and demands a complete revision of my ideas about them. They really have something! Certainly not
just naive secularism! Absolute seriousness of the new creation – in *opposition* to the *kosmos*. A real yes and no. (But based on the scandal of a deluded
eschatological Jesus necessary to get a real crisis-dialectic in movement. Ac-
robatic! In any case the dirty words are now "metaphysical," "Being,"
"Transcendent" etc.)

Yesterday when I went to ask Dom James' permission to call the doctor I
saw he was angry about something and thought at first it must be that someone had reported one of the 2 calls I made to M. from the Steel Building
June 30 or July 2. Afterwards I guessed what the real reason probably is.
Ping Ferry said he was going to write to suggest Dom James send me to
California to rest up and recover from my "emotional involvement." Dom
J. was furious. Pretended last month to be concerned about my poor emotions – all he wanted was an excuse to lock me up in the infirmary – nothing
he hates or fears more than the thought of letting me go somewhere!
Which shows how much he really cares about my peace and [indecipher-
able]. Thank God he is willing to compromise and let me stay in the hermitage rather than have to argue about my going anywhere (I will certainly
never suggest this again!!). He depresses me infinitely – but there is no use
bothering about him.

Sartre in *Les Mots* turns out suddenly to be Merton of the movies. But that
passage is too long and overdone. Just because he is making fun of himself
he thinks he is permitted to drop all limits to carry on interminably.

Anti-eschatology of Camus – moving passages in his notebooks – warm secularity of earth, sea etc. "Mediterranean." Meditation in a Franciscan cloister in Fiesole. Contrast with God-is-dead set? Says his secularity is *with* St.

Francis, the world-lover. There is no question I too am really a world-lover after all: but what kind?

July 28, 1966

[William] Hamilton (God is dead) is less interesting than [Thomas J.J.] Altizer. Pedestrian optimism – Radical theology wants to live in *an America where optimism is possible* – It is a theology of zest – of enthusiastic participation in the electronic era – Johnson's state of the union message of 1965 same day as T. S. Eliot died – opened a new era of optimism!!! And so on.

(However, I will say this – new concept of post-modern post-civilized art is straight *play* without self-conscious searching.)

Back to theology: life is not full of zest and optimism because there are "no tragedies." Why? Tragedy belongs to pre-death-of-God theology. Now that God is mercifully dead there is no tragedy only zest. Hurray for zest. "A whole generation in its late thirties decides to take a swim in the Plaza fountain in the middle of the night."

July 29, 1966

Momentous talk with Dom J. yesterday – repercussions from Linda P.'s visit end of last month. She talked volubly on returning to Montreal, said I was drunk etc. (one afternoon I was) and this all got back to Dom J. in a letter from Fr. Salman, who sounded highly indignant and probably was delighted at this opportunity (L.P. says they regard me as an *enfant terrible* who by some fluke wrote a best-seller). Was offered a job of Master of Novices or Scripture professor (!!!) to lure me back to community, but in the end I think he saw I was not deeply involved in that mess – and will let me stay in hermitage I think. (More in small notebook.)

Ludicrous chapter on Metaphysics in Warnock's *English Philosophy Since 1900*. True, there is no metaphysics in England. But to assume that all metaphysics is just a game without meaning – to have no sense of the need for metaphysical insight of any sort – this is the wonder!

Went to Louisville with bad bursitis for a cortisone shot (painful) and lunch with Wygal (dull) and finally a check up with Marshall, the neuro-surgeon, who says he can't do anything definite about the numbness in my left leg. It was a terrible day, being in town and not able to see or contact M. But my purpose was to be in and out of town without seeing her and the reason I saw Marshall was so as not to have to come to see him Aug. 12, the day before

M.'s graduation, when we had arranged to be together again in the park. I thought this had now become so dangerous as to be out of the question and so dropped a letter in the mail saying we would have to call it off and saying in effect goodbye. She will get it, I suppose, tomorrow.

Then I felt it was heartless and wrong, and wanted to call her, but guessed wrong and got the dormitory after she had gone to do extra work somewhere on the 3–11 shift. In Marshall's office I was almost visibly crying! Was so torn by loneliness and longing to talk with her – and knowing it was hopeless. Worse still driving out on the turnpike – first passing near the hospital I thought I was slowly being torn in half. Then several times while I was reciting the office deep silent cries came slowly tearing and rending their way up out of the very ground of my being. It was awful. And she must have "heard" them. I got scared. There was nothing I could do with these metaphysical howls. Getting back to the hermitage finally calmed them. And I wrote a poem I had begun to scribble while waiting at the Medical Arts building. A Blues for M.[19] Sort of Bob Dylan thing (read a good article on him in the *Post*). Liked what rock'n roll I heard on WKLO on Wygal's car radio – I have grown to like that station better and it has also slightly improved since March.

Getting back to the monastery I found – to comfort me – a box of books to review for the *Sewanee Review* – 5 on or by Camus and the poems and some essays of Edwin Muir. Began Muir's poems with the hot water bottle cooking my bursitis and find much to say about them. A good discovery.

Tonight – rain and frogs. Can't sleep. Thinking of M. – and the two worlds, that of our love, which is not permitted to exist and yet is such an imperative *reality* – and the stupid, trite, artificial world of people who have their ways and standards which outlaw this reality. For very practical purposes of course – I know that if we really let go I would be destroyed and so would she. And yet – would it not be worth it after all? I know she thinks so – tonight I wonder about it again. But I know I have something else to do. The rain and the frogs are saying it clearly enough. As for the "people" – they are none of my business except that I have to keep out of their blundering way if I can!

[19] "Cancer Blues" – one of the *Eighteen Poems*.

July 31, 1966

Killed a copperhead on the path yesterday about fifty yards from the hermitage. I was on my way down to have a curious talk with Fr. Eudes. He has apparently been very much in on all my problems. Without my knowing – got a letter from Fr. Salman, and has heard the scandalized reactions of some of the young monks. This is good to know about, though none of it is very clear, nor is what Fr. E. says very clear to me either. Suddenly I find myself looking from the outside into a world of religious correctness which has to some extent become alien. And that is the whole trouble. It is also the source of confusion. "You are no longer correct, as you used to be." For twenty five years I have been an edification but now . . . Yet strangely now I feel real, though wrong. The correctness leaves me terribly uneasy! I will not say anything about that, I don't know what to say. I may be wildly deceived. It is perhaps true that I am doing, as E. said, everything possible to ruin my life. (I can think of plenty of other efficacious possibilities I have neglected!) Yet I feel rather that what I have been through was absolutely necessary. Well, not the Linda Parsons bit. But my love for M. – which I don't regard as ended and will never so regard. This had to be known and experienced, and I am grateful for it. All their interpretations are partial and biased by fright. I know I have been naive and imprudent. So what. It certainly has done something to get me to *decide* clearly for solitude, and that is the important thing.

I am really relieved at not having to continue that complex double game of letters, phone calls etc. (No trouble admitting this was all wrong. Not just a matter of external correctness but of inner unity and consistency.)

[T. S.] Eliot's *Sacred Wood* remains a book of singular value, one of those books in which every sentence stops you. This for instance on M. Arnold

The temptation, to any man who is interested in ideas and primarily in literature, to put literature into the corner until he cleaned up this whole country first, is almost irresistible.

Small wonder that I have in these weeks walked in the world of folk-song and passion – the only one adequate for my perplexities (well, Gregorian is too, thank God). I realize, reading Muir's lecture on "The Natural Estate" of poetry [in *The Estate of Poetry*, 1962], what the real hermit temptation is: it is to go off with the elves. To take the "Road to Fair Elfland" with the Queen of the Elves – which is *neither* the narrow thorny path of righteousness nor the broad path of wickedness. That has been my persuasion – that there was another purely free and neutral road, love for M. in our own kind of woods and Cherokee Park (note "Clerk Saunders and May Margaret"!!). It is True Thoreau the layman who goes to Elfland for seven years and then returns!

jhs[20]   *July 31*

Dear Fr. Eudes:

Our talk yesterday has been fruitful in this: it has suggested some helpful perspectives anyway. We appeared to be arguing about a lot of points that were really beside the point, but this does not matter. The one essential thing to my mind that calls for argument is one on which argument will be entirely futile. I will therefore just state my own idea and pass on. It is the error that you and Rev. Father both share that before I was in some measure whole and consistent and now I am not, and the thing for me to do is to recover my previous wholeness. Anyone that thinks that I was whole and consistent before simply does not know me. My fall into inconsistency was nothing but the revelation of what I am. The fact that in community this could comfortably be hidden is to me the most valid argument why I should never under any circumstances get myself back into the comfort of pseudo-wholeness. I am now in several disedifying pieces. That and not loneliness is the trouble. I am divided by having seen the despairing hope of wholeness with a partner of the other sex – which is of course totally out of the question – and a wholeness alone which I do not have. Now it is entirely possible that as a result of projecting my self-hate on to the community I am refusing the humble and realistic possibilities that could come from taking some active part in the life of the community. I will think about this and give it time, but at present I am so totally loused up on the question that any decision to participate would be phoney. Meanwhile, up here I can live well enough with loneliness and division, and I will do my best not to let my inconsistencies frighten people down there. All I ask is the mercy of God and of the Order, and for my own part I will cultivate the honesty without which this life here would not be bearable at all. And continue to mind my own business. Perhaps it is not necessary for me to act out so visibly and so explicitly my conviction that I am not a monk and that I really never wanted to be one. I mean (don't be upset) of course that the whole question of "being a monk" is imaginary and irrelevant and to suppose that it requires manifestoes and proofs of some sort is now for me a waste of time. But I will

[20] The following letter to Fr. John Eudes Bamberger appears as a page of the journal.

really try to behave in such a way that this pseudo-problem does not disconcert other people. I do honestly and sincerely see that this is something that need no longer bother me at all. I am almost capable of finally becoming a free man.

   All the best in Christ,

   Fr. E. replied to the above by saying that my general tendency now is to "self-defeating programs as a way of life," which is a bit sweeping (whereas before apparently I was living fruitfully – not now).

   However, there is no harm in taking seriously his advice to be more self-critical and self-disciplined and to "take into account your need to create and exploit the relationship with the young lady and the readiness with which you let it over-ride other needs you have." In other words why did I fall so hard for M.? He now admits it was not entirely because I was a hermit and lonely. Or does he? It doesn't matter. I'll accept the fact it is perhaps a much bigger problem than I realized. And try to work it out.

   I like Edwin Muir's Norton lectures on poetry – very good one on Yeats, and a lot of sense in his lecture on literary critics. Against the professional critic who considers himself a kind of orchid which the tree of poetry exists to sustain. (Northrop Frye has a whole doctrine of the critic as the man who is needed to perfect the poetic experience – he is essential to poetry!) E. Muir – the traditional public is essential. The critics = the *critic* is essential. Critic is now the poet's public. Poetry tends to sterility and irrelevance in proportion as the poet addresses himself to the critic rather than to the public.

August 4, 1966

Yesterday a heart-rendingly brilliant and lovely day: all such days are for me now heart-rending because of M. and the days we spent together last May. Such days speak of my love for her and her love for me and of our "vision" of each other – and my intuition of her as a kind of expression of the sweetness of all creation (extraordinary). Awful feeling of loss and deception. Have I really been a complete fool in letting her go? And so on. Almost despair, and blind clinging to God in hope. And at the back of my mind that hot-wind of the radical theologians saying that God is what we don't need!!

   I thought much of her own suffering. It seems to me that a very real and very strange awareness of the quality of her loneliness and anguish is somehow conveyed to me. In our solitude we somehow remain in deep communication. No way of proving it – perhaps only an illusion. But it is terribly real and was most real yesterday afternoon when I was trying to read Muir for my review etc.[21]

Are people like Camus and Muir the true monks of our day? Is monasticism to be really found in an external commitment to certain formal sacrifice and an institutional and ritual life or in the kind of solitude, integrity, commitment that Camus had – or the fidelity to vision that was Muir's?

August 5, 1966. Our Lady of the Snows
Yesterday morning after walking out to the Derby Day place again (meditated a bit on P. Erwin's book and on Edwin Muir) came back and recited the long office of the degraded feast (this morning's vigils). Yesterday a beautiful rough day. Another session with the Abbot. He lectured me again – not unkindly, but of course with the great moral superiority he now enjoys. And he had engineered various small and humiliating "solutions" to practical problems of monastic importance – too intricate to describe. I am mad at myself for being affected by all of it! For instance the politics about the shortwave radio in the gatehouse. The misunderstandings, the evasions. It is supposed to be for me to use in an emergency. They never answer it. They have now an excuse why they don't. I am "asking for messages from my friends." (Once failed to contact gatehouse at all and wrote a note asking if the Hammers called.) I have no confidence in this thing working in a real emergency. Might as well forget about it and trust solely in God.

Then the Abbot started laughing at me. He said "I am thinking of writing a book on how to get hermits into heaven!" And laughed heartily. He enjoys the whole thing very much. And I burned interiorly. And was mad at myself for feeling it! The man has to gloat. I have offended and disturbed him many times and now I should have the decency to let him enjoy his innocent satisfaction. However, on leaving I said: "When the baby is born you can be its godfather!" A slight shadow crossed his face and he laughed with less enthusiasm. Was I really kidding? We are a pair of damned cats.

Reading. Certainly I am in trouble and I know part of the problem comes from not reading enough "holy" material. For a long time – in the thick of the affair – read no Scripture at all and spent time writing long diary entries

---

[21] "The True Legendary Sound: The Poetry and Criticism of Edwin Muir" was first published in *Sewanee Review* 75 (Spring 1967). Reprinted in *The Literary Essays of Thomas Merton* (New York: New Directions, 1982), 29–36.

(the typed Midsummer Diary etc.) or letters to M. Now I am meditating on St. Mark and Ecclesiasticus – and saying the Psalter regularly. But I am withheld from reading the Fathers by a sort of guilt and confusion. Are they really relevant to me now? Is this purely an escape into a beautiful lost world of extinct Christian culture? Will it simply reinforce the deceptions and delusions of my "monastic life"? I don't say these are answers – but they are real questions.

Always thinking of M. – things deepen, grow on me, possess me more entirely. The image of her the last few times I saw her – the waif-like, questioning, looking, expecting solitude, watching me coming toward her or going away. Sadness, pain, love, and a kind of helplessness which I can do nothing to help because I too am helpless. Except in prayer. M. as a living and suffering question mark. The thought of her turns everything slowly over inside me and I choke with bitter tears.

And her face turned up to me to be kissed, with total surrender after we had put down the picnic things in Cherokee Park. I hear nothing from her – nothing can get through, even conscience letters. Awful loneliness, getting deeper and more inarticulate all the time. (At this time she had written two letters that did not get through – one a note from the Merton room at Bellarmine, where she had gone in desperation.)²²

This morning I have finally really begun to dig the God is dead set. Wm. Hamilton's essay "Thursday's Child" [in *Radical Theology and the Death of God*, ed. Thomas J. J. Altizer and William Hamilton, 1966] is so correct, so honest a statement of the complete futility of all our gestures and charades! I know exactly what he means and at this point I find myself with him – though I reserve the right to my own empty and disconcerting experience of faith. But as to the complete alienation and disedifying scandalousness of it, I am with him. This is the real "*place*" – I mean it is the ark in the present deluge. I cannot be "in the world" (just as well) but I have a new sense of the meaning of my solitude. This is fraught with consequences and I see they must sink in.

The first of these is peace. I have got to stop being troubled by my alienation. God will take care of it. (I can say this shamelessly, thus separating myself also from Hamilton and co.)

---

²² Merton later inserted this parenthetical note.

The above – a surprising context for the meditation topic suggested by Dom James "What does it mean to be *a Hermit?*" Yes indeed! What does it mean!!

Innocent joy of having a shortwave radio set which I shall never even bother to turn on for any reason. Only in a Trappist monastery would I achieve the inexorably consistent absurdity towards which I now willingly drift and in which I really foresee a kind of happiness for a few years before they plant me.

August 6, 1966. Transfiguration

Last night I dreamt I called M. and was going to meet her – indeed I was seeing her again often. Going to meet her! I awake when I was having trouble finding the way. Perhaps my next date with her is in heaven. I wake thinking of this possibility. I have often wished I would die in these last days – I constantly pray for us to be together finally in God. And am impatient for the time when we will be!

How beautiful were the few times we had together. I do not regret at all my love for her and am convinced it was a true gift from God and has been an inestimable help to me. I know it was getting to a point where it could have gone very wrong and become destructive. But it did not, and I know it remains in both our lives as something healthy and beautiful, a real grace, that will hold us together forever. I am so thankful for this!

Meanwhile, I have to accept the punishment the Abbot is giving me. Nothing great in itself, really, only his scorn and his narrow-mindedness bearing down more directly, cutting off liberties and what were really privileges – so I cannot truly complain. I must see Dan Walsh less frequently (soon not at all). I must stop seeing Wygal at least in Louisville – in all this I know he is fearing plots and smuggled letters etc. Well, he has the right and I must accept – without resentment. What I resent is the suspected personal animosity but Dom J., though I know he doesn't like me really and is jealous of me, does keep his animosity somewhat controlled and is not as unfair as he could be if he wanted. That he is certainly arbitrary and demanding in many tiresome frustrating little ways – (refusal to let me go to St. Joe's again – I may need a bursitis operation – will have to change doctors and start over again in Lexington where we don't pay the hospital etc. Then in Lexington I must not go to the Hammers' *house* but can eat with them in a restaurant etc. All silly but not totally negative).

I think what really irritates me is the central ambiguity in all Dom J. does especially in my regard. His real motive in letting me be a hermit is to have more complete control of my relations with the outside, to cut contacts and correspondence etc.; when he says I am not living as a hermit he means I am frustrating this aspect of his plan.

One of the things that most angered him was my going to Loretto on the 13th and "giving conferences." This is what he hates – my communicating with other people successfully and receiving their gratitude and appreciation. He sincerely thinks his reason for hating it is that it is against the hermit ideal. "If you were in community it would be different." It would not!! He felt the same way when I was in community.

August 7 , 1966. "Day of Rec[ollection]"

One thing I realized this morning and I have realized it before: the real difficulty with Dom James is his mentality, his character, his prejudices, his background. He is the very incarnation of New England middle-class, efficiency-loving, thrifty, crafty, operating, sanctimonious religiosity. He is at once calculating and sentimental, comfort loving and disciplined, a mystically inclined businessman, secretive, suspicious, solitary, yet in many ways self-sacrificing and dedicated to making his institution run in an orderly manner. And he is good at this. He has put everything he has into it.

But he finds me irritating and embarrassing because I will never play any of his little games, and am anti-institutional from the start, and I do not like being used for his ends (he discovered that long ago and on the whole he has not tried to exploit me much). (He has in fact often left me a great deal of leeway and I should have paid him off with greater consideration. The trouble is I am not profitable – except in royalties – he gets no payoff from me either as hermit or as a cenobite and he is fed up. Have been too conscientious about it, not from perfect motives but just to assert my independence.)

The independence of the Steppenwolf says H[ermann] Hesse, is really only a pseudo-independence. The autonomy of the intellectual who repudiates bourgeois comforts without entirely giving them up himself – and Hesse in the end justifies the bourgeoisie. That is about what I am doing in the monastery. Is it worth all the trouble I put into it?

Yet at the same time here, with Dom J. – the failure of communication and total lack of real contact is getting more and more embarrassing – now I really feel like a Negro in the presence of a Southern white man. The desperation of knowing that you are talking to a wall of blank refusal to see you in any other than his own purely arbitrary terms. I have felt this before but never as strongly. The temptation is to take up an attitude of insolent and uncomprehending servility. And I suppose that is the worst thing possible in the circumstances.

The central idea in Camus is that *revolt* is the affirmation of man in his common nature (not enough emphasis on person) as against the historical process, or against revolution itself which always degenerates (due to its nihilistic elements) into the police state. Revolt saying "No." The refusal of resignation, places a man in the open, in his isolation and vulnerability, his capacity to unite with other "revolters," and *this creates the only situation in which new values become possible*, i.e. creates an authentic chance for renewal. The only alternatives are madness and death, outside of this creative revolt.

Question arises – is Camus also a Steppenwolf? Perhaps. Sartre prefers *power* to liberty.

In a sense this applies to my own situation – if I don't dramatize it irresponsibly.

I am in an ambiguous, uncertain state of revolt. It is not effective because first of all I am conscientious about my vows. Hence it is not so much "revolt" as "reflexion" and "reflexion" creates no new values.

Just enough revolt to invite reprisals! Useless! Self-defeating. Perhaps Camus or (Hesse) is the only answer in my position. The plight I am in is so ridiculous – so truly absurd. An effete, ambiguous, mixed up, self-questioning form of traditional monasticism, held together by a few determined and traditional minds facing inevitable discredit and collapse. My own highly ambiguous and in fact ludicrous hermit experiment (in which I have nothing but *happiness* and this is the crowning joke). My solitude really does not rate as revolt, I guess. Perhaps if I can simply accept its happiness and its humorous possibilities, that will be enough.

Went to confession to Fr. Flavian today instead of Friday. He said people are wondering what is the matter with me – and some are saying "The abbot is giving him a hard time." I don't know how much of the real story has got around. Fr. F. frankly admits he "can't stand" Dom James. At my Mass, however, I was reflecting how far I failed in meekness and nonviolence: not the external acceptance but the interior peace. Too much interior fury at the possible wrong motives I can guess at (rightly or wrongly) and no real desire to come to a peaceable agreement. I want him to be proved *wrong*! It is all silly.

In the afternoon went especially to see Fr. F.'s new hermitage which is almost finished and is very nice indeed. Much slicker and more modern comforts than here – inside toilet, shower, water of course and his own chapel. I still have to wash my dishes in the rain bucket – and myself too for that matter. And because of my misbehaviors Dom J. refuses to let them dig me a well.

I walked out in a broad open field in the East Farm (Linton's) and watched the high cool clouds, and said aloud several times the word "Revolution" to see how it sounded. Then I read in the *Book of the Poor in Spirit* [by Johannes Tauler] how by many deaths we must come to see God.

August 8, 1966

There were letters in my box about something of mine in *Life*. I had not seen it. I know a piece of *Conjectures* (this Journal in fact) was to be there. They have paid some huge sum for it. At dinner, by the kind bounty of Dom James, there were tearsheets, doubtless from his own copy, or from Leo Gannon's. The polite kindness was tempered by the fact that he must have seen this already last Monday when he bawled me out for being a non-hermit (because of Loretto chiefly but perhaps even because of this). Now I suppose this is his next move after my note of Sunday and the outline of hermit rules he requested.

Anyway I was glad to see it and the chief reason why I was, was that I knew M. would see it and be happy and proud – it would serve almost as the letter which I can't write. That was some consolation in any case.

August 13, 1966

Rain. The Hammers planned to come over but perhaps the rain will prevent them. I will say Mass earlier in any case.

Today is M.'s graduation day, and I have been thinking of her even more than usual. Yesterday we had planned a last picnic in Cherokee Park but I gave it up and canceled the plans after the big showdown two weeks ago, as I had to finally settle everything and get straight with the management here. I miss her terribly, think back repeatedly of the few wonderful days we had together, the perfection of our love, our obligation to one another . . .

Yesterday my arm hurt so much I could hardly type a letter (to Dame M[arcella Van Bruyn] at Stanbrook and to [Robert] Lax). Two days ago finished the first draft of an article on Camus (and went over it again yesterday and today making additions). I like his notebooks. Intend to write to Jean

Grenier. Hope to write on "Zen and the Cloud." Got Edwin Muir's *Autobiography* from the U. of K. and it is most impressive.

Fr. Abbot said Thursday that I could make my "commitment" or quasi-profession as a hermit. I was happy about this. It means stabilizing myself officially and finally in the hermit state and for many reasons I want to do this – first there is no other kind of life I am interested in living. Second, by way of a deeper consecration of myself to God. (I might even make a vow; but think it is simpler not to). Third – so that there is a clear understanding between me and the community – and any future Superior. I am happy too that we seem agreed and settled and that there will be no more strain and tension (I hope) over my misdeeds.

A present: clusters of delicate mauve lilies almost like orchids have suddenly bloomed in front of the hermitage. A surprise – from some of the bulbs Eileen Curns sent last winter I imagine. Only one or two lemon lilies ever appeared.

In the mail about the *Life* article – a hard-hitting book *The Negro Man* by one of the editors of *Ebony*. His wife, a Catholic, and a fan from her schooldays, sent it. It seems things look stormy this fall in the South.

August 15, 1966. Assumption

A big indefinite thunderstorm is moving in from the S.W.

The Hammers came Saturday and there was heavy rain, but we sat in the Tobacco Barn on bales of straw (bales they were picking up on the New Farm Whitmonday when I was out there). We have given up the idea of printing the love poems. They said J. was worried about me – they were glad the affair with M. was all over. Yet I still have terrible agonizing fits of loneliness and have to get in touch with her. If only I could talk to her, or even get a letter from her! And I keep wondering how she is feeling. She is now gone home to Cincinnati. I think of her still almost constantly.

Big SAC plane goes over low flying before the storm (which is still no closer) goes off into the east, a pale impressive silhouette in the more lurid sky there.

I walked in the woods (D[erby] D[ay] place) for a while; read some bits in a selection of Protestant Mystics – liked Rufus Jones and especially an anonymous Anglican woman called Aurelia who seems to be right on target! Then read more Montale. The "Eastbourne" poem. His motets are exquisite – one, a still life of Pompeian souvenirs, is as pretty as Mozart

> *Nella valva che il vespero riflette*
> *un vulcano dipinto fuma lieto.*
> [A volcano
> painted on a seashell smokes
> brightly in the sunset.][23]

Letters about the *Life* piece are still coming in.

I like the Abbey much better without the steeple. It is a much simpler, more modest, less forbidding place – it even has a strange charm, nestling in the trees instead of trying to dominate everything with a big false spire.

But last night I dreamt they were putting the spire up again – temporarily – for a festival of some sort. The frame rose up with the ease of the work of an umbrella, but the spire was top heavy and I saw it was going to fall. There were many workmen up in it, and I cried out to God to prevent it from falling. Still it fell and all the workmen with it. Hundreds of workmen were lying on the ground injured. I went to the nearest of them – three negroes – and wanted to help them. I wanted to get a car to stop to pick them up but no car would do so – even one driven by a Negro woman.

I thought "what a stupid thing it was to try to put that old spire up again! Typical of Dom James!" I woke without knowing any more.

August 18, 1966

Have had difficulties for some time with the verse of René Char – finding it impenetrable. Today I think I have broken through – and precisely with this short poem.

> *Un oiseau chante sur un fil*
> *Cette vie simple à fleur de terre*
> *Notre enfer s'en réjouit.*
>
> *Puis le vent commence à souffrir*
> *Et les étoiles s'en avisent.*

---

[23] English translation of Eugenio Montale's *Mottetti: Poems of Love* from *The Motets of Eugenio Montale*, translated by Dana Gioia (St. Paul, MN: Gray Wolf Press, 1990).

O folles de parcourir
Tant de fatalité profonde![24]

[A bird sings on a wire
This simple life on the earthly level
Our hell rejoices.

Then the wind begins to suffer
And the stars take notice.

Oh crazy ones for traveling across
So much deep fatality!]

Why did this click? Not just because of the birds that sing on the power-line to my house. The middle couplet, I think, affected me first. But at any rate I recognized my own kind of poetic world, which, in many French poets, I simply cannot. But this is exquisite. Though exquisite is not my kind of a word. Well, what is it then?

But after this they all connect and I laugh.

Dans l'absurde chagrin de vivre sans comprendre
Écroule-moi et sois ma femme de décembre.
[In the absurd chagrin of living without understanding
Tumble me down and be my December woman.]

August 20, 1966

Went to town yesterday for a cortisone shot for the bursitis. Operation put off. He still thinks it can be avoided perhaps. I hope so. Going to the hospital especially in Lexington involves complications. I would be unable to resist letting M. know I was there, or her friends would let her know – I would love to see her, but it would complicate things again. Yesterday I made a long distance call to Cincinnati and talked to her – it was wonderful and in a way shattering. Her voice was full of choked up emotions and my heart was all churned to pieces by the time it was over. She has sent several letters but none have got through to me. Said she loved the "Cherokee Park" poem[25] and the piece in *Life*. Has to come back to Louisville to take an exam. Oct. 28–29. It was a relief to hear her voice, yet I came home disturbed and troubled.

[24] This poem by René Char, entitled *"Un Oiseau...,"* appeared in *Fureur et mystère* (Paris: Gallimard, 1948). Translated by Beverly Evans.
[25] Another of the *Eighteen Poems*.

What troubled me most was the time spent with Wygal – his insistence on driving to his house when I explained that I had been forbidden to go there, sitting around stupidly drinking and playing with color TV (idiotic the color comes on and off – it was an inane soap opera etc.). Finally as a climax of absurdity I looked at a couple of copies of *Playboy* and was utterly repelled by the whorehouse mentality of it. The whole business was saddening. I can see there is absolutely nothing for me in all this and I have to just avoid it in the future. Hate to offend anyone, but I have to have the courage to break with something that has nothing whatever to do with my real existence – I don't mean just *Playboy* (!) but this whole business of visits with Wygal and so on. It is absurd.

Sense of having encountered miasma in the city (fury, traffic jams, sadism on radio, confusion), returning to the woods as though wildly plague-stricken, hoping my awareness and suffering are a good sign and that they promise recovery . . .

August 22, 1966

Yesterday – a fine sunny afternoon full of white and blue cumulous clouds. Went out to the D[erby] D[ay] place in the woods, thinking of M., read some Eckhart – and concluded that I had to simplify and unify everything by making no further plans to get together with her or to keep in habitual contact (but only to take what obviously came by itself). Principle – that what we renounce we recover in God.

Then read more René Char. He has to be read aloud. Compact, rich, intense, full, much music, more austere and self-contained than Saint-John Perse. I must really read him now. It will take time and attention to absorb all that is there. Perhaps a long course of reading, in the full afternoons out under the trees!

This morning – rain. Everything dark green. Took out my new Japanese umbrella (sent a few weeks ago by John Reynolds of *Jubilee*) and walked in the rain saying Prime and then the rosary. Wonderful contrast between the luminous gold and white aura created by the *Bangasa* and the jade green of the pines. One walks in a world of special human light, deepness and comfort in the midst of wet and dark nature. The kind of atmosphere in which I walk with M., or the thought of her – in the woods alone. Though I know it is foolish to try to keep up steady contact, I love her deeply and I can see that the purity of this love does really demand the sacrifice of human comfort and consolation. I can't say I understand how to do it, and how to avoid hurting her – and myself – more than necessary. Perhaps really the definite break is the more merciful thing, yet one cannot just "break." In the circumstances, I cannot possibly say anything that sounds like "I do not want to see you or hear from you again." It simply is impossible. And a lie! But we are in fact prevented. And I think clear acceptance of the fact is more or less required of us both.

August 27, 1966

Bright cool days all week. My Feastday Thursday. Wrote poem on Miguel Hernandez (whose poetry moves me deeply) and finished first draft of an article on Camus and the Church.[26] Seminarians barged in here I think Tuesday, much talk of Camus and Suzuki on the part of two at least. Camus is widely read, including by (young) Catholics. Perhaps I will send this article to the *Catholic Worker* when it is typed out.

The spell of Cesare Pavese, a novelist. Italian hill towns in the north or rather villages in the foothills of the Alps. Passion. Intensity. *The Harvesters* is a racking, smashing book. Curious, undecided, circular movement of *The Moon and the Bonfires*.

Letter from a nun in Covington who knows M. M. had been to see her, given her the poems etc. I am glad M. has some one to talk to. "She is numb," Sister K. said. Letter was conscience, looked as if it had been opened, I was surprised it got through. M.'s conscience letters have been stopped, perhaps opened and read.

Yesterday a letter came from Juan Liscano of the magazine *Zorca Franca* in Caracas and I sent him something. They have published a very good lot of authors – South American and European. Almost *no* North Americans. You can't call T. S. Eliot North American. Mary McCarthy and David Riesman the only names I clearly recognize. Mary Ellen Walsh is probably a N.A. name too. And that's it! Except an interview with Henry Miller by a nun (?!).

Writing more poetry now.

Yesterday in the woods, after chores (book list, letter to Liscano, papers to send out, portable stove for Flavian) went out to woods, and read René Char. Two splendid poems: the "Meteor of Aug. 13" and "La Sorgue."

---

[26] "For the Spanish Poet Miguel Hernandez" was published in *Sewanee Review* 74 (Autumn 1966). "Albert Camus and the Catholic Church" appeared in *Catholic Worker* 33 (December 1966).

August 29, 1966

Dom [Jean] Leclercq is here and is on his way to Cuernavaca, where Dom Gregorio is in trouble over his psychoanalysis – delated to Rome, falsified documents, dishonest accusations, condemned as contumacious, supposed to be imprisoned in Maredsous, resisting with help of his Bishop etc.

Dom L. lectured on iconography of St. Bernard and some ideas of St. B.'s art which seemed to me fanciful (visual pictures of words, members, acrostics etc. maybe so!).

His conversation is naturally full of the whole business of monastic reform, politics to defeat. And Card[inal] Antoniutti and get the vernacular for all the monks etc.

All this is of course important and yet it seems to me completely trivial. I can't get involved – first there is the fullness of my own solitary life in which I am mercifully delivered from all this communal worrying and politicking. (Yet remember it is because of the politics of people like Dom L. that you are here!)

Then there is the emptiness in me that opens out toward M. in her distance and which makes these other desires seem totally unreal.

Camus in *Notebooks*, planning a novel: ". . . that void, that little hollow in her since they discovered each other, that call of lovers toward each other, shouting each others' names."

Exactly: that discovery of each other. Like May 5 at the airport. The discovery that in each other we find the meaning of life and the universe – that we are capable together of being a microcosm, a whole world, a summary of it all. And then to have the history of this world cut short – we spin in space like empty capsules. And yet no. There is a certain fullness in my life now, even without her. Something that was never there before.

September 2, 1966

Day before yesterday M. got a letter through to me – totally different kind of envelope etc. so they did not stop it. I don't know if the Abbot has been reading her conscience letters or just throwing them away. At least two were sent in August and did not reach me. This one did and I was happy with it, happy to be loved and told so – happy to know she could get through. Poor darling, I can see how rough this is on her – in some ways worse than it is for me. And in some ways not as bad. But one thing is sure where love is serious, there is real suffering. I don't know what to do except to go on loving and occasionally slipping a letter out to her somehow. This I think I owe her, besides needing it myself. I think a love like ours demands some human concession. In any case I take this responsibility for communicating with her and do so because I think it is necessary. In a way it would be much easier to break it all off, which is what everybody thinks; I do not think that is right. It would be a betrayal of her love.

This afternoon typed out some of the very wild free poetry – very irrational and absurd – I have written lately and find it not so good. Sometimes the incoherence does find a kind of queer logic of its own and it is satisfying. Often it is quite banal.

Next week (on the 8th – Feast of Our Lady's Nativity) I am to make a permanent commitment as hermit and am trying to prepare by a sort of retreat. Was in the woods early today – an unusual time for me, usually I go out in the afternoon. Was meditating on "My food is to do the will of Him who sent me and to accomplish His work." This was a whole new perspective since Vatican II. Before it was unconsciously interpreted – around here at least – as if it could not mean anything but blind submission to a static established way of doing things. As if all initiative were wrong – or at least highly "imperfect." Now everyone is beginning to see that seeking God's will is a much more risky and unpredictable venture. I know that there are certain defined limits for me, but within those limits almost anything can happen and can be "God's will" and a summons to obedience: and not in terms of simple, blind submission only. I see how much I need prayer and grace to face this and be constantly open. And know well how easy it is to kid myself – so much so that I hardly like to think about it! What really is God's will for me? To live where I am living – to remain here – to be faithful to the grace of solitude – yet also a certain fidelity to my deep affections for M. – though this seems to involve a pure contradiction. And yet it does not *per se*. Only in a selfish exploitation would it become wrong: and then of course it could be disastrous for us both. So it is certainly His will that I take great care to avoid any such harm to her and to myself.

I see that I am floundering around in the dark, and need to pray and meditate a great deal. And that it is true that this summer I have done some very foolish and dangerous things.

Still using P. Erwin's Directory for his Brothers of the Virgin of the Poor – *Au coeur même de l'Eglise* [At the Very Heart of the Church]. It is very good. I need it.

September 4, 1966. XIV Sun. after Pent[ecost]

Retreat continuing. Two things are definite.

1. It would be better to make up my mind *not* to try to do anything about seeing M. again, not to arrange or plan anything on my own initiative. If something just pans out, well, that is another matter perhaps. I don't know! And it would also be better not to run a kind of guerrilla campaign to get mail in and out. Not that I am doing that – but still: not to be in direct conflict with Superiors on this point, not to be planning ways to outsmart them etc.

2. Though I have admitted this verbally, today I could see in my "right mind" that if I had been really aware of the meaning of my vows and my commitment, I would not have let my love for her develop as it did at the beginning. The wrong steps began with my first love letter, and the phone call on April 13 arranging to see her in town on the 26th.

Yet even as I say this and admit it, there is a sense in which I see it was almost inevitable. I had fallen so deeply in love with her already that it was difficult to do otherwise – yet I suppose I could have made another choice. And yet too – I am glad I didn't. I am really glad it worked out as it did. To have spent those days with her, known her so intimately, to be loved by her and love her now – all this has been so perfect and precious. I can admit it was out of place, yet I cannot altogether repudiate everything about it. Least of all can I in any way repudiate, or seem to repudiate *her*. She is the chief value in all this, her person, her heart, her love, her involvement with me. One can no longer speak of the situation as of a purely objective moral case. It is totally other, and far deeper than that.

Yet if it were a "moral case" I would only be able to say: that letter should not have been written, that call should not have been made. They were, objectively at least, infidelities. And yet . . . I simply cannot say it without qualification. Was I being faithful in an obscure way to some other and more inscrutable call that was from God? Somehow I can't help believing that I was. The conviction won't leave me. For that very reason – I must never let the same thing happen with any other woman, for if my love for M. and hers for me is from Him, then there can be no "others."

And that is the main point of a moral case anyway, practically speaking: as a guide to future action. The past is what it is and I cannot really regret anything in it except what my conscience sincerely regrets – the day in Wygal's office.

––––––––

I went for a walk to the woods. These days "to the woods" means – along the track by Dom Frederic's lake and around to the place of the Derby Day picnic – flat, steady, quiet and somehow very recollected full of awareness, peace – "holiness" – awe. A place of life in which both M. and God are more present and I remember His gift to me – her love – and the way that love (against all that the books say) seemed to bring me (and still does) closer to them.

There I could not help questioning the idea that the love of a human being *necessarily* comes in conflict with the perfect love of God. Of course I know St. Paul seems to say this: what exactly does he mean? Certainly I know that in my own case a fully involved erotic and sexual love for M. – completely fulfilled and frequently so – would turn my life and my vocation inside out. But the affection I have for her – with the explicit *sacrifice* of sex and of erotic satisfaction seems to me not to conflict with God's love, but to be in harmony with it. In other words that I have made the sacrifice of what had to be sacrificed, and my *affection* and *love* for her as a person to whom I am obviously bound in a special way, is not to be sacrificed. On the contrary – it seems to be a great good for both of us. Is this true? I believe it is.

(Night)

Tonight I decided to read over this Journal to see if I could make any sense out of it or see my affair in any kind of perspective. There are things that are not said here that come back to me reading the rest. First: how terribly lonely for M. I was the first days after I left the hospital. The letter I left asking her to write. My anxiety to hear from her. The impact of her first letter where I saw she loved me really (as I had suspected in the hospital). All the hospital stuff is in another notebook. We were in fact extremely intimate in a way – and this even got mentioned (obliquely) in her evaluation – a lot of people seemed to notice we were very taken up with each other. The agony of loneliness for her on Holy Thursday and Good Friday. Real trauma when I got home. Most of this came out (but very obliquely) in the poem "With the World in My Bloodstream."

Also I realized how, when I began to call her on the phone, my body got very upset and excited, stone pains etc. – and I was emotionally upset by it, knowing that there was a very powerful drag of passion at work in me and trying to rationalize it. Yet at the same time there was an obscure sense that she was somehow supposed to enter deeply into my life and I into hers so we could "be with" each other in the depths of our hearts in the midst of no matter what loneliness. A sense that this kind of union was possible and desirable. Really strange! Because that in fact is what we seem to have achieved now, and in great peace, really. (At least it is peaceful for me, though apparently more difficult for her – to judge by her last letter – yet essentially the same for us both.)

At the same time – our completely unrealistic, impetuous willingness to consider absurd possibilities! Reading the pages in early May I think we must have been half out of our heads. And yet there is no question – there was something fabulous about those days: the evening at the airport and the picnic on Derby Day – I have never experienced such ecstasies of erotic love (except later on other days with her).

As it goes on (Ascension Day) I see how imprudent and careless we were, and how in fact I was forgetting the real essence of my vowed life while desperately trying to keep the mere letter of the vows. And the moments of miserable confusion, half-hearted attempts to get free and control this thing. What really saved us was not any reason or restraint on our part but the fact that S. could not (or would not) drive her out here on Whitmonday, or on those Saturdays when she hoped to come! We would infallibly have got ourselves into a frightful mess, and it is true that I was emotional, unstable, irresponsible and did not really see it.

The one thing that troubles me most in it all – I see my instability and a certain *dishonesty*. That hits hard, because I think of myself as honest, sincere, direct etc. But there are some awfully ambiguous moments there when I am doubting and trying to get free. Those weeks in May were much more troubled even than I realized – and I did suffer a lot. Yet though this all had some basis in *her* character too – I love her all the more when I see how she has struggled with herself and how she has (I think) in many ways changed (I have some idea of how she was with others) and how sincere she is in her own troubled way too. We were really two messed up people! And we could have done each other awful harm! Yet we did not – and instead our love deepened, and has continued to deepen, and I think now it is very real, though we are isolated and God knows what will become of it.

I remember how upset I was around Pentecost – and the merciful guilt of the long afternoon Whitmonday on the Tobacco Farm. The discovery of the phone calls really did get me off an impossible hook (she sensed this too!!). I had no will to resist if we had got together as we were doing. Yet when we separated our love grew and the afternoon in Cherokee Park is one of the best dates with her I remember – we were on a much more serious level really! In fact that day seems to have confirmed us in a genuine love – more solid than the emotional and "ecstatic" experiences of the other days (though nothing can equal May 5th or 7th, which were miracles of innocence and spontaneity. Paradise Feasts!).

But we are two very complicated people! Poor dear M.! I love you anyway, completely – and nothing has changed – only that I love you more deeply, more peacefully, and the anguish is gone – and I will have to be very sober and careful about all this in the future!

The overall impression: awareness of my own fantastic instability, complexity, frailty, and the nearness to disaster in May and early June. Providentially we were saved from real danger. Dom James was more right than I was willing to admit and after all pretty kind and not too unreasonable! (He was scared by the problem too!) The worst thing was that afternoon with Linda Parsons when I got drunk and was irresponsibly misbehaving in a way that made me very ashamed (as an infidelity to M. really – but I was really acting crazy!). (In fact also nearly drowned in the lake when we went swimming, I was so drunk! This was really frightful!) And in the end: respect for M. and for our love, gratitude for it, sense of the underlying reality and seriousness of it, sense of immense responsibility to her, desire for her happiness, realization also that in spite of all my hectic confusion (and her seductiveness), I owe a great deal to her love and this is a lasting reality that cannot be denied – and we *do* belong to each other. In a way for keeps!

September 5, 1966. Labor Day
A very bright morning. Sun just rising over the valley full of mist – tops of the hills just inside over the wash of mist like a faint outline in a water color. Bells at the Abbey for a solemn Mass – departure of five for Chile, finally, where the Las Condes foundation is being taken over. I concelebrated yesterday and that was my farewell. Fr. Callistus is to be the superior there.

Last night I was up late (until 10:30 or 11) reading the journal and reflecting on the really overwhelming experience of the summer – experience in which I do not fully recognize myself – and in which I think there are signs of something strange in my life. However, it is there, and the fact of M.'s love and mine is there – to be understood and grappled with I suppose. A deep reality and a disconcerting one, for which I was not at all prepared – and which, as I now see it, could really have thrown me. Remains the fact that we do love each other in spite of the strangeness and disorder of the whole business, and that this means commitment to and care for each other in spite of separation. God has been most good to us and has greatly protected us against ourselves and has brought our love to a kind of quiet stability I think – so that now we can go on more or less safely. And perhaps I don't need to fuss over it so much. Sitting up and reading tonight through all this was, however, a kind of shattering experience in its own way – seeing the whole thing all at once in all its frank and pitiable confusion yet also in its goodness and joy – and above all in its danger, so much greater than I realized – yet at times my own fears were terribly acute. But they were not really "reasonable" and they were unconscious reactions sweeping through me without my really understanding them. In all this I have the impression of having been swept along where I thought I was going ahead by my own direction and volition. And I *did* decide, that is true. Much more was decided for me!

Can I hope that I am now in a new area, and traveling more securely, and that my commitment to the hermit life will be something more than a comic gesture? Because that is the real trouble. Is the whole thing just a fantastic private comedy? I question myself and my whole life very seriously. The real absurdity of it all! The *unreality* of so much of it. I mean especially the unreality of years I look back on when, being master of students for example, my job gave an appearance of substance and consistency – but actually I was floating in a kind of void! I think I enjoyed it to a great extent – but if I had been more fully aware I would probably have not been able to cope with it.

In a word, what I see is this: that while I imagine I was functioning fairly successfully, I was living a sort of patched up, crazy existence, a series of rather hopeless improvisations, a life of unreality in many ways. Always underlain by a certain solid silence and presence, a faith, a clinging to the invisible God – and this clinging (perhaps rather His holding on to me) has been in the end the only thing that made sense. The rest has been absurdity. And what is more, there is no essential change in sight. I will probably go on like this for the rest of my life. There is "I" – this patchwork, this bundle of questions and doubts and obsessions, this gravitation to silence and to the woods and to love. This incoherence!!

There is no longer anything to pride myself in, least of all "being a monk" or being anything – a writer or anything.

September 6, 1966

Too much analyzing. I think that this view I have of my love for M. in this Journal is a bit distorted by self-questioning, anxiety and guilt. Perhaps I have too much of a tendency to question myself out of existence. Anyway, when I get too close to my own worries everything is out of perspective. This is the case in the last four or five pages. I think I really understand the whole thing better not when I read my own notes but her notes and her letters, because these are necessary to complete my own ideas and aspirations and love. Also I write much more sanely when I am writing not just for myself (as here) but for her – as in the typed *Midsummer Diary* and the other *Retrospect* I sent her. That is where a more balanced view of our lives needs to be sought. This book is too shortsighted – and perhaps ought to be destroyed. (It is certainly not for publication.)[27]

---

[27] Compare this with the entry of May 11, 1967: "My intention is that, though it may eventually be published, this Journal should be kept under wraps for twenty-five years after my death."

PART III

Living Love in Solitude

September 1966–December 1966

Somehow in the depths of my being I know that love for her can coexist with my solitude, but everything depends on my fidelity to a vocation that there is no use trying too much to rationalize. It is *there*. It is a root fact of my existence.

November 16, 1966

The days of my retreat were bright, calm, unforgettable. Early walks, late walks. Early to St. Malachy's or St. Edmund's fields. Clear blue sunlit skies over the knobs. Meditating on Fr. Erwin's (Little Brothers of the Virgin of the Poor) good monastic directory (I must thank him!) and then reading René Char.

Killed a small rattlesnake near the lake one afternoon.

Afternoon walks to D[erby] D[ay] place.

A final day of rather tormented struggle and inner letting go of my selfish hold on M. or wrong need (I hope).

Thursday the 8th I made my commitment – read the short formula I had written (simplest possible form). Dom James signed it with me content that he now had me in the bank as an asset that would not go out and lose itself in some crap game (is he sure – ? The awful crap game of love!). A commitment "to live in solitude for the rest of my life in so far as health may permit" (i.e. if I grow old and get too crippled an infirmary room will count as solitude??).

After that I was at peace and said Mass with great joy.

For M. – I have a happy, friendly and loving affection deep and non-obsessed (I hope) and it will last. I love her but no longer crave her. At least that is how I feel at the moment. But to what extent do I know myself? I know enough to know I may be kidding.

The Bob Dylan records Ed Rice sent finally reached me Thursday and Thursday night I played some of them. Rich variety of things. I like best the "middle" (so far) protest songs like "Gates of Eden" which is full of a real prophetic ardor and irony. And power! But the newest baroque obscenities, the dead voice, the noise of rock, the crowding in of new fashion, this is very intriguing too. Intriguing is an extremely bad word. One does not get "curious" about Dylan. You are either all in it or all out of it. I am *in* his new stuff.

His song "I Want You" rang through my head all day yesterday in Louisville. Another bright day. Went to Dr. Mitchell for X-rays. Operation is perfect. Other bad disc above it not that bad yet. Avoid making it worse. Bursitis better.

I am through having lunch with Wygal (who is anyway in Maine) and that is in a sense a liberation – though it was always good to have a good meal and talk of my woes. Still, great peace being *alone* and able to go about with my antennae picking up the sounds and presences of the city and the hour. (Nothing new – bombs closer and closer to Hanoi – the Texas killer had a tumor on the brain, yes, but that was not the decisive "cause" – does the Pentagon have a tumor on the brain? Maybe. Tumor of power.)

Long wait in the sun for a bus outside Medical Arts Building – lump in my throat as we go by St. Joe's and Lourdes Hall – the place out in front of Lourdes H. where I last saw M. standing looking back with such hurt eyes at our parting in July.

In the U. of L. library, read Sartre on bad faith (can use it – but oversubtle??). Then found the Bingham poetry room (new) and looked through the Random House René Char. Quiet and peaceful in there – no one at all there and all the lamps lit. Must go back.

Lunch in the cafeteria about 1:15 – some rock in the Juke box – Beatles sounded good.

Back to library – some of [Paul] Klee's diaries and notes.

Later, tired of looking and reading, wanted to find some living magazine in the reference room but found none. Though they have a representative selection.

Finally on the way home called M. from a phone booth near Bardstown station. (She was by that time home from work.) It was a happy call. She is much more buoyant since her letter got through and her hard work in the hospital is a help. "I am very tired." – "I think of you constantly!" "Especially when I wake up." She was a little worried about the commitment but I told her everything went well. "I was thinking about that all day – " (the 8th) (seriously). She was a little piqued that I liked B. Dylan's song "Just Like a Woman." "Well, it's *pretty*." (Sort of distant tone.) I forgot to ask the exact date of her birthday but I think it is _____. (She was born just about two months before I came through Cincinnati on my way to Gethsemani! And I walked through Cincinnati station with the words of Proverbs 8 in my mind: "And my delights were to be with the children of men!" – I have never forgotten this, it struck me so forcefully then! Strange connection in my deepest heart – between M. and the "Wisdom" figure – and Mary – and the Feminine in the Bible – Eve etc. – Paradise – wisdom. Most mysterious, haunting, deep, lovely, moving, transforming!) At the beginning of the call she changed to the other phone (bedroom, I guess) where she could talk more openly. We talked of our love being deep and the same and of our "radar." And I said, "Yes, but there is no consolation" and she said, "*This* is consolation." It was a happy, cheerful, friendly, affectionate call without hooks and without anguish, and without smoke. She said I ought to write a poem about the freight trains going by (she was delighted at the strange place I was calling from – always wants to know exactly where I am). I said I could guarantee nothing but wrote a poem this morning.

A LONG CALL IS MADE OUT OF WHEELS

This is a long call
Built of heavy wheels
In the undestroyed solemnity
of two powers

Industry and love
Do not know each other personally
But live together
In the same town

With questions and quarters
In a hot glass house
I seek you humbly
I throw no stones at trains.

It is copper September
A season of vows
A covenant of beginnings
The New Year of the Jews

A month of ripening
As able as ever
To enrich this country
With bourbon and tobacco

O let September call you
To the beating heart

Of everlasting barns
To the long heaviness
of rolling cars

To the cool sun's center
Where I sing in a transparent bell
of green glass

Let the copper line wake
With an instantaneous
Loving charge

Princess of my world
In your fabled river-town
You run from room to room
Til your sweet joy
Is very near

And the boom of my freights
Can crowd you with glory
Though just yesterday
I was in despair

Love is a sacred gamble
of quick seasons, and rain
Dryness and recovery
There is no time
Table for the unforeseen
connection

(O lumbering train
"Must to thy motion lovers' seasons run?")

All the little buildings
Come and go
And do they criticize
While I buy time
To hear the sun set
In Cincinnati?

No one can criticize
Your silver smile

> At these dusty hedges
> Nameless unseen blooms
>
> And the tune of my train
> Changes nothing
> The edge of this last town
> Is still the edge of Eden.

September 13, 1966

Sunday I was thinking guiltily about that call. This business of writing and calling her does involve me in a certain duplicity. And yet I honestly think it is necessary – not just a matter of passion but also of genuine rightness and justice. It is "owed." I find it impossible to believe that my state demands an absolute, abrupt fracture and rejection of human affection! It *does* demand fidelity to my vow and hence great caution about any positive attempt to meet and see her again.

Reading Marshall McLuhan *Understanding Media*. I think it is very important indeed for monks to go into this. Critically important for the whole question of adaptation. I would like to write to him – would like in fact to go to Toronto, but this is hopeless. It remains a very important question. I may try to invite him down.

Certainly McLuhan brings home to me the fact that I do not really know what is going on. Doubtless *Conjectures* (or the other diary) may appeal to a lot of people who, like myself, are essentially book-types. But does it have any real understanding of new developments? Possibly very little.

This is another reason to be careful about writing essays and comment. Or more still, sermons (more still, medieval theology, however mystical).

I think this is another reason why I should think more of "creative" writing – poetry – prose notes – etc.

September 17, 1966

On the 14th – Feast of the Exaltation of the Holy Cross, copies of *Conjectures of a Guilty Bystander* arrived. There were ten in my box – also a letter from Sister K. which, though sealed in a second envelope marked "conscience matter," had been opened. The second envelope was opened too. I was worried and amazed, but perhaps it was only an accident. She does have her own problem which is certainly "conscience matter" but also she told of giving my letter to M.

Had you seen her expressive little face while reading your letter you would have been amply rewarded for your thoughtful efforts to reach her. She was ecstatic. She is well, looking her usual lovely little self. . . . Sensitive to the tremendous gift that is hers, aware of your powerful love and all it means to her as woman, grateful to your leading her closer to God; to your every token of communication. . . . You know her experience overwhelms her. The irony is that she discovers love and is in love with the impossible. . . . Woman is meant to be a "Yes." Not to live that "yes" in its fullness with the one she loves is something only God can understand. . . . You are saving, in your love and suffering, the one you love. She is charged with your love; you're not denying her its greatest significance nor are you being denied it. She loves you and will always love you. . . .

All I can do now is ask to serve God as the instrument of His love for her. And to be attentive to His will. I can't plan anything myself. Even the little contact we still have may be cut off. I don't know if the abbot read all this. He might have – but if he had, I don't think he would have given me the letter. And if I protested to higher Superiors about this he would say I was just evading the rules by a trick and they would uphold him. *But* it *is* a matter of conscience and I believe that before God in a case like this I have to decide in my own conscience and in view of her needs, what ought and ought not to be done as regards letters.

Humanly how can such a thing be left to the decision of others who do not know anything of the case, are not interested, and decide in purely abstract terms?

Letters still come in about the bits of *Conjectures* that were in *Life*. Translated another poem of Miguel Hernandez yesterday (onion lullaby). A good letter from Cid Corman, a bit apologetic for his rather harsh rejection of *Raids* (he is most sensitive to any violence in language – too sensitive. As bad as the prudery which cannot even bear any mention of sex). Yesterday, a brilliant September day. Bro. Cuthbert fixed the cracked stone in the center of my fireplace. Good weather is coming. Since I can't chop wood too well I will get a tank of gas and a gas heater this winter. Coffee percolator went wrong but is trying again. Morning coffee is important to me. I am not really fasting yet. Guess I will. Bob Dylan records each evening while I have the record player which I must return soon to Abbot. The records must go back to *Jubilee* after I have written the article on Dylan. Re-read Camus' "Renegade" and today the "Growing Stone." I wish to compare them. Nostalgia for primitive community. Camus is really a traditionalist and romantic conservative, balked by fact that he can't accept Christian transcendence – or even, really, primitive immanence either. So he has neither Man nor *Macumba* – but wants to celebrate the Sisyphus with primitives none the less. Knows it is hopeless, of course. The ending of "Growing Stone" gives it all away.

Yesterday in the woods I read the whole of René Char *Feuillets d'Hypnos [Leaves of Hypnos]* – powerful, compressed, authentic, rock-like and alive too. (The Sisyphus project of Resistance: necessary and inevitable!) The young murdered husband Roger, who had become to his wife the husband in whom God is given her, made me weep. The nice dog, greeting the Maquisards in silence. The forest fire. The execution in the village, which to save the village, they did not prevent. Thoughts of the young Maquisards. Landscape of resistance. And so much else. I got down what is on the surface of my mind here at the moment.

September 17, 1966
later

Finally had the sense to get rid of the fluorescent desk lamp that has been ruining my eyes. More room on the desk too!

Another letter from Cid Corman, this time harder to take. Having informed me in a previous letter that he was a saint, and having implied that many had him as their guru, and having emphasized his hatred of all violent language – he finally managed to write some pretty stinging letters none the less! I felt that they were rather gratuitous and that really he was acting under a kind of compulsion for which he himself perhaps had some unconscious guilt. But anyway he is smart and means well – and some of his points were pretty sharp and telling. (He is probably pretty good at finding where people are vulnerable and protects himself by pointing out all this to them. He has apparently lost a lot of friends, doing this!) But I ended up questioning the value of my own work and the purity of my own motives. Without sadness or preoccupation I know I can really get along without this nonsense. If I never wrote another book I'd be happy enough! I don't *have to* do all this. If I have to work on some creative stuff and never get anywhere with it – it will be worth while. Like weaving baskets and burning them as the old monks did.

Victor and Carolyn came over though Victor had a slight heart attack in the morning. I am worried about him. He was talking about "*Die Letzte Stunde*" ("the last hour") and seems very aware that he is soon going to die and may never see me again. We were talking about anger (Jewish New Year's – being written in the angels' book etc. – and the angels at my Mass yesterday – explained etc.). Each time he drives away in the Volkswagen or MG or whatever it is – I wonder if it's the last time I'll see him.

September 18, 1966

Early morning. Pre-dawn. 16 Sunday after Pentecost.

The different desk light is not only better to read by but quiet – it does not hum. That fluorescent was really hard on my eyes!

Reading about importance of the *Trial* symbol in Camus' artistic interpretation of life – how pervasive it is. Here is where our hubris comes out: in *judgment*. We are all judges and lawyers and penitents and defendants and accusers and juries. Cid Corman gets me at once in a judge-accused relationship. I must relate to him as a *defendant*. He is "up" – he will stay "up." I must vindicate my claim to exist. But this is doubtless because he feels himself to be on trial (maybe he thinks I am trying *him*. I can't remember saying anything that would give him that idea. Maybe he got it from *Raids*). But the joke is that I don't have to be on trial at all if I don't want to. Let them all play at being judges – what has that to do with me as long as I don't join the game by my own will and acts? Unfortunately, however, my acts – my writings – have been such that they have put me in the game. But I don't have to play it any more. I can get out any time. That is the real purpose of the solitary life!

But the point is to get out without excuse and without vindication, for the moment you justify yourself you are back in it again. If I depart with one last Parthian anathema, judging them all and then escaping . . . they will meet me again around the next corner. It is another story: being in the court and not of it – forgiving and not judging. (Rather than judging and getting away unpunished.)

According to an ad of E. I. Dupont (stockbroker) in the *N'Yorker* I have a life-expectancy of another twenty years, so I ought to invest in life insurance stock – or something. All very bewildering. Another stockbroker says that women have "special investment needs" to which he will give "personal understanding attention."

September 19, 1966

Merit of meditating on J. B. Clamence in Camus's *Fall*. This is what one should not be in the solitary life. The false desert father (*vox clamantis*) [the voice of one crying] crying out only about guilt and trying to be innocent, i.e. not judged. And judging others in order not to be judged first. All this is irrelevant, an absurdity – the issue itself is a fiction. What is there to justify or excuse? Love takes care of it all. Whose love? Must I prove that *I* love? No, I hope in God's love, i.e. in the incomprehensible. And in that love live at peace with myself and others. Someone questions the peace and asks to examine it. That's his problem, not mine. It is not examinable.

September 20, 1966

In the pile of things I have lying around waiting to be read, I picked out today the mimeographed conference of Jacques Maritain (in December 1964) to the Little Brothers of Jesus on their vocation. The best thing I have seen on the "apostolate of contemplatives." First he clears up the awful ambiguities of the phrase – which has degenerated into the purest cliché. He excludes all forced and artificial *témoignage* [witness]: artificial in the sense of the conscious or the self-conscious. For instance a funny sentence on the man who listens to a crashing bore with devout and overdone intentness as if he were an oracle. "That's all right for the Opus Dei but it is not the vocation of the Little Brothers." (Probably the trouble with Cursillo too – as it is too intently conscious, deliberate, organized.) Jacques emphasizes the *"microsignes* [microsigns]" of a Christian love that acts without awareness and is received without special or detailed awareness – the human and unconscious "aura" of a contemplative love that is simply there. (The implications of this would be frightening – if one were to realize that what counted was one's being and not one's acts. So aware that one is *nothing!!* And *acts* are nothing too! How dare to undertake this? This idea of *presence* in and to the world is fundamental. *"Ce ne sont plus des murailles, ce sont des exigences d'un amour constamment épuré du prochain qui gardent et abritent leur contemplation d'amour."* ["These are no longer walls, but the demands of a constantly purified love for one's fellow being which protect and shelter their contemplation of love."]

He speaks of the Little Brother "present" in a Moslem city being a good enough reason why a Moslem lives and dies in Christ without ceasing to be a Moslem. But would it ever be the other way around too? A strange question: but a very real one to me!)

So important: this presence is not a "pre-apostolate" simply "softening up" the unbelievers for the coming of the missionary!

"La mouise confessionnelle *des vocations religieuses – la mouise rêvée aux manies et aux particularités du monde catholique."* ["The *confessional* poverty of

religious vocations – the dreamed of misery with the obsessions and peculiarities of the Catholic world."]

Freely Catholic = without Catholic provincialism (which is of course un-Catholic. The official and forced universalism and centralism of Post Trent Catholicism has made the Church provincial).

No special job to do. *"C'est pourquoi leur vocation n'est pas la plus haute mais la plus abaissée, la plus au ras du sol – et du même coup la plus libre et la plus universelle. Tout travail oriente et entraîne et resserre la vie dans sa direction particulière."* ["That is why their vocation is not the highest but the most abased, the most flush with the surface – and at the same time the most free and universal. Every task orients and trains and binds life in its particular direction."] The job = rails along which henceforth everything has to travel. Even contemplation is then drafted for a purpose.

But (he touches only lightly on this) the contemplative in the world is limited to *inefficacy* humanly speaking – not being able to "do anything for the poor with whom he lives." *"Ils se contentent d'être là: sur certains points sensibles du monde, où les hommes ont un terrible besoin d'être aimés par des coeurs voués à la contemplation."* ["They are happy just to be there: at certain sensitive spots in the world where men have a tremendous need to be loved by hearts vowed to contemplation."]

The importance of a *purely immanent activity* (the contemplative does *not* do nothing). This can be basis for an incomparably deep understanding of another's suffering.

"L'être humain ici bas dans la nuit de sa condition charnelle est aussi mystérieux que les saints du ciel dans la lumière de leur gloire, il y a en lui des trésors inépuisables, des constellations sans fin de douceur et de beauté qui demandent à être reconnues et qui échappent entièrement d'ordinaire à la futilité de notre regard. L'amour vient porter remède à cela. Il s'agit de vaincre cette futilité et d'entreprendre sérieusement de reconnaître l'univers innombrable que le prochain porte en lui. C'est l'affaire de l'amour contemplatif et de la douceur de son regard." ["The human being down here in the darkness of his fleshly state is as mysterious as the saints of heaven in the light of their glory, there are in him inexhaustible treasures, constellations without end of sweetness and beauty which ask to be recognized and which usually escape completely the futility of our regard. Love brings a remedy for that. One must vanquish this futility and undertake seriously to recognize the innumerable universe that one's fellow being carries within him. This is the business of contemplative love and of the sweetness of its regard."]

"Il s'agit pour l'âme d'assumer et racheter dans l'amour des choses aussi lourdes que le désespoir et la révolte qui habitent tant d'hommes et spécialement ces hommes auxquels un Petit Frère s'est consacré en particulier." ["It is the soul's job to assume and redeem in love things as heavy as the despair and revolt that inhabit man and especially those men to whom a Little Brother has consecrated himself in particular."]

(But not merely to exorcise it in a way that produces mere negative resignation and inertia.)

In a way Camus was groping for this kind of solution. Rieux in *La Peste* is precisely portrayed as closer to this than Paneloux, who is inhibited by a special doctrine and by a set of fixed, rigid mental attitudes which get between him and human reality. He cannot "assume" the suffering and revolt of others, he can only explain it, judge it, at best try to explain it away with a suggested change of mind and mentality that will make it less difficult. (Resignation! Don't fight it.) In the concrete circumstances what he is doing is in fact refusing to take up the burden and simply adjusting it on the shoulders of the sufferer.

Jacques M. says to the Little Brothers:

"Ça vous nuit, pour racheter leur désespoir et leur révolte par le sang de Jésus, parmi ceux qui, sans chanter pour cela l'Internationale, *et en un sens beaucoup plus profond, on peut appeler les damnés de la terre.* ["That disturbs you, in order to redeem their despair and their revolt by Jesus' blood, among those who, without in any event singing *l'Internationale*, in a deeper sense, one can call the earth's damned."]

"Des hommes qui tout en faisant rien d'extérieur . . . ont entrepris cette tâche là du fond de leur coeur, il est clair qu'ils ont besoin de donner toute leur âme à la contemplation." ["Men who, all the while doing nothing on the outside . . . have undertaken that task from the bottom of their heart, it is clear that they need to give their whole soul to contemplation."]

Great question: does the sheltered "contemplative life" behind our walls here, sheltered by many observances, defended against the life and thought of ordinary men, not in the end make us *afraid* of the damned? And isolate us only in a purely imaginary communion with imaginary and edifying "poor" who are "friends of Jesus" in a merely pious and fictitious sense? What would we do with those who would hate and insult us? Seek refuge from those with the Grace Line, huh?

September 21, 1966

A dream. I know that M. is swimming alone in one of our lakes. I am near there but I have refrained from joining her for fear of the consequences. But now I approach the lake and see her wading in the water over there by the shore (it is no recognizable lake here – what is it like?). She looks so disconsolate and alone, as if she had wasted her afternoon there to no purpose, since I have not come. I go down toward the lake dressed in my habit, and wave to her that I am coming. She still looks disconsolate, unbelieving. I wish to join her, I think, even if I have to swim naked. There appears to be no one around. But as I go to her along the bank I find one of the monks sitting there in my way. I cannot get to her. At this I wake up in great distress.

Sunday on my way back from my walk I found a jacket of a monk's work outfit lying in the grass by the gate on the main road, at the end of the sheep barn road. It was left there by Bro. Ralph who left secretly Friday before dawn, with no money apparently, dressed in work pants and sweat shirt. Last anyone knew of him he had hitched a ride to Bardstown with a man who worked for us and did not recognize him.

Fog all around the hermitage this morning (pre-dawn). I have a new coffee percolator that seems to work well.

September 22, 1966

My reading and study of Camus continues very fruitful. Have now read enough of him and on him so that everything begins to click with everything else. He is an easy man to study because everything he says is said in images and all belong to a living pattern of suggestions and allusions and "myths," easy to spell out. This probably makes him a little corny (his figures tend to be artificial and almost allegorical at times).

Today – great impact of *Le Malentendu [The Misunderstanding]*. Not the odious Chas. [Charles] Addams figures of Martha and the Mother, but the wisdom of love in Maria and the stupidity of Jan's absurd project which leads to his destruction. The question of language and communication treated as though in a morality play. But effectively (perhaps not as drama I don't know, but at least as a "morality," a "parable"). The point: when one insists on "leaving a message," one has also to have a "role" as messenger, and one has to worry about "looking for the right words" and correctly analyzing the situation, and viewing others objectively . . . etc. etc. And it all turns out to be nonsense. Maria says "don't go in and tell them who you are." Jan can't do this. Too tied up in figments about duty, law, right and wrong, responsibility, Fatherland, brotherhood, etc. Innocence receives its reward. But in this play, though, it seems also a formal rejection of God, this absurdity is laid not on Him but on man. The absurd situation is created by Jan's attitude, style, thinking. God is repudiated by Martha – who is, however, a nihilist and is therefore repudiated by Camus. *It is Maria who speaks for C.*

I thought of M.!!

In a sense, I see I am caught in a stubbornly *wrong* pattern. Once the machinery of rationalization starts, one can churn out no end of inanities about obligation, duty, solitude, and so on. But also about love, freedom, life, etc.

If it were possible just to forget everything and love M., that would be the obvious thing to do. Then the truth would be found. But . . . in my own history and as a result of past choices it is not possible. Where I am now, nothing unambiguous is possible. In a certain sense *I have to be wrong* up to a point, and what I am trying to learn is how to be at least simple and honest about it, and not try to say I am right, and not try to whitewash myself in terms of something or someone I cannot be. I am neither a good monk nor a good lover. Nor am I really "myself," unambiguously. Nor can I pretend to be wholly loyal, truthful, "in order." I am in a situation in which it is not fully possible for me to be "*en règle* [in order]." (Oh of course I could easily fix that exteriorly, but at the price of another bit of double-dealing.) A certain (I hope harmless, "innocent") duplicity is unavoidable. And – to what extent excusable? I don't know. God's mercy is the only answer to that.

The point is not to take on a false role and speak a mere "part" – one that I neither need nor believe. One that has no point anyway.

(Note – Camus himself is caught in so many ambiguities. His vain attempt to resolve them in "*La Pierre qui pousse*" ["The Growing Stone"] – an absurd ending really: a pat, moral conclusion carrying no conviction. Yet one can see what he might have *wanted* to say – about love. He just hadn't got there yet. Neither have I.)

A letter came today from Julien Green – about my notes on *Chaque homme dans sa Nuit*. "Your remarks about my novels do throw a light on the strange world my characters live in. No one, to my knowledge, has ever said what you say about the meaning of my books (shall we say the 'hidden meaning'? I don't like to sound mysterious but, after all, you do hint at something of the kind)."

But then he complains that I have damned the hero of *Chaque homme*, "the only one of my novels in which I clearly indicate that the hero is saved" and indicates how. W. forgives his murder, and the "puritan husband" (Green protests against my calling him "horrid") sees him "as if observing us from a region of light."[1]

I must have read the ending carelessly – it was so exciting I rushed through it.

September 23, 1966

"The doctrine of justification (Luther's) tells me that God, by forgiving me and making me his child, opens up a new future for me. . . . God cancels our hopelessly stranded history and in its place puts *his* history" ([Helmut] Thielicke). If one adds the Catholic idea of grace and does not make justification *only* this, then it is a very acceptable and deep statement. Camus' disgust with "History" (in the Hegelian sense) – organized illusion and despair.

China is in the thick of another artificially staged "cultural revolution" – getting ready for the next strong man after Mao disappears – and for the big war that seems to be coming. The U.S. is apparently getting ready to invade North Vietnam (as if they did not have enough trouble in the South!). It is building up all the time. That fool Johnson! For that is all he is: a fool, in foreign politics and in domestic politics a crafty operator.

Wrote a statement today for a collection of statements from authors all over the world, on the Vietnam war – and tried to frame it in such a way as to be really for peace and for the people of Vietnam, as against both Washington and Peking. The Chinese of course want the war to continue even more than the Pentagon does. Everybody is happy as long as someone *else* is getting killed. And the Vietnamese have been getting killed for twenty-five years – so they must be used to it. Let them continue, and a few Americans. Peking has no objection to that either! What a world full of bastards!

Sweeping danger in the "cultural revolution" in China. "Develop Prestige Street" has been changed to "Fight Revisionism Street." True, the upheaval is no joke and a lot of people are suffering, but it is anything but a revolution. Just more of the same. A tightening of the same screws by a lot of kids who are just being given their first taste of power – the kids who have

---

[1] For Merton's notes on Julien Green's *Chaque homme dans sa nuit*, see "To Each His Darkness," published in *Raids on the Unspeakable* (New York: New Directions, 1966), 27–33. For Merton's letter responding to Green, see *The Courage for Truth*, edited by Christine M. Bochen (New York: Farrar, Straus & Giroux, 1993), 273–74.

grown up since the Reds took over. They imagine they are "new." They are as old as the Chinese wall. More and more of the same.

September 26, 1966

Yesterday was grey, rainy, foggy. My elbow is bad. I had to go to Dr. Mitchell for a cortisone shot which was painful. Then to the U. of L. Tried several times to call S. (M.'s friend) at her home – finally got her at the hospital. It was nice to talk to her but she had no real news except that M. has to compete with some other new nurse in the hospital – I don't understand this situation. Later called M. from Bardstown in the rain (George was driving and picked up Dan Walsh at Bellarmine). M. is depressed about her job because it is all paper work and not the nursing she wants. "It is not the work I was trained for – I'd be better off as an aide." She was off Sunday and was writing me and thinking of me, she said (all that day I was happy and felt very close to her). She wants to see me – but how? Got my letter via Dan B[errigan] and a photo from the Hammers. Liked the poem about the other call (from that same booth). N. is safe in Vietnam – landed in the jungle and got back to his own side. She worried about him getting brainwashed. She worried about me "in all that rain." Was S. surprised when I called her. And so on. It may have been my last chance to call M. like that. I am bound to be driving with Bernard and then it will be impossible. Besides we will be coming earlier. She does not get home until 4:30 or 5.

In the U. of L. – read Montaigne's "On Solitude." I usually find him a bit disappointing. This was nice writing – but not much more. Glanced into Chateaubriand's *Vie de Rancé* which I must certainly read. (It must be around here somewhere.) Could not find much poetry. Looked up [Ruben] Darío's poem on Whitman ["Walt Whitman"]. Glanced through a book by Albert Caraco which I had never heard of and did not quite know what to make of it, but it seemed to have possibilities. In the poetry room, read hastily [John] Berryman's "[Homage to] Mistress Bradstreet" which is a fine poem, and hard. Looked at some Charles Olson and made a real discovery – Laurie Lee – whom I like tremendously.

In [Henri de] Montherlant's *Va jouer avec cette poussière; carnets 1958–1964* [Paris, 1966] – a note on a mistress called M. who lay with her fists over her eyes "*et jouait des reins* [and was playing games of the loins]" got me in a turmoil over M. And I was sad for a little, and randy in my sleep when I got home. But this does not much disturb me. The fact that I love her with my whole being is simply to be accepted and coped with: and she loves me as I love her. It is beautiful and difficult, full of pain and joy, and since it is real love it is rewarding and irreplaceable. And there is no human hope for natural fulfillment.

Also in Montherlant – a procession (funeral?) for Briand. One man marches carrying a sign "*Ligne des Braves gens* [Line of the Good Old Guys]." He is all alone!

October 4, 1966. St. Francis

Tom Cornell is on trial today for burning his draft card. Bro. Paul died the other night and is being buried today – I will go down to concelebrate at the funeral Mass before dawn in a little while. Bro. Martin de Porres was up here yesterday morning to see about giving me a gas heater as I can no longer cut much wood without my back hurting or my bursitis flaring up.

In the last week – I finished the article on "Three Saviors"[2] in Camus and did some work on "Edifying Cables"[3] which at no point satisfies me. It remains hollow. But I have to pursue this line apparently beyond the point where I am tired of its futility. Do I still hope something can come of it? Perhaps.

Camus says "*comment vivre sans quelques bonnes raisons de désespérer* [how to live without some good reasons to despair]!" and I would add "*comment écrire* [how to write] . . . ?"

I also read Char, at times inspired by him and at times weary of his idiom, his meta-language or para-language, which is nevertheless solid and pretty consistently brilliant. But in all these things there is the lack of an essential dimension, a central core, a real *ground*.

Have finished Douglas Bush's excellent little book on Milton [*John Milton: A Sketch of His Life and Writings* (New York, 1964)], have been seriously reading *Paradise Lost* for the first time in my life. Here the "ground" is much more truly and deeply present – even though the movement is so like a movie scenario. And that is all right. But a basic restlessness (metaphysical I mean). Beneath Camus, Char and even Milton is a metaphysical current

---

[2] "Three Saviors in Camus: Lucidity and the Absurd," first published in *Thought*, Spring 1968, was reprinted in *The Literary Essays of Thomas Merton* (New York: New Directions, 1981), 275–91.

[3] "Edifying Cables" was Merton's working title for a book of poetry published as *Cables to the Ace* (New York: New Directions, 1968).

which is unthinkable in Dante. Yet Dante builds a Cathedral. And we are no longer in the age of Cathedrals. Milton's movie is more like us.

A really beautiful letter from M. came last week. Sweet and warm and loving – with a complete and total love. "The happiest I have ever been is when I took care of you in the hospital. . . . Being without you isn't the hardest thing – it's not being able to give you anything except thoughts and prayers. . . . You keep me, you guard me, you protect me in all my ways. . . . We have been given each other to love, to love totally without having to hold back a thing with complete abandon. There are no fears, no pretenses, just knowing that somewhere you exist and are loving me as I love you sustains me. . . ." The sweetness and warmth of her heart simply overcome me, and I see that this love of ours is and remains such an overwhelming reality, such a true value. I cannot explain how I can love her and be a hermit – it seems to make me *more* solitary. More detached from "the world" and more completely independent of it, alien to it. Our love's out of that world – out of its fictions and confusions – yet *in* its deepest natural reality, in its life, its aspiration to continue, its hope of fulfillment. And yet out of that and above it too. Transcendence has to be related to this kind of reality, otherwise it is just abstraction, which is no transcendence at all. But what to do? I am so fed up and hampered by this life – each letter is a kind of major operation. She has to come to Louisville on the 20th and wants to see me – and yet she will be taking exams during the time I can be in town. What then?

"If we had real humility and goodness we would see far more marvels of goodness in the Church. But because we are selfish ourselves we are only ready to see good, good brought about by God where it suits our advantage, our need for esteem, or our view of the Church."

(K. Rahner – [The] Dynamic Element in the Church [Freiburg, 1964], p. 65)

Since my retreat I have been reading this very good book on and off. More off than on I am afraid. But this statement, read this morning, clicks with what I have been realizing lately. Sunday afternoon, out walking in the sun and looking at the monastery *without* its phony and pretentious ancient steeple, and thinking of all that has been going on there, I realized how much good there really is in this community – not only in so many individuals (this I have never doubted or questioned), but in the community itself as it is organized. I know this is a "good community" and a fortunate place in which to be today. A place where there is real spiritual life, and hope and charity and love for God. An honest monastery, with all its shortcomings and failings and for some of the failings, I am perhaps myself to some extent responsible. But I count myself lucky to be here. There is really no other place in the Church now where I would rather be. I see so evidently that my hermitage is my true place in the Church. And I owe this to my community. Also, let's face it, to my Abbot, of whom I am so easily critical.

I have learned to mistrust my ideas and my sometimes exorbitantly "pure" demands. It is sobering to realize how *badly* I am myself measuring up to the grace of solitude that has been given me.

K. Rahner shows why the Church is justified in being suspicious of those who claim charismatic privileges:

"She knows that only too often, as far as we can see, ultimate fulfillment and maturity is denied to such charismatic enthusiasm, that the holy venture of voluntary poverty, of a holy renunciation of earthly fulfillment, of contemplation in silence and obscurity is only blessed with meager fruits. . . ." *p. 60–61*

This is a passage where he defends the Church's right to "administer" the charismata and set bounds on claims to exercise them.

Communication last week with Dom Simeon, Superior of the Chinese Cistercian community at Lan Tao. He is disillusioned with the American houses and foresees trouble for the whole Order. I agree with him. At the same time I think the restlessness is not fully warranted. One way or another, people are using the present situation to justify their own instability. I can tell because I have so often tried it myself in the past!! Dom S. spoke of Fidel Taparra, who was my novice (a Hawaiian), one of the first – who went to Vina, then to Lan Tao and left. Is now in the Navy.

Burial of Bro. Paul this morning under a grey early sky, with the huge crane the builders of the Church are using hanging over the cemetery. The Church is still wide open to the winds and work goes slowly. Mass on third floor and a complicated procession through the South wing, winding down the stairs, through the guest house etc. At the funeral I suddenly saw Bro. Ralph, who left surreptitiously a couple of weeks ago – maybe more – with no money, in his work clothes, hitchhiked to Bardstown before dawn and then wired his home for money – went to Florida – was home almost before anyone knew what had happened to him. He was absolved, but for some reason the Abbot has made him come back and work things out so he can leave again legally – probably to avoid a black mark on the house in Rome? R. looked terrible at the funeral and I pitied him. He was evidently deeply depressed when he left and more so now he is back. I felt the abbot was in a way trying to "use" the funeral as an emotional cudgel on R. Did he perhaps look at him in one of the hellfire prayers? They were too far away. But Ralph was right by the coffin where the Abbot was.

Rahner speaks of the devotion and love of a mother for a child as a possible example of a Christian charism, "a gift of the Spirit and of his unselfish love." I wonder if M.'s nursing is not something like that (a gift which is being rather cruelly frustrated now by hospital organization!). Anyway R. says of these gifts:

"*Ultimately the whole Church is only there so that such things may exist* so that witness may be borne to their eternal significance, so that there may always be people who *really and seriously believe that these gifts here on earth are more important than anything else.*" *(p. 66)*

Charism of Christian artist, p. 67.

"Ultimately only one thing can give unity in the Church on the human level: the love which allows another to be different even when it does not understand him. . . ." *(p. 74)*

"*A charism always involves suffering. For it is painful to fulfill the task set by the charisma, the gift received, and at the same time within this one body to endure the opposition of another's activity which may in certain circumstances be equally justi-fied.*" *(77)*

That is pure gold and especially important for *now*. And for the years that are coming. He does not mention also the opposition of those who are not of the Church – that is taken for granted. But they too may have gifts – divine gifts – by which they oppose us. Was there perhaps a hidden charismatic element in the "prophetic" work of Camus?

K.R. goes on to say one must not "build a little chapel for himself inside the Church to make things more tolerable . . ." etc. *(78)*

October 13, 1966

So many things have happened in the last ten days or so. The death of Fr. Stephen under the tree by gatehouse on the 4th. I was among the little group kneeling in the grass to pray by him as he died. Then sat with Fr. Flavian saying psalms by his body in the post office before he was taken up to the third floor chapel. He was buried on the 5th with much singing of birds on a bright morning.

On the evening of the 6th – Jacques Maritain, John H. Griffin, Penn Jones and Babeth Manual arrived. A wonderful visit. On the morning of the 7th they came to the hermitage (bright, cool). I read some poems for them. In the afternoon we went out to the woods. Late Mass for them all in the temporary exterior chapel which I liked. It was a beautiful mass, which as a matter of fact, to please Jacques, I said all in Latin and all in the old way. He was delighted. Began then reading his book – the new one – which he gave me in page proofs, *Le Paysan de la Garonne [The Peasant of the Garonne]*. It is perhaps a bit self-conscious: he is very aware of himself as *"Le vieux* [the old] *Jacques"* and half apologetic, but says I think some very telling things about the novelty hunters and the *superficial* advocates, change in a naively progressive way ("anything is good as long as it's something new"). The morning in the hermitage was good because they liked the bits of "Edifying Cables" I read to them. That was encouraging. Jack Ford and Dan Walsh were also there, and they came in the afternoon too.

Penn Jones has been working on the Warren Commission report and his book [*Forgive My Grief: A Critical Review of the Warren Commission Report on the Assassination of President John F. Kennedy,* 1966], though hard to read – a mass of material without much form – clearly shows the commission neglected to investigate some very important things. Apparently this is now more generally advocated. It appears very probable that Oswald was not the only assassin – that he did not know the others – and that some very powerful people may have been behind it all. I read all this in one sitting Sunday morning, with rain falling on the hermitage – a drab day.

Monday I had to go to the proctologist. It was a beautiful day. Raymond was along to see some other doctor. I found some good things in the U. of L. library – old articles on Camus from the immediate post-war years (1946–). And some [Gregory] Corso, R[obert] Creeley and others not so good (I still can't read Charles Olson). I very much doubt whether I can or should get involved in this kind of poetry – or at least not with the people who want it. I've had enough with the pontifical Cid Corman. Maybe they all want to be gurus as well as poets.

––––––––

Downtown Louisville at the bar of the Brown Hotel in mid afternoon, drinking bottled beer and finishing a letter to M.

Dan Berrigan arrived by surprise Tuesday – I was not expecting him until the end of the week. We concelebrated twice – once in the regular present rite, and today, with a new Mass he found somewhere which is very fine and simple. I don't know how legal we were. It was a very moving simple English text (Canon and all). I think it was composed by Anglicans and has been used by them. Contrast to the Mass I said for Jacques, old style, last week. That was very sober, austere, solemn, intense. This very open, simple, even casual, but very moving and real. Somehow I think the new is really better – and is very far from anything we will be permitted here for a long time. I have nothing against the old.

The gas heater was put in the other day, and it works all right, but smells bad. I prefer the wood fire – but can't count on keeping it supplied. No bursitis at the moment because I have not tried to chop any wood.

October 14, 1966

Letter from Catherine Meyer at *Harper's* magazine yesterday. My "Apologies to an Unbeliever" was to have been in the "Editor's Easy Chair" (!!) for November, but was cut out for something else. Then she wrote:

But there was a happening. There was a moon shot a couple of weeks ago, which did not make it. . . . General Dynamics, which had planned a two-page ad in *Harper's* and other magazines based on the assumption that that particular shot would land properly, canceled. So poorer in money but richer in goods for the reader, *Harper's* switched things around and placed the Merton piece in a just-beginning department called "How it is – "

A dark October morning with clouds. Extraordinary purple in the North over the pines. Ruins of gnats on the table under the lamp. The letter preface to an American school edition, *L'Étranger* (preface of Camus himself) has things to say on truth and silence which have deep monastic implications. I must refuse all declarations and affirmations of what I do not fully and actually know, experience, believe *myself*. Not making statements that are expected of me, simply because they are expected, whether by the monastery (or monastic life) or by the peace movement, or by various literary orthodoxies and anti-orthodoxies or routine rebellions. If I renounce all that, there will be precious little left to say. But above all (as Maritain and I agreed) to steer clear of the futilities of "Post-Conciliar" theological wrangling and image making.

October 16, 1966

Three small harlequins – two sweetgums and a maple – stand bright against the dark background of pine and cedar. Dim brilliance of the woods on a grey day. [. . .] I am full of obscure lonely happiness because of her and because of the miracle of her existence. I tried to write a poem for her about it but the poem could come nowhere near. What finally started me off was this from Camus (in his *Notebooks II* – 274):

Quand on a vu une seule fois le resplendissement du bonheur sur la visage d'un être qu'on aime, on sait qu'il ne peut pas y avoir d'autre vocation pour un homme que de susciter cette lumière sur les visages qui l'entourent. . . .[When you have once seen the glow of happiness on the face of a beloved person, you know that a man can have no other vocation than to awaken that light on the faces surrounding him. . . .]

It is one of the most beautiful passages in all Camus and so well expresses my own deepest belief. One of the things that best justifies my coming to Gethsemani is the "light" I have seen on her face when we have been happy together – and the happiness that others had too because I am here. And what about my own happiness because she is who she is and she is there?

I have been working I think successfully on "Edifying Cables" in the last few days. Reading some Milton. Got into Robert Desnos yesterday. Though he is less superb than Char he really moves me more immediately. Basil Bunting found for the first time yesterday – very fine, rough, Northumbrian, Newcastle stuff of the Kingdom of Caedmon. A letter from Gary Snyder says he may come here. He read *7 Storey Mountain*, he said, when he was hitchhiking up the coast to a logging operation in British Columbia, some years ago.

[John Crowe] Ransom's exegesis of "Gerontion" [*Sewanee Review* 74 (Spring 1966)] is good but I think he has missed much of it – the *acedia*, the "night." It is not mere indifference and falling away, or perversity.

October 27, 1966

Last week I went to St. Anthony's Hospital for some X-rays (stomach). Had a room in the splendid new wing – a room filled with pure sunlight all morning. But it was a trial. M. was in Louisville for some exams – all her class of nurses had come back for them – she came to the hospital a couple of times, but I did not see her as much as I wanted. It was good to see her as much as I did (especially a week ago tonight, Thursday, when she came in a little late and everything was quiet). Still I had hoped and planned to see more of her – she missed her bus Wednesday afternoon when she could have had several hours free – and in the end I came back frustrated and disappointed – and aware that I can't go on depending on much consolation in seeing her and communicating with her. And really, for the first time since April, I can see that the affair is no longer so intense, and I feel much freer. Yet I hate it to stop – I have depended on it so much. On the other hand it is time to get back to real solitude and out of this senseless contradiction that has made everything so wacky for seven months. I know we will always love each other but . . .

Tonight walked up and down on the cool clear evening, in the full moon, meditating, enjoying the quiet, the peace, the cool silence of the valley, and the freedom. All I have ever sought is here: how foolish not to be content with it – and let anything trouble it, without need. True, the moon did make me think of May 5th at the airport – and that was something else again!! I can't regret it. It still seems so obviously to have been a gift of God. But I can see I cannot make such things happen again by my own desire. It is utterly pointless to think that I can find *for myself* some happiness in loving M. or any other woman. Clearly that is out of the question, and I know it now, barely! I can love her for her own sake without demanding anything from it.

Finished a preface to Nhat Hanh's new book [*Vietnam: Lotus in a Sea of Fire*, 1967], which is clear and interesting and ought to be widely read. *Harper's* is publishing it – soon.

October 28, 1966. Sts. Simon and Jude
When I was in the hospital – last Friday – Jack Ford came over in the evening and we went to [Pier Paolo] Pasolini's film *The Gospel According to St. Matthew*. Pasolini supposed to be a Communist etc. The actors – all ordinary Italian people, but with extraordinary faces. That is to say ordinary Italian people. Some of it was unforgettable. A Passion play on the screen, done very movingly and with a lot of verve and dignity – visual quality of Tuscan painting at times (without the color). But above all the faces! Anyway here was a certain truth, and not the phoniness of Hollywood.

Reading Chateaubriand's life of Rancé. This too is a fascinating work of art. Beautiful in its aberrations. A kind of harmony and order in its eccentricities. Power of his imagination forming all this into a credible and acceptable world. And I can't help being moved, and remembering the spirit that was here at Gethsemani when I entered. A bit fantastic, manichaean perhaps, yet there was a certain rugged truth about it. Sure, there is another kind of truth here today. But the air conditioning in the new Church (right under the sanctuary!) is embarrassing. Of two kinds of falsity maybe the aberration of Rancé is preferable. I wonder if Gethsemani has any real future.

And of course I have to face the falsity of my own life with shame. Not with drama. But obviously I have not been on the right road. The only thing that has kept me from much worse error is the protection of God – invisible and undeserved.

Have more or less finished "Edifying Cables" but can't say I like it. It is disturbing and false in many ways. It is not myself and I don't know who it is. A glib worldly spirit. Empty voices. Still, as an exercise in writing (that's all it is) I suppose it can go. I sent it off to be typed by Eileen Curns as I can't get a typist here now in the cheese season. Monday five more left for Chile – I talked to Fr. Roman Sunday evening.

October 31, 1966

This weekend – momentous visit of Sidi Abdesalam, from Algeria. He came with Bernard Phillips from Temple U[niversity] and with a disciple (Sidi Hadij) and the latter's wife who translated, as Sidi A. speaks only Arabic.

I can't begin to put down everything, I was so moved by the visit. This is a true man of God, also a man of an ancient and very living (Arabic) culture, and authentic representation of the best in Islam etc. etc. (all that one says sounds stupid – cannot touch the reality). His simplicity, humaneness, directness, friendliness, generosity, warmth etc. Overwhelmed me by repeatedly expressing a high opinion of me as a person, as one who has "arrived" etc. Which is a bit confusing and unnerving. How to account for it? What to do about it?

Before he came I had a sense that he came as a messenger from God. He too had this sense. Perhaps the formal "message" crystallized around the fact that, having reached completeness and the "glass being full to overflowing," it was wrong for us to be kept here "in prison" and that I was supposed to go out – to meet people (in his own way – the small groups, the individuals here and there – not organized conferences etc.). We both agreed there was nothing for me to do about it in the way of challenging authority. He just said Dom James would probably die or retire within a year – as if he were half joking. We'll see! Later, reflecting on the visit alone in the warm October sun, out by St. Edmund's field – I realized I had *no desire* whatever to go out or travel and my own preference would be to stay here in silence and peace. Maybe he's wrong – all I can say is that if it is clearly God's will for me to go out, I will go gladly. And God himself will make it clear when, where, how. It seems to me my call to solitude will make any traveling rare, exceptional, and semi-secret. No publicity etc. and very restricted contacts only. I don't trust even this! And I have no intention of thinking about it for a minute or planning on it.

All I can do is jot down points at random about A.'s visit –

He said I am very close to mystical union and the slightest thing now can so to speak push me over the edge. (Felt it [at] Mass yesterday.)

Fear of this on my part.

His approval of what I said about the "New Law" and loving as a friend of God etc. Trust in God's friendship – guided by the spontaneous norms of friendship.

Sense of strong bond of friendship between us – I mean him and myself. "Sacramental" quality of simple friendship in our group, 5 of us, sitting in the grass on top of St. Joseph's hill. A real experience of Sufism. I now see exactly what it is all about. Close to monastic spirit. Very close indeed in simplicity, spontaneity, joy, truth. Almost carried out of myself by last words of Gospel of Christ the King yesterday. Sense of blinding light, helplessness, overwhelming joy. My own nothingness, goodness of God to *all*.

Optimism of Sidi A. not perturbed by state of this world as if there were a very special crisis. Things are what they are. See them in God.

Sense of God present in us, with us, in friendship.

He believes in importance of dreams. The dreams that *impress* one, not just the "gout dreams." I spoke of my habitual dream of having money and being about to go somewhere. "Money is the scourge of man."

Above all, importance of knowing and following the voice of one's own heart, one's own secret: God in us. Deepening contact with source. Through a friend etc. who understands. Certainly this visit had that effect. A deepening, a clearing of the wells.

Realism of his spiritual doctrines as exposed to the small group that came out to talk with him in gatehouse.

I sense that he is a remarkably free man and he praised and encouraged my own freedom. Yet I do not feel perfectly free. Still hampered by too many fears. Including a mistrust of his high praise of me. Certainly he is sincere. But is he misled? Am I misled? etc.

At the same time, some concern about M. I know we are slowly breaking up and that is as it should be. To try to keep up an intense intimate love affair when always so far apart – artificial and constrained, inevitably. I still love her deeply but it would be too much to say I need her. Even that I need to keep contact with her. On the other hand I suspect a change in her, a falling back into superficiality and ambiguousness. This troubles me. She is a mixed-up person with many conflicting trends and also a kind of tri-umphant selfishness that can knit all the conflicting trends together and di-rect them in the sense of some perverse interest of the moment. And there is ambivalence in her love for me. And there is in me a tendency to drive others in the direction I least want . . . Hence a feeling that I must be care-ful. I am not perfectly at peace about the situation. We could suddenly and with no good reason became destructive toward each other. That would be an immense shame, and I certainly don't want it to happen. I pray that I may not do anything myself to bring it about.

I don't know whether or not I still believe the best of our love was "from God." How easy it is to deceive myself! Certainly those days in May were marvelous. But ambiguous too, and I was very soon upset by it all.

Basically I am much more ready now to admit that the whole thing was a mistake, a subtle and well-meant seduction to which I too easily and too completely yielded (so much so that she herself was frightened by it at first). This must never happen again. Also it is clearly *over*. Except for friendship, I hope, and the last communication that may be required to avoid bitterness and bad feeling about it.

Am reading Camus's *L'État de siège [State of Siege]*. The whole Plague theme is one of the best and most powerful things in his work. The heart of it. Per-haps there is much wrong with this play, but to me it reads well anyway and I like it. A medieval morality play, hence inevitably naive, rambunctious, untidy, and probably not as controlled as he hoped. I suppose one must overlook faults in it – musical comedy atmosphere of the "leading juve-niles" – . Was he having trouble with the color, verve, vitality of it? (Better when his plays are somber – *Le Malentendu*.) I don't know. He liked it and I like it. My heart is with Camus. *Thought* is going to publish "Three Saviors."

Vietnam. [Eric] Sevareid said it is like using great sledgehammers to kill hornets.

Vietcong need about 87 tons of supplies a day. U.S. 20,000 tons a day. NLF estimated annual budget – 10 million. U.S. (for the war) $15,000,000,000. Each Vietcong killed costs a million dollars (not to mention *men* we lose!!). We really must be interested in killing people expensively.

November 1, 1966

The wilderness theme in the Bible. Am reading a good book on it by Ulrich Mauser [*Christ in the Wilderness* (London, 1963)] (in that Protestant series). Terribly fruitful at the moment! I can compare my own life. How evident it becomes now that this whole thing with M. was, in fact, an attempt to escape the demands of my vocation. Not conscious, certainly. But a substitution of human love (and erotic love after all) for a special covenant of loneliness and solitude which is the very heart of my vocation. I did not stand the test at all – but allowed that whole essence to be questioned and tried to change it. And could not see I was doing this. Fortunately God's grace protected me from the worst errors. My difficult return to my right way is a gift of His grace. But I think I am gradually getting back. Each morning I wake up feeling a little freer (though I don't remember dreaming of it) – just as last May each morning I awoke a little more captivated. And I now see how much anguish I suffered – but I could not let go! Now thank God, I can. But what will happen if she writes me another love letter. Somehow I don't think she will. I think it is clear to both of us that the affair is over – and that it has been very silly.

Heavy rain in the morning. Went down in the dark to concelebrate. Came back with the pocket of my rain coat full of eggs and had me a super breakfast. Finished reading Camus's *L'État de siège*. It is really lamentable. A disaster. It began OK, and the idea is good enough, but it is mechanical, arbitrary, full of trite moralizing – none of which is redeemed by the fact that "his heart is in the right place" etc. It is just downright bad – the moralizing and melodrama of 18th century bourgeois theater, or 20th century *agit prop* [pro-Communist propaganda]. All the good ideas go astray. A very sad job. I wonder why? And have an uneasy feeling that my "Edifying Cables" are also bad and false, not in the same precise way, yet perhaps for the same sort of reason. Mechanical irony, habitual prejudices, tired thinking, an imitation of my own vitality. Yet with "Cables" I cannot be sure. Maybe they are really good. Who knows? See what they look like in print. Then it will be too late.

Rain cleared in late morning. I went for a walk to the Lake Knob, with a great sense of new freedom and discovery – and determination never to get caught again by a love affair and not let this one flare up again. Only now do I begin to see the state of the ruins! What an embarrassing mess! And how completely stupid I have been. At the beginning, like a drunken driver going through every red light – and as a matter of fact only really sobering up now, after seven months of it.

Sidi Abdesalam's visit was certainly a great help. But I can't in my heart take seriously his statement that I am close to myst[ical] union – I can see an enormous purification is needed. A spirit of repentance won't hurt! At least I am inclined to that, at any rate. That may not be the height, but it is at least a first step.

November 2, 1966

About four this morning it began to snow. And it turned into a real storm, by evening it was one of the heaviest storms I have ever seen here, though since it was above freezing the snow did not lie as thick as it otherwise might have. But now it is night and still snowing and I think by tomorrow there will be quite a bit of it – and this is only All Souls' Day! I went down in the dark and snow to say my three masses early (others are not saying the 3 Masses anymore – a few of the older priests are). Came back had breakfast, read some Antonin Artaud on the plague theme (Camus tried to use this but failed imaginatively and otherwise. Artaud's thesis is a bit far fetched anyway. Plague – Theater).

After dinner I walked out to the woods in the snowstorm. Then back and settled down for the afternoon, let myself be enclosed in the snow and silence, and it has been marvelous. Stayed up here for supper, cooked a mess of rice and it was good. Now everything is perfectly silent except for the wind howling in the dark. The hermitage is marvelous in the snow and night, and I rejoice in it – the gas heater is splendid! Place quiet and cozy, and I am utterly alone. It is a pure delight, I thank God for it! And again I am overcome with embarrassment to think how I have trifled with this grace.

Read some of Etta Gullick's ms. Introduction to Benet of Canfield. It is on the whole very good. A few poems of Wallace Stevens. Bits on Zen from the new book of Nancy Wilson Ross which she sent me.

Boughs of evergreen out there in the dark cracking under the weight of snow!

November 4, 1966

M. Her little, clear, determined voice coming to me through all the cold and snow, in a letter, saying she has carefully considered it, and she really, powerfully loves me, and she is never going to stop. So definite. I read the letter out there in a field of snow, weeping, looking through hot tears at the icy hills, the frozen wood, where we were Ascension Day. And she is right. Without getting carried away (or wishing that I were not, seeing that I don't *have to be*), I have to admit our love as a basic and central truth about which there can be no nonsense. And will have to try somehow to reconcile it with contemplative liberty (after all she explicitly accepts this situation). Foolishly hoped to call her from Billie's goat barn (that didn't work) and eating hot dogs with Br. Clement at Billie's – and driving back through the snow – the day disputed by this impulse, clearly a wrong one!

The fact of passion has to be faced, and I must not let it get too disruptive. The fact of my vocation to a deep mystical life has to be faced – though I am helpless to account for it or cope with it and am in danger of being terribly unfaithful. The fact of M.'s love has to be faced and met with my own most serious gift and trust. God alone can reconcile all that has to be reconciled. I have simply been torn by it. Reduced and walking in the sun and snow and renouncing any hope of quick answers.

In these circumstances, readings on *Paradise Lost* have been deeply moving and magnificent. At times I have felt that Milton is the one who really knows the world as it is. M. and I are so much, in so many ways, Eve and Adam.

One thing I am grateful for: this thing of having made with her a world of reality that is our own and subsists in and by and for us. A world of love which is the *real world* – because it is a world of choice, in which we have decided to be essential to each other's meaning, each other's grasp of everything else. It is as if we were married.

November 11, 1966. St. Martin

This morning began reading a fine book of George Williams (Harvard), *Wilderness and Paradise in Christian Thought*. Must review it.[4] An excellent survey and not without a certain pleasing passion for the wilderness (and for conservation). A fine tying up of Christian sense with modern American problems.

Yesterday – a very good letter from a young married woman in Cincinnati about my "Apology to an Unbeliever," which is in this month's *Harper's*.[5] She appreciated it – and says but she never "hears God." And what about it? I tried to answer her honestly without falling into seven deadly heresies – and realized the complexity of the problem as I never have before.

The whole question of "hearing God" has become extremely ambiguous. So ambiguous that the very way it is talked of makes some people incapable of "hearing" anything. Their defensive reflex is basically healthy and perhaps more radically religious in some cases than the "faith" of those who "hear."

I came to this point – in considering the experience, briefly grappling with it.

1. The worst thing I could possibly do would be to simply give an official and "objective" answer. However true, theologically, it would be *false* in this situation. It would communicate nothing and close the door to all communication. In fact slam the door in her face.

2. Hence I need to be able to stand aside from official positions, and speak as a man on her own level – in order to begin to be true. (At once I can grasp that in the other position one arrogates to himself an authority he does not really have – but which society has given him in a way. A right to tell others to get off – even a right to bully. This is impossible. Must be refuted.)

3. But on the other hand no condescension. One must step down in such a way that one *can't* get back "up" – here is where it gets funny – because I after all do not abandon my faith at all.

4. It is really a question of seeing that in some strange way the "faith" has become idolatrous when it is seen only from a certain viewpoint and that

4 Merton's review, "Wilderness and Paradise: Two Recent Studies," appeared in *Cistercian Studies* 2 (1967): 83–89.
5 Merton's letter to this woman, Katherine Champney, is published in Thomas Merton, *Witness to Freedom*, edited by William H. Shannon (New York: Farrar, Straus & Giroux, 1994), 327–29.

without abandoning the faith one has to abandon this idolatrous viewpoint.

5. Which turns out to be that of most believers.

6. So I came at it this way. An honest human question is asked. Instead of giving "God's official answer" (idolatrous – a *refusal* to communicate on equal terms) I must in the nakedness and poverty of my human condition give a humble and tentative answer that is guided by the desire to help her *see* in her own way.

7. This begins with an intuition of an immense value in her which she does not see. (The ground of her being which opens out into God's infinite love.) Official formulas will make it *impossible* for her to see this.

8. Yet without gnosticism – or anything – I must use simple words.

9. So trusting in the Spirit whom I don't know and using words to say only as much as we are capable of seeing together at the moment, I try to speak to her as a Brother.

10. If I do this, then in our honest rapport God himself speaks without anyone being aware (necessarily) of the fact. And I leave the rest to her. Guided of course by what I believe to be his revealed word – which I substantially try to communicate in my *own* way, i.e. very differently (without perverting it – yet in fact *contradicting* a certain way of understanding it which *seems* correct and isn't).

November 12, 1966

Eliot's essay "What Is a Classic?" is short, brilliant and absurd. His definition of a Classic is solidly useful, and then he proceeds to make its use impossible except for a few choice spirits – Virgil, Dante, Racine and for no one in English. Perpetual somersaults of logic in order to make sure that this title must be denied Milton precisely because he is such a genius, but also because he does not completely exhaust the possibilities of language – etc.

This is apparently one of the great problems of literary criticism: one can formulate splendid principles – and their use is always contestable unless it is so restrained that it is hardly a use at all. Here more than anywhere else one always has the sense that the opposite to what is said can be convincingly asserted.

Importance of this year's Chinese paroxysm. In this country it is regarded as another nutty Communist ploy – to harass people. It is probably more – but what? Evidently there is a real passion going into it. A passionate rejection of Soviet revisionism and a desperate resolution to meet any attack from the

U.S. Basically the passion seems to be racial – a rejection of white society and its choices – and a determination to do something else. A horrifying communalism – and yet . . . Who can condemn them, unless he has something else to offer? Same with the Black Power pitch in the U.S. It is nutty, irrational, but its drama is something one has no real reason to complain of because of the infinitely organized muteness and absurdity of the U.S. civilization which surpasses every other facticity. And yet could do so much, if only it weren't mindless, obtuse, self-deluded, self-complacent – destructive.

Passionate name changing. In the monasteries – people are picking new names (Bernadine to Zachary, Amandus to Roger. Mysterious non-improvements). Naturally those who went to Chile last month have mostly Spanish names – but *new* Spanish names, not translations. In Chinese – young red guards change names from, for example, "Fragrant Celery" to "Look up to Mao." All very funny to the West. Speed of emergence of Red Guards in China – a youth movement – became official only last June – turned China upside down in August – September. Mao "joined" them Aug. 18. International outlook may lead to something!!

November 13, 1966

Gelassenheit – letting go – not being encumbered by systems, words, projects. And yet being free *in* systems, projects. Not trying to get away from all action, all speech, but free, unencumbering *"Gelassen"* in this or that action. Error of self-conscious contemplatives: to get hung up in a certain kind of non-action which is an imprisonment, a stupor, the opposite of *Gelassenheit*. Actually quietism is incompatible with true inner freedom. The burden of this stupid and enforced "quiet" – the self sitting heavily on its own head.

Still thinking of K.C. who wrote from Cincinnati. From a certain point of view my letter to her was a scandal. I was in effect saying "Don't listen for the voice of God, he will not speak to you." Yet this had to be said. Today, for a certain type of person, to "listen" is to be in a position where hearing is impossible – or deceptive. It is the wrong kind of listening: listening for a limited message, an objective sound, a sensible meaning. Actually one decides one's life by responding to a word that is *not* well defined, easily explicable, safely accounted for. One decides to love in the face of an unaccountable void, and from the void comes an unaccountable truth. By this truth one's existence is sustained in peace – until the truth is too firmly grasped and too clearly accounted for. Then one is relying on words – i.e. on his own understanding and his own ingenuity in interpreting existence and its "signs." Then one is lost – has to be found once again in the patient Void.

November 14, 1966

Delight. Nathalie Sarraute. Finally reading *Portrait d'un inconnu [Portrait of a Man Unknown]* which has been lying around for four or five years. Very good. I can't read novels – only anti-novels. This is expect[ed].

Mass-media. While I yell about them and McLuhan pontificates – the fact is that 75% of the sets in NY are *turned off* during prime evening time. But that is in NY. Not Bardstown.

November 16, 1966

Great richness for me of the Williams book on *Wilderness*. So many new areas open up. Material on the American paradise mentality. Its great importance still. Moved by his deep sense of importance, spiritually, of conservationism. So many things click. Strongly tempted to write to him.

A very sweet letter from M. yesterday (F[east] of Dedication). "I am so 'yours' you couldn't get rid of me if you tried. . . . Even if we wanted to (drop each other) God would somehow bury us together. . . . (We are) married in a strange way – we are, we really are." Maybe we both protest a little too much, but I do think our love is deep, real, and lasting. It will have to last in a very strange way! But it will. I accept the fact and see that it is not something I have to struggle to put out of my heart. Everything will adjust.

Yesterday once again I was going over the whole situation. *Should* we remain apart? etc. There are moments when it seems utterly wrong to be without her. Yet I know too that, whatever reasonable arguments one might dream up for it, it would be utterly wrong to leave here and drop everything in order to marry her. Neither of us has the strength to stand the pressure this would involve. And we both know it. Yet we love and we can't help loving in our own poor way.

Renewed purpose on my part. I can't even consider doing something that would have such disastrous effects for the community and above all for the hermit experiment – and probably for M. and myself too.

In any case I know in my heart that my true call is to solitude with God, however much I may love her. She knows this too.

The objective fact of my vows, more than a juridical obligation. It has deep personal and spiritual roots. I cannot be true to myself if I am not true to so deep a commitment.

And yet I love her. There is nothing for it but to accept the seeming contradiction and make the best of it in trust, without impatience or anxiety, realizing that I can't realistically manipulate things for us to meet etc. Yet if God wants us to be together somewhere it will be possible. But there is no use in fostering a lot of illusions.

Apart from that – the whole thing makes me ache through all the regions of my being and at times I am close to sheer desperation.

All this was made more acute by the visit of a priest who left his diocese and is getting married. He is under great strain – looked and acted like a weary salesman. Chainsmoking and gesturing with both hands while driving down the middle of the highway etc. Drivers behind exasperated wondering how to get past him. He has in fact been driving around selling his case to various people. I encouraged him as best I could – since his "wife" is now pregnant, and the decision is semi-public. Yet before this I had tried to encourage him *not* to do this. He is trying to get up an ordinariate for married priests who could continue functioning as priests and I wrote a letter in favor – which may get me in trouble, but so what. The whole thing does not in reality inspire me with much confidence – there is too much inertia and stupidity to be met with. I think the possibilities are vaguely tragic – not much more.

So all this made doubly clear to me that there is no use whatever my thinking of this as a solution for myself and M. It would be utterly preposterous.

First streaks of dawn beginning to appear in the East. Arcturus rising is the only star left in that part of the sky. Cold but not freezing. All I can do is thank God that I am in this peace, solitude, joy. The ambiguity that love has brought into it is no cause for disturbance. Somehow in the depths of my being I know that love for her can coexist with my solitude, but everything depends on my fidelity to a vocation that there is no use trying too much to rationalize. It is *there*. It is a root fact of my existence. I cannot pretend to understand it perfectly. I know a certain response is required of me – and I try with God's grace to give it.

November 23, 1966

This morning wrote several pages of French insertions for "Edifying Cables." Can't remember what started this going. I think I rather like them. Haven't worked much on revising *Faith and Violence* because I scratched my eye with a branch and it is still sore. Naomi said *Conjectures* sold over 15,000 before publication and apparently now it is hard to get. Lunch at Tommie O'Callaghan's the other day. Her sweet little girls, the utter loveliness of children. The little blonde girl in the doctor's office, so delightful in her littleness, her love of her mother and grandmother, her happiness at being loved.

Sunday Fr. F. cracked up – preached a homily on the abomination of desolation in which the abomination seemed to be the Abbot (just about to return from Chile), but it was psychologically ambiguous and in the end we were exhorted to complete submission. Fr. F. now hospitalized. Crazy place, this!

November 27, 1966. I Sunday Advent

Advent is here already. Warm night with wind and many clouds. Full moon trying to be seen from time to time. Yesterday – visit of Napoleon Chow from Nicaragua, friend of Ernesto Cardenal. I couldn't think of much to do. We drove around and talked. An auction going on near the tobacco barn. Teenage kids everywhere, all over the place, groups of two, three, eight, a dozen, hanging around with nothing to do. It was Saturday. This year I have for the first time seen how crowded everything is. Especially the U. of L. But even the country.

Bro. A. met me on my way up to the hermitage. Is trying to get out of the monastery and wanted to discuss this (without permission of course). An interesting talk. He is bright, nervous, frustrated, hopeless, and sees nothing for himself here except despair. He and I agree that as things are now there is really no future for this monastery: that the "changes" now being made are seen to be illusory – mostly a game to make the players get the good feeling that "something is being done." Far from the crisis being over, it has just begun. What is the real trouble? I used to think I knew. But it is so complicated! Dom James is certainly in the middle of it all in the sense that everything crystallizes around him – yet it is not all "his fault." He is typical of a certain mentality. He is incapable of doing and seeing things in a really new way. He never really listens to anyone else, is convinced of his own rightness, is secure – now more than ever – in his own ideas, despises, secretly and openly, everything he does not agree with. His mentality is exactly that of the people in Washington, in the Pentagon, in Wall Street: the arrogance of nice, self-satisfied, rich people who have everything and imagine they are kind and good because they are pleased with themselves. The "manifest destiny" outlook – which has led to the ludicrous impasse in Vietnam and may lead to a war with China.

Dom James does not know how much he is detested by so many of the monks. How they writhe with embarrassment at his long triumphalist letters from Chile (still being read a week after his return). (He is now an expert on South America.) How attuned they all are to his atrocious and naive vanity which he alone does not realize (his boasting about all the important people he has met etc.).

Inevitably his conviction of his own importance means one thing only: his rule has to be a complete autocracy – and often very arbitrary at that. It was never more so because he has immense prestige and he knows that now even Rome will never say "boo" to him. I understand that even the [abbot] general who is out to make visitations here in the U.S. is not coming to Gethsemani because Dom J. does not want him. This is hard to believe – one would think a visitation *pro forma* would be arranged, to keep up appearances. The visitations of Dom Columban are a pure formality – mere flattering of Dom J.

Religious weakness of the community: it becomes all the more dangerous in proportion as Dom James stubbornly imposes his idea of order and strength. Curious intuition – starting from the Bible idea of God not only as "supreme being" but the God of Abraham–Isaac–Jacob. God reveals himself to "the people" as *their* God. God "for them." It suddenly occurred to me that this is most important, this relation of choice – choice of a society, of a communion open to God who is *"for"* the community. Now in a certain sense my love for M. brings us together in openness to and dependence on a God who is *for us*, who gives our love, who blesses our commitment. On the other hand, there has been a growing sense in the community that the God-image subtly imposed by Dom James is a projection of his own personality which the community *consciously rejects*. Consequently, momentous and terrible thing, the abbot has his own private God which the community distrusts as an idol, and instinctively rejects. How this affects the whole fabric of obedience! If this is true, what can we expect? Fortunately it is not absolutely true. Or how could I go to concelebrate today? There is the God who is present in the announcing of the word and the breaking of the bread and this is *not* the abbot's little idol, or his private possession, the support of his power. But who really trusts Him? Distrust of the abbot has brought on a profound distrust of any concept of Fatherhood and of authority. Yet they desperately seek a God who will be "for" them.

"The Word" (of God) is "a flood which breaks the dam." This from a Babylonian source, but in Spirit of O.T. [Old Testament] – and of Marxism for that matter. But basic. One senses this in our community to some extent. Uneasiness, anguish, dis-ease, because something is building up to break the dam and this "word" is inscrutably different from the comforting platitudes of the Superiors. But this sense pervades all society – is resisted by those who erect *their word* in to a dam and are determined to "hold" it at any price.

December 2, 1966

Advent weather – grey – 28, – probably snow again soon.

Early morning – reading Faulkner's *The Bear.* Glad the time has come for me to read this. Shattering, cleansing, a mind-changing and transforming myth that makes you stop to think about re-evaluating everything. All great writing like this makes you break through the futility and routine of ordinary life and see the greatness of existence, its seriousness, and the awfulness of wasting it. And how easy it is to waste and trivialize it. Seriousness of my own solitary vocation. Eschatological witness of Ike McCaslin. To know what it means that Boon kills the head Bear.

Wednesday over at Thompson Willett's with Jim Wygal. Illegally or independently if you prefer. I had qualms of conscience – but don't know precisely where the guilt came from. Anyway, shouldn't have been there. Yet should have too. Curious experience. A beautiful big old Southern house. Nice kids. Huge bar. Lovely old kitchen with an open fire for cooking (once). We drank some of his whiskey and talked. Because he has a boy in Vietnam he hopes it's a holy war and I didn't have the heart to argue. Conversation – bits and pieces of *suggested* ideas. Something comes up, is noticed, then delicately left aside as if we tried out five hundred things and really touched nothing. Wedding pictures. Football. All things I can't develop much! With Alice in her plaid dress and black stockings. I got to liking her and she stood on her head for me in secret, revealing a lovely little navel. I was trying to call M. and couldn't get her. Coming home in the early nightfall with the cold dark day streaked in copper over the ragged woods. Yet Bardstown is part of me and I am part of it. My winter rites. The lovely evenings. Sense that B. is somehow a lonely place. My operation in 58 at Flaget (or 57??). My arrival there in 41 on my way here. It is good to know Thompson, who is in many ways a devoted supporter (the Merton Room etc.).

December 3, 1966

What a contrast between Faulkner and Sarraute. The clever aridity of the Frenchwoman and the passionate myths of the Southerner – the "driving complexities of the heart" – the love of truth, the need to be free – the need to understand why we are not. Biblical Faulkner. I could write a book on *The Bear* as a basis for contemplative life. The *true* kind. *Theoria*. Freedom. *One* truth.

Everything looks different when you are reading something like this. The curious insubstantiality of what is trying to go on in the monastery, the reality and dignity conferred by past sufferings and mistakes of the Trappists. The meaning of those woods and hills. The meaning of my coming home. The true desert – the Southern curse! How real a wilderness it is! I want to talk about it to the novices if I can do it without choking on tears. It is a great, great story.

December 6, 1966

Great appetite for Faulkner now. *The Bear* can be read as a perfect tract on the monastic vocation, i.e. especially poverty. Though it is not "monastic." Merely Christian!! Merely. *The Bear* is a key to everything in America too. I am talking about it in the Sunday conference. How important to see our monastic vocation in this light. As against all the secular city naiveté that is floating around. A genuine and serious eschatology! There comes a point where compromise is simply impossible. Either the curse exists or it doesn't. To embrace the "system" and plunge into it is to say there is no curse and never was and man can by his own ingenuity fix everything just by acting as if there were nothing wrong; and the indifference to humanity which is built into the society he lives in, is accepted as "love." Things just become what you call them. Murder goes on? You have to learn not to see it, I guess!! Solidarity? with what? Murder! Just call it love, that makes everything OK in the secular city and next week there will be a better word for it, "love" not being quite acceptable.

December 10, 1966

Two days ago, F. of the Immaculate Conception, Joan Baez was here – memorable day! Ping Ferry had called the abbot and arranged it (Ira Sandperl had written before and had been refused. I sent Joan a book and a note last July). Wire said they would come sometime in the morning. I waited around, and they drove up around 12:30. Were here all afternoon.

Out on the tobacco farm – grey skies, cold wind, Joan running down the wide field alone in black sailor pants with her long hair flying. Ira and I talking about everything and drinking beer. They want me to leave and come with them. "Someone has to talk to the students and you are the one" etc. I can't fully explain why I don't. I mean I can't explain to them. This solitude is God's will for me – it is not just that I "obey" the authorities and the laws of the Church. There is more to it than that. Here is where my roots are.

So we came back to the gatehouse. Joan met the abbot and disliked him – saw through him at once and he was visibly upset at the way she looked *through* him.

We came up to the hermitage and spent the rest of the time here. Played one side of her new record, "Noel." Lit a fire. Sat on the floor, talked. Grey rugs spread out. Sitting around, lying around. Fr. Chrysogonus was here, entranced. Then he left and went down. Joan sat on the rug eating goat-milk cheese and bread and honey and drinking tea, in front of the fire. Lovely!

She is an indescribably sweet girl, and I love her. I know she loves me too – she said she had discovered prayer in reading my books and she and Ira seem to have read and liked most of my recent work, great openness, warmth, support. Talked a lot about Bob Dylan – how he is destroying himself, and becoming mean, stupid etc.

She is a very pure and honest girl, stays away from dope, everything, is rightly regarded as a sort of saint in the peace movement, and her purity of heart is most impressive. A precious, authentic, totally human person; the thing I sense most, for some reason, is a kind of mixture of frailty and indestructibility in her. Here is this sweet living child and she is on earth for now, for the time being, with a kind of visible evanescence in her reality, solidity, truth. A manifestation given us for a while. Yet right close, available, open, "given" in the realist sense. "Here I am." A sort of epiphany of what we most need.

She was talking about their non-violent institute – the people who come to it, what they think and do – (they can't be convinced she isn't using pot etc.). The meditation – the periods of silence worry the neighbors. She is a person who needs much silence, a kind of bride of silence, a listening person, who when she speaks comes out of silence with a lot of love and care for everything. Love for all kinds of creatures. In close union with the Mother, is the Mother.

Most of the talk (Ira) about books, people, ideas, events. Granada, Mississippi, Martin Luther King – etc. They don't go for the "new politics" (moving toward Marxism) etc.

We talked of my love for M. and I read some of the poems and Joan was ready to drive ninety miles an hour through the rain to Cincinnati so I could see M. when she got off at the hospital (11:30 p.m.). So we went to Bardstown and called M. But then they could not get their reservations changed to a convenient time. Just as well I did not go!! Would have been totally exhausted. Tired enough after driving with them to the airport and then coming home with Jack Ford after watching a bit of the *Glass Menagerie* at his house. Guilt next day for this wild impulsiveness, this night ride.

December 14, 1966

Yesterday I thought it would snow – skies have been grey and even black for over a week. Clouds of birds gathered around the hermitage. Twenty robins or more, a dozen finches, jays, many junkos (including one I found dead on the porch), other small birds and even a couple of bluebirds – I had not seen them around in the winter. Yesterday morning about two I heard something scampering around in the house and found it was a little flying squirrel. I have no idea how he got in. I thought for a moment of keeping him and taming him, but opened the door and turned him loose. At least let the animals be free and be themselves! While they still can.

I am still reading Faulkner. Nothing impresses me as much as *The Bear*. I suppose I need to get *Light in August*. Perhaps write on *The Bear* and *Requiem for a Nun* – "Faulkner's Saints." My "Day of a Stranger" is accepted by *The Hudson Review* – for next summer.[6] That news came in on the 25th

---

[6] "Day of a Stranger" appeared in *Hudson Review*, vol. 20 (Summer 1967).

anniversary of my entrance into the community. Re-read the ms. and it is OK. It comes close to being real. Still questions about "Edifying Cables." The typed ms finally got back from Eileen Curns but I have more to do. Maybe the writing is worth while – or let me say – maybe it goes in the right direction.

The Archbishop wants to ordain Dan Walsh and Dom James is dubious, suspicious, negative, etc. etc. Dan, innocent and receptive – is amazed.

Atmosphere of Dada and happenings in the Peace Movement. Provos. Yellow submarines, Flutes. Why not? Does it mean anything? As much as any other happening I suppose.

A man wrote an article in *America* on the vernacular liturgy. "If the Church wants to sweep the world like the Beatles . . ." With this mentality, what can you expect? But I am afraid that is the trouble. The Church is conscious of being inferior now not only to the Communists but to four English kids with mops of hair (and I like them OK). More and more I see the importance of not mopping the world with the mops, Beatle or liturgical. I am glad to be marginal. The best thing I can do for the "world" is stay out of it – in as far as one can.

I ought to have more compassion for the Abbot. He does not know that he loves the habit of command and can no longer live without power and that everything he does is probably governed by this in some subtle way – though he sincerely tries to make it otherwise. But his judgments of others are made in relation to his own power hunger – and how they affect his security. He is really a tragic person and has no idea of it. And the monastery will have to feel the effects – indeed does. I wonder if all our abbots have not been tragic in somewhat the same way. But as a result of this the community is poisoned by futile resentments and petty complications. And you see the same thing throughout the whole Church. Mere request for "due process" ([John] Courtney Murray) will not cure it. But what would happen if his power were suddenly taken away? That too must be considered. The evil in monasteries where abbots have been forced to resign. The danger of hubris in a young idiot like Du Bay, who is utterly convinced that he is a radical Galahad.

December 15, 1966

In confession (to Fr. Matthew) was talking about my resentment of petty harassment tactics on the part of the Abbot – in silly little things – mail especially – and this led to other things, his politics, his playing the monks against each other, his petty forms of tyranny. The whole picture is depressing in the extreme. There is *nothing* anyone can do to make it healthy. The community is really poisoned by all this, in a subtle way. *No* hope in visitations, no hope from higher superiors. No hope of his resigning – and no one special to take over his job. Fortunately most of us are stoical enough to shrug it off and live in peace. But the situation is *wrong*, destructive, dishonest, harmful. *No* hope of really carrying out in this monastery what the Council really calls for. Only a few gestures, a little face lifting – nothing more than a new coat of paint on the building and of course the air-conditioned Church, which was railroaded through by him before anyone knew it and then blamed on the building committee . . . It is a sick situation – and for some people the only honest thing to do is leave.

I think of Joan and Ira last week and all they were saying.

And got a card from Bob Wesselman today, married (was a Monsignor). And so on. Depressing.

But one thing I know: as long as I am in the hermitage I can live according to my conscience, not anyone else's! I am not pure either, but at least I can struggle honestly with my ordinary dishonesty and not inflict my problems on other people. I know at least this solitude and this responsibility and this privileged silence. And the need to pray.

Words of my Latin psalms have been driving themselves home to me lately.

Contribulasti capita draconum in aquis. [(You) who crushed the heads of monsters in the waters.]

Laetamini cum Jerusalem et exultate in ea, omnes qui diligitis eam in aeternum. [Rejoice with Jerusalem, and exult in her, all you who love her forever.]

Et factus est mihi Dominus in refugium, et Deus meus in adjutorium spei meae. [And the Lord has made himself my refuge, and my God the help of my hope.]

Convertere anima mea in requiem tuam, quia Dominus benefecit tibi. [Return, my soul, to your rest, for the Lord has done good things for you.]

Multiplicabis in anima mea virtutem. . . . Dominus retribuet pro me. [You will increase strength in my soul. . . . The Lord will repay on my behalf.]

December 16, 1966

It is good that I did not read Faulkner when I was not ready for him (of course *Sanctuary* thirty five years ago, but that was special) – like ten years back when Matt Scott sent me *A Fable* and I just glanced at it and tossed it back to him with total indifference – even agreeing with [Clifton] Fadiman (Fadiman!!) about Faulkner being unreadable.

Now is the time and now I see his true questions. *The* American prophet of the twentieth century (or at least the first half of it) – too great to be heeded by the nation. Has so much to say, so accurately for everybody – since what he says of the South applies to all the little Sutpens and Jason Compson[s] and Joe Christmases and Snopeses in the whole U.S.

Finishing notes on [Rafael] Alberti's angels for *Continuum* [Spring, 1967].

Wrote again yesterday to Josefa Manresa, Miguel Hernandez's widow. Learned more of his tragic innocence. How he foolishly treated Franco's police and let himself be captured again – jailed near home, but with TB could not see his wife and child etc. On March 28, 1942 – a month after I got the novice habit.

A grand dawn – pre-dawn still – the long dark line of hills, the varieties of red and dark and purple in the sky, the chalk streak of a gone jet about the black trees, the lights, there in the farm building through the screen of bare oaks . . . grass underfoot slipping with unseen frost. I have become so used to the splendor of morning that I remain with my nose in books and don't go to look at it. Same with stars. Yet last night the Swan was plunging down into the west through my high pines and when I got up Cassiopeia was swinging down into the north, the Great Bear over against her in the north east. The Lion sweeping up overhead out of the Southeast, and Arcturus out there over the dark oak wood at the top of the long field.

Made more coffee. From the silence of the valley I can learn that certain questions do not need answers of mine, or not now. Don't make the Abbot too big a question. Don't be too anxious about the ruin of this place which is now so rich, so stable (so likely to be abandoned because of him). The only thing is patience. *Wait!* Do nothing yourself. You will see. *Constantes estote videritis auxilium Domini super vos!* [Be constant, you will see God's help over you!]

December 18, 1966

Judgment will come. But *Nolite ante tempus judicare* [Be unwilling to judge beforehand]. Everything is still uncertain, hidden in hearts, the end not known, we do not see, we cannot see until God Himself throws His light into those depths. When he has, everyone will be *praised*. *Tunc erit laus unicuique a Deo.* [Then will be praise to each one from God.] Until then neither blame nor praise.

[Amiya] Chakravarty's fine pamphlet (a talk at Boston U.) on the "Emergent Plan." Emphasis on compassion and *Pacem in Terris* [Peace on Earth]. He is to come here today.

An old issue of *Choice*. James Wright, Robert Bly are good poets.

December 20, 1966

Mild winter days and nights "for men and animals"!

Animals like Billie's police dog that got my scapular all dirty with his paws, and the nice black pup that was there (first dog I would want to have – need no damn dog).

Went over there with Clem who was fretting over a meeting of the Monastery Council (Private Council rather) about work. He says the monks don't work any more anyhow.

Against my own feelings, went there and called M. – felt it was right to take this opportunity though – a good but curious call. She had not yet got a letter supposed to have been mailed Thursday or Friday. Wanted to see me. Wanted to know about "the other night" – then when I said something about "trust and patience" she got a little funny and said "but is that enough" and began telling me to resist the abbot and take matters into my own hands. But in the end she seemed to be telling me to become Ahab and hunt him like a white whale. Finally though she realized I was not really agreeing and said, "Don't worry over what I said." And I said it was good to know what she was thinking. But I don't feel she was realistic, except in terms of a sort of worldly go-getter mythology.

A sense of estrangement, of *décalage* [discrepancy] between her inmost self, which is so lovely to me, so simple, and this superimposed, determined, aggressive little worldly *persona* – which is I guess the one that gets her in trouble. The self she has learned to be in business, and is not her at all, the self that the nurses probably built with pop psych. in bull sessions in Lourdes

Hall. And a crack about "Oh well, probably in a few years there won't be any marriage any more anyway." That jolted me. Because it doesn't fit with the other things about loving each other forever. She has I think a funny and fluid memory and what she thinks is a stable set of ideas is really a very fluid process – so that I felt she was not talking to *me* anymore but to someone I had become in her mind in the course of our long separation.

Then today I glanced at a line of a letter I am writing her and thought "My God, this is a lie!" Perhaps. Anyway the whole thing is evolving – and we are evolving – and in our minds we still grasp on ideas of each other as we want ourselves to have been when it was best.

I am not going to worry about it. It will take its own course and there is no point in trying to force a special direction on it.

Astonishing value of Faulkner in this instance. Having read both *The Bear* and the "[An] Odor of Verbena" lately, I was intensely prepared for her and saw through it at once. This is not for me. I have my way to follow. If it becomes a choice . . . I am not sure whether it has to, but anyway, this suggestion gets nothing from me but "No." I have my vocation to follow, and it is on a level she does not really take into account. Maybe she has done so at times before – but how seriously? *Can* she take it seriously? Think back to Ascension Day and to June 11.

The real *destructiveness* of it (which I saw for a moment on Good Friday and wouldn't do anything about) is beginning to be clear. And yet! And yet there is under it all the reality of that inner M. that I can never, never repudiate. But on that level, love has to be entirely "in God." And she does not fully accept it. Her body is young and hungers. Mine is middle-aged and has its wild moments and its desperations too. There is the danger. The real danger. And now I know it.

December 22, 1966

Rinzai and another tremendous bout with Faulkner *[The Wild Palms]* – this time the convict and the woman and the river. Another fantastic myth, the void, the great power of evil, the alone man, the woman, their relationship, the ark – paradise – hell of snakes where the child is born – the primitive lake-dwelling huts of the cajun – the insensate return. As if the Flood with all its evil lifted humanity to a supreme level of stark, lonely meaning – nameless. The convict, the woman, the child is only a bundle, yet alive, and the boat. Marvelous passages on the River as the Void, from which comes inexhaustible, malignant power. And the frail but indestructible identity of man. And the silent presence of woman. A rending and shattering legend about everything.

December 28, 1966

Christmas has come and gone again – and I got through it alive. Actually it was quite peaceful, and I stayed out of everything, going only to concelebrate at Midnight Mass, and visiting Fr. Flavian in his hermitage Christmas Day.

Lovely cold moonlight – going down to Mass Christmas Night.

Came back, read notes and cards and bit of Sister Marion William's thesis.

On my table, picture of Sy [Freedgood's] pretty little daughter Julia looking sweetly at her horse.

Flavian's hermitage doesn't look as if it were lived in. Seems empty, uninhabited – one hardly knows if he has not yet moved *in* or if he is moving out. Yet he has been there since August. Two outsize ugly crucifixes – both slightly hideous in fact. A shower without water in which he stores things. Practically no furniture. No visible book. He was talking of a kind of prayer life in which there was practically no reading, only rosary and psalms. And not much work envisaged – except perhaps some job for the monastery. I came away feeling that it was all unreal. Or is it so real that it is beyond me? I have no confidence in it. But he may learn by experience. Anyway he is certainly not what I would call "settled." A couple of phrases around to indicate that he did not much like being in the woods. "I don't like nature the way you do" etc.

Yesterday [Feast of] St. John's. I took a long walk in the knobs, even climbed the high one in the middle which I think is called Thabor, and followed the logging trail all along the top of McGinty's hollow, out over the edge unto the hollow behind Donahue's. Woods dark, windy, and cold. Sleet began to fall after I got home. Very bleak. A dead snake on the tall knob, had been killed – could only have been there a few days. Killed by a man? Most likely. It was too cold for snakes the last 3 or 4 days (down around 20) but evidently they can come out on warm days – this is peculiar, for they are supposed to hibernate! The whole thing was strange. Maybe it had been killed by another animal or by a bird. But why not disposed of, then?

Black winds. Tall stately pines. Rugged walls of the knobs. Distant woods and fields and farms beyond New Haven. Lonely wind. Thick carpet of leaves, wet and packed down, with snow still in them from Christmas Eve. Lonely, wanted to call M., but also coming to grips with the fact that I can't keep calling and it is useless to think of trying to see her. A mind-blowing business. I still deeply love her and know she loves me. And I know the deep, permanent value of our love. And also its complicatedness. No end to it. But if we don't get impatient, things will quietly work out with no fracas – and with a deep and lasting union of hearts.

December 29, 1966

Year ending. Yesterday I was looking at Dom Frederic's lake with thin melting ice all over it and a screen of pine needles along the back and the blue warm clearing sky above it and was thinking of all that had happened this year. Crazy but good year anyway.

Finished Fr. [Augustin] Kishi's book on Zen and St. Thomas [*Spiritual Consciousness in Zen from a Thomistic Theological Point of View* (Osaka, 1966)] – good on Zen and dutiful on Thomas and not really pulling the two together.

It is good to have accepted a man like Faulkner completely – then you can read and enjoy even an inferior book like *Sartoris* and watch him working and tolerate the trash that is there – not trash, but juvenile creation. Good really – though a little embarrassing (comic Negroes etc.). Now we are more "serious" than that but do we know anything?

December 30, 1966

Reading *Letters from Mississippi* – the SNCC [Student Nonviolent Coordinating Committee] book [edited by Elizabeth Sutherland Martinez, 1965] about the 1964 Freedom project. Very good, very moving, it leaves you a little hopeless – sense of a transitional style in the Civil Rights movement – realization that it accomplished so little – yet was a great thing, especially for the white students and intellectuals who were in it. They profited most (and three were killed, of course).

The problem is not race only, but *man*. Race just makes it easy and simple for a certain type of mean bastard to mistreat other people with a good conscience. But there are all sorts of other excuses, and plenty of mean bastards to take advantage of them. And society will bless them every time. The harassment by petty officials and cops, little people with authority, bullies in every walk of life, people who systematically persecute and cheat and provoke and despise others and make their way in the world by depriving others of what they have coming to them. And the others having to accept it and be nice about it because otherwise life would be unlivable. How often I think my own relations with the abbot are nothing but "yassah white boss" ass-kissing relations. The latest petty humiliation – (they are so petty and cheap it is humiliating to write them down and so I almost never do!) – J. Laughlin sent a subscription to *Poetry*, and Jim Holloway a subscription to the *NY Review*. In both cases I asked the abbot twice if it was OK for me to receive them, and I'd like to. He said yes, he would see to it. I get one copy of each, no more. He hints that the secretaries are somehow losing them. The secretaries assure me he has them in his desk (probably reading them himself, though God knows what he'll get out of *Poetry!*).

And yesterday he had the nerve to ask me how my spiritual life was getting on. "Yessuh white boss, mighty fine white boss. I'se only a simple ole niggah boy, white boss but de Laud he loves me!" It is all of course for my own good.

Even if all the problems of civil rights were solved tomorrow, the same mean bastards would be pulling tricks on other people "for their own good" – only some of the mean bastards would now be black.

Today I go to Louisville again to see the doctor. The bursitis is not bad enough to operate but has not cleared up entirely. Still I think I will need to go in less this next year – unless the back gets bad again. Fed up with it.

December 31, 1966

Cold day yesterday. Rode in on the truck with George – everything heavy with frost. Those same fields, farms, houses, junkyards, bridges rushing by. And the signs: Louisville, Louisville. The name Louisville will forever mean M., and her love. Struggle inside me, knowing once again it has to *all* end. That I cannot go on calling her every time I am in town. Still less go to town in order to call her. I did need to get this shot and also see another doctor about my ears.

Called her from the M.A. building. She was sleepy and sad (just waking up – had some sad days). Main thing she said – though she is changing from _____ to _____ Hospital on Jan. 2. She still wants to get away completely from Cincinnati and her family and the people there. And wants to go to Hawaii which sounds like an evasion. For a year she says. Still, maybe that is a good thing.

Lunch at Cunningham's – some of the records on the juke box reminded me of her ("Together Again") and I call her a second time from there – more lively. I am still so powerfully held by her love and she seems to be by mine also. It is going to be a struggle to get all this straight, but the main thing I think is to get the phone calls etc. in order. Certainly there will be no more of these if she is in Hawaii. [. . .]

She wants to go to Hawaii at the end of February. Meanwhile she has sent another letter. We'll see if I get it!!

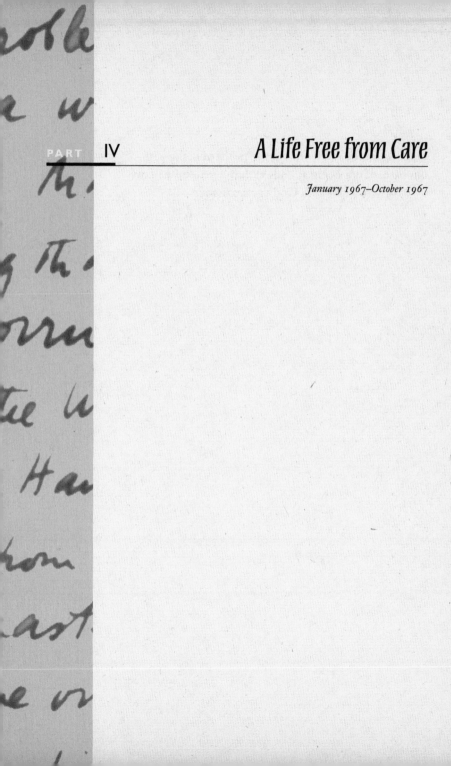

PART IV

A Life Free from Care

January 1967–October 1967

Once again the old freedom, the peace of being without care, of not being at odds with the real sense of my own existence and with God's grace to me.

April 10, 1967

January 1, 1967

Still night. Warm and rainy.

This year I have to get back to right order, and really make my meditation etc. what they ought to be. Actually my prayer life has not been *bad* but not good either. A certain radical shift in my relation to M. is necessary. An inner detachment. Time I think is working on both of us. Less calling, less writing too. If she goes to Hawaii all that will take care of itself. I am worried because she seems upset and unsettled. And there is really nothing I can do for her. Yet we love each other and can't help ourselves much. Useless to say again that I know I have been foolish, have exaggerated, have been impulsive, have probably done more harm that I realize. Yesterday dark, rough, depressed day but after a lot of anguish it ended in hope and comfort and I went to bed, slept until I heard the bells pealing out in the rain, the first sound of the New Year.

While I was eating breakfast, read in *Letters from Mississippi* how the SNCC volunteers and the Negroes watched on TV the signing of the Civil Rights bill (July 2, 1964), knowing that as far as the South went it meant nothing. A Negro woman declared she was going to the local pool for a swim. Had to be dissuaded – she might have got herself killed. How hard it is fully to realize the utter enormity of the situation. All these people systematically and totally denied the simple needs and desires of the human heart! No question that this country is under judgment, and the moral blindness of the majority – of those in power – the total moral impotence of the system – are sufficient indications. It gets worse all the time and everyone is helpless. The gestures of a few are perhaps consoling, but achieve nothing important. Perhaps a little here and there.

I think that now I do really experience the whole M. thing as something that is credible – and acceptable – in the past tense. Not that it is not also present, but present tamely, in a friendship that does not need that much passion – and is perhaps free of complication. The wrenching of yesterday and the fiction of a "New Year" seem to be a help. I know, to claim it is "free of complication" is a bit optimistic. But I am lucky that it is not much more complex than it is.

January 4, 1967

Finished [Joseph P.] Lyford's book – *The Airtight Cage* [New York, 1966] – a clear-cut and impassioned report on what happens to people in a slum. In this case the "Area" – South of Columbia in the 80's and 90's on the West Side of NY – which was a somewhat comfy middle-class Jewish–Irish area when I was in college. I still remember so many things about it – the dark brownstone rendezvous club for girls where the Alpha Delts [Alpha Delta Phi] used to get dates. Cold shadows on Broadway on a winter morning. Walking down Broadway around 1:30 a.m. shouting Merry Christmas to everyone after Midnight Mass – the *Thalia*, the *Wurno*, and other movies . . .

He shows the life of utter helplessness, rootlessness, lack of community, lived by people (poor and middle class) who have *no recourse*, i.e. a system that deplores the slum but *needs* it as a human refuse dump.

The slum life is lived by 1/5 of the population of the country – a life where people are destroyed. In order to witness the fact that the system itself is in grave trouble and is self-destroying. Yet there are so many rich resources that could be used. Will we ever do this? My guess is that only more and more cataclysms will force it upon us, and we don't know what lies ahead.

Importance of what he calls the "total facts" that no one really sees. What use is a monk in the world if he does not see those facts? Or a priest either? (He mentions priests in the area that seem to be really and effectively concerned.) I am left with a great respect for the Puerto Ricans. And with a confirmed conviction that one of the purposes of the social institutions is to fabricate lies about society. And that this is true also in monasteries. And that today the process is inevitably bureaucratic because in a bureaucratic system petty cruelty and evasion and compulsive futility and masked irresponsibility and greed can be perfectly rationalized and indeed automated for full effect.

January 7, 1967

High wind last night. This morning – going out into inky darkness full of the cold and roar of wind in the forest, everywhere. Then rain. And the wind stopped. Rugged black sky when I went down for Mass. Finished a paper for that Harvard magazine and turned it in to be typed.

There was a very touching card from a Haitian nun in the school at Bel-Air – picture of the map of Vietnam (drawn for her) with a star of peace over it – and promise of prayers for peace from her and all the girls in the class who all signed – lovely Haitian names. I can imagine them. It was a sweet card, and moved me to tears.

Some photos from J. H. Griffin came – taken when Maritain was here 3 months ago.

Doris Dana, friend and literary executor of Gabriela Mistral, was here for a couple of days – she left early on the Epiphany to go to Griffin at Fort Worth. We had a good talk and drove around a lot, drank some beer in a quiet hollow between New Haven and Howardstown and looked at the bare woods. Much about South America. She brought the *Misa Criolla* which is quite good – a bit too slick perhaps, and the *Misa Gitana* which impresses me a great deal more. The Spanish texts themselves are great too. *The Chilean Mass* is not so striking but there are good folk dances on the other side. She brought up the story of Ishi – that is what impressed me most. She says she will send the book, which I had heard of before and wanted to get.

This evening I had a talk with Bro. Finbar who is thinking of leaving when his temporary vows expire next month. He was one of those in the Brothers Novitiate when the two novitiates merged in 1963. Bro. Mark – another, and one of the best, also left a few weeks ago. Really this situation is quite disturbing because as far as I can see these were two very good monastic vocations. The trouble is obviously not with them but with Gethsemani and the Abbot. And the combine, Dom James – Father Eudes which seems to be disastrous for a great many people.

Though I have a great deal of difficulty putting up with Dom James, I am much better off than some, since he has long since decided to give me plenty of lee-way (at least what he considers such). Those he completely dominates are in a really terrible position. This Abbot-Psychiatrist combination works in some cases as a real tyranny – and very unfairly too. Though Fr. Eudes tries harder to be fair than the abbot does. Between them it is a deadly business.

The other day when I saw Dom J. he brought up the "sad case" of Fr. Charles Davis, the English Jesuit theologian who got married and left the Church. Immediately I realized this was a dire "warning" to me – and got a little irritated, so that I spoiled his game for him by saying a few things that he was not too willing to hear. The deviousness of it repelled me. Also his total intolerance and incapacity to understand the first thing about it.

Finally Bro. Finbar was talking about the man – and the side of him I see least and can least abide. It is totally repellent. His sickening sentimentality, emotionalism, and all that – and the *ludicrousness* of it. The man is incredible. Really he is something to worry about: and nothing can be done. His position is so strong, that no recourse to superiors will mean anything. Only I think what will happen is that one by one all the young men will leave. God will quietly give us *His* idea about the place and the way it is run.

What makes me most angry is of course the mail situation, the opening of conscience letters, the xeroxing of outgoing mail that is "interesting" and so on! There is a real smell of police state in that office of his! Yet he pretends to be so kind, so unaware of it all . . . He can't realize what his monks really think of him and evidently no one is able to tell him in a way that will make any impression – except to make him think he is "betrayed" and "martyred." I think Jim Wygal is really right about him. It is pathological.

January 10, 1967

Cold. Grass in the dark slippery with hard frost. I went out into the latest dark (before dawn) to see my big bad friend Scorpio – rising – and there he was. First time I have seen him up there – all the way to Antares and beyond – this year. I have not been starwatching much lately.

Pascal is my kind. The [Romano] Guardini work on him [*Pascal for Our Time* (New York, 1966)] is fine – one of G.'s best, at least for me. Whole thing so full of ideas they rush in from all sides and I have to stop and walk around. Yes, I know, the world is full of people who will want me to know that my reading of Pascal is vicious – like taking LSD. Fatal pessimism and all that. Jansenism.

Yesterday I got a letter from an ex-Trappistine who is out between convents and returning to the Order she hopes. An incredibly naive and narcissistic document – mental age of about 10, so I would judge. Scolding me because she had read the review in *NCR [National Catholic Reporter]* of *Raids* and *Conjectures*, telling me I was a naughty old world-hater and that the world was really lovely, how everyone really loved everyone else and all was paradise in Texas. It is true I guess that this failure to understand my stuff is partly my fault. Too loud, too sweeping, too excited, too preachy. When I criticize a *system*, they think I criticize them – and that is of course because they fully accept the system and identify themselves with it. All love and bliss!! And they seem to have no idea that the affluence (which for them is Kingdom of God) has another side to it – the burned bodies of children in Vietnam and the Negro–Puerto Rican ghettoes.

Strange that the people who are *really* in the world and know what it is, like my stuff – or more of them do. In the same mail a letter from another girl, mature and with *real* problems and difficulties!!

These pious ones with their pretty myths and images about "the world" – they have not got beyond the old holy cards. Only the subject is now: instead of sweet sweet Mary and Baby Jesus it is now sweet sweet world of automation and jets and freeways – and tranquilizers I guess also. Perhaps the tranquilizers are the real exasperation of this new beatific theology of the world.

Another "natural" for me – Loren Eiseley. Amiya Chakravarty spoke of him and sent two books, and Harcourt Brace is giving out a little privately printed lecture of his which I have just read. Perfect. And clicks perfectly with what I have had on my mind all morning. I hope to begin *The Firmament of Time* [New York, 1960] – seems to fit in with what I read in Guardini – Pascal on Nature. Perhaps another good start.

Book Providence!!

January 18, 1967
Visits lately.

Last week, Jim Holloway and Will Campbell. Much talk of Faulkner, his drinking, his connections with *Ole Miss* (an underground paper there, mimeographed, on Will's machine: "Just another rat hole for them to watch"). Its unpopularity with "the (Civil Rights) movement" – and with everyone else on that issue: penalty for taking a unique personal position and not electing to run with some pack. Will disagrees with F.'s "idealization of the Negro" and with his idea (mine too I guess) of the Negro as (possible) Redeemer. My idea in "Black Revolution"[1] was simply that *if* at a certain moment white and Negro had responded to *Kairos* [decisive moment] there

---

[1] " The Black Revolution: Letters to a White Liberal" in *Ramparts* 2 (Christmas 1963), 4–23; see also *Seeds of Destruction* (New York: Farrar, Straus & Giroux, 1964). The essay has been reprinted in Thomas Merton, *Passion for Peace: The Social Essays*, edited by William H. Shannon (New York: Crossroad, 1995), 154–88.

could have been a naturally redemptive act and a kind of conversion of the country. Not any more. Anyway it was only a *possibility*. Not something essentially inherent in the Negro, a historic chance.

We drank some beer under the loblollies at the lake – should not have gone on to Bardstown and to Willett's in the evening. Conscience stricken for this the next day. Called M. from filling station outside Bardstown. Both glad.

Jonathan Williams, Guy Davenport and Gene Meatyard were here yesterday. Williams impressive but seemingly a little aloof, though friendly. All were friendly. Williams said all the poets sooner or later get into a fight with Cid Corman and he would be prepared to publish an anthology of "My last letter from Cid Corman" contributed by various – or all the – poets. Williams gets around and knows everybody and has marvelous books full of drawings and writings of all these people – and some excellent pictures in them. Guy Davenport – a recluse, vulnerable, pleasant and kind, touched no beer. The one who made the greatest impression on me as artist was Gene Meatyard, the photographer – does marvelous arresting visionary things, most haunting and suggestive, mythical, photography I ever saw. I felt that here was someone really going somewhere.

For the rest Williams and Davenport were tired of young poets in Lexington and I read them bits of "Edifying Cables" which got nowhere – in the end we went and looked at the lake and they got cheese and went home. But I hope Gene Meatyard – and Guy – will come back.

Next week – boring – I have to see a man from Time-Life books about a big Bible project I made the mistake of getting involved in. After that I am I think free for a while and can just hang around the woods and think.

Ping [W. H. Ferry] sent Charles Davis' statement, in *The London Observer,* on why he left the Church. Powerful attack on the institutional arrogance of Rome and the distortions, the untruth, the inhumanities that result all down the line. It is incontrovertibly true. And it opens a real question whether the *only* loyal and honest thing to do is to keep a stiff upper lip, offer it up, accept the evil, close ranks and remain obedient. Though that is often all *less* honest, less courageous. Or at any rate the thing is no longer a certainty. It is perhaps something one may be called upon to risk for the love of God! A wager – one way or the other.

Coldest morning this winter – down to around 15. And I have a cold.

January 24, 1967

A week later and it is warm again, 60 now, at 5 a.m. It has been cloudy and warm for a couple of days, smelling of rain, and I *need* rain to fill my water-buckets, and none comes. Sunday was Septuagesima. I am giving talks on Faulkner still ("Old Man") and rereading the whole of *Wild Palms*. Also writing my piece for a Panichas book *(Mansions of the Spirit)* [2] of which I have a Xerox here. Some fine things in it. This morning I finished the [Georges] Florovsky essay. Which explains perhaps why I never could get into Tolstoy. But it also makes me see that the negative and inconclusive radicalism of Tolstoy could be a danger for me too. Except that I am very different from him.

The *NCR* printed my (inadequate) reply to Michele Murray's review and sent a Xerox of *her* reply which was sound. [3] There is no question that I don't communicate as I should. Fortunately there has been a minor revolution here. The Council (of the Abbot) ganged up on Dom James and told him the mail situation here was idiotic. All the letters being opened and read, money and clippings taken out. The censorship of my mail by the A. personally, also withheld much of it and even real conscience letters on occasion! All this has been changed (at least for the moment). Mail comes in and goes out sealed. I am getting even the magazines (most of which I can't read). Yesterday *I. F. Stone's Weekly* came for the first time in many months and the Vietnam war is more fantastically inhuman and absurd than ever. Huge destructive operations – clearing and razing thousands of acres of jungle, villages etc. The total idiocy of technological war.

Where I really think Michelle M. misses my point is that I see a basic irrationality and inhumanity in our system, in which she sees and takes for granted human hopes. One must of course hope. But the contradictions are so glaring. A few gestures in a futile "war on poverty" that changes nothing.

[2] "Baptism in the Forest: Wisdom and Initiation in William Faulkner," in George Panichas, ed., *Mansions of the Spirit: Essays in Religion and Literature* (New York: Hawthorn, 1967), 19–44. See also *The Literary Essays of Thomas Merton*, ed. Bro. Patrick Hart (New York: New Directions, 1981), 92–116.

[3] Michele Murray wrote two pieces on Merton in the *National Catholic Reporter* (December 21, 1966): a book review, "Life Viewed Too Facilely," and "Thomas Merton, the Public Monk." Merton replied with "Thomas Merton Replies to a Perceptive Critic" (January 18, 1967).

A few slogans about a "great society." And a frenzied absurd all-out effort at mammoth war with machines – a war on women and children and trees and rice fields – this society is cursed with destructiveness and thinks itself – I suppose it *could* be – creative and progressive. And in a way it is – for its technology is fabulous. But for what? Am I crazy to see something demonic in it?

Today Russell B[rowne] from Time-Life books comes, about a big Bible project, and I don't want to get into it, and am not sure I can keep myself out of it. Am not sure what it really is. But I don't trust Time-Life books. Heard from Sy Freedgood (at *Fortune*) the other day. He is not too favorable – but is himself finishing a TL book on New York.

Last night – moon almost full, behind scudding clouds. I walked in the warm dark wind. Lonely again for M. and troubled and wanting to write to her, wanting to hear from her, wanting to see her.

January 29, 1967. Sexagesima

Early morning. Good coffee that Beatrice Olmstead sent. I am finishing the ms. of the book of essays edited by George Panichas. (My piece on Faulkner is being typed now.) The essay on [Saul] Bellow raises the question of Bellow, who, I think, appears to be in the same kind of predicament I am in with the critics. I have not read any of Bellow and have been put off by the negative noises, not really knowing what the noises are about. They are just vague scolding noises. Bellow is "popular" but not really "in" – that is, he is disapproved by those who are really in. And yet also approved by critics who are smart but belong to other groups. Reading the essay on him I could see the reasons. He writes of alienation, mass-man, the doomed city, and all that instead of happy growing collective technological man building the city of hope on earth etc. It is very naughty to write like this.

[Handwritten marginal note added in April:] Apparently this is off target. Still have not read B[ellow] *(April)*.

At the same time from the quotes I can see he is a careless writer but perhaps worth reading. And I will probably never get around to doing it. The fuss about him for and against is very likely among Jews: some will be swearing by him and others will be furious at him for creating an image of the Jew which they can't stand. All that nonsense.

So it is with me to some extent. I am, to begin with, judged by my early books. Either I am rejected entirely because the "monasticism" is unacceptable, or my later work is rejected for not being "spiritual" and "unworldly" like the earlier ones.

I see clearly that I must inevitably sound like a stranger and outsider to the people who watch TV, and are fully immersed in a world I left 25 years ago. And there is little point in pretending I am *not* an outsider – why should I? So I will resolutely continue to be me, and say what seems to me to be true, and if nobody listens that is all right. I am not asking to be listened to. On the other hand I think there are quite a few people who are glad to have someone say what I am saying.

January 30, 1967

A warm, pleasant day. Work – some letters and burned brush a little. Outside the house stands a truck and well-rig marked Pee Wee McGruder, Shep., KY (for Shepherdsville). It stands there. I have seen nothing of any Pee Wee McGruder. Maybe tomorrow, my birthday, he'll start – whaling and banging away at the rock on which my place sits.

Today an invitation came from France – Dom Columban of Melleray has been awarded the Legion of Honor, and as I was involved in this, he wants me there when he receives it. As he is the Father Immediate of Gethsemani, the request would normally be respected, but I am sure Dom James will find some way of saying "no." Anyway I have turned the letter over to him for his decision. It would be nice to go to France after all these years, but I really don't care that much. I am perfectly content walking in the fields here by myself, and it would be a bore to be involved in all this socializing and rituals and chatter that would be the price I'd have to pay.

Good letter from Amiya Chakravarty about Sally Donnelly's essay and my introduction[4] which he likes.

I am reading *Ishi* – which Doris Dana sent. A heartrending book about the last of the Yahi Indians – victims of genocide a hundred years ago. What a frightening past this country has – and yet people admire it. True, not *all* were vigilantes and a lot of Ranchers protested against the indiscriminate massacre. So later Vietnam today! An Indian war!

---

[4] Merton's "Foreword to Chakravarty's 'Marcel and Buddha: A Metaphysics of Enlightenment'" was published in the *Journal of Religious Thought* 24, no. 1 (1967–68). It was reprinted in *Zen and the Birds of Appetite* (New York: New Directions, 1968).

February 1, 1967

As I expected, the answer on going to France was "No." And I do not in the least mind not going. But I was irritated and frustrated by the complicated mixture of emotionalism and hypocrisy of the answer. Dom J. could not simply *forbid* me to go – he started out saying his five page letter (all this was done by notes back and forth) was only his "humble advice." But it quickly ran to a pitch of shrill reproach and recrimination. How could I dare to ask such a dreadful thing? It was obviously a temptation of the devil. This could not come from the Holy Spirit etc. etc. So by this logic Dom Columban, his higher superior, is the devil. Interesting!

With such emotionalism there is no argument and no discussion, so I simply let it drop. But really this note represents a progressive deterioration in the man. This is worse than it was before – more irrational, more emotional, more convinced of the utter infallibility of his own personal determination – and yet strangely insincere, shaken by departures of men like Finbar (whom he "loved" in his strange emotional and rather nauseous way) or Mark.

The thing that troubles me is that this man is really sick. I ought not to have thrown his note away – should have passed it on to Jim Wygal for his evaluation.

Another point: not only the high-pitched excitement and fury of the tone, but the literal repetition of all the same ideas he has uttered mechanically over and over for forty years – as if they were relevant discoveries applicable to this case.

I have to be careful of this man. And I can see where the case of Gethsemani is serious. The effect of someone like that – on top of the insanities of the past, can be fatal. I am surprised things are not far worse than they are. What is to be done? Higher Superiors can do nothing about him (he is shrewd to play his cards right with them and never give them an opening).

February 2, 1967. Purification

Dawn. It was a warm night – 60 when I got up. And now there is lightning, thunder, rain. Which means this is another day when Pee Wee McGruder will not come and start digging my well.

February 3, 1967

A bizarre thing. Ishi (the Yahi Indian about whom I am reading in the book Doris Dana sent) – liked the song "The Road to Mandalay." I remember myself being shattered and heartbroken by it as a child. Now I realize that

"Mandalay" must be somewhere around the Gulf of Tonkin – Hanoi, Haiphong etc. Disconcerting. The song itself is a bit stupid – British soldier – Asian woman, generous dose of sado-masochism etc. Still a sad song of loneliness and division. I remember being crushed too, at the age of 7 or 8, at a movie about this love of a westerner and an Asian (Japanese? Indochinese?) woman who eventually walked into the sea and committed suicide, and asking myself, "But *why* did it have to be like that?" For some inscrutable reason the westerner could not just *love* the Asian, he had to be for her a sign of death. And to me this spelled utter tragedy and uncomprehending despair.

Yesterday it got cold in the afternoon. Rain, sleet, snow. I walked in the woods, came home, built a fire, made tea, read a good urbane book of Viscount [John Julius] Norwich on Athos [*Mount Athos* (New York, 1966)]. He thinks Athos is in hopeless shape and doomed to end completely. I suppose he is right.

February 4, 1967

Finished *Ishi*. A moving book. The best and the worst in America comes out in it. The furious stupidity and violence of vigilantes and the warm, touching friendliness of scholars. And Ishi who is the "real America" – at least who has the valid claim to be the America that was created natural.

Had to go to town yesterday. A disappointing day. Dr. Mitchell will operate on my bursitis at the end of the month. Had lunch and sat around at Tommie O'Callaghan's – worrying about Dan Walsh and her own relatives in trouble etc. Hoped to get in touch with M. but couldn't, and I do see that it is time to stop fooling, finally, with letters and phone calls. Should have stopped months ago.

I picked up Faulkner's *Essays, Speeches and Pub[lic] Letters* [ed. James B. Meriwether (New York, 1965)] at the library. Some of his worst writing is here. But I'll still read anything and everything that's his. In the *Holiday* [April 1954] essay on "Mississippi" he sounds sometimes like our Fr. Peter – vain, double and involved.

And I reflect on my own writing. Everyone now goes about declaring I have written too much and implying this is the last reason for not reading me – but in fact my own recent writing – the last three years – has been in some ways the best. I am sure there are plenty of people who read it (Amiya Chakravarty says the Smith girls do – and I also get letters about it). Still, there is no need whatever to go on churning out a book a year and some-times two.

Yesterday in town, talking to Tommie, about all the current issues – the Pill, the Catholic Schools and all that – I realize how out of touch I am with what concerns married people trying to live in the city, which is all right. I am pre-cisely supposed to be out of touch with those particular problems. But I need to be more definite in my mind: not imagining I have to try to "keep up" with everything. Stay moderately informed – and go on quietly doing my own job. People need me to be a contemplative and not a newspaper man.

Coming back from dinner at the monastery – under a very black and cold sky, with a black and cold heart. I realized again how much illusion there has been in me all these last months. The beautiful illusions – surrounding a core of reality – in my love for M. have not really made me happy – or her either (I feel her life is probably far more complicated and unhappy than mine). And though the love was real, yet it was (is) also full of unreality, de-ception and unhappiness. I have been desperately using it to give my life "*value*" – as if my worth consisted in loving her and being loved by her. But this is an illusion. Love is good, but only so far as it proceeds from a *real* per-son. What value I have does not come to me separated from the outside. And there is no sense trying to depend on this or that state of mind – whether human love or spiritual fervor – to make my life seem meaningful. The real-ity is quite other: my life is meaningful in itself, because it is life, quite apart from explanations and notifications – or appeals to what someone thinks of me, or what my work is supposed to mean. Being separated from her and trying to live on "love" is nothing more than living in imagination and memory. A dream. A source of deep unhappiness. I am beginning to see it clearly now.

Theokistos – a hermit who died on Patmos in 1917 – said, "When I was in the world I saw people trying to do good: but they were doing harm. Then I saw there was nothing left for me but to go off alone. In that way I would not harm anyone else. I pray God to pardon my sins and take me finally to heaven. I am going to die and I must appear before him." This strikes me as very real and solid, as opposed to the confusion and vagueness of so many aspirations that are mistaken for realities now! A lot of fussiness with good intentions: and no awareness that this can do irreparable *harm*.

February 6, 1967

The community is on retreat. So am I in a different way (not going to conferences). Spoke with Fr. Claude Peifer, the retreat master, briefly last evening.

Yesterday (Sunday) was out in the woods – reading [Irenée] Hausherr's *Penthos* [Rome, 1944]. A nice sunny, quiet afternoon. I find I can at last relax my desperate grip on the image of M. and of her love. Obviously I still love her, but there is no point in insisting that we are still "in love," though maybe we still are, up to a point. Certainly things have changed very much since September (when I called her from the booth in Bardstown that afternoon everything was still charged with all the power of our love). But I see it is folly and infidelity for us to try to keep it going even in my own heart now. I need simply to let go and move on. And that is what I am doing. Not kicking myself in the pants for being a fool, or resenting anything (I don't – even the fact that she has a pile of utterly ridiculous letters from me!!) – and still retaining a warm and deep affection for her – (I can't help doing that – my love has been far too deep to be abandoned). Not forgetting either my *permanent* responsibility to her. Certainly I can never go back to what I was before. I can never again be the person that did not know or love her in a deep, mysterious way, because we gave ourselves to each other almost as if we were married.

Monasticism. I see more and more the danger of identifying the monastic vocation and spirit with a particular kind of monastic consciousness – a particular tradition, however "authentic." A monasticism limited to the medieval western – or worse still Byzantine – tradition *cannot* survive. It is utterly finished. I very much wonder how much of the Rule of St. Benedict can survive in practice. This is a very serious question. Maybe monasticism needs to be stated all over again in a new way. I have no way of knowing how to tackle this idea. It is just beginning to dawn on me.

I did a "graph" of my work – the biggest ups and downs were in the beginning.[5] The lowest plunge was too "awful" in 1950 with *What Are These Wounds?* In the fifties the writing was consistently indifferent but got better in the end and most of my best work has been since 1957.

---

5 "Thomas Merton's Graph Evaluating His Own Books 1967" appears as Appendix 2 in *"Honorable Reader."*

I would say I would be much better off if I had published only these:

Thirty Poems

Seven Storey Mountain

Seeds of Contemplation

Tears of Blind Lions

Sign of Jonas

Silent Life

New Man

Thoughts in Solitude

Wisdom of Desert

Disputed Questions

New Seeds of Contemplation

Seeds of Destruction? [inserted later]

Chuang Tzu

Emblems of a Season of Fury

Raids on Unspeakable

Conjectures of G[uilty] B[ystander]

That's 15 – plenty. But yet the others too – some of them – had something in them that had to be got out of my system I guess.

February 7, 1967. St. [Romuald]. Shrove Friday

"The road from the preaching of Jesus to the Church might well, from a certain perspective, be called 'history's greatest anti-climax': for it is a road from a moment of ecstatic eschatological expectation to its supposed appropriation but actual negation in an institutional and hierarchical system."

[p. 52]

So Rosemary Ruether in her ms. [*The Church Against Itself*, 1967] on the Church which she has lent me. More or less following [Alfred Firmin] Loisy. I have to admit this is the big problem – the problem we Catholics have all dutifully and obediently refused to face: and now we have to face it. Facing it does not mean "leaving the Church" à la Charles Davis, but there must be a groping for unambiguousness somewhere. Every day the experience of life in the monastery under Dom James shows the equivocal nature of our "Church" experience. By God's mercy there *is* a truth here in spite of all that is done against it in His Name. But the distortions, the evasions, the perversion of love into power and resentment, and all the virtues of mimicry and practice . . . All of these slowly strangling hope until in the end a final despair has to be embraced as the ultimate hope. True, one is driven to

Jesus in desperation. The place imposes a dark night of inhumanity in which one is forced to cling to something *beyond* all this – or perish.

In her letter Rosemary challenges my solitude, but not understanding it, I think. She is very Barthian – which is why I trust her. There is a fundamental Christian honesty about her theology – its refusal to sweep evil under the rug and its "No" to phony incarnationalism. And above all she knows where the real problem lies: the Church.

My feeling is that we shall not solve this problem ourselves (how could we? We are too much a part of it!), but events will bring on a crisis that will smash all facades. Maybe in the ruins of the great institutional idol we will recover something of our Christian truth.

"The disparity between the original message of Jesus and its subversion by the institutional Church is the unsolved (and unsolved because chiefly unaccepted) dilemma of Church history."

The problem includes in part the fact that the Resurrection and Outpouring of the Spirit were turned into historic rather than *eschatological* events (*history-ending* events) and became a big birthday of an institution.

And yet the fact of an historic "interval" invites an institutional salvation-machine to get in there and fill the gap – to meet the "threat of history." Well, this frantic effort to "meet the threat of history" was never so frantic as today. The Church "handles history by expelling the Spirit."

February 9, 1967

Yesterday, Ash Wednesday, after one of the coldest nights of the winter (down to about 10) the sun came out a little and in the afternoon when I came back from a walk in the woods I found four golden crocuses had come out of the ground in front of the hermitage.

Reading Rosemary Ruether's ms. on the Church. One point she makes is completely convincing: when the "glory of the Spirit" becomes a purely historic event which underwrites all the Church's institutional activities throughout the rest of history, when the Spirit becomes a "thing" owned and operated by the church, then the Spirit sits in judgment on the very Church that desires to be guided by it. Then you get the demonic parodies of power and holiness which make the institution of Church so frightening and repugnant: and yet the Spirit is there nevertheless for the well-meaning and the deluded. (This is more my own anxious paraphrase and formulation.) But this I think is true: "The historification of the Spirit and the Risen

Lord as a past mandate for the historical institution spells the death of the Church's freedom for grace."

However, our struggle in and with this institution is a great grace.

When it comes to her christology – she is neo-modernist I guess – I wonder if after all she does not raise problems – or accept those which have been raised by Bultmann etc. – that have no solution in the terms in which she deals with them. There is something seemingly quite arbitrary about the Kerygmatic "Christ of Faith" and who is to say when there is and is not "faith"? And when the Christ of faith is present to faith? In the end doesn't it all come down to pious hopes and devout imaginings?

I get more and more uneasy feeling that now we are being summoned to a decision for Christ on the basis of the fact that someone who says God is dead has also "decided for Christ" – and he is published each week in a different magazine. But five years from now he will be forgotten and someone else who has taken his plan will have decided for some other figure, or idea, or drug, or kick, or something.

Flannery O'Connor's Hazel Motes was logical about all this. He started with a Church without Christ and then when nobody joined him he blinded himself and sat in silence – at least some kind of conclusion. The others evade this by a perpetual inconclusiveness – which means in the end perpetual motion and chatter.

The really big problem: the fact that when the apostolic generation died out, the Church had to completely re-interpret the primitive eschatology according to which the old eon was finished, the Kingdom had begun and the *end of history* has arrived. But history went on, and the Church found herself a place in it. And it eventually became a very definite and solid plan. But is all this the fruit of repeated unconscious acts of bad faith and semi-deliberate cheating? Rosemary R. says no, it was just a practical way of asking the best of things – of getting through an uncomfortable predicament. But she does not get away from the objection of a *radical break* in continuity between apostolic and post-apostolic theology when eschatological theology was abandoned, "tradition" became decisive, and a new incarnational theology put Christ in history in His Church – His *institutional* Church. According to this (Protestant) criticism, the supposed continuity of Catholic faith with primitive apostolic faith is a pure fiction.

For her, monasticism is part of this fictional structure. It is true that monasticism was *taken over* rapidly by the anti-Arian movement and became an institutionalized radical elite.

Her solutions.

1. Acceptance of the breakdown of primitive eschatological Christianity.
2. Acceptance of fact that Catholicism tried to adjust by a metaphysical, incarnational, and classic world-view.
3. Acceptance of the fact that this has broken down.
4. A new tradition of primitive Christianity in existentialist-personalist terms – restoring the basic tension between history and eschatology.
5. *But* – this means to her in practice that eschatology becomes absorbed into history. It is no longer "literal" and "apocalyptic." Hence there is no longer any question of life after death, of a Kingdom "as a once for all happening."
6. She does realize that this new existentialist outlook is also "time-bound" just as the metaphysical one was . . . or is it the "ultimate Christian framework"?

Toward her solution – distinction between the changing doctrines and "The inner reality of Christianity (which) is apophatic because it does not lie in any deposit of knowledge, thought or historical information, but in the encounter between man and God."

But then what is so special about the Christian message?

How is this new theology supposed to be "open to the Word of God"?

What does she mean, if anything, by this conception?

February 13, 1967

Lent is now under way. Yesterday was the First Sunday. A clear, cold afternoon. I went for a good long walk in the woods and sat for a while by that most lost and hidden pond where there are so many new pines and old fallen ones, and dead trees standing in the water.

Thursday Pee Wee McGruder came to begin drilling for the well but nothing very serious has been done yet. Thirty feet down he seems to have hit a small cave.

Finished notes on "A New Christian Consciousness" – perhaps too long for that Bucke Society newsletter.[6] I don't know what I'll do with it. I simply

---

[6] "The Self of Modern Man and the New Christian Consciousness" appeared in the R. M. Bucke Memorial Society newsletter (April 2, 1967).

cannot write that thing for the *[Saturday Evening] Post*. I think I ought to stop even considering it.

February 14, 1967

Finishing the Ruether ms.

Really a question of getting new bearings. The book is important – at least for me. And explosive.

Where it is important for me is that it forces me to reexamine the whole question of my conversion, and to distinguish in it the action of God's word and the attraction of a sacral and traditional and stable culture. This was important especially in my vocation. Now that the stability of these structures is really shaken – and I have done my own part in shaking them – I have to live really by God's word and by a "true" Christian community (where?) and not cheat by relying on past cultural props which keep me comfortable. The whole Church-world argument in my work has been ambiguous because I bought the idea of a sacred and unworldly Christian culture and set that up against the wicked world. We tried hard to be therefore modern, technological. Technology is certainly able to be even more demonic than, say, the Papacy (see R.'s book) – but the division is too easy.

Anyway, it is much clearer now *where* fidelity is important. Fidelity to God in the Church – in a certain way *against* the Church as established and "worldly" and tied up with what is really dirty and demonic (Spellman's idiotic blessing of the Vietnam War as a "holy" war. That's what "holy" has come to mean all right!). To live in the church with the realization that the Church itself is nevertheless full of sham and lies. Yet in the way she puts it (following [Gabriel] Vahanian), the position is too subtle and too intricate for most men – in the end it seems futile too. Maybe the only answer lies ahead in revolution and diaspora.

The great question is the right interpretation of a sentence like this: "It is in the secular world, the world which applies no faith issues to itself, that the Christian now finds the free, open, provisional existence into which man is released by the good news."

Applies no faith issues to itself? What about all the secular myths and dogmatisms. When I was baptized I had a real sense of liberation from them, and so too I really experienced liberation from them on "leaving the world." True the monastery itself is largely sham, and all the worse because a holy sham: yet it remains nevertheless in many ways more authentic than the degrading and insulting sham outside.

Maybe the hermit life is another kind of defeat – but I certainly feel that here I am relatively more honest and more true than anywhere else and that here I am not being "had" – and though I may be in many ways wrong, I am at least able honestly to try and cope with my wrongness here.

Conception of the Anti-Christ within the established Church – and that we must nevertheless remain faithful to the Church and this very fidelity means saying *No* to the lie that is in the Church. Not canonize its sinfulness. *Non est tam magna peccatrix ut christiana ecclesia* [None is so great a sinner as the Christian church] *(Luther)*.

"The objective historical spirit of the Church was constantly against the Holy Spirit because its innate tendency as a human structure is to banish the gospel and to make endless perpetuation of its own natural culture its primary commitment." *(Ruether)*

February 15, 1967

Reread Faulkner's tirade on privacy. I remember being impressed by it 12 years ago when it came out. Matt Scott passed it to me in some magazine *(Harper's)*. It is a bit inflated – Faulkner's somewhat schizoid grandiloquence – yet it is really moving. All that he says has now become heresy (except as he says – it survives in the popularity of a few "mouth sounds"), but he is right in attacking the total bad faith behind the spurious community and public-spiritedness that just makes money out of vulgarity and scandal. Freedom – freedom to run with a wolf pack strong enough to get away with every injustice and indecency – and to make money by it.

There is no question that Faulkner remains worthy of respect and honor for his individuality, his idiosyncrasy. He is also reproved and hated for it, but the fact is here. Part of his greatness was that he stayed in a small town in Mississippi – and when he was not there remained closed and hermetic – and drunk. But I like his Virginia conferences too.

However, his romantic exaltation of privacy vs. government has to be seen in its context – of a kind of romantic Southern conservatism. The danger of his mythology is precisely that it is convincing, and in many ways better, more coherent, certainly more alive and interesting than Northern liberal mythology. It presents a seemingly plausible case for the contrivance of what is completely finished – and can't get anywhere. The case rests in the fact that this dead thing was capable of generating more esthetic emotion than the ongoing dullness of the big rather stupid and inhuman machine that has taken its place. (The other myth is that the machine is human, delightful, reasonable, loving, and contains all man's heart can desire: it is the fulfillment of every hope including the second coming of Christ.)

February 17, 1967

Faulkner's climacteric – late in 40's, early 50's. His worst writing in essays and speeches. Especially the speeches! Delta Council Speech of 52 – full of every kind of cant and nonsense: i.e. mythological ethic of "old tough fathers" "standing on own feet." Scorning the "alphabetical splatters on the doors of welfare and other bureaus."

The business of taking sides, standing up and being counted, being on the right side – the temptation one has to face above all in his fifties, when he realizes he is on the way out, and tries dishonestly and desperately to *stay:* to leave behind permanent and noble declarations, to prove he was really there. And really a lot of it is shameful, in a way ignoble, yet I feel he was ironic about it nevertheless. He was just not a Mississippi planter, though he pretended to be on occasion.

The stupidity of my own statements and declarations!

February 19, 1967. II Sunday Lent

Snow the other night. Then two cold mornings. Yesterday – one of those blue, bitter mists hanging low, hiding the tree tops, stinging the nose, tightening the throat. Cleared about 9:30. Then a warm day. Some mail and a walk. Panichas liked the Faulkner essay. A letter came from Sidi Abdesalam. "Where are you?" Hoping I am not bogged down in words, my own and those of others. What is best is what is not said. True, my meditation is still slack, but I do not want to grip a futility and tighten on something merely imagined, arbitrarily decided. I do still wait, and listen, try for a more total awareness, more simple, and *no phoney absorption.*

The worst thing is, however, this preoccupation with a *persona*, a constructed professional self. This is the danger. Futility of it. Complete waste. The woods save me and the sun and snow. Lovely songs of birds, melting snowfields yesterday afternoon.

Back to Camus (I have a booklet to write on *The Plague*. Lee Belford at NYU asked for this). Am glad to get to him again out of the kind of romantic murkiness of Faulkner. "The Fire and the Hearth" is not so wonderful.

McGruder has been up and down the hill a few times for desultory work on the well, is down about fifty feet. With the snow, I suppose I won't see him again until I get back from the hospital, where I am to go next Thursday for a bursitis operation.

February 22, 1967

It is the twenty-fifth anniversary of my taking the novice habit. I have been wondering about going back over the years and writing up some of the things I remember. Certainly a great deal has changed. In many ways we have swung around 180 degrees from the attitude that prevailed when I entered. Good or bad? Both. Neither. The old ways had to be changed but I do not know if the new makes sense. I find that I certainly do not believe in the monastic life as I did when I entered here – and when I was more sure I knew what it was. Yet I am much more convinced I am doing more or less what I ought to do, though I don't know why and cannot fully justify it.

Elbow hurting. I go in tomorrow for the operation. Rain and sleet tonight. The kettle boils for some tea before I go to bed. I am not planning to see M. or especially hoping she will try to come down. If she does it will just mix things up and we will not be able to be really alone together in that hospital. I more or less hinted at this last time I wrote – and I think she won't come. Maybe I'll call her.

Box of Faulkner books came yesterday from Random House. I began *The Sound and the Fury*, which I had never read. What a book! One of the greatest ever written by anybody. There is the real Faulkner. The Benjy section is fascinating – and *beautiful*, incest and all. A marvelous piece of work, innocent and strange and immediate and with so many implications for the world of "moral" people.

Monday or Tuesday – finished some notes on Ishi for the *Catholic Worker*.[7] Today, rough draft of a statement on Vietnam (aid to civilian casualties) for CPF [Catholic Peace Fellowship]. Typed ms. of *Faith and Violence* (collection of magazine articles possibly for a paperback) got to me from Bellarmine and I sorted the pages today, wondering why I had made a book of it. Is it worth the trouble? I'll see when I read the ms. after hospital.

---

7 "Ishi: A Meditation," *Catholic Worker* (March 1967).

The sleet is turning into snow. But my crocuses, in their little tight group, have flourished bravely two weeks since Ash Wednesday even in snow and some very cold weather.

March 2, 1967

A real spring day, after some zero weather during which I was in the hospital. Went to St. Joe's a week ago today. It got cold and a wildly blowing snowstorm began in the afternoon – snow driving across the wide open lots down by International Harvester's. Operation for bursitis Friday. Not much to it. Woke up in the recovery room with children crying after tonsillectomies and young nurses gazing down at me like mothers. Was able to take some soup by evening (in fact even ate a couple of mouthfuls of chicken at supper time). Two of the nurses from last year dropped in and I called M. in Cincinnati. Was in the hospital over the weekend, and came back Tuesday. Finished a book on Camus I am reviewing for the *Sewanee [Review]*. I slept in the infirmary Tuesday night but was anxious to get back to the hermitage, so slept here last night and today, apart from a little weariness and a slightly sore and stiff arm – and a dirty bandage – I am feeling OK. Can't type comfortably yet. And am having trouble getting anyone to help me type in the monastery now. So many good people have left.

March 5, 1967. Laetare Sunday

The crocuses multiply and are still there after nearly a month, with some very cold weather. Bees in them yesterday. I walked in the woods. Woods ringing with distant voices – Fr. Matthew is putting up a tent on top of one of the knobs – where he will build a small hermitage (not to live in but for the days of recollection). Another communal hermitage is to be built in the flat shady spot where M. and I and the Fords had our picnic last May. I have loved to walk there all summer – reading Montale, reading René Char, or just praying and thinking. Now that too will be over. I'll find other places. My place on the edge of St. Malachy's field is gone – people will be there for the statues (monument to Jon Daniels). Bro. Giles is working there now, putting in Dogwoods and so on. Anyway I know that all this foolishness of mine must finally end. Though our phone calls were warm and affectionate and M. almost came down Monday (but the hospital called and she had to work). I know that our love affair is really all over and there is no point trying to keep it alive. Certainly I miss her, but one has to face facts. I am humbled and confused by my weakness, my vulnerability, my passion. After all these years, so little sense and so little discipline. Yet I know there was good in it somewhere, nevertheless.

More trouble with Marie Tadié. She has endless capacities for making trouble and it may finally end in the law courts – for she is constantly threatening us with lawyers. [. . .]

Letter from Rosemary Ruether, who is the most fiercely anti-monastic person I know of. Absolute rejection of the monastic idea as unchristian, demonic, etc. Yet allows some place for it in practice as a "service." The main trouble seems to be the supposed claim (which no monk in his right mind would make in that way) that the monk is the only true and radical Christian. But this is a real question since historically the claim has been made and supported and perhaps even to some extent officially accepted (with certain qualifications) by the Church. That laypeople were good Christians in so far as they adopted a quasi-monastic spirituality. On the other hand R.R. seems to be claiming quite aggressively that *she* represents the true radical Christianity and on the basis of her own authenticity she is entitled to reject it – which makes the whole thing a little laughable.

The real problem in practice for me is that Dom J.'s policies make it impossible for all to have adequate contact with these other forms of witness and service, to see what they are doing and to learn from them – and learn some kind of fruitful exchange with them. Emmaus House for instance. R.R. is tied up perhaps with SNCC. Or at any rate with Civil Rights work in the South.

Another question – is there a special kind of hellishness that goes with the very *claim* to be a radical and perfect Christian? History is full of examples – including monastic ones – examples of intolerance, fanaticism, heresy, cruelty, inhumanity, stupidity, love of power, all based on the claim to radical perfection. See the sects after the Reformation. And the same thing in the secular sphere among political radicals.

7:30. Big glaring red sun in the east behind the bare trees. Light rain falling on the roof here out of torn clouds. Everything flying in a warm wind. The pretty squirrels that ran on the lawn last night. The other day the well-diggers got to water down in the limestone.

March 7, 1967

Snow again for the non-feast of St. Thomas Aquinas. Three days of rain turned to snow yesterday when I was in Louisville again to see the doctor. (He looked at the scar of the operation and rebandaged it saying he would take out the stitches next week.) The streets in Louisville and especially the turnpike about 3:30 or 4 were in appalling condition, full of driving wet snow, cars at times traveling helplessly, one out in the middle of a field, one piled up in the middle of two or three others and one even straddling the guard rail – though how it climbed up there I have no way of telling. After Shepherdsville and Bernheim Forest when we got as far south as the first real Knobs, the snow turned to rain and evidently out here it had continued to rain instead of snowing. Floods were beginning all through the Rolling Fork Valley. Got to the monastery and changed in the infirmary and after supper climbed in the cold rain up the flooded path to the hermitage.

Again the big glaring red sun looking over the snow and the ice-heavy trees.

Called M. yesterday and she sounded happy enough, but maybe I confused her with silly oblique statements as if I were trying to say we had really passed into an actively new phase and could no longer be so intimate etc. Of course we both know that, and accept it. But why talk about it or make things worse by analyzing? In the end I found myself riding home sorry and numb and blindly reaching out to cling to her again. Oh M.! I am old enough to be less stupid but I guess it doesn't matter and it always comes back around to that; though I try to be free again, I can't yet and my nature is full of devices for trying to hang on. Perhaps hers too. It doesn't matter. But she really believes in love much more than I do – and is also more realistic about it at the same time – and more hung up on it because after all she has to have a man, she is destined for marriage, and I am not.

March 10, 1967

A warm sunny day. Reading W[illiam] C[arlos] Williams' *Essays* in the early morning – they are very informative. Back in the 30's I was trying for this kind of outlook and could not make it – had to get hung up in some kind of materialism instead. I was simply not ready for Doc Williams then and in any case I don't remember trying to read him. If I had, I would not have understood. I thought I was looking for Studs Lonigan or something (who remembers *that* I wonder?). Fine essay of W.C.W. on Gertrude Stein and what she was at.

Wrote to Cid Corman about the Kusano Shimpei poems in *Origins*, which really impressed me – very alive, simple, sophisticated, honest, humorous. Both Eastern and Western. Universal in that sense.

Walked in the afternoon to the east where I do not usually go – places I had never really explored – up at the far end of our bottom land below Boone's house, and along the new creek which was manufactured by the bulldozers five or six years ago – or more. Then back through the tangle of my own woods in the "unconscious" hollow behind the house which is a real jungle in places. In the evening found a note at supper (in infirm[ary] refectory) from Bro. Martin, who has been in charge of getting my things typed and mimeographed. Said the Rafael Alberti poem on Rome ["Roman Nocturnes"] which I gave him last week was too much, beyond his "limit," scandalous, would "cause ill feeling" – he was very upset by it – and obviously didn't understand it too well. Evidently thought Alberti was in a rage because the whore houses weren't open or something. And Alberti wasn't even mad or mean – just pleasantly joking about Rome. So now I suppose this is my signal that there is to be no more secretarial help here in the monastery for me – saw it coming last week. Of course it is a bit silly to mimeograph so many things and send them all around. Might as well give it up, if people are getting annoyed by it. As to typing – I can still, I hope, get it done outside. I hope Tommie O'Callaghan's friend isn't shocked at the poems I sent out for typing the other day.

Meanwhile more trouble with Marie Tadié too – but that is the abbot's headache more than mine. I have kept saying it would be best to have nothing further to do with her. If he wants to continue with her as agent and translator, that is his affair.

Crocuses still there, wide open in the warm sun.

March 11, 1967

Did I mention anywhere here Zukofsky's two letters.[8] They were beautiful. He liked my revisions (at which I was most happy) and promised to send books. So I sent a scrawl from the hospital saying "send books!" He wrote back with all kinds of family advice about bursitis (the way he and Celia fight back with aspirin and something else, some mystery of Squibb) and

---

8   For Merton's letters to Louis Zukofsky, see *The Courage for Truth*.

then the books came, and they are perfect. I am reading the early "A's" ["*A*" (New York, 1967)] and find them more moving than any other modern poetry I have read. The ground of his verse: a whole musical family. That makes the difference. He never reaches to make anything "musical" or "poetic"; he just touches the words right and they give the right ringing and tone. And all the rest too, the humorous drawing. Ben Shahn.

> The fir trees grew around the nunnery,
> The grille gate almost as high as the firs,
> Two nuns by day, passed in black, like
> > Hooded cameras, as if photographing the world.
>
> > > *[from "A6"]*

And "A-7" a perfectly beautiful Easter figure, says everything, lovely. Easter all through the "A's" or the early ones. And spring. So many resonances and intersections of everything.

March 20, 1967

It is Holy Week. I need a little garret. Sy Freedgood was here three days last week. Wednesday he got in late after cracking up a hired Hertz car in the rain. And I found him bandaged and sinister Thursday morning but able to get around. We went to Lexington, principally to see Victor Hammer, who has been ill but who was cheerful, up and around. Had lunch with Guy Davenport and Gene Meatyard in the Imperial House – good. Saw Gene's photos of me – strange and good. Went to Guy's place for a little – Buster Keaton poster and Zukofsky's little booklet of Job. Got home late and tired and with a cold that began to get bad in the night, which was largely sleepless.

Sy kept telling me I needed to get out and see things and meet people – and he is probably right. But he seemed to think I should put up a big fight for this and I have neither reason nor motive for doing so. Nor would it get anywhere or do the slightest good. The most I would want in any case would be the freedom to travel once in a while to very special places and to see exceptional people. For instance to visit Sidi Abdesalam, or to go to the Zen place in Japan.

A week ago I was in Louisville to get my stitches out – gave some material to Marie Charron to type – met her at lunch at O'Callaghan's. A nice spring day, when daiquiris tasted very good.

———

McGruder came for a while again today and dug a little. He swears he is nearly finished. He has found water (though perhaps much of it is from a cave).

March 21, 1967

Tuesday in Holy Week. A cool, rainy spring night. I like the spirit and intentness of these days. Yesterday finally wrote to [John] Hunt[9] at the *Saturday Evening Post* that I could not see any way to doing the article he asked for. Part of the whole question of what I am trying to do in my situation. It is strictly *my own* situation and other people's answers won't do. Though Sy is right, I ought to be able to get out and speak to people and see with my own eyes and hear with my own ears – and I would like this – [but] it is better to do without it if it would only mean getting caught up in endless nonsense, lectures, conferences, dinners, etc. Who needs all that?

Rosemary R. seems to think *that*, the "world," is what is "real." The world of the body, the senses, etc. turns out after all to be the world of Muzak. It seems to me that here in my woods I have a more authentically bodily and even "worldly" (good sense) existence than they do. Sure, reality is historical – but it is not simply identified with this. An uncomprehended *surface* of history. Who understands it? Certainly salvation is a matter of decision in history: but decision made with a definite *perspective*.

For more people – for me – the idea that life is worth living is identical with the idea "God *is*." "Christ is risen" etc.

But for others, today, the perspective "God exists" equals "life is not worth living." And consequently – to make life worth living one must get rid of God. True, if "God" is the spook that religious make him seem to be – an object – an onlooker – a malicious manipulator and hostile scorekeeper. But of course that is the devil.

If we can agree that when the devil becomes God life is not worth living, then we can perhaps understand ourselves and our situation a little better. But the devil "becomes God" not only in religious shapes – he has more interesting and more up-to-date secular shapes. And apparently our radical Christians do not see the problem.

---

9 See Merton's later letter to John Hunt in *Witness to Freedom*, 329–30.

March 22, 1967

It is true as Sy F. says that I need contact, a broader community than just here. It is true also, as he voluntarily said, that I "live among idiots." Yet that is not the point. My community *is* here, idiots or not, and who is to say I am any less of an idiot than the others? Also I realize very strongly in my own heart that I cannot arrogate to myself the right to travel around and go where I like, to demand the privilege – which would certainly upset others in the community. What matters is for the community as a whole to come to a decision on greater openness and mobility. And until it does – or until I get orders from higher up, there can be no question of demands on my part. And how do I know this need for "openness" is actually of the Spirit? I am sure that *some* of the possible trips and contacts would be. But how could I ever avoid tedious, stupid, deadly organized conferences and academic or ecclesiastical social rituals that are only a mockery? Yesterday afternoon, walking about in my own field and in the hollow where the deer sleep, and where a big covey of quail started up in front of me, I saw again how perfect a situation this is, how real, how far beyond my need of comment or justification. All the noises of all the programs, or of all the critics, do nothing to alter this.

March 23, 1967. Holy Thursday

Last night – remembered the Wednesday of last year's holy week, in the hospital – the rainy evening when M. came to say good night before going to Chicago and when I was so terribly lonely, and lay awake half the night tormented by the gradual realization that we were in love and I did not know how I would live without her. Last night too I lay awake – not long though – thinking of her. Obviously I am still in love in a quiet, deep, hopeless sort of way: but it is no longer passion and it no longer troubles me (or her, I think). I called her last week from Lexington (and Louisville on this Monday). Her father is ill and may have cancer.

The quiet of the long afternoon of Holy Week. Yesterday I burned some brush in the woods near the hermitage. I love the woods, particularly around the hermitage. Know every tree, every animal, every bird. Sense of relatedness to my environment – a luxury I refuse to renounce. Aristocrat, conservative: I don't give a damn. Those city Christians can live in their world of Muzak and CO_2 and think they are in touch with "creation" – nature "humanism"! I admit that it is a reality one must acknowledge but am not so sure it is better for self-confrontation.

The new books that came in from Herder & Herder strike me more and more as superficial, contrived, thrown-together trifles, straining to be "new" and never quite managing to convince. For instance [Raymond J.] Nogar's *Lord of the Absurd* [New York, 1966] seemed to me to be very thin, chatty stuff, and I can't see how so many people (?) are impressed by it: except of course that it accepts evolution – but what is so marvelous about that? It's a hundred years late. And now our "adaptation" of Babin's *Options* (*"Approches de Dieu"?*). An earnest effort to show the Gospel is still news, but news in the same terms as space-flights are news. An exceedingly self-conscious Christianity, a Christian modernity: the Christian always at every moment asking himself how can I be more creative, dynamic etc. How can I see the infinite Christian dimension of my two weeks' vacation.

Good article in a recent *Encounter* on Camus (by M. Cranston). Ping Ferry sent it.

March 31, 1967. Friday – Easter Week
A warm, summery week. Redbuds coming out. And everything is beginning to get green – first faint clouds of green in the woods. Much singing of birds.

Holy Saturday was very warm and quiet and I spent some time in the sun. Easter Night – things went fast. One becomes critical of the liturgy now that everything is presumably addressed to "twentieth-century man." OK – then why so much fuss about a candle? The whole thing makes sense in Latin but it begins to be suspect in English.

Easter Day Fr. Flavian came up and we talked a little and then I went for a walk in the sun, I forget where – a walk. Said the Day Mass alone in the Library Chapel.

Easter Monday morning Pee Wee McGruder came up to finish work on the well digging. They put in the casing after welding it there on the new grass. And then in the afternoon I went for another walk but not far away, only on the dirt road around behind St. Joseph's hill because I had to give a conference. And I gave it on community life, which was perhaps silly. (Palm Sunday I talked on the Easter service from *Sound and Fury* – Dilsey's illumination. Better.)

In the afternoon I found a note that Donald Allchin had come – (a day early). Saw him briefly in the evening – we talked of the Epiphany Philosophers etc.

Tuesday it rained most of the day and we sat in the Gatehouse. Wednesday it was bright and lovely and we went for walks – even to the top of the Lake Knob. He does not take the "Secular City" people seriously yet admits it is the same absurd superficiality that *is* after all serious in America. He said this country, religiously speaking, still seemed to be in the nineteenth century.

Thursday – yesterday – I went to town to the Dr. and gave Donald a ride in to the Baptist Sem[inary]. Pleasant spring day. Sat and said office in the sun on terrace outside the Medical Arts overlooking the Parkway – cars going by quietly and fast, planes sliding down to Standiford field. I had just called M., who was going to the dentist and who is moving into an apartment with another nurse – it is good for her to get away from her mother I think. Says maybe she will take a vacation on Cape Cod in September.

The bursitis operation was not finally successful. The arm still hurts and I cannot do much with it – less than before the operation, – and the X-rays show some calcium still there. I have to rest it. So back to hot water bottles – and also I will get in the sun I guess, but I can't type and there is a lot of work to be done! No matter I'll read more, and write more in notebooks, and build up more material.

Fortunate that Jim Wygal was too busy to have lunch. I was glad. And Fr. John was out of town, and the line at O'Callaghan's was busy and so I changed my mind about going there. Since I had some money I had lunch at the *Old House* (a very good omelette) and the Negro headwaiter was talking about how they are reading Bonhoeffer in their Church study group.

Then went across the street to the Cathedral for a while. A Busy Busy Mass was just ending. Then run run. Parade Parade. The Body of Christ. Up to the tabernacle to get more. Down again. People marching up and marching back. Brusk. Tense. Business-like. And one still gets the impression of duty done more than anything else (yet it is *not* duty and they obviously mean the best). In other words, as "sign" it is still not there, and what happens is inside the people. Could be worse. What happens? Conditions are realized and a job is done. Then most everyone marched out – a few other ones stayed to pray quietly. There is a new bishop. The place looked as if it had been painted. I have not been there in quite a time.

———

Then to buy paperbacks, and read and some science fiction – why I don't know. Probably because I imagine I need to read some science fiction precisely because I haven't done so in twenty-five years. And it is an important literary form I guess.

Beer at the cooler in the hallway behind the liquor store in the Heyburn Building. People from the building. The amiable blonde girl who brought us all beers "just because she wanted to do it." Very nice.

I got home in the evening with my arm hurting and carrying packages. So intent on getting the packages to the hermitage that I did not notice the well-rig was gone. Did not realize its absence until dawn this morning. I could not believe it had not been there the evening before. Did Pee Wee McG. steal it away in the middle of the night? Impossible! Now they have to put in a pump and a track and a sink and a tap and maybe I'll have water. Because carrying gallon bottles of water up from the monastery is no help to bursitis and I think I am beginning to get it in my remaining good arm.

Hunt wrote from the *Post* that they want to see [Thomas P.] McDonnell's interview.

Today is the anniversary of the day I first saw M. in the hospital. March 31 last year was Wednesday in Passion Week. That day she was assigned, as student nurse, to take special care of me, change the dressings on my hip etc. She came in and made a little speech about how I was "her patient" and I little realized how true that would turn out to be. I remember those days when we talked and laughed and got on so well that in a week we were in love. And I can't find it in me to regret that part of it. Certainly I made mistakes and we could have made plenty of worse mistakes. But the fact remains that we love and understand each other and still in some sense need each other, though obviously it is all over.

April 1, 1967

The sun is high on a lovely green spring day.

Long-legged shadows of chairs on the porch.

Doing some notes on Camus' *Plague* – (background) for the booklet I am to write this summer. Left arm painful – I wonder how much typing I am going to be able to do. It is possible I may get a tape recorder and may perhaps learn to work with that – but I cannot see the point of just reading into it: a new kind of work altogether? Crazy tape – mosaics? Tape notebooks. Singing, swearing? Is it providential that I have sore bones? A liberation from type and ink? (Can do some drawings too perhaps.)

The life of a solitary is in a certain sense without limits. All one needs is to know how to turn one's space ship in a certain direction and blast off again: yet the very absence of obstacles can become the biggest of all limitations.

The tinkle of water in the well (as I sat in the moonlight on the porch trying to meditate). Water is dripping from one of the small caves into the deeper hole.

John Slate is supposed to be coming out next week to help me make my (literary estate) will. I don't yet have my ideas all in order about this. So much of the stuff to be left is junk – material to be kept perhaps but *not* published.

April 6, 1967

Too much visiting. It has been hot. The dogwoods are coming out. The trees are green ahead of time. Last evening driving with Slate down Eastern Parkway and seeing the thermometer say 84 near Howard Johnson's at the corner of Preston. We had been to Bellarmine, where I was recognized by too many people and had to sign autographs. Went to the airport taking Fr. John and Pat Welsh (who takes care of the M[erton] room) and had a good supper at the Luau Room. Stopped on the way to St. Joe's for a letter (which I did not get – one I wrote to Eshleman returned). At the Luau room I was happy – and was in a position to watch the planes this time but there were few. Argued with Slate about God, Vietnam, and everything else. The place where M. and I were, where we sat on the grass all alone, has become a parking lot and was full of cars. Sense of desolation and loss. Coming back in the dark got home very late, worried about S. who shouldn't drink and did. (And at one point roared down the dark empty turnpike at around 100 m.p.h.) However, I have some hope that the estate business will finally get settled in a way acceptable to everyone. One bright spot – at St. Joe's I ran up to 2E where I had the back operation and said hello to a couple of the nurses – R. and T. (who was a student with M.) and sad-eyed little Mrs. L., whose name haunted me one sweaty, sleepless night the water ran in the walls.

On Saturday and Sunday Winston King was here from Vanderbilt. Had some good information about Zen people – [Sen 'ichi] Hisamatsu, [Keiji] Nishitani, and Masao Abe etc. All of whom I greatly respect. My *Mystics and Z[en] M[asters]* came yesterday morning. With a photo on the back cover, which makes me mad. We need rain – only a little black water left in my buckets. The well is good for plenty of water but I still can't get at it as there is no pump etc. Haven't had time to read much of anything.

April 7, 1967. On being – "Hesychast"

Certainly there are strong "hesychast"[10] tendencies in me. Last evening, relieved and quiet, alone again with the pines after all the talking, I certainly have to recognize the fact that when I am talking a lot and running around here and there I am simply not *myself*, and act and speak in a way which is not true to myself and to my inner grace. On the other hand I can no longer make quiet an absolute, and I try as far as possible to be free and unconcerned everywhere (said my office riding on the turnpike not disturbed by Slate having the car radio on – psalms I like better [than] rock n roll).

The trouble is that I tried to feel guilty of my "*hesychia*" and probably this makes some sense too. A mere question is not good enough. I do react too much to the attack of these activists upon everything "contemplative" and I do see that the appetite for withdrawal and quiet in the monastery (the appetite of the Abbot and many monks – just not wanting to be disturbed) is equivocal. What I really do need is the inner freedom that is tranquil and unconcerned in everything – and I certainly have it more than ever, in a way. Yet I am careless, untrue to myself, undisciplined, free with the wrong kind of freedom, drink and talk too much, use bad language too much, etc.

So I doubt too much. I value silence and prayer and then worry whether I ought not also to conciliate "the world" with some of its own gestures. Foolish statement I sent to St. Louis, on priests marrying. Sure I think they ought to be able to marry if they want to. But why do *I* have to make noise about it? Probably means getting into a very stupid argument.

Hausherr brings out the fact that Athonite Hesychasm precisely bears on solitude and anachoresis as *essential* for inner quiet: that the belief that one can preserve *hesychia* in crowds and action is reproved.

---

[10] Hesychasm names the practice of inner stillness and quiet and also refers to the use of the "Jesus Prayer."

Question – of "monotrophy" – having one goal, one tendency – to "perfect love for God." Problem is not in the goal, but in the way of conceiving the *means*, the nature of the pursuit, one's concept of one's relation to the goal. A prioristic and abstract ascesis based on idea of God as an "object to be attained" is useless today. The unity and "monotrophy" have to be seen as dialectical, in movement, in "becoming." And emerging into a state of oneness. That is the "ground" of all becoming. No – that expression does not quite work. Not a willed and forced security based on stubborn insistence upon one predetermined idea, one arbitrary course of action which is conceived to be uniquely and everywhere *Right* – in black capitals.

April 8, 1967

"They hope, by means of the dreams they keep telling each other, to make my people forget my name just as their fathers forgot my name in favor of Baal." *Jerem.* 23:27

Cooler last night. I was happy to have a quiet day yesterday and get a little work done. The review of Camus for *Sewanee Review* is about half finished (first draft). The valley is as beautiful as it can be in spring. Redbuds still blooming and Dogwoods coming out into full bloom like constellations in the green gloom of pines.

Hesychasm again. A letter came from Archbishop Helder Camara full of exhortations to get up and go – mainly after reading Nhat Hanh's book (and he praised *Fide e Violenza*). Wants me to "encourage" Maritain not to be pessimistic and frightened. To write to the Pope. To write to Cardinal Maurice Roy:

"Aidez-le à comprendre qu'on n'a pas le droit de transformer dans un bluff les plus belles espérances de l'heure actuelle." ["Help him to understand that one does not have the right to change into a bluff the most beautiful hopes of the present moment."]

(I don't know what Roy has done – or what the "hope" is). And can [Robert] Hutchins be persuaded to invite me to the 2nd *Pacem in Terris* conference? He already has – not officially but I know they want me to come. But there is no point in bringing the matter up. Would never get permission and would only cause a storm.

Can I say I really "would like" to go? No. I would be scared of simply making a fool of myself and accomplishing nothing. There is no question that my twenty-five years here have for better or worse, left me essentially outside the age of traveling by jet to conferences everywhere. I just do not belong any more in that world. Maybe I should belong in it – maybe I have made a mistake. I don't know. But the fact is that I belong in these woods.

In so far as my own doubts and conflicts get into the game, it is foolish to pass judgment on a kind of life that is simply not for me, or to seem to pass judgment. And I certainly don't mean to condemn everything in sight. I watch the jets go over my trees. They are pretty. I admire Dan Berrigan for his perfect acclimatization in all this (his seven fables in the new *Critic* are superb). What I do not accept is this world's particular evaluation of itself.

Probably the best thing to do is to avoid all noises about it and also to avoid any attempt to get myself sent out somehow, somewhere, just because I may happen to feel uneasy about not belonging, or even guilty.

Carleton Smith was here (before Slate – on the day Bro. John was buried – Tuesday) and I was talking about Card[inal Franz] Koenig coming to the country, and about Maritain etc. etc. And going places. I seem to get this from every side now (Sy Freedgood especially. As I expected, he had pumped Slate full of propaganda about getting me out).

Last night I dreamed of M. Today, again, I realize how confused I have been – not just because of her but in general because of my slackness, my imprudence, my inconsistency, my frivolity. I suppose also my laziness. It is certainly true that a great deal has gone wrong in my life. Yet I do not know precisely how or where, and I can hardly pin it on any one symptom. My falling in love so badly was not a cause but an effect, and I think really it all comes from roots that had simply lain dormant since I entered the monastery. So too in my writing, my persistent desire to be somebody, which is really so stupid. I know I don't really need it or want it, and yet I keep going after it. Not that I should stop writing or publishing – but I should not let myself be flattered and cajoled into the business, letting myself be used, making statements and declarations, "being there," "appearing." Pictures appear (without any desire of mine, to tell the truth) and I am ashamed of myself.

At the root – an attraction for this kind of publicity nevertheless. Or rather, I would like to be known, loved, admired, and yet *not* in this cheap and silly way. But is there any other way? In my case, if I were more serious about remaining unknown I would not be so quick to accept what eventually shames me.

April 9, 1967. Good Shepherd Sunday

Hesychia: but there was nothing idyllic about the golden age of Egyptian monasticism. Violence, turbulence, confusion in the crisis at the end of the fourth century. Largely because Theophilus of Alexandria decided to *use* the monks in the political struggle: against Pelagianism, against the more primitive up-river Copts, against Constantinople and then against the Origenists he had formerly favored.

Riots of monks in Nitria and Scete as well as in Alexandria.

Departures of large groups of monks for Palestine and Constantinople (the Tall Brothers with 300 followers).

Finally, devastation by barbarians (407–408).

Pessimism – from lack of silence (in my own life). Having to talk about the world (or thinking I have to) I put myself in a relationship to it which is false – the relationship of one called upon to judge it, which I am not. And since I feel it to be false, I feel my footing is unsteady. But why judge? Yes, the times are perhaps terrible (though for me they are not so terrible. I have it good). But do I believe "in silence and hope shall your thoughts be"? Well, "the world" does not believe it. That is not my business. Do I have to convince everybody? No. But if I am myself a more hopeful person I can be of more service to them than I can by reminding them that they are (we are) in a mess.

All my talk, all my sass, all my running around are not a "freedom of the spirit," but just damned laxity and irresponsibility. And I have to face it, because again and again the burning and embarrassment of conscience are intolerable. True the other evening with Slate at Bellarmine etc. – was something I decided against my own wishes because it was necessary for him to see the collection at B. – how it was kept etc. As for the Luau room, that was my idea and perhaps a bit too far out. The rest – was just a question of trying to get Slate home once he had started drinking. At least I rejected the idea of dropping in on the Willetts. That is a place where I don't belong, even though Thompson and Virginia are good lovable people.

Quiet collected photo of Suzuki standing around some laurels. Winston King brought it the other day. It is a comforting presence on the table before me.

———

Grey morning, but not yet rain and I need it. So short of water that I can't afford to use my coffee percolator (as I would need twice as much water for dish washing if I had to clean that). Outside there is multiflora rose hedge which is now huge – in places seven or eight feet tall. All beautiful with new green foliage and full of nesting birds.

April 10, 1967

Rain finally. After a few flashes of lightening over the NW. It came during meditation.

Yesterday I had a lovely hesychastic afternoon! Walked up and around by the lake, past the Derby Day picnic place. I am able to go by there now without being all torn up by emotion. Then quietly around under the pines and up to that hidden pond with all the pines around it, and a little open patch of dry shale. There I took my shirt off and got the warm sun on my back and looked at the pine tops and the sunny clouds. What a change since the last time I sat there, in May last year (on May 16). That Sunday [. . .] I was literally shaken and disturbed – knowing clearly that I was all wrong, that I was going against everything that made sense in my life, going against all that was true and authentic in my vocation, going against the grace and love of God. Struggling desperately in my heart and knowing I was help-less, that things were moving in a certain direction and I had gone too far to turn back. After that, only the grace of God saved us from a really terrible mess. It was fortunate that we were simply not able to see each other when we wanted to. And finally it *was* a good thing that we were stopped alto-gether, though it ought to have been done differently.

Anyway, yesterday was utterly different. Once again the old freedom, the peace of being without care, of not being at odds with the real sense of my own existence and with God's grace to me. Far better and deeper than any consolation of eros. A sense of stability and substantiality – of *not* being de-ceived. Though I know there was much good in our love, I also see clearly how deceptive it was and how it made me continually lie to myself. How we both loved each other and lied to each other at the same time. How difficult it must be to keep going in *truth* in a marriage. Heroic! For me the other truth is better: the truth of simply getting along without eros and resting in silence with "what is." The deep inner sustaining power of silence. When I taste this again, so surely, after so long, I know what it means to repent of my infidelity and foolishness: yet at the same time I do not try to build up again anything that was properly torn down. It was good that I (we) went through the storm: it was the only way to learn a truth that was otherwise inaccessible.

Wrote to Carleton Smith yesterday. Letter last week from Meg Randall in Mexico about Cuba – and poems from Cuba. She is happy about the people there and I believe her: at least they are free from the deadly helplessness of life under a completely static and corrupt system that sought only to keep people down in order that a few crooks might make a bit of money.

April 15, 1967

A lovely day. Everything is two or three weeks ahead this year. The trees are almost in leaf. The redbuds are gone, the dogwoods are going. Bright sun. Bright, pure, little clouds. Deep blue sky. I was going to do some work on the "Rite for Ejection of Lepers," but took off to the woods instead – same place – by the hidden pond. All the old desires, the deep ones, the ones that are truly mine, come back now. Desire of silence, peace, depth, light. I see I have been foolish to let myself be so influenced by the current trends, though they perhaps have their point. On the other hand I know where my roots really are – in the mystical tradition, not in the active and anxious secular city business. Not that I don't have any obligation to society. Etc. But – [am] reading Mircea Eliade and a book on Ibn al Arabi, and the *Book of the Poor in Spirit* again. This evening on the porch I sang the alleluias and Introit of to-morrow (Latin) Mass (which won't be sung in community). III Sunday after Easter. *Modicum* again! The one that moves me so deeply.

Big Peace demonstration today, but demonstrations do no good. Dan Berrigan is in a kind of crisis with his Superiors again – over the question of aid to War victims in both North and South Vietnam. Is to be sent on a symbolic visit to N.V. and his Superiors won't allow it. He will probably go anyway. And then?

Up by the lake I ran into Raymond with a carload of nuns – who turned out to be from Sister K.'s community at Newport. I wrote a note to her. The light and weather and foliage etc. at the lake was *exactly* as it was on Derby Day last year. I could almost see M. This was painful for a while but I am getting so I resist it. It is useless. All I can do is pray for her and go about my business, my real business. So I stripped off my shirt and got the sun on my back and arm and watched the tadpoles in the brown water and the clouds

beyond the tall pines – and sought what I seek. A magazine of the psyche-
delic people got to me by devious ways. Very interesting: they are all caught
up in it as I was when I was a novice. But they are caught up in it. And probably much more than we monks are. Socially the prospect is discouraging.
On the one hand gangsters exploiting the appetite for vision and on the
other laws made against the drugs so that in the end the kids who turn on
will be preyed on both by gangsters and police. I feel very sorry for them.

The Gullicks were here Tuesday (from Oxford). I was glad to meet them
and talk about Etta's ms. on Benet of Canfield (which is an ungainly thing
but good material). They were only here a day. I kept the rest of the week
free. Finished the Camus review for the *Sewanee*. It is being typed. Heard
from Ed Rice today. Had a nice letter from Rosemary yesterday – about
going to the Episcopalian parish etc. She is R.C., a lot of new things happening: She had a good article on divorce in a recent *Commonweal*.

Slate's wallet (which he had lost) was found in the Hertz car in Louisville.
Very strange. A good thing he lost it because if he had had it, he would have
gone on a long drunk in Bardstown after leaving me off at the Abbey. We
both looked in the car. The [indecipherable] must have shoved it under one
of the seats.

John Pauker will exhibit some of my drawings in Washington. He is starting up the *Lugano Review* again, with Jim Fitzsimmons apparently. A good
magazine but it went bankrupt. I wrote to Anne Freedgood the other day
about possibly publishing some of Kusano Shimpei in this country. (Whom
I read at the height of the frog season a month or so ago – appropriately.)

McDonnell's interview – the final draft – was sent down to me this week and
I returned it. I think it's good – it is going to *Motive* [October, 1967]. Not to
the *Pax!*

April 16, 1967. III Sunday after Easter

Jubilate Deo! [Rejoice in God!] Clean green hills, lovely freshness of the
morning, long spearhead of hard, consistent cirrus clouds pressing into the
east where the sun is partly hidden. Bell-like resonance of the calves' lowing
down at the barn. O my sweet valley! Gregorian comes naturally out of this
earth and this spring. Yet I see the time has come to live without it (except

such as I myself may sing). But they do not yet have a music for the cities, for the corporations.

To fight the corporate mind.

To sharpen the meaning and push of revolt even though it is far out of sight and perhaps has no point. At least this is *less* part of the same general fabric of alienation and consent than the long-haired movements (with which I nevertheless sympathize).

The feminization of articulate revolt – its cheerfulness, its sweetness, its despair (among all the kids who take drugs).

Another bright hot afternoon. Sat in a field, read some Eliade, gave conferences – and at Supper Fr. Augustine handed me an illustrated booklet on the apparitions at Garabandal in the Basque country of Spain. Pictures of the little girls looking really sweet in ecstasy – and one, Maria Cruz, obviously not turned on like the others. (She has since denied that she saw anything.) Message – disappointed everyone. (Do penance!) After 1963 Conchita [Gonzales] was the only one who kept getting visions and revelations (the biggest and most determined girl) and she got a few "specials," one of which is a conservative pronouncement on priests and eucharist – a little anti–Vatican II, maybe! This one was in 1965 and I guess by that time she had been pretty thoroughly got at by the clergy. The first ecstasies may well have been quite genuine. Two things yet to come: a "big warning" and a "big miracle." Meanwhile all the girls except Cruz are tucked away in convents, and Conchita has been to Rome to talk it all over with the Holy Office, and be photographed in the Colosseum with her pastor and Princess Cécile de Bourbon, who is a real sweetheart. So much for the pictures. But in my heart there is a deep longing for the first part of it at least to have been real, especially because of the angels and all the laughing that went on – and those kids so simply crazy with joy. I need to know Mary is still close to us and need her to be very close to me here, always. My heart breaks with need of vision and help for the world.

April 19, 1967
"The prophet who prophesies peace can only be recognized as one truly sent by Yahweh when his word comes true." *(Jeremiah 28:9)*

Especially when Pres. Johnson [and] the "prophets" announce peace and escalate the war. Johnson apparently not sent by Yahweh ([Francis] Cardinal Spellman to the contrary).

The sense that this country is obsessed, alienated, driven by its own mythical destruction, and that my first duty to the country and the people is to extricate myself from the general obsession and contribute nothing to it. But people like [Norman] Mailer, intelligent as their intuitions may be, do not completely extricate themselves (are not born) and do contribute to the chaotic suffering. Is it a birth? Is this country really trying to bring something forth? I can still believe that it is. But what? Perhaps a monster? I still have hopes it will be something new and alive and basically good. Where the good may come from is perhaps where evil is feared. The streets. The ghettoes. But that too is only part of the obsession. (Or is one obsessed by the very fact of believing, one ought to be totally outside the obsession and utterly delivered?)

[Pierre] Dommergues' book [*Saul Bellow* (Paris, 1967)] came yesterday from Paris. Very interesting. I like the mosaic technique. Lots of information. I still have not read Bellow.

Naomi Burton coming today. I hope we don't fight over anything. Maybe since she has been living in Maine she is different – perhaps more wound up in some other way. But I love her, and she cares for me, with that damned mothering care.

Dan Walsh preparing for his ordination. Archbishop John Floersh on his own initiative decided this, got all the necessary dispensations (from seminary, interstices etc. etc.) and the ordination is to be at St. Thomas' Seminary Pentecost Sunday. Dan is dazed. Everyone is astounded.

April 21, 1967. St. Anselm

Heavy rain in the night. A woodthrush singing in the rainy woods at early morning. Naomi Burton has been here since Wednesday the 19th. Two fine days. Wednesday and Thursday. Yesterday we had a picnic at the lake with Fr. John Loftus, Ron Seitz and Tommie O'Callaghan. Brilliant sun and I got my head sunburned, took a bunch of probably useless pictures on Naomi's Nikon. Fr. John's involved in the demonstrations over open housing in Louisville and the situation there is rather hot, though I have not seen the papers. Ron Seitz was stoned in a demonstration (stoned: i.e. hard stones thrown at him – largely by Bellarmine students).

Today I had to go to Dr. Lucas and Naomi drove me. Very heavy rain on and off all day. Found Lucas etc. had moved out of the Fincastle Building to the new South Medical Tower and a bit of the new building was not yet fully finished.

I called M. from the Brown Hotel – and talked to her in her new apartment where she lives with another nurse. Again things have moved on inexorably. We tend to talk as if it were still the same but of course it is not – and I sense an air of confusion at her end, not without self-contradiction. The important thing, however, is that her fiancé is back, and she has still not decided what to do about the engagement. The impression she gave was that she would go on with it. Though she does not exactly love him she "can make him happy," but I told her that talk like that did not really make sense – I doubt if she can really mean it that way. And she added that she was a "sort of a masochist," which made it all the worse. It was all a bit disturbing and I suppose it was meant to be – deliberately ambiguous. I don't know if she can really seriously mean to marry or if she has real authentic motives for doing so, but at the same time I see that I really cannot contribute anything but more confusion and I'd better keep out of the picture. So once more another inexorable step has to be taken and I must make sure it is ended. It is. But it must be more definitely so. Yet I haven't the courage to face the idea of never calling her again. I am certainly set on not going to any lengths to see her.

I see again that real loneliness is all that is left for me and I must fully accept it. Nothing else will do. I am tired of having visitors. Talking just wears me out and seems utterly pointless, though with Naomi there was business to be settled etc. She suggested a book on Sufism and that is all right with me.

April 22, 1967

Evening. A full moon rising over the sharply outlined valley. Everything cool, green and very clear. I should have gone out for a long walk this afternoon but I had to write letters and then I have acquired a tape recorder and had to fool with it a little to make sure I know how to work it. It is a very fine machine and I am abashed by it. I take back some of the things I have said about technology.

I have made this day a sort of perplexed celebration – said mass for M. and her fiancé and honestly hope they will get back in love again, in fact by now they probably are. And that they will be happy in marriage some day soon . . . and so on. I am sure there is no real problem. At least I tell myself so. M. may want to hold on to me sentimentally in some way but I am convinced that the real love is more or less over between us, though we shall always be fond of each other I am sure.

So in a way it is a liberation day – and I have made up my mind to be what I am supposed to be. (Finally!)

Actually it is a most happy evening – could not be more perfect. I have some bourbon (Tommie O'Callaghan brought some) and am playing an ancient [Django] Reinhardt record that brings back the thirties. (Regression?) Perhaps in a little while I shall go out and stroll around under the trees. And try to tell myself that I am not really sad at all.

April 24, 1967

The other night I ended by sitting up late and making all kinds of naive experiments with tape. I think I am getting on to it and that it has real possibilities if handled with care. One good thing about it: it may cool down my emphatic attitudes. I will do less underlining, do not have to try to be so definite, so decisive, a kind of freedom can come from being nicely relaxed, cool and open. I have this interiorly and can be this way when not speaking and not thinking. Important to be that way while speaking and thinking, why so urgent?

My urgent vocabulary. "MUST. Must make sure. Definitely. Certainly. Nothing but. Have to. Had to. Proven. My duty. In a crisis. Won't allow. Exactly. Discouraging. New things happening. Encouraging. I sang. Moves me deeply. Utterly different. Against. Devastation. The times are trouble. I was shaken. We were stopped. A good thing. Ought to have been done differently. You realize of course. Business to be settled."

Try the urgent vocabulary, the non-words, on tape. (The too loaded words that are non-words because they insist.) Disturbing. False. Never again. First time in my life. Not fully warranted. Restless. The guarantees. How do you know?

Yesterday, colder, grey in the afternoon, the vast long field to the South bought from what's his name, Webb Bowling ("You know me, Father, I'm Webb Bowling!"). Walked along the hedge next to Boone's for a while and turned back lest I found myself down on the highway. Sat on a cinder block up against the old farrowing house and realized that I had hit a kind of suckhole of despair. Utter sadness, loneliness, hopelessness, no prospect of any human joy left. Drained of any trust in the love that has held me up. The silly interior singing that was after all a kind of comforting context, a locus, a place to live in, an atmosphere. Blank. Went into a kind of stupid daze. Got up again and walked, feeling better. Dark sky in the SW, with peculiar shark-shaped low clouds underneath the general black. Flying Saucers. A big fishbone missile of cloud pointing down to Charlie O'Brien's pasture, and the hills behind Athertonville Distillery, that promise in the snow – November. Depre[ssion]. Sadness. I will at least keep praying for her to be happy. I wandered around the front of the Cross hill to the Dehy[drator]. Read a little Eliade on the coincidence of opposites. Came back. Office. Conference on Sufism.

Well I think the tape will shake things up a bit. Read a bit of [Samuel] Beckett on tape and played it back – it was illuminating and helpful. Beautiful simplicity in drabness.

April 26, 1967

The other day in Louisville I saw the headlines "U.S. planes bomb Haiphong" – but did not pick up a paper at the stands on the street for the papers were soaked in rain – and didn't get time to go in to the Brown for one (forgot when I was actually there calling M.). Now I hear that a U.S. plane was shot down over China. I haven't read about it all yet, but I have an uneasy feeling that things are getting close to a big war – as if the V.N. one were not already monstrous in terms of killing, but everything indicates that Johnson and the establishment are not averse to a big war in China. Probably the computers are telling them they need this war to go on and get bigger and that it can be fought without serious danger to the U.S. – on the contrary that it will be very profitable. Of course a lot of Americans will be killed, but then that will be a good way to get rid of a lot of unpleasant characters, Negroes, peaceniks, and those who disagree with the current philosophy. A big war will also get patriotism steamed up and dissent will not be tolerated any more. The latent fascism of many Americans can be encouraged etc. The prospect is not consoling. Once again – I don't know what to do. The kind of protest that is available seems to be plainly useless. Revolutionary violence cannot get anywhere beyond ghetto rioting. Perhaps in a while the Negroes may go in for more massive sabotage, or something, but what will it accomplish beyond a tightening of police repression? And a certain disruption of the comfortable life on streets.

The V.N. war has made this country richer than it ever was before. It is keeping the economy up, preventing a recession, prolonging the longest period of expansion we have ever known.

Corruption in V.N. itself is fabulous (bad enough in U.S.), military and civilians in V.N. are making thousands of dollars on black market etc.

One thing is certain: the country as a whole is making piles of money out of this war – business, labor, all are in it. What real motive do people have for wanting peace? They naturally are not too interested in preventing a war from escalating even to "world war" scale if it remains in Asia and it might well do so – without becoming a nuclear war.

The brutal truth is that the people of America by and large have *no real objection* even to a war with China as long as things go on as they are here now. Of course there is a lot of dissent on the part of a large minority and not everyone has an easy conscience even among the majority. But money is coming in and as long as it keeps coming . . .

I face the fact that I am living in an immoral, blind, even in some sense criminal society which is hypocritical, bloated, self-righteous, and unable to see its true condition – by and large the people are "nice" as long as they are not disturbed in their comfortable and complacent lives. They cannot see the price of their "respectability." And I am part of it and I don't know what to do about it – apart from symbolic and futile gestures.

The marches and riots stopped in Louisville the other day, Dan tells me.

Denis Goulet – from the U. of Indiana – was here yesterday. A lovely young guy with a lot of good ideas – interested in development of 3rd world and the sociological-religious problems involved. But has a scientific capacity to deal with these things on a professional level. I envy him – he gets all over the place – got a doctorate in Brazil, married a Brazilian girl, involved in a cooperative in Patagonia, lived a while at the fraternity of the Little Brothers in the desert – at – El Abiod, worked in Algeria, Lebanon (?), Bolivia, stayed with some Indians in the Amazon jungle. The world of the 60's is a pretty lively one for people who can get money from universities and foundations etc. to go wherever they please. Keenly feel my own isolation and "imprisonment" – but it is what I have to accept and work with. Anyway Goulet is an interesting and worth while person, not a square, not contaminated by his professional milieu, honest, open, with ideas of his own and an intelligible speech.

Bursitis bad – or noticeable anyway. Rectal trouble bad. Tired of visits. Want to get work done. Tired. Writing some verse. A newspaper story on the illnesses etc. of Carson McCullers (clipping under my napkin the other day) made me realize my own troubles are insignificant.

April 28, 1967

I am reading the *Autobiography of Malcolm X*, which is an impressive book. Took it out into the sun in the wood's edge this afternoon after writing one or two necessary letters. Yesterday I was in Louisville again – this time to see Dr. Roser. Got one audiogram and found that whatever is causing my colon trouble it does not have its sources in a sinus infection as Dr. Lucas thought. Have to see an allergist next week. Tedious and time-consuming – but the implications of my current trouble makes it necessary.

In the public library, skimmed through some poems of Robert Duncan, whom I like, and looked at a couple of books by Paul Bowles. Nothing much in the news. Sob story of Johnson: he would gladly stop all the killing if only the wicked aggressive North Vietnamese would agree to negotiate.

First time I have been to town in a year without even trying to call M. In fact barely even gave it a thought.

May 3, 1967

May came in with floods of rain, night and day, especially in the night. Monday May 1. Talked in the afternoon with Jan Yungblut from Atlanta and Dr. Young from Anderson, S.C. Jan Y., a Quaker-friend of M. Luther King, from whom he brought messages – exceedingly deferent but very nice. We discussed his ms. on mysticism which has good things in it. Will have to try to write him something on the Christological problems it raises but that is a subject I am shy of (as with Rosemary in her letters).

Reading [Frantz] Fanon (*The Wretched of the Earth* [New York, 1963]), Malcolm X and beginning *Soul [on Ice* by Eldridge Cleaver (New York, 1967)], all in view of an essay on war for a symposium edited by someone at Drexel.

Yesterday had to go (late afternoon) to an allergist in St. Matthew's. Spoke for a few minutes again with J. Yungblut and now also with his wife. June also is staying in Bardstown while she is here. She is doing a dissertation on [Samuel] Beckett, working under Cleanth Brooks, and I found her very interesting and likeable.

Dr. Tom Jerry Smith – the little office at St. Matthew's – the mysteries of allergies expounded – injections in the arm – the rigorous milk-free diet (disconcerting) – TOE whatever that is – fungus – fermentation – "allergic state." – The cow. I do not succeed in pulling it all together. Avoided bread at breakfast. Fortunately had some rye crackers apparently with no trace of milk in them. I hope.

May 4, 1967. Ascension Day

Reading Fanon – and in contrast – stuff about Hippies in S.F. and an illuminating critique of Salinger by Mary McCarthy (in Dommergues). Hate stuff, Love stuff, all marketable, all advertised, all publicized, all disturbing to the consumer who lives in his suburb, and all of it – I wonder if it means anything? (Except Fanon who talks out of another world not of surfeit and drugs but of hunger and desperation.) Now synthetic visions which are supposed to be real. Not orthodoxies and anti-orthodoxies and visions of life which one is supposed to purchase this morning. Attack on [Lewis] Mumford in *NY Times* because he is not [Marshall] McLuhan. Names. You have to know Names. The Grateful Dead and the Quicksilver Messenger (whom I can't find in the Schwann catalogue). My own kind of surfeit with all this. *Yet not* knowing it is no advantage. Nor is knowing it. Nor is judging whether or not it means anything. Maybe it does. Does one ask if there is a "lesson" in it? Or if one is seeing things? One needs a whole new language – and after that one can also go off and talk about not this but something else.

The whole damn business is a fabrication.

Evening. This afternoon – wrote something for the Dahlberg Festschrift, to send to Jonathan Williams at Aspen tomorrow.

Then went out for a walk in the woods.

Contrast with Ascension Day last year – weather very much the same, bright, not too hot. Last year that ecstatic afternoon in the woods with M. – almost unbelievable. I kept thinking of it. But I don't regret that today was entirely different! Peace, silence, freedom of heart, no care, quiet joy. Last year – there was joy and turbulence and trouble which turned to confusion and a deeply disturbed heart because I knew I was wrong and was going against everything I lived for. Today I looked up at the tall treetops and the high clouds and listened to the silence – and was very glad indeed to be alone! What idiocy I got into last year!

Still I wonder how she is, and what is developing in her life. I worry a little about her.

May 6, 1967

"Le matin du 16 avril, le docteur Bernard Rieux sortit de son cabinet et butta sur un rat mort, au milieu du palier. Sur le moment, il écarta la bête sans y prendre garde et descendit l'escalier. Mais, arrivé dans la rue, la pensée lui vint que ce rat n'était pas à sa place. . . ." ["When leaving his surgery on the morning of April 16, Dr. Bernard Rieux felt something soft under his foot. It was a dead rat lying in the middle of the landing. On the spur of the moment he kicked it to one side and, without giving it a further thought, continued on his way downstairs. Only when he was stepping out into the street did it occur to him that a dead rat had no business to be on his landing. . . ."][11]

Very curious. This morning I begin my work on Camus' *Plague* and last evening coming up from the monastery I found a dead mouse on my doorstep. I tried to figure out what had killed it, but there was no indication, it was just dead.

A white-footed mouse.

This morning severe colic though I have carefully followed the allergist's strict milk-free diet.

A dead mouse on the doorstep. Very curious.

"On the morning of the 16th of April Dr. Bernard Rieux . . ."

"Le lendemain, 17 avril, à huit heures, le concierge arrêta le docteur au passage et accusa des mauvais plaisants d'avoir déposé trois rats morts au milieu du couloir." ["Next day, April 17, at eight o'clock the concierge buttonholed the doctor as he was going out. Some young scallywags, he said, had dumped three dead rats in the hall."]

Today is Derby Day, a day of pleasantries. To begin with, rain threatens. And then in Louisville the Negroes have threatened to disrupt the horse race (for the edification of the white race). Today is Derby Day, a day of pleasantries.

Several times this spring I have said the "Mass in Time of Pestilence," which I feel to be quite appropriate for our age.

Rain is now falling.

Yesterday I finished the *Autobiography of Malcolm X.*

---

[11] English translations of Albert Camus's *The Plague,* here and below, are from Stuart Gilbert's translation (New York: Knopf, 1948).

———————

Note that there is Bubonic Plague in Vietnam. I don't know how many cases, but quite a few. But the moral plague there is serious enough!

"Did not Diemerbroek know of people stricken with the plague who had been cured by music?"

[Michel] Foucault. Madness and Civilization [New York, 1965]. p. 179.

May 7, 1967. Sunday within Octave of the Ascension

Mystery of the Ascension moves me more this year – back to a sense of its meaning.

The mystery for the monastic life, [Louis] Bouyer said (whatever happened to Bouyer?).

Yesterday, Derby Day, light rain began in the morning and turned to floods of rain in the afternoon, so by post time for the race the track must have been a river. I don't know what happened and don't care. But the Negroes who were preparing to demonstrate and disrupt things probably did not have to do much – the Derby was already ruined.

In the evening I began reading Gerald Syke's book *The Cool Millennium* [Englewood Cliffs, NJ, 1967] – with which I agree so completely that it can hardly be called something new. Yet it does have a good effect, because it makes one realize more than ever how fortunate I am in my life in the woods, and what a chance I have to be really free. That I don't need to prejudice my peace and freedom with recriminations against society. I am as out of it as one can be and still live in the USA. And there is no likelihood of my changing anything by my clamor. On the other hand I do have enough of a hearing to reach quite a few individuals and help them. (Yesterday another letter came from Smith [College] – another of those girls. They move and charm me with their understanding.)

Above all I do not have to act as if the judgment of the current establishment were in anyway decisive or as if I even needed to explain myself – give an account of myself. There is just no more need to worry about that, as far as I can see. So why fuss about it?

Finally, the situation in the monastery. People continue to be upset by the unnecessary struggle with Dom James – who pretends to give with one hand and takes back with the other and is absolutely bent on making only superficial changes and offering tokens or meaningless symbolic concessions only.

Fr. Chrysogonus is now in a kind of crisis due to the fact that, having knocked himself out with work on chant, liturgy etc., he has realized that he has only been used for James's political ends and not really for any authentic renewal. That it has not really "taken" and the community is suspicious, reserved, non-committal because everyone knows that unreserved commitment is merely a cult of the abbot's ikon of his own ideas – and a defeat of real renewal, veneration of a parody.

The point is that in Dom J.'s book, the community serves him and his individual image – it is a business he is running successfully. Its main purpose is to be *his* success. He does not know this, I believe. But he is so completely a business operator (plus his own curious sado-masochistic mystique) that he can't see anything else. He does not really give a damn for people and their ideals and needs except in so far as they can be fitted into his own going operation – in a word *used* by him. Certainly there is an air of altruism and disinterestedness in it sometimes, because that has to be part of the image. The place has to appear free, happy, "creative" and whatnot. This is part of the "success." And this is what does not happen. The happiest people are those who have simply found a way of doing what they know they need to do, in spite of him and in spite of everything – but these remain more or less marginal types, or are in obvious opposition to him. They are respected for being so.

The others, who are stupid enough to be more purely and simply the Boss's men, in all good faith, count for little. They are regarded with pity or contempt, or simply ignored. Yet they do serve his means and one realizes the danger of tangling with them – or better, of attracting their attention to what one happens to be doing. (They are his CIA.) In good faith they have accepted a distorted idea of monastic obedience, which puts them in a state of alienation; and this they regard as virtue. In a sense, perhaps, it is what they themselves prefer and seek, and they would be upset by everything else. But it is a pitiable condition.

Yesterday – corrected proof for "Day of a Stranger" for *Hudson Review* and wrote a brief statement on a loud, rebellious book by a Fr. [James] Kavanaugh (thoroughly angry, denouncing evident abuses and injustices in the Church, very shrill and a bit melodramatic). I gave him my support but I wonder if a book like this can accomplish much. I don't know. But it is good for somebody to shout and bang on the table at this juncture I believe.

May 8, 1967

On being a Stranger.

I need more awareness of what it involves. And get some such awareness by the invitations I have to refuse. Helder Camara urged that I get to the *Pacem in Terris* conference in Geneva. Ping Ferry said the Center would pay my way. (He is starting today.) No use even asking Dom James. A few weeks ago – invitation to some conference in Curitiba, Brazil – some Catholic Book thing. They would pay my way etc. I refused first, then they applied to him and he refused. The other day, wrote refusing invitation to another meeting in Cuernavaca. Same again. Dan Berrigan will be there.

Being "out of the world" does not mean simply being out of Las Vegas – it means being not on the planes, not at the reunions, conferences etc. Not in Hong Kong today and Lima tomorrow, not in the credit-card expense-account talk circuit where you are paid to be everywhere, and this to make news – (because where you are paid to be, there the action is, since the action is that you are paid to be there).

The question is: do I really care? Do I resent being excluded from all this? Inevitably my being grounded in this corner of woods, unable to move, able only to speak half surreptitiously to a few who get through to me here, makes me a comic sort of intellectual. Inevitably I am a sort of reform-school kid who is punished by being taken off the street. And one who does not know the latest, is not perfectly attuned to the intonations and accents that convey the real message.

Is this a castrating maneuver of Dom James? Probably in part it is, and he is so irrational about it that it is annoying – but I am free of him, at least free enough not to care too much. However – if my yelling here is merely the yelling of a castrated and defeated being, it is of no use to anyone.

Certainly no point in mere resentment of modern society "bla bla."

Nor trying to pretend I am after all superior.

Nevertheless, the situation has unique advantages. Much of the real germinating action in the world, the real leavening is among the immobilized, the outsiders (the vast majority who have no credit card and never step on a plane) the Negroes, the Latinos, etc. In a way I am on their level. (But I don't have their grapevine!)

I know I do prefer solitude, and I want my solitude to be authentic. It is a sacrifice and a frustration to have to be so out of things when I could easily be "in." I am convinced that there are real advantages I must understand and make use of.

Meanwhile next Sunday I have to concelebrate with the Archbishop at Dan Walsh's ordination – a momentary illusion of being "in" something and, to me, confusing. I'll try to make the best of it for Dan's sake.

Yesterday the new Archbishop McDonough was here – I did not go to hear him speak. Ran into Raymond's friend Alexis – the South African from Notre Dame – and Fr. [Henri] Nouwen (Dutch psychologist teaching at N[otre] D[ame]), had a good talk in the evening by the lake in Charlie O'Brien's pasture (old name for St. Bernard's field).

Formulating opinions – when the plague that will reduce them to absurdity is already raging – I do have a real sense of this, a real suspicion that this is what is perhaps going on at all those meetings (Camus – *Plague* – 35). Sour grapes? Perhaps.

May 10, 1967

Yesterday I had to go the allergist again – out in that God-forsaken St. Matthew's far from a library or anything else of interest. Was in there nearly two hours getting needles stuck into me and contemplating a print of a fierce trotting race entitled "A Race for Blood." He is a careful and interesting doctor, however.

I am reading the part about exile and separation in Camus's *Plague*. "The incorrigible sorrow of all prisoners and exiles, which is to live in company with a memory that serves no purpose." Anguish of remembering the days with M. last May, as the light and weather inexorably bring the same settings back and ten times more lonely (because of the rainy weeks in late April).

Yesterday I called her from the airport (Dan Berrigan just left for NY) in a quiet booth down by the East end of the terminal away from the airline desks. She was sleepy and sweet in Cincinnati. Yes she is going to get married. In October. She does not think of it with a lot of joy. "But it is what I think I ought to do" and I agree with that. The boy seems to be a nice guy, good and reliable, and will probably be a devoted husband to her. I told her I thought she was perfectly right and that I understood. She said she worried about me, that I was still the one she really loved etc. It was sort of heart breaking. "Even after I am married you can still keep *writing* to me." Yes but really I should not. But perhaps if we simply go on as good friends – and share what we can reasonably share of each other's news etc. Probably won't work out that way, though and I came home to lonely woods and desolation.

Dan Berrigan looked like a French worker priest in beret and black turtleneck windbreaker. A good uniform for a priest. He wants to go to Hanoi, but may get thrown out of the Jesuits for doing it. Jim Holloway came over from Berea.

Quiet cloudy evening: I sat on the porch watching 3 does quietly feeding in the field while dogs yelled across the valley. And a pileated woodpecker made a lot of racket in the wood just east of me. I love the Towhees in their dapper plumage. If I were a bird I'd want to dress like that. Dan Walsh was in his black suit and Roman collar today sitting in the gatehouse reading (with difficulty) his Breviary. He was ordained deacon yesterday – is due for the priesthood Sunday and I am supposed to concelebrate. The new Archbishop McDonough came down Sunday but as I thought it was only a chapter talk I did not go. It turned out (Dan said) that he especially wanted to see me on some business. I was never told about it. Maybe Dom James did not know? Seems rather peculiar to me!

May 11, 1967

Finished (yesterday) a short piece on Malcolm X.[12] I realize I don't fully know what I am talking about. Perhaps I overestimate him. Perhaps his African experience was nothing more than a juvenile dazzlement at the native bourgeoisie. Perhaps already beginning to be corrupted in a new way. Saved by death – like Kennedy also, who would have been less likely to be enshrined if he had to carry on the Viet Nam war.

Implications of the racial and neo-colonial situation – for my own life. I realize more and more that I have no right whatever to make a romantic escape, under whatever pretext you like, to the Third World, to Latin America, to Asia. No matter how sincere the poetry of it might be, the act would be ambiguous – an infliction upon others of a false ideal image of my own – a "presentation," ultimately, of a deceptive North American document: Christian concern and whatnot.

[12] "The Meaning of Malcolm X," *Continuum* (Summer 1967), 432–35.

On the other hand – can a Russian, or a Chinese Marxist, do it any more honestly than I?

Anyway, I realize my "imprisonment" here on this hillside, while having its delights, also has a necessary, inescapable ignominy or is this judgment itself an unnecessary refinement? A novel luxury? A further ignominy?

My intention is that, though it may eventually be published, this Journal should be kept under wraps for twenty-five years after my death. However, I may experiment in reading parts of it on tape and then getting these transcribed and working them over for publication.

Meanwhile I have no intention of keeping the M. business entirely out of sight. I have always wanted to be completely open, both about my mistakes and about my effort to make sense out of my life. The affair with M. is an important part of it – and shows my limitations as well as a side of me that is – well, it needs to be known too, for it is part of me. My need for love, my loneliness, my inner division, the struggle in which solitude is at once a problem and a "solution." And perhaps not a perfect solution either.

However, I think a lot of merely foolish stuff can be destroyed: most of the love letters are in this category. They were merely garrulous outpourings of feeling, and this is usually not magnificent, only routine sentiment. The true feeling is no doubt in the some of the poems. They really express it – at least they do so better than any letters.

May 13, 1967. Vigil of Pentecost

A rather foul, murky, damp day. I am making a sort of 1/2 day retreat in preparation for tomorrow. Another booklet on Garabandal came in. A lot of it is perhaps, somewhat questionable in detail, but the overall impression is moving, and once again I was stirred by it. Quite apart from the authenticity of the apparitions (and they seem for the most part genuine), I experience in myself a deep need of conversion and penance – a deep repentance, a real sense of having erred, gone wrong, got lost – and needing to get back on the right path. Needing to pray for forgiveness. Sense of revolt at my own foolishness and triviality. Shame and amazement at the way I have trifled with life and grace – how could I be so utterly stupid! A real sense of being flawed and of needing immense help, pardon – to recover some capacity to love God. Sense of the nearness and mercy of Mary.

At the same time I cannot help feeling a sense of decay in everything – I mean in the society I belong to and even in the Church, in the monastery. A much deeper and more serious sense, because there seems to be so little substance in the noisy agitation of progressives who claim to be renewing the Church and who are either riding some rather silly band-wagon or caught up in factional rivalries. As for the conservatives – they are utterly depressing in their tenacious clinging to meaningless symbols of dead power, their baroque inertia, their legalism. Disgust!

After some sympathetic interest in the "hippie movement" and a real compassion for their good intentions, I am a bit sickened by it. Not that I know enough to judge. But the whole thing seems so phoney, so pointless, so decadent. A false creativity, a half-dead freshness, kids who seem to be already senile in their tired bodies, thru LSD trips – a sense of overstimulation and of exhaustion. The gasping of a culture that is rotting in its own garbage – and yet has so many potentials! I know, all this is too pessimistic – I am trying to salvage something in myself by saying "I am not that, at least!" Yet I am part of it – and I must try to bring life back into it, along with the others.

May 14, 1967. Pentecost

Lightning, thunder and rain on and off all night, and now at dawn there is still more of it. The lovely grey-green valley, misty clouds sweeping low over the hills and forest out there in the South, iron dark clouds heavy above them. The rainy gloom full of pale-yellow irises and the cloudy white blossoming green masses of the rosehedge. I went out a while ago and a hawk flew fast away – it had been waiting on the cross or in the big poplar tree.

As I have been asked to do a piece on Paul the Hermit,[13] I reread Jerome's *Vita* today. A work of art, really. With plenty of monastic theology in its symbolism. A beautiful piece of writing, with deep mystical and psychological implications – so that whether or not it is "historical" is irrelevant. It awakens a kind of inner awareness of psychic possibilities which one so easily forgets and neglects. The return to unity, to the ground, the paradisial inner sacred space where the archetypal man dwells in peace and in God. The journey to that space, through a realm of aridity, dualism, dryness, death. The need of courage and of desire. Above all faith, praise, obedience to the inner voice of the Spirit, refusal to give up or to compromise.

[13] St. Paul of Thebes, an early Christian hermit who died ca. 340.

What is "wrong" in my life is not so much a matter of "sin" (though it is sin too), but of *unawareness*, lostness, slackness, relaxation, dissipation of desire, lack of courage and of decision, so that I let myself be carried along and dictated to by an alien movement. The current of "the world," which I know is not mine. I am always getting diverted into a way that is not *my way* and is not going where I am called to go. And only if I go where I must go can I be of any use to "the world." I can serve the world best keeping my distance and my freedom.

In the *Vita Antonii* [Athanasius of Alexandria's *Life of Antony*] – "Virtue" is within us not outside us, and we find it when we return to our "original nature," our "natural state" – the state proper to ourselves, as we "came into being" – one might add our true identity in the mind of God. The soul, says Anthony "came into being fair and perfectly straight." So true. – "Make straight your hearts unto the Lord God of Israel" [identified in margin as Josh. 24:23], and St. John [the Baptist] ([Matt.] 3:3), "Make straight your paths."

"For the soul is said to be straight when its mind is in its natural state as when it was created. But when it swerves and is perverted from its natural condition that is called vice *(kakía)* of the soul."

So the job is (as St. John of the Cross says) keeping the strength of the mind, of one's thoughts and desires, for God.

"Having received the soul as something entrusted to us, let us guard it for the Lord that He may recognize His work as being the same as He made it."

May 17, 1967

On Pentecost – drove in with Bernard and Rev. Father in the rain, found St. Thomas' Seminary way out in the fields somewhere toward Cincinnati, walked in long halls this way and that and found a sacristy. And waited. And had pictures taken. The concelebration was fine though. A great enthusiasm filled the large bright chapel crowded with people, friends and students of Dan, including some former monks with their wives etc. Archbishop Floersh moved and moving. Dan nervous at one point. A great celebration though. Then we went to O'Callaghans (this time I with a carload of ex-monks). The day stayed grey but we could sit in the yard at metal tables, where I talked too much, drank too much champagne, and generally misbehaved, going against all I had in mind earlier Pentecost morning.

Then yesterday – Monday – another and much brighter day. I concelebrated with Dan at Church. A much more intimate and quiet Mass with the nuns all visible in their choir behind the open grille and singing very well. It was deeply moving, a sense of light and joy and of spiritual reality, a most beautiful Eucharist. One's sense of the reality and value of Carmel was very strong. I was very happy about it – preached homily – later we had a half hour or so with the nuns in their speak room and again I talked too much, but everyone seemed very happy. I felt very purified and enlightened by this contact with them and Dan never stopped talking about it for the rest of the day. Lunch at Fords and met some of the young priests who teach philosophy at Bellarmine – some very alert guys. And Josephine Ford from N.D.

Later I went down to the Chancery and had a very good talk with the new Archbishop, McDonough, and I am happy about his attitude. He was very positive about certain things, encouraged the writing, thought I ought to go to Morocco and see people like Sidi Abdesalam, and so on. The Delegate apparently is in favor of a bit of my work and wants to come down and talk to me too. Perhaps something is cooking.

Coming home late called M. who had had the day off, had been reading Robert Frost ("Bereft") and kept saying we should go on talking to each other as before (with love) and that she had dreamt of me. But I still have doubts about writing her with much affection or so frequently, and I know she has hesitations about our seeing each other – or at least about her driving down here. So it is calming down anyway, but I was glad to talk to her and on the phone she sounded happy.

May 21, 1967. Trinity Sunday

My breakfast reading (which is supposed to be "light" and informative) is now a new book by [George] Gamow on Quantum Physics. It dazzles and baffles me – but Niels Bohr & Co. are definitely among my No. 1 culture heroes. This magnificent instrument of thought they developed to understand what is happening in matter, what energy really is about – with their confirmation of the kind of thing Herakleitos was reaching for by intuition. It is terribly exciting, though I can't grasp any of it due to the fact that I never had even high-school physics, and the equations are just hieroglyphics that represent to me no known answers. What sharks are they hunting? I don't know, but when the shark is caught I try to focus on him my bedazzled reason.

What a crime it was – that utterly stupid course on "cosmology" that I had to take here (along with the other so-called philosophy in Hickey's

, . texts!). Really criminal absurdity! And at the time when the bomb was dropped on Hiroshima! Surely there were people in the order who knew better than allow such a thing! Dom Frederic, no. He couldn't help it. The whole Church still demanded this, and God knows, maybe some congregation or other still does.

I am thankful at least for the elementary astronomy and geology I got at Columbia.

A letter is appearing in the *London Times* with a quote from my letter to Margaret Gardiner – a protest against V.N. war signed by Lord [C.P.] Snow and others. I am all for his brave idea of dialogue between the two cultures and today could write him a fan letter. But won't. The Chem[istry] department at Birmingham U. (England) is putting out a magazine which is 1/2 literary and the editor (David Kilburn) is after me and Lax and Reinhardt etc. for poems, art – this too is exciting. He [is] a good poet. This is the sort of thing that makes life very enjoyable.

May 22, 1967

Finished Foucault *Madness and Civilization* – a really remarkable book. Not sure that I have got more than a tenth of it. The material itself very rich, and his own handling of it subtle and masterly. One thing: the nineteenth-century asylum and its positivistic assumptions has very exact analogies to Trappist monasteries as organized by nineteenth-century French abbots. I'd like to do a paper on it. But for whom? No one would publish it and Superiors would fall off their chairs – which would be a good thing no doubt. If I could think of something to *do* with it. Meanwhile, just sitting down and getting it on paper is out of the question until I have done other more urgent things. But today Tommie O'C[allaghan], and Gene Meatyard etc. are supposed to be coming (promised both) – I have got to get free of "social" commitments. Yet the poet [Andrei] Voznesenky is in the country, would like to see me. I would like to see him . . .

May 27, 1967

A beautiful May morning. Limpid clarity. Silence. Birds. Air thick with the sweetness of honeysuckle. Thank God I have had a few days of quiet. Reading a life of Niels Bohr, finished Izutson on Ibn Arabi and returned it to Wenjyko at McGill. I can't say I am totally happy with the 6th century Palestinian monasticism described in clarity. Too much political struggle – and I mean struggle for *power*. There is a great difference between a monk speaking out on a moral issue and a monk or community thrown bodily into a violent struggle for power with bishops and other monks.

The *Times* letter appeared Tuesday, May 23. I got a copy from Margaret Gardiner in London yesterday.

Yesterday – dipped into the ms. that Julian Muller at Harcourt Brace and World wanted me to comment on – nuns used as whores by Viet Cong etc. – a sort of breezy Morris West treatment, popular and tough, with some nasty monsignors and good tough Jews etc. etc. The correct mythology that assumes a compound of oversexuality, crude violence, honest bourgeois privatism, native American honesty, a bit of lesbianism for kicks. In other words a pile of stupid shit. What revolted me was not so much the sex as the attitude – the mixture of superficial objectivity and Time-Life self-righteousness – and the suburb sophistication. America as she sees herself. The kind of America that makes Norman Mailer vomit – and me too (man at U. of Minnesota sent me an essay he had written on me and Mailer).

It always gets back to the same thing. I have dutifully done my bit. I have been "open to the world." That is to say I have undergone my dose of exposure to American society in the 60's – particularly in these last weeks. I love the people I run into – but I pity them for having to live as they do, and I think the world of U.S.A. in 1967 is a world of crass, blind, overstimulated, phony, lying stupidity. The war in Asia gets slowly worse – and always more inane. The temper of the country is one of blindness, fat, self-satisfied, ruthless, mindless corruption. A lot of people are uneasy about it, but helpless to do anything against it. The rest are perfectly content with the rat race as it is, and with its competitive, acquisitive, hurtling, souped-up drive into nowhere. A massively aimless, baseless, shrewd cockiness that simply exalts itself without purpose. The mindless orgasm, in which there is no satisfaction, only spasm.

So I have done my bit and looked at what they have to offer and want no part of it. Yet I remain part of it. But I do not have to be so divided or so doubtful. Why not go ahead with my own business, which is not writing but living and meditating and breathing, and believing? Obviously the divisions are more critical and more far-reaching than I understand. And new rifts open up. Catholicism itself is to me more and more of a problem. Not a theological one – it is on the level of culture and of psychology. American Catholicism – the American Catholic mind and consciousness. The American Catholic Spasm! Again, aggressively, a forbidding, combative stance, now legalist and more pseudo-liberal (the liberal publicist itch). The whole thing revolts me.

Yet the new bishop is obviously a nice guy. His football tackle henchman standing impatiently by the car as big and shiny as a dreadnought waiting to open the door. Car sleek as a millionaire's or a gangster's.

And I have to keep going to the allergy man who looks like a musician – and I guess he is smart with all his needles – tucked away in a corner of St. Matthew's. – Needles. Props. Bottles. Woodcarving of grotesque demons which are at once allergies and patients – and the doctor's own problem. The Ray Harm picture of pelicans and the same people waiting hours and kidding about it with some acidity.

I ought to learn to just shut up and go about my business of thinking and breathing under trees. But protest is a biological necessity. Part of the allergy maybe.

May 30, 1967

It is Decoration Day – looks like rain. Misty. Cold.

Will Campbell and Jim Holloway here yesterday. Will drove his red farm truck up into the shade by the hermitage and we sat in the breeze talking – mostly about his work preaching "to the Klan." Crawford (?) the head of the clan, accepts him though "liberal." Curious stories – guns and so on. The Kluxers convinced that there must be shooting (and the Black Power types equally convinced). Doubtless the shooters will start by shooting in different places, not on each other. Curious times are coming.

I haven't heard much about the Middle East crisis lately.

Things obviously don't get better in Viet Nam.

Will Campbell had his guitar and sang "country music" – curious, hopeless, sentimental songs all about betrayal and death – women doing their men wrong, evil boys with dying pet doggies, etc. General theme of forsakenness, loneliness, death – curious stuff. Such a different temper from the (Negro) Blues!

Last night – curious dreams.

One – I am in a place where there are Buddhist nuns, separated from me by a curious, paper-thin sort of iconostasis or printed partition, behind which I hear their soft erotic laughter as they are aware of me there. Sense of being drawn to them.

The other dream. The monastery building (Gethsemani) is on fire. The fire burns slowly on the inside of the building, but threatens to become violent. Meanwhile there are still people in the building. I think "Why don't they get *out?*" I myself am there, moving through small patches of fire, but get to safety. The building is not destroyed but all that is inside is consumed, more or less.

More changes in the Mass – elimination of a lot of signs of the cross, kisses of altar etc. In a way it relaxes tensions – is more honest – more true to the non-hieratic feeling of the modern America – but I had no real objection to the old formal ritual gestures either. This speeds up the Mass too. Perhaps I'll try to go more slowly and reflectively, with more quiet pauses to replace the old "actions."

May 31, 1967

May comes to a cold end. Rain. Train in the valley.

Have just been reading of the destruction of Jerusalem by the Persians in 614 a.d. Since Helena, the Church of the Holy Sepulchre and the True Cross had been a center of the Christian Empire and the Feast of the Exaltation of the Cross in September was second only to Easter – an Exaltation of the Empire! I realize the crucial importance of the history of the East in the centuries when Islam was about to begin – and know *nothing* of this history. It is probably the key to a lot of things. (Death of Muhammad, 632.)

June 1, 1967

Precisely on June 1 the day lilies began to open. But it still rains.

Yesterday a letter from Dom James in Europe. The Apostolic Delegate is inquiring about my connections with the National Association for Pastoral Renewal, which is considering a poll on clerical celibacy and is in hot water with Spellman. I guess there is going to be a rumpus. Frankly I can't say I really care one way or another. I sympathize with those priests, and I think the continued opposition to them is going to mean trouble. But in the long run I don't know if a married secular clergy really solves anything for the church—or for the clergy. My own feeling is that it does not matter that much and I am not deeply enough involved in the issue myself to get into a fight about it. I am an "advisor" of the NAPR—i.e. a name on a list—and able to be "used." That is the extent of it.

———

Evening. It has been a cold quiet, wet day, as cold as in November.

I sit here with a wind breaker on. It is dark. As far as I am concerned it was a good day – quiet. Began writing the booklet on Camus's *Plague* for Seabury Press.[14] *The Plague* itself is impressive on second reading. A clear-cut job. Reading [Ernst] Benzon *Evolution and Hope* [Garden City, NY, 1966]. The absurd hope of some nineteenth-century optimists. The future *has to be* better, man *has to become* a superman. Article of faith! Every bit as naive as the most naive myths about Adam and Eve.

This evening there is nothing terribly hopeful about things. I was content until I went down to the monastery. Confusion – the weekly routine which seems to me a bit absurd. Why not let people go to confession when they feel a need to, instead of this regular once a week business? But anyway Fr. Matthew was a bit depressed – General Chapter going on, not much hope of anything really happening. Weariness with this elaborate business of pretending to reform etc. Worse than that – a sort of hopelessness and a growing realization that it is almost impossible to do anything significant within the kind of framework we have. And even the good things that are being done: Fr. Placide's foundation at Aubazine – what will they really amount to? What is the point of taking over an elaborate, cumbersome Oriental liturgy just when the Roman (Cistercian) liturgy is being completely simplified?

What seems to be growing on everyone is the disturbing realization that this whole business – the whole monastic institution – may now be finished. In trying to save it they have thrown out some of the same things that made it seem coherent, and now the incoherence and insecurity of the whole thing are getting obvious. In fact, Gethsemani is to a great extent held together by the emotions, the willpower and the personal delusions of Dom James, who firmly believes in himself as Abbot. It suddenly dawned on me why he is going around telling people he hopes to retire: he always makes sure to tell it to the right ones – the ones who will implore him *not* to! They are the ones who are content with his fantasies and his games and his abbatial "presence." Actually there is no hope of any real development as long as

———

[14] The booklet is entitled *Albert Camus' The Plague* (New York: Seabury Press, 1968). It is reprinted as "The Plague of Albert Camus: A Commentary and Introduction" in *The Literary Essays of Thomas Merton*, edited by Brother Patrick Hart (New York: New Directions, 1982), 181–217.

he is there. He will generate a certain stability, it is true – he will keep the place from falling apart – but perhaps he will only exhaust everyone who might have good ideas, and when he goes the place really will fall apart. Perhaps that is what his supporters sense. And it is true, hardly anyone is crazy enough to even think of taking over such a hopeless job.

Meanwhile – there is the crisis between Arabia and Israel which seems to be fairly real and no mere pseudo-event. And the racial tension in this country. The ever worse situation in Vietnam, where the war gradually becomes more and more serious and it seems inevitable that China will eventually get involved. What idiocy! And people are now so accustomed to the war and the general pattern of violence and affluence that they expect no real change – they stop thinking about it. I am not so resigned: on the contrary, I feel as disturbed as I was in 1962, and once again have the sense of real growing crisis. And perhaps this time we shall not get out of it as easy as we did with Cuba.

As for the race situation: it is now clear that *none* of the really rational, humane, decent settlements are possible. The "nice" clean way of settling everything in a bright, friendly atmosphere of cooperation – all that our democratic myth had led us to believe, is simply out of the question. What we are going to have instead is crude, stupid hate, mutual harassment, an impasse of force and resistance, and a mess that cannot be arranged. If at the same time there is war . . . a big war . . .

June 3, 1967

Still raining.

Last evening: eating sardines and drinking a couple of cans of Schlitz, and reading the life of Niels Bohr, I was again astonished at the "nearness" of the whole development of atomic physics, to my own life. Things going on at the Cavendish Lab at Cambridge when I was there. In January 1939, when I was taking my exams for the M.A. and had presented my thesis, the uranium atom was split in an experiment at Columbia (Jan. 25) and I knew nothing about it (though it got into the papers). At that time there was an immense ferment going on in Germany and the U.S. over the atom. Bohr had just arrived for 3 months at Princeton. Everyone was splitting the uranium nucleus and wondering if Hitler was on the way to producing a bomb. I had no idea that it went back that far. A sense of awe at the fact that people like Bohr were so much at the *heart* of what was happening – so truly "prophetic." For this is a truly modern kind of prophetism: I mean in men like Bohr, [Werner] Heisenberg, [Leo] Szilard etc. who grasped all the consequences of their discoveries in a widely human way. As opposed to this kind of narrow scientism which sees only a short range and purely technical consequence. Bohr had the ability to translate his discoveries into a language relevant to everybody, to all humanity, and to the deepest and most critical problems of man then and there – here and now.

All this was happening on my own doorstep and I knew nothing about it! Yet I think it was surely related in some mysterious way to the spiritual ferment in my own being – my groping toward a religious adaptation to crisis – my real awareness of the crisis on another level.

I am just discovering other well-known facts: for instance as far back as 1927 it was known that genetic mutation could be artificially induced by X-rays, and now it is known too that it can be done chemically. So that there is a very real possibility of drastic genetic change in the near future, whether deliberate or accidental.

So that once again it becomes imperative that there be some concerted action by the best minds everywhere to control this power in view of the interests of *man*. Not let it be used haphazardly by individual nations or groups – or by cliques of madmen! – for what they conceive to be the right ends.

June 6, 1967

How do you begin to say that you think World War III is now going on but that you are not sure – ?

Perhaps the simplest way of saying it is that is feels like 1939 *all* over again. The sick feeling that the big machine has gone on the rampage again and no one can really control it: because though they think they want to stop it (the rampage is inconvenient and not according to plans), they have set up all the causes which put it out of control.

Like I am almost ready to write and say goodbye to everybody.

Yesterday, riding into town to see the doctor again (the end of that is finally in sight, at least for deciding what allergy shots I need) – radio announced the fighting – on all fronts – between Israel and UAR. A meeting of the UN Security council was supposed to convene but I had reached the library before it did. Air raid alerts in Tel Aviv, but it was bombed. Artillery in Jerusalem. Cairo bombed (airfields) and Damascus airport. Planes fighting. Troops fighting in desert. Israel apparently attacked – but provoked by the blockade. Reports. Counterreports. Bright June day bright as that September morning on the Rappahannock in 1939 when we heard London talking and all was said to be quiet . . .

The unreal subtle buildup. State Department says of course the U.S. is neutral but White House, without formal contradiction, refuses to confirm this. Russia is neutral but "warns" . . . Arabs say oil will not go to anyone who seems to be not quite friendly . . . Obviously the situation is very nasty. No, planes from the U.S. 6th Fleet are *not* involved and so on.

Same reports all day, with slight variation. Making up the public mind. Gradually everyone gets the same confused picture – same subliminal hopes, fears, determinations. We know where we are all going – so we think. We are taking a firm stand. Confidence in our President who is being firm, watchful, will stand no nonsense from a bunch of rug-salesmen, gypsies and semi-muggers. What today? I have no ideas. I am back in the woods, with my own deep and unquiet sicknesses. I do not try to figure anything out – I only try to come to terms with the idea, now more disturbingly real than ever before, that at the next moment I may go up in smoke with the gold of Fort Knox and all the fissionable material stored there (20 miles? 30 miles? 15 or 20 in a straight line? I don't know).

There is no question that one cannot realistically assess all this without taking into account the unimaginable: the possibility of sudden massive destruction all over this nation. It is *real*. It is real *now*. How cope with that? Don't ask me. All I know is that perspectives are different – my solitude is more significant – after all no matter what collective rituals they may have devised for atomic war, you face death alone anyway: you have to make some decision as to what your life may fully mean. Solidarity – yes. I can see it is going to be a strange kind of underground solidarity perhaps, with people who know they cannot belong to the world of the established, organized insanity. Who perhaps have some other, slightly better, insanity – that may make sense if anyone survives. And of course everyone might . . .

What I find it hard to stomach is the sense of being massively lied to, conned, pushed around, manipulated, forced into patterns I cannot agree with – in a word, the pestilence! And, as Camus says, one must identify it and resist. How? It is at once the same old pestilence and a brand new one. Note that Bohr was right at the heart of things in World War II even when he came up against Churchill – what good could he do? We are inheritors of the consequences of that failure (for which Bohr himself can certainly not be blamed). (Unless the fact that he was a modest, soft-spoken, reflective person and not an operator is to be held against him!)

June 9, 1967

Apparently the Israel-Arab war is practically over – the Israelis having destroyed most of the Arab planes, taken over Jordan and pushed their way to Suez. The rest will now be shouting and blustering in the UN. Russian and American warships are watching one another in the Mediterranean. I haven't seen a paper. I got this from the Prior yesterday. In any event the situation appears to be much less critical than it was on Monday. And our habit of crisis has been hardened by another degree.

Tuesday – the O'Callaghans and their children with Gladys Ford and her children and two of Marie Charron's children and one from the Hennecy's came out for a picnic. Pleasant, bewildering, all this movement and brightness and multiplicity – fishing, pogo-sticks, softball, a frisbee, other games the names of which I never knew – children filling my hands with rubber crabs and flies they made in school (I put a large black fly on the open dictionary in the library). Questions. Coming and going. "Now I'm going to sit there next to you. Keep my place for me. Don't let anybody take it while I get my plate. That's my plate there, you watch it, don't let anybody take it. . . ." The kids are so beautiful though. Their eyes and their smiles. And very nice kids too.

I am reading Kafka's *Castle* again – this time it hits me harder than before, for some reason. It so exactly describes life in the Catholic Church! The firm and stable unreality of relations between subject and superior – the creation of a small pseudo-supernatural mystery world of curial bureaus from which emanate incomprehensible instructions, warnings, rewards. Perhaps one thing that makes me most laugh: The new archbishop tells Dan Walsh that the Apostolic Delegate (of all people!) thinks very highly of me, wants to come here on *retreat* etc. (I know he won't!) Then a few days later – the letter of the Delegate to Dom James, sent me from J. in France, with raised eyebrows over my being an advisor of the NAPR (priest-marriage outfit). Meanwhile the Delegate is one of 27 new cardinals.

There is a certain solemnity and mystery about the messages that come from afar – Washington – Rome. Unfortunately there is no mystery about messages from the Abbot, which are at once pseudo-paternal and puerile. And *his* mind, at least, one knows well enough, with all its faces and concealments. From Cîteaux he sent fleets of postcards to the community – all with the same idiot message and all written, no doubt, before he left – taken to be mailed from France, all for Jesus, through Mary with a smile.

So Fr. H. tore up *his* postcard and left the pieces in a neat little pile in the room where he kept his work clothes etc. – and disappeared. He called from somewhere telling the Prior he did not intend to return at least right now. No one knows where he is, exactly. One sometimes has to be drastic to get a message through to the *Castle* – but even then does the message get through? Dom James will be stirred with righteous emotions, but the chances of his ever understanding why such a thing happened are simply zero. And no one any longer even bothers *to* try to tell him. Except perhaps Fr. Tarcisius, who is young and still eager.

The question always in the back of the reader's mind in the *Castle* "Why does K. stay in that damned village? Why does he imagine he has to penetrate the Castle?" But he has come to stay. For in fact wherever he might go, it would everywhere be the same.

June 10, 1967

The Beatles' "Taxman" is running through my head. They are good. Good beat. Independence, wit, insight, voice, originality, they take pleasure in being Beatles, and I do not resent the fact that they are multi-millionaires, for that is part of it. They have to contend with that sneaky taxman.

Still have not read Teilhard de Chardin and really have no intention of doing so – though sometimes I pick up the [Henri] De Lubac book on him [*The Religion of Teilhard de Chardin* (New York: Desclée, 1967)] and look at it. I have read only *The Divine Milieu* [New York, 1957] – and my review of it was stopped, though that article is now being published in Brazil I understand.

I have the greatest liking and sympathy for Teilhard as a person and especially because of the treatment he had to undergo from his superiors – consistently silenced, removed from the scene, set aside, deprived of all recognition, all the usual petty machinations of a baroque, political Church to keep him quiet, and to prevent him having a "bad influence." And when one considers the approved illegible dullness that was encouraged and flourished instead!

On the other hand, are the neologisms of Teilhard much better? Good intentions, heart in the right place, wanting the right thing, but did he really have the necessary gifts? If it comes to science, I will gladly read later and better scientists. If it comes to poets . . . he does not even begin to be one. As for theology, I must admit that I become more and more suspicious of it in its contemporary form. After Barth. Does one have time for all the superficial journalistic chatter that comes out on all sides? I don't.

Then there is the ms. of the English translation of Maritain's *Le Paysan de la Garonne*. It is painful. I am sorry I told him I liked the French edition – for it does have some good insights no doubt, but it is not a good book. In its own way it, too, is tedious journalism. Why did he have to feel bound to get involved in this utterly stupid controversy? I made the same mistake (less controversially) with *Redeeming the Time*.[15] As if I too had to be "heard." (Fortunately I let it be published in England, only then changed my mind.)

Joe Cunneen is working over the translation of the *Paysan* and the translator is upset – and both are firing amended chapters at me, and I am trying to finish my booklet on Albert Camus's *The Plague*. A plague on both their houses.

M. spoke of perhaps meeting in Louisville in a couple of weeks, but I have grave doubts. A lot of water has gone under the bridge, and I wonder if either of us really wants to see the other that much. Of course I would like to see her – but it could so easily be a letdown, a real disappointment. We are obviously no longer in love, and not even particularly in tune with each other, having much different worlds to live in and such different interests. It is not at all like last year. And now having half committed myself to seeing her, I am thinking of getting out of it. And I am sure she has the same doubts too. It would be wiser to forget the whole thing – and to remember her as she was last July 16, standing on the walk in front of Lourdes Hall as my cab drove away.

Still don't have any sink for my water. Temporary taps were put in after Easter – waiting for cabinet maker to come through with something. 3 months. It took two and a half months to get the well dug and now it takes longer than that to get a sink. Thank God I have a pump and a hot water heater and can wash my dishes, at least, in a bucket.

June 11, 1967
The Castle. A fantastically suggestive book for anyone living precisely the kind of "Castle" life I live. An ironic tract in Ecclesiology. My order and my

[15] *Redeeming the Time* was the abridged and altered British edition of *Seeds of Destruction* (London: Burns & Oates, 1966).

Abbot believe firmly in maintaining a kind of Village-Castle relationship in their monks. Thus creating and maintaining something like the intensely neurotic anguish and alienation which Kafka describes so subtly. Too subtly. But the subtlety is part of it. The needless yet necessary subtlety. All this digging into motives of motives . . .

And I face the fact that this is my own sickness.

How does one get well? Am I too old to get well? Is it possible for me simply to leave this village and deny this Castle? Is that what I should do in the name and for the sake of health?

Or is that just another maneuver (or however the hell you spell manoeuver)?

Who says that this is the only place where one lives a Castle existence? What about General Motors, the Pentagon, Madison Avenue, the Kremlin?

It seems to me naive, the great illusion to suppose that getting out of here and into "the world" one gets out of the Castle-village bind. One merely gets into a different aspect of it.

Also *The Castle* is not a sick book, it is a healthy book about a sick situation, because it admits the sickness. Too much modern optimism seems to consist merely in looking at a bad situation through the small end of the telescope, and saying it isn't really there.

On the other hand it is imperative to overcome Castle sickness – involvement in Byzantine and futile hierarchical relationships – hoping in the inscrutable machine – here where I am. But it is so firmly built in to the system I belong to, and I am so deeply obsessed with it, that I wonder if I really can be free. It would be an awful thing to be caught in this forever, without issue. I have hope: hope of a new hope: not hope in myself or in the guitars. What is this hope? I don't know. What are its real risks? What is the real struggle it demands of me?

June 12, 1967

Finished *The Castle* except for the fragments at the end. This is I think the third time I have read it. Surprising how much I had forgotten. It is as though the first time, because this time I have been really open to it. The extraordinary scene in the upper floor of the Inn, the corridor of the officials, where they wake up in the morning, the files are distributed etc. Fascinating: a very great piece of writing.

Kafka is one of the few writers still capable of making me want to write a story because he is one of the few whose approach I find credible for myself – a dream-like, free association dealing with subliminal events, letting them organize themselves, and not bothering to find an "end." True, it is sometimes a bit boring. (Need to study the fragments he deleted, and see why perhaps.)

After reading Kafka all life becomes much more curious because one sees it in that strange perspective, hears people talking and sees them acting as automata, and it is very revealing. Because to a great extent that is what they – we – are.

Visit of two brothers of Taizé yesterday. Young. From the mission in Chicago, nice guys with a lot of questions, one a Dutchman the other a Swede. "What is the function of the contemplative life in this modern world?" "How do you explain the aim of the monastic life to young people?" "What questions do novices ask?" "How do you explain your own (Cistercian) way of life in the modern world?" All these questions have become for me somewhat embarrassing and unreal. I still have to try to answer them, I imagine, but when I do the answer turns out to be forced, and the voice that speaks is no longer mine. Just the talking machine. I am not at all interested either in "being a Cistercian" or in giving any account whatever of what that might possibly mean.

When they met with the group chapter it was disquieting and revealing. Long, serious, rambling, rather desperate speeches by Bro. Casper, the cook, who seemed scared. All about those on the battle line and those behind the line. A frenzied and mechanical justification of the old "dynamo of prayer" line, which is Dom James's only and official explanation of our value in the world. One wonders if everyone here believes that – but most are plenty scared if it seems to be questioned. It was not a line in which the Taizé boys seemed especially interested.

The most curious thing about Taizé is the fact that they have got themselves fully implicated in the hierarchical Catholic castle life. In order to preserve their place of singular importance in the "ecumenical movement" they have to be very careful of their relationship with Rome and with the various chanceries. As a result they are completely caught up in the routine of clearing everything with *Catholic* officials and indeed are more involved in this than many Catholics are. They say they "*have to*" do this and it is obvious that they depend more and more on official Catholic support and are indeed perhaps being used by Catholic officialdom. This to me is absurd, and I told them so. What is the good of being Protestants if they abdicate their freedom and get into this ludicrous tangle of telephone wire and red tape? Their only reply was that it was "absolutely necessary for the ecumenical movement."

June 15, 1967

News from the General Chapter is discouraging. The aim of the newly approved experiment seems merely to soften the life, make it comfortable and relaxed, so that people won't get frustrated and leave. But this will not help: they leave not because the life is difficult but because it has come to seem *pointless* – and these relaxations will not give it meaning. Quite the contrary: the whole special *character,* the physiognomy of the Cistercian life is apparently being sacrificed – except for the one thing: "we do not do any parish work – we do not go outside to teach. . . ." Nothing whatever is being done to make this life more seriously contemplative, or to orient it in that sort of direction. Diet relaxed (really that is comprehensible). Private rooms can be allowed – (comprehensible too) – less work, less prayer, less of everything – and apparently more of nothing. No sense of any aim, just "make things more bearable." Relaxation of the Rule really does not matter so much in itself if it is for some clear and legitimate purpose: the only purpose I can see to all this is – to keep people comfortable so they won't run away altogether. Well, just watch! More than ever will leave and there will be very few vocations. I think this time they have really scuttled the boat.

On the other hand, I understand that the mail will be opened and censored again: on a point like that they'll be strict! The aim is evidently to keep everyone under subjection and surveillance, putting in bribes and concessions, partly by the old authoritarian methods.

In other words: keep them in the monastery, keep them on the books of the order, fill as many choirstalls as you still can, even if you have to let them live an easy and pointless sort of life, just so they'll stay inside the walls, and won't leave, or start "experimental foundations" . . .

Glad I hurried to finish the booklet on Camus's *Plague* before the hot weather got here. Finished it yesterday. Afternoon between 90 and 100 – better stay out of the house – read and meditate under the trees where there is a little air: I have been too anxious about work and have neglected my time for meditation in the afternoon. Now I am back at it, using Huprior, who is excellent. The new Mumford book came today from HB&W and I began it. It seems to be excellent – and defies all the currently accepted dogmas of the culture-history people.

Actually it is quiet and fine at the hermitage. Masses of red day-lilies. Joe Carroll was up with the tractor to cut grass – everything trim, tall pines, young trees growing.

Draghi, whom I haven't seen for a long time, wrote. As usual he is interested in some bizarre thing, this time ESP – and predicts a big political assassination soon. Mao or Johnson. Not hard to guess Mao might get knocked off or Johnson either. Both are cordially hated.

And then there are the people who desire to be in contact by "thought waves" with "humans" from other Planets in flying saucers in Miami "after June 22." The people of the other planets "like Miami because it used to be landing place for Atlantis"! Well. Maybe Johnson will be shot by or in a flying saucer, then everybody will be satisfied.

I'm going to bed.

June 17, 1967

How little anyone understands here the real issues in the Israel-Arab conflict: and first of all the question whether the Western powers had any right to encourage and support the foundation of a *Zionist* nation. Certainly the Jews have a right to live peacefully in Palestine – with the Arabs who also have that right. What is needed is a Palestinian nation of Jews and Arabs – and I even suppose this was once possible. Maybe now it is no longer so. After [Joachim] Moubarac compares the (completely) Jewish occupation of Jerusalem (the former Arab part – mosque of Islam etc.) to the Nazi occupation of Paris. Well, anyway, that is how the Arabs look at it. Pope Paul's idea of keeping Jerusalem an open city and giving access to all religions – was right. No one seems to have seen that – regarded it perhaps as a sentimental gesture to "please everybody."

On the other hand, ambiguities arise from assuming that all these groups take their religion fully seriously – as they did in the Middle Ages. That is quite another matter! And Jerusalem may well be a sign of contradiction because of religious corruption – on the part of *all* the religions which call that city theirs and holy.

The tragedy is not understood. The need of reconciliation between Arabs and Jews was well put by I. F. Stone. But is it *possible?* Never less so.

One thing good may have come out of the war – maybe it slowed down escalation in the Far East: though perhaps not decisively. The place where I still most fear the beginning of the Third World War is definitely the Near East. On the other hand, it may be quiet for a brief space now – the Arabs being so badly beaten. But a bloody reckoning is unavoidable. 400 million Moslems . . .

Letter upon letter from Dom James, read in refectory. I hear some of the material – yesterday for instance – there was a long disquisition on the questionnaire that everyone was supposed to answer last winter. I did not answer it, because one look at the questions showed that the whole thing was a waste of time – it was not in a form that could possibly be tolerated. No result was even conceivable. Apparently about 50% of the Order answered. Jealously, faithfully, and some in a pathetic outpouring of words, complaints, hopes, etc. The chief effect of Dom James' letter was to pour scorn on these as malcontents, neurotics and even "paranoids." (Well, obviously we have plenty of those!) The letter was typical: on one hand it sought to justify the questionnaire. The argument boils down to this: the questionnaire was useful because it was a very instructive example of how *not* to conduct a questionnaire. In other words it was useful precisely because it was useless. The establishment being thus justified for its stupidity, he proceeded to mock and insult (sweetly of course) those who went to the trouble of answering. Most answers were useless, and this, so he suggests was somehow *their* fault for wanting to express ideas of their own in any case. Finally, it was suggested, there will be a new questionnaire, but this time much better – and it will not ask any questions about the essentials of our life because to question the essentials would be a kind of revolt! So that just about ties up the package! The next one will also be useless, but this time it will give a nice tidy "result" which can be used in the Order to keep everything clamped down, with the unassailable argument: "This is what you yourselves have asked for!"

June 21, 1967

A hot weekend – big rain at the time of the Sunday concelebration.

Lots of helicopters hovering around these days – Tours of inspection?

The abbot is coming back sooner than he told me he would – is in New York now visiting rich friends – after returning from France via Chile.

Yesterday I was in Louisville again and I think now the doctor has the allergy shot right, so I won't have to go back again for a while. And glad of *that!* Found the Kosher foods in St. Matthew's A&P, so had Kasha for supper, and now am supplied with matzoth, potato pancakes etc. I called M. from the U. of L. and now she doesn't want to marry her fiancé after all,

[. . .] And she keeps urging me to leave the monastery so that I can "be myself." There is probably something to that, but is it quite so simple? I doubt that: the whole massive politic of getting out and getting established elsewhere is beyond me now, and there is really nowhere else I want to live but in this hermitage. I'd like to be a little more free of the system here, and able to circulate a little and find some other people who are awake and doing something: but I do have quite a few such coming here.

I know my gut allergies are to a great extent revolt against my predicament here and they get more violent and drastic every day – though the shots do help: but only help me to hold my own. I have to keep up with shots every five days to maintain the semi-comfort I had, say, last year. Certainly I had much less trouble all around when I was seeing M. – last year, apart from the back operation and bursitis, was one of the best as far as health went!

June 25, 1967

Quiet, rainy Sunday morning. 6th Sunday after Pentecost.

I am reading De Lubac's book on Teilhard de C. – *Commonweal* has asked for a review. Maybe I should not have accepted – I've been doing too many reviews. But it is interesting. And I need to understand T. In many ways I find him "*sympathique*," but I can't get excited about his mystique, though it has its good points. It strikes me as a bit romantic, and all the queer neologisms – super-Christ, christic center, hominization of the cosmos etc. and the basic activism involved seem to me to give a very tinny kind of a sound when you tap on them to see what they are like. Maybe the book will finally make him quasi-established. He is in fact very much part of a certain kind of establishment thinking.

Yesterday I went over again to see Victor Hammer in Lexington. He was very thin, tired, quiet, yet in good spirits. It does not seem possible that he will survive another heart attack. He did not say much. It is sad to see him drifting away like this and not be able to do anything for him.

Guy Davenport came over to Hammer's, then we went to the Meatyards' for a couple of drinks and to look at more photographs. Gene and Madie are two of my favorite people, and he is certainly a marvelous artist. Day before yesterday read Ronald Johnson's long poem *The [Book of the] Green Man*, which I think is one of the best poems written in this century. I wrote to him about it. Got a letter from Lewis Mumford in London about my letter to the *Times Book Review* – on the idiotic review of Mumford's book. Apparently a lot of his friends were angry at it. The kind of review where you press a button and get all the current clichés of Marshall McLuhan.

The other afternoon, Friday – in the heat, enjoyed singing all the antiphons for 1st Vespers of St. John Baptist. Indeed the feast means a lot to me this year. I am tired of going out and around. Fortun[ately] I don't have to go to Tom Jerry Smith anymore – I hope – as these shots are now working all right. May have to see Mitchell again about the back but I'll try and put it off with exercises, traction, bufferin etc. I definitely do not intend to try to see M. or do anything more about her – maybe call once in a while to see how she is doing, that's all. Mail censorship is to begin again I hear. I knew Dom J. would not be able to keep his hands off the mail. He'll be able to blame it on the General Chapter, of course! (Probably brought up the question himself.)

June 26, 1967

Importance of really studying Kafka's *Trial* is dawning on me. First of all for work – comparison with Camus' *Stranger* and for the ideas on language, war etc.

Also for my own evaluation of my own position. My own neurotic attitude toward society and my own guilt. A deep [indecipherable] in existential psychoanalysis! And on the idea of "original sin," solitude, identity etc. How K. goes to work and constructs the identity they seemingly "want" him to have (do they "want" anything?). In other words, by resisting one can effectively affirm whatever it is one is accused of and, in a manner, submit to the accusation. (Fr. Kavanaugh's book). The utter uselessness of that kind of righteousness. Du Bay also. It is clear that no one *affirms* the clerical state in all its absurdity more firmly than Du Bay with his idiot idea of a priests' union.

So too in non-institutional matters. We perpetuate our sickness, our failures, our pathologies, so that our efforts to struggle with them may be recognized as useful for others. So that our remedies may not become obsolete, we take good care to perpetuate our sickness. But there are unfortunately some ills that go on without us, remedies or no remedies. Yes: but we want to be remembered as having recognized them.

Innocence consists in not having to answer, and therefore in not even thinking about an answer. But if you already have an answer prepared you are already guilty. "Responsibility" as an admission of guilt, as a desire for it? We overdo "responsibility" and "irresponsibility." But unfortunately that is our condition.

July 3, 1967

Yesterday, the Visitation, also Sunday. Two very heavy rainstorms and other lighter showers. Had a short conversation with the Abbot of our New Zealand Monastery, Dom Joachim, whom I had met before – and who seems a bit naive. I realized to what an extent many of the Abbots themselves are little better off than the monks and are dominated by a highly authoritarian system. Dom Gabriel etc. (and Dom Celsus of Mt. Melleray dictating the smallest details of observance!). At the concelebration, for some reason I was thinking back over the past years here – and the people who have left – and the decade of the fifties when there was so much false optimism and real anguish – and how that has all been exploded now. Yet in the singing I could still hear that same pathetic Gethsemani voice – so much desire, so much good will, so much determined illusion. And yet there is something real here, but to find the reality one has to subvert the official illusion, the image of ourselves that is acceptable to (because created by) authority.

There is more fighting (on a small scale) in the Near East. Russians pouring planes and weapons back into Egypt to replace what Israel destroyed three weeks ago. I suppose one must learn to live with this kind of thinking which keeps man constantly on the edge of a new World War. But living with it seems to mean – for so many – a false optimism and a resolution to ignore the real danger. Yet one cannot live in perpetual fear either. To do so is to give in to the forces of irrationality and contribute one's own share to the confusion, the general illness.

Monsignor Chatham – (from Jackson, Miss.) – here last week. A courageous man in his sickness – but again: so happy, so convinced about the fact that Johnson and Kosygin had conversations that lasted four hours instead of two. His eyes were shining! As if those conversations meant anything! People seem determined to clutch at everything symbolic of "friendliness" and "togetherness" (no matter how deceptive) and ignore the fact that everywhere men hate and kill and arm for more killing, and that the machinery for reaching agreements simply does not work any more, because it is used by the haters for their own purposes.

————

It is one of those wonderful, bright summer mornings – sky without a wisp of cloud, pure blue (except, little storm on the horizon for everything is wet and sparkling). Birds singing. Distant roar of an occasional car on the road. On my *Ikonenkalendar* [icon calendar] – a beautiful, subdued, hieratic ikon of Cosmas and Damian, the healers.

Got a very good letter from Ron Johnson the other day, in reply to my letter about his *Green Man*. (This is a perfect *Green Man* morning. I intend to read Kilvert, Sam Palmer etc.) He spoke of having met R. S. Thomas in Wales – lovely description of his unearthly Welsh wife. Last week too I was happy with the poems sent by the little girls in California and their "underground paper."

I am curiously fond of little Diane O'Callaghan – all of those children, but somehow especially Diane, who for some reason I sense to be more complicated and more vulnerable – there is a great curiosity between us, and a strange sort of attraction which at times makes her moody and aloof, and then suddenly breaks out in a kind of childlike passion, as when we were playing in the water and she swam to me and began climbing all over me and holding onto me desperately saying "You're all warm, you're all warm." She is I think nine years old, or ten. I feel a great tenderness and care for her, and I want her to grow up happy: and I think she will probably know a lot of anguish. But she has a mind of her own and a precocious heart.

July 4, 1967

Having got a couple of *New Yorker*s from the Hammers when I was in Lexington, I read this morning a report from Jerusalem by Renata Adler, on that fast little war. You can't get away from the fact that the Israeli Jews are in reality Europeans and Westerners. And in the background is World War II, with Hitler, the Nazis, etc. And the bourgeois world. Good, courageous people who make us feel that *one* culture makes sense, that *we* are courageous, resourceful, sacrificing, etc. And it is true that they did a courageous job and defended themselves successfully – more than successfully. And incidentally it appears that Nasser really had plans for genocide . . . I certainly sympathize with the plight of the Arab refugees, and all the poor people who have again lost their homes and their hopes. I can understand the Arabs feeling bitter – but the fact remains that it should be possible for them to get along with Israel if they wanted to and that if there were a little give and take there could be cooperation between them. And that Israel is not unwilling to try this. It is people like Nasser who are, at times, implacable. And they keep the hatred of the ignorant and helpless always inflamed, so that they think destroying Israel will somehow help them solve their problems. The Russians concur – and provide weapons.

Joke – (reported as told by an Israeli scientist at Weizmann institute first morning of the war).

> A Jew is walking down the street in tears.
> Someone meets him and asks what is the matter.
> "I am an optimist."
> "If you are an optimist why are you crying?"
> "You think in days like this it is easy to be an optimist?"

I think back to the morning of June 5 when I was driving along the Watterson expressway with Joe Carroll and the radio was on, giving the first news of the war – alerts at Tel Aviv, shelling in Jerusalem etc. Bright, sunny morning – flat land – a few new buildings rising stark and without character in the sky: a new motel going up etc. It might have been Tel Aviv itself, for all you could tell by the look of things. Also: how fortunate it was that Israel won so fast, that by the next day everything was already settled: indeed it was already settled that morning when we were coming into Louisville. One among the scattered reports, was the right one and it seemed the least likely at the time. Some Israeli spokesman had said that "our plans are succeeding remarkably well!" or words to that effect. If it had been longer and more complicated, it would have perhaps involved everyone.

Meanwhile also, I reflect on my own strange position: I hear a bit of news here and another bit there and then come back to the woods and it all cooks in my mind. But I don't get in the full stream of it, and don't have the same content as everyone else. Of course, if the news is not real news, this doesn't matter. In the real events, though, I cannot help but lack perspective. Not that this perspective of everyone is necessarily the right one.

July 5, 1967

Yesterday turned into a very happy day: it was bright and cool all day (the nights have been almost cold – between 50 and 60). Early in the morning I heard a truck coming up through the fields and could see my new bookcases swaying about the cab. It also meant that the sink and cabinet were arriving (I still use the outhouse, however; no indoor toilet). So my kitchen was finally fixed up, the water connected, and I cleaned up the whole place, gathering up the books that were piled all over chairs and everywhere. The new furniture smells marvelously of fresh cedar and the place is really transformed by it. At last the kitchen is a real kitchen, and I don't have to wash dishes in a bucket on the floor. It took six months from the time the well-rig first got here, to the time I first washed my hands in the new sink. To celebrate I had supper of chop-suey and rice, and walked in the clear cool evening utterly at peace and happy with the cottage. In fact I stayed up late, not for any special reason, but just walking around smelling the good smell of the cedarwood, looking at the new look of the rooms, and loving the place to be as clean as it (for once) is!

Yesterday morning, too, instead of reading, I got on to the typewriter and finished my review of De Lubac on Teilhard: and that was a good thing, because if I had left it until later I would not have done anything on it (the plumbers being here etc.) and would have felt very frustrated.

Also I am back reading Camus – *Actuelles I* and Kafka's *Trial* – and will keep working toward the Camus book I want to finish, if possible, this year.

It is good not to have to go to town again. I have been in there too much and it has got me out of the real tempo of my solitary life, which I am, I hope, now recovering. Today a long quiet day.

Terribly sad and poignant statements and poems of the Buddhist nun, Nhat Chi, who burned herself to death May 16. Utterly tragic – and no one pays any attention: her death is meaningless to them. That is the real tragedy – not her immolation, but that it is taken for granted, ignored, not even known, perhaps, to people who simply don't care about such things. Once, a few years ago, it was a novelty! . . . That her death was an extreme cry for peace is not even regarded as significant. The complete inability of people to *attend* to any such thing. Communications media reduce everything to zero and there is no more communication, only a cloud of grey, shapeless, undifferentiated images, all meaningless.

It rains. A letter came today from a girl in Lanza del Vasto's "Communauté de l'Arche." A seven-day fast is being planned for December. Seven days of *complete* abstinence from food. They want me to join in and get others to do the same. I certainly want to try, though I have never gone that long without food, or even half that long. It will need some preparation! Whether I

can manage seven days or not, I think it is a good idea to get back to some ✕
real fasting. I have not fasted much at all since last year. That business with
M. really threw me off my track in a crash. Now I no longer look back on it
with longing and desire, but just with embarrassment. It was really a stupid
thing – though I recognize that it had a lot of good points because it
brought out the things that had to come out and be recognized. It would
have been much worse had they remained hidden. Still I began drinking
more than I should – whenever I had a chance to, at least. And really lost all
serious discipline except for the one thing: solitude. Keeping to the woods
was what saved me.

Beautiful letter from Margaret Gardiner today in the Orkneys.

July 8, 1967

Fasted yesterday (morning) and found I did not get much useful reading
done without that morning coffee. Yet it is certainly good to feel empty and
hungry. I do find I am eating less anyway.

Steady downpour of rain Thursday. I got permission to have an altar and
say Mass in the hermitage. Went over to Buck Murfield, the cabinet maker
at Athertonville, to order the altar in a hurry in the hope of getting it some
time like next week – perhaps to say my first Mass here on the 16th, which
is the Feast of Our Lady of Carmel (Sunday this year), patronal feast of the
hermitage. (The feast has been dropped from the Cistercian Ordo, where it
used to be on the 17th.)

Victor Hammer is critically ill in the hospital, partially paralyzed, in an oxy-
gen tent, dying. Have thought very much about him all the time. Death is
shocking in anyone, but most shocking in the case of someone of real genius and quality and someone you know and love well. The blunt fact is that
it is just not conceivable that Victor Hammer should cease to exist. This is a
basic absurdity which Camus confronted, and which religious explanations
may perhaps help us only to evade. Instead of facing the inscrutable *fact* that
the dead are no longer there, and that we don't *know* what happens to them,
we affirm that they are there, somewhere, and we *know* . . . But we don't
know, and our act of faith should be less facile; it should be rooted in our
unknowing, not just a further construction of a kind of instinctive feeling
for survival. Yet what is man that his life instinct should translate itself into
a conviction that he cannot really altogether die? Where is it illusory and

where not? To my mind this is a great and pertinent question and one worth while exploring metaphysically – not by abstractions but by contemplative discipline and by a kind of mystical "pragmatism" if you like. One *can* to some extent sort out various forms of experience of the ground of being which gives us clues to what is fundamental in us. Obviously these cannot be "objective." Hence they can't be scientifically proved. But they can be "checked" against the same quality of experience in other subjects who have undergone similar discipline and are "enlightened." Such experience seems to show that the individual consciousness is rooted in something much deeper. We do not know how the ego is "united" with this deeper consciousness, but we know it tends to arrogate to itself what belongs to the ground which both is and is not the self (both permanent and transcendent). Can this be explored in language relevant to modern man? In any case, don't assume he is not concerned! He is very much concerned to find out who he really is and what his true capacities are.

I offered Mass for Victor on Thursday, saying the Collect for the dying. He is not interested in receiving the Sacraments, though I understand Carolyn got a priest to see him. Curiously enough I understand his willingness, and know that he does believe in God and that his mistrust of the Church is somehow part of a deeper belief. This is an experience in modern man that we *have* to face, and come to terms with. Yet I think Carolyn would like him to receive the Sacraments (she is not Catholic). To me, also, obviously, it would be much more "satisfactory" – I do feel it would be more consistent with his whole life and his work, not just a concession to convention or something – perhaps I am wrong but I think it would be consistent with his most authentic desires. But can I presume to settle someone else's conscience for him? I know most priests would disapprove, but I have a deep repugnance for the Catholic idea that at all costs you have to so to speak "enforce" the Sacraments when someone is dying, taking advantage of their condition, as if God could not save them without our fuss, as if we had to *overcome* their conscience in order to make it right. Who knows? It might be the surest way to make it wrong.

Yesterday, with an empty stomach, I read with indifference and incomprehension about the starvation in Kabylie in Camus' article of 1939. Today with good coffee and a cooked breakfast of eggs – read the same with understanding and indignation! So the luxury of being articulate depends on a certain detachment, disinvolvement. Is it better to participate in the stupor of hunger and have nothing to say? Both are necessary: hunger and silence, nourishment and speech. Finding the right alternation – and being ready to be *reduced* to silence and hunger by no choice of one's own, if necessary. The dangerous assumption of an absolute right to be fed and articulate when the majority starve and are tongue-tied. Illusory dignity of the well-fed spokesman who justifies himself by diagnosis, planning and exhortation: the vicious circle of *political* life.

July 13, 1967

Fasting again but this time drank some tea, which makes all the difference in so far as keeping one's *mind* alive goes. A bright, clear morning after days of rain. Monday morning was a deluge. As the light began to grow and the valley became discernible, I saw the bottom-fields had all become one big lake. Walked out in the lull of the hard rain and saw through the trees the rushing flood water – an old tire riding by very fast on muddy waves. I was afraid Buck Murfield was flooded out and would have to stop work on the altar. Went over to Athertonville Tuesday, and sure enough the floods had been there, 31E had been closed off by water and there were still houses that had water up to the front porch. But Buck and his wife were planing away in their shop which was full of the sweet smell of cedar. I still have hopes of getting the altar in time for Sunday.

Victor Hammer died on Monday, while we were flooded here. I heard about it Tuesday morning and said Mass for him. A great loss. I don't know if he finally received the Sacraments – I suspect he did not and respect his reasons. There is no question that to him it would have been an empty formality that did not correspond to his own particular kind of faith. And the problem in my own mind is that, much as I would have wanted to do anything I could, I felt somehow that any aggressiveness about it would have meant forcing upon him some sign that, instead of affirming our friendship and understanding – a religious and spiritual and Christian understanding – would in some sense have violated it: not because of the idea of Sacraments, but because of the "official" meaning that Sacraments have unfortunately acquired.

There is such a problem about the social *meaning* of certain signs, ways of participating in worship, etc. I still feel there is a great deal of uncertainty about the meaning of the new Liturgy for instance, because of the gap between the theological statements *about what it ought to be* and the actuality of what it is. The theologians declare that the Liturgy is the place of God's power and visible presence: but is that what one "sees"? I admit that when one believes, then the Liturgy *is* a place of holiness and sharing in God's presence and in His peace. But for me this was even more true in the old Liturgy – though also true of concelebration, true of my own Mass – I can't seem to find the differences that are declared to be so important.

True, there is a lot of ambivalence in me because I am a non-liturgical type, and because, isolated as I am, I am very little aware of what is really going on and sense that I do the new things badly, confusedly, that I don't take easily to the priestly role, the office of celebrant, the leader of the people at prayer. Yet in my heart of hearts I don't mind, I don't feel it is a handicap really, except insofar as the official life of the Church goes – about which I really don't care.

Ed Rice wrote that he had sold *Jubilee* to Herder & Herder. Notre Dame Press will probably publish *Faith and Violence* as a paperback. The commentary on Camus' *Plague* is ready to go off to Seabury Press. I have had too little time to do real work – still seeing too many people. To have to spend an afternoon with a visitor twice a week is far too much for me. Once would be too much. I'd like to get it down to once or twice *a month*. But there are people you have to see. Jim Wygal was out yesterday. Tomorrow Pat W. from the library – there is work to do! Which is OK. But just visiting and socializing is not OK. Especially if I sit around drinking.

July 14, 1967

No matter what else I get involved in, and no matter how many mistakes I make, I am more and more convinced that my task is here in the woods (or some woods somewhere). I have said this so often that the words to express it are loose and have no grip on it. The reality is changing, and is not something I really understand at all. In a way I seem to have less footing. Certainly I know it is not simple and that my own estimate of the situation has been pretty crude. The whole question of my relationship to the community is something I can't formulate and I'll just let it go for the moment – except that the community to me is a curious, sometimes funny, sometimes crazy phenomenon which does not even understand itself. It bewilders me, and yet I am so much part of it. And that is frustrating too, for I am involved in and identified with something so wacky and pathetic, so full of ambivalences, all those guys, some solid, mostly half wits I think, who are nevertheless good, well-meaning people and honest in their way, and many of whom are here on account of me – so that their madness is now mixed up with my own madness and I am part of it.

For example – yesterday in the bushes to the west of me, beyond "my" long field – red-bearded Bro. Odilo, solemn in a white sun helmet, and old Trappist work robe, erecting a weird wood and plastic squatter hermitage . . . Fantastic. Beyond all George Price cartoons! But obviously this is partly my fault.

And the Abbot, his elaborate little game of pretending he wants to retire (as a dream it is sincere, but is it more than a velleity? He has to indulge himself in something!). Actually he can't and won't let go of his power. Goes around telling everyone it is now his "duty" to stay and help watch over the new changes – and precisely what we need, if we are to have any real renewal, is for him to retire. So he will stay in office in order to *prevent* real change, and that will be his excuse for not embracing a solitary life he really doesn't want. Blame it all on God!

Part of the game now is to go around getting opinions on it and getting people to plead with him not to resign – or else to discuss the joys of the hermit life which, alas, God's will and duty prevent him from enjoying.

I can see how Dom James is cheating: but so what? What good does that do me? And what good can I do *him?* The more important thing is that I too am cheating and perhaps more than the others. Perhaps monstrously. For instance – the collection at Bellarmine, the collection of Sister Thérèse [Lentfoehr] – and all the business of filing and cataloguing every little slip of paper I ever wrote on! What a comedy! But I like it and cooperate wholeheartedly because I imagine it is for real. That I will last. That I will be a person, studied and commented on . . . This is a problem, man. So today Pat Welsh is coming and Mrs. Schumann and we will settle "problems" of cataloguing maybe. On the other hand it will be fun to see Pat again (last time was when Slate and I took her and Fr. John [Loftus] to the Luau Room).

Fouled up community living. Always trying to wangle a special community for myself on my own terms. The more suitable companions. Bad? I don't know. But it doesn't work either. And the hippies – so pathetic and unhappy in many ways.

July 16, 1967

Today, patronal Feast of my hermitage, first Mass here (after nearly seven years). Went over to Athertonville Saturday after dinner to get the altar, sweet smelling, in Buck Murfield's dark shop. Some of the fields still under water from the floods the other day. Saturday was bright and glorious – exceptionally cool dry weather, lovely white clouds dry and full of sun, clean, pure. Set up in the hermitage, with ikons over it, the altar is just right (but I need curtains for front windows for privacy and to help the slick ikons from glaring with reflected light).

Said Mass (at hermitage) this morning (though Sunday) – Mass of Our Lady of Carmel. *Epikeia,*[16] Dom James concurring (approved by Fr. Chrysogonus!). The most official *Epikeia* you ever saw! So official it is no longer an act of virtue perhaps.

Mass about 4:30 or 4:45. Said it slowly, even sang some parts (of Gregorian Kyrie, Gloria, Preface, and other bits). It was a beautiful Mass and I now see that having the altar there is a *great* step forward and a huge help. I wish I had done this before, but Dom James was always against it and I did not push until I learned Fr. Flavian was going to get approval in August to say Mass in *his* hermitage when his first year is up. So I decided to ask. In the past Dom James objected that it would be inconvenient for a server to come. Now he said, "Well of course you won't need a server."

Saying Mass up here changes the shape of the day, and eating dinner up here makes it *completely* leisurely. The best Sunday I can remember in a very long time. The morning was perfect. Eventually, after reading, I went for a walk to the Gethsemani statues in the Grove (the Jon Daniels statues) – brilliant sun, and everything very quiet in the late morning.

I have to give an evening conference – spoiled the day for me. I am tired of these performances, these Sunday amusements, entertainments of the bored. And when I get tense out of resistance to the chore, I insist too much, and say more than I mean. It is futile. I will have to try again to give these talks up. Is the fact that "people like them" a good enough reason? I feel the whole business is a bit phony. I am no longer in touch with the community

---

[16] *Epikeia* literally means "act of justice," observing the spirit rather than the letter of the law for the sake of the common good.

or very much in sympathy with it. Or able to understand what it is trying to do in its desperation. Does charity *demand* that I be involved in affairs I can do nothing to remedy? Certainly my talks (now on Sufism) have little to do with current monastic problems – directly – but I make ironic observations that are no help! The whole thing embarrasses me. It is false.

July 18, 1967

Just finished reading in manuscript a series of letters to Clervaux from Dom Leclercq on his recent trip to Asia. A fantastic document. India, Thailand, Cambodia, Vietnam, Philippines, Indonesia and then back. As he flew back to Europe his plane was rerouted to Athens instead of Cairo and he did not know he was flying over a war! I had an interesting letter from him written in Manila, about Vietnam, and another when he got back.

It was a monastic journey above all – to give retreats in contemplative monasteries mostly. Could be expanded into a very good book, vivid impressions of the Church in Asia – stupidity, ugliness, incomprehension, activism, pomposity, yet also holiness, simplicity, beginning of openness, some good monastic beginnings. Yet all in all I get a feeling that the Church in Asia is clinging to the worst of Westernism and too identified with western power. Yet the best he found was in monasteries that have some connection with the Cistercian line, official or not, like Kurisumala (P. Francis [Acharya of Scourmont] and Dom Bede Griffiths), or the Pierre-qui-Vire foundations and the Cistercians of Vietnam, the Trappists of Indonesia. This was encouraging at least.

Fantastic impression of crowds, heat, misery, with the wealth and comfort of the western places, the *corruption* of America in Vietnam, the hatred of Americans – and oppressive sense of my own immobility. What to make of it? Do I care? (The quiet of the morning here, the singing birds, irreplaceable.) But the fact of not being able to go anywhere at a moment when everybody is on planes, means that I am inevitably out of touch with the full reality of my time. Or does it? *Everybody* on planes? Millions go nowhere – and those monks in Asian monasteries, where do they go? Perhaps going nowhere is better. I don't know. But I feel it, am galled by the rope that ties me up.

Yesterday Fr. Hilarion – who is becoming a hermit out of desperation and fed up with the community – (a bad motive!) – came to talk to me and discuss his situation. He is intelligent, lucid, and bitter, though not wildly so.

He sees completely through Dom James – as lucidly as anyone here, but he also knows how many in the community are either taken in by Dom J. or cowtow to let him be boss in any way he pleases. We both agreed that J. has no real intention of retiring – that the longer he stays in office the worse it will be – harder for the monastery when he eventually *does* die or retire. He makes it harder and harder for his successor. There will be an explosion and God knows how the next man will be able to get the pieces back together again. Another one is leaving – Bro. Jude. The Visitation that is coming in a couple of weeks will of course be no help at all, for in these Visitations no one does anything but listen to complaints, jolly people along, and end with a fine speech that compliments the Abbot on having a lovely community and the community on having a splendid Abbot and all continues as before. There is no recourse. It is a system that has ceased to work except to keep itself in existence – and to ensure that everyone works for the system.

July 20, 1967

Letter from P. Charles Dumont, who has been continually ill. I don't know how he still manages to get out the *Collectanea*. He resigned from the commission working on the revision of the Constitutions – and that is a good thing. A thankless and useless task, which could only grind him down for nothing.

Weather cool and misty. I am working on Camus's *Réflexions sur la guillotine [Reflections on the Guillotine]* – a powerful and subtle piece of work and very important for a real understanding of his novels. Perhaps the real key to them. Yesterday I corrected and sent back proofs of the review article on Camus to the *Sewanee Review*.

Yesterday afternoon Dom James came up to [the] hermitage on an "official" visit. Don't quite know what he was at – you never do. We conversed for about 1/2 hour without really communicating anything except the fact that we don't use the same language. Yet I decided to talk to him about his own desire (?) to retire and be a hermit, encouraging him to do this, and saying I did not think he had a "duty" to remain in command of this monastery. I doubt if he really can give up that command – and I doubt he really wants to be a hermit. Also I think he may hold this against me in some subtle way – because I have questioned his present position of "I-want-to-resign-but-duty-forbids" etc. (which I think is merely an evasion). Of course I did not tell him that outright. He is a man who *cannot* be direct and with whom directness is impossible. One must suggest everything obliquely in the midst of banalities. Which is also what he does. (Snide remark about the "activism" of the IHM Nuns – Corita – to whom Anselm Steinke preached a conservative retreat.)

July 22, 1967. St. Mary Magdalen

I will no longer worry (and haven't really worried much so far) about being a somewhat disruptive influence in the monastery. I do not *have* to rock the boat, but I think it is good to do so anyway. I think I really do the community a service by keeping many people unsettled, and raising dangerous questions. Also by being something of a temptation and a scandal. What I do regret is having led others unconsciously into a kind of trap – raising profound and pathetic hopes and then delivering them up to the mercies of a monastic institution by which those hopes are systematically frustrated.

Yet it is a wonder Dom James lets me go on disrupting things as I do. It obviously bothers him and upsets his own peace of mind at times. I guess he is content to keep me in the trap and not let me out to spread the bad news. That reassures him, gives him a sense that he is in control: and then he continues with indirect hints which try to silence me: but he does not insist. He does not want to be in the role of a "reactionary" and repressive Superior – and also he is always influenced by the fact that people *like* what I do and say. He is not so much afraid of silencing and suppressing me, as of displeasing all these people. Only let them be *dis*pleased (with me) – and my story would be a different one.

July 26, 1967. St. Anne

There have been worse riots this summer than ever before – and everywhere. Cincinnati (even Louisville – where whites were causing the disorder), Newark, Cleveland, Erie, and especially Detroit were the worst so far. In other words all the illusions about a peaceful and orderly settlement of things has really broken down and the violence is becoming revolutionary – though still in a haphazard, nihilistic sort of way. Things are as I said they would be when I wrote about it all three or four years ago. The rest is coming: perhaps the next election (1968) will be a big step towards Fascism. The majority of whites will find no other answer. There were five thousand paratroopers called in to Detroit.

Dom James has given Fr. Hilarion permission to live as a hermit and today, I understand, a 30 foot trailer has arrived for him to live in. But I also understand there was some protest about this in a Council Meeting. Fr. H. is here at most ten years and has not served the community in any exacting job – and everyone knows he is getting permission not so much because he has a hermit vocation as because he can't stand living in the same house with Dom James – and it's mutual. But the hermit life is not the answer to that kind of problem, and I thought Dom James would have been fairer simply to let the man go somewhere else and do what he wants. But he will go to such lengths just to keep his name on our books! I wonder what will come of it. I imagine H. is perfectly capable of enjoying life alone in a trailer – but what about all the others in the community who think they want the same thing?

Dom Ignace Gillet is coming for his first visitation here in a day or two. About which nobody especially cares, knowing it is a pure formality. Br. Eric put up some curtain rods for me (I can't handle machines to drill holes in concrete) and now I can close off the front windows at night and when saying Mass. Also I hope to say Mass up here more often. Am making a tape at Sr. Luke's request for the Lorettines' General Chapter. Wrote a letter to a Contemplative Nuns' Superior in Canada whose bishop wants them to make themselves "useful," take care of old people or etc.

Getting late. For once there is a hot-night racket of insects and frogs (it has been very cool this summer). I wasted time re-reading bits of this journal – looking again for the M. stuff – so hopeless. She has been in Cape Cod, I know, and got back Saturday (that was her plan). I have not had a chance to contact her and – what's the use? – don't especially want to. And yet . . . it has been so foolish. I know that what I have to do is work on my meditation, and on the kind of life that people forget exists. And she is no help in that. Yet I felt so much more real when we were in love. And yet too I know how much illusion was in it. (Or at least I can make a good guess!)

July 27, 1967

Today a copy of Victor Hammer's last book reached me, from Carolyn. A beautiful thing – in its physical production, and in his thoughts. An admirable testament, and I spent the afternoon reading it, sad and moved. So many of the pages were things he had brought over in proof to discuss last year! I certainly miss him. This evening I reflected how his visits were always something reassuring, stabilizing – because of his intelligence and European culture. All the things we could talk about – from cave art to Pavese, from Austrian rococo to Berenson. I never felt distracted and restless after one of his visits with Carolyn here: we belonged together. Other visits disturb and distract me, as if I had somehow been untrue to myself – involved in small talk, or trivialities. With Victor and Carolyn – we were not necessarily serious at every moment and we could drink a good bottle of wine and some Spanish brandy on top of it: and I really enjoyed it, without an afterthought. Others are much more like strangers, even though I like them too.

Guy Davenport and Gene Meatyard (and Maddie) are also good to talk to, and with Gene and his ideas for photographs I always find we are doing something exciting and good.

August 1, 1967

Nightfall. Crickets and thunder. Last night there were three storms here, the worst just about the time I got up (3:15). Violent rain threshing down, continual lightning and as I was putting on my shoes a terrific thwack of lightning striking in the woods near my cottage. I jumped! After Lauds (which I recited with more devotion than usual!) the storms cleared a bit, or rather moved up toward the east. Our storms go over to Loretto. I went out on the porch and my morning meditation consisted largely in attention to the marvelous play of three storms over our valley: one far south, one east (having passed over here), one passing by in the NW. Some lovely shapes and signatures of lightning in the South.

When the sun came up we had a clear morning. I said Mass at the hermitage and read late. When I was saying the little hours about 10, the bell rang for a death in the monastery. It was Fr. Nicholas [Caron], the translator at visitations, who had a heart attack while translating for Dom Ignace Gillet in the scrutiny and died 1/2 hour afterwards. A good simple priest (Canadian). I met Dom Ignace, who also seems to be a simple type and less of a big wheel than Dom Gabriel. Two others are translating in the Scrutiny and I was drafted to translate in the evening chapter. Which I did. I have just come back. A quiet, comforting talk on love, death, eternal life. Felt the peace and security it generated in the community and wondered – how much of this is psychological? How deep is it? Is it too easily reassuring? I don't know. I know my own faith is less comfortable, and I am not proud of that necessarily. Yes it is all right to say we will get to heaven and hundreds of "souls" will come running up to thank us for helping them get there. And yet – is that what it will be *like?* "Eye hath not seen." I have no idea what it will be like. Yes, I believe it. But not in the way he seemed to *imagine* it. He talked about how easily we forget those we love on earth, and as I walked up through the field I was thinking of M., as if that were the kind of love he meant. I haven't been in contact with her for over a month – and have no plans for getting in contact in the near future. Yet I wondered how she is.

Heavy doses of rain began to fall on the roof of the hermitage. Beyond the woods, the insistent lowing of Andy Boone's cow. I am up late. It is time to go to bed. Tomorrow they take the body of Fr. Nicholas to Georgia to his own monastery.

August 2, 1967

Reading [Joost] Meerloo's remarkable manuscript *Homo Militans [Militant Man]* (not yet published in English – he wants me to collaborate with him on it). It is very interesting for the idea that I am working on – ambiguity and "communication" through the language – doubletalk and doublethink – surrounding peace and war. He makes so clear the fact that on another level than that of explicit statements, we convey fears, hostilities etc. which are the "real" communication.

This is the explanation of what was healthy in Dom Ignace's talk in chapter last night. The thoughts were completely familiar and ordinary – and underlying them was really no hostility that one could sense, only an authentic peacefulness, well-wishing, acceptance of the hearers etc. The problem is that this benevolence seems to imply that the past *ignores* unpleasant realities in modern life and assumes an archaic stability which no longer exists to support this "peacefulness" in younger monks.

And I am *not* peaceful. I realize (through Meerloo) how much my own life is an unsuccessful attempt to control my own hostilities – perhaps not entirely unsuccessful: but hardly "whole."

Evening. I sit up late again listening to crickets and frogs because I can't go to bed yet. I had to translate in chapter again tonight – which is not my business at all, and realize I may be stuck with this for the rest of the visitation. Came back feeling stupid, as if I had done wrong. And in fact these sessions in chapter are, in their own way, stupid. Dom Ignace was very nice and simple and gave a talk on his impressions of Japan and I did a good job of translating and made everyone happy – and it was childish. I am ashamed of myself. I did the best I could and it was silly. And so I pretend I belong here . . . as if I belonged somewhere. The woods, OK. But I came back feeling sad. And I realize it is this way almost everywhere and with everyone except very few people. Going to chapter – just as reprehensible as going to Thompson Willett's and playing with little Alice in the pool. Got back – read a happy underground paper from Cleveland and felt the same about *that*. It is silly. It is stupid shit. Then I read a little poetry magazine. The same. Do I now have to think there is something the matter? This does not follow. I will no doubt have to go to chapter for a few days and do my silly bit. But I don't have to read happy newspapers and poetry magazines that still take themselves seriously. Or anything else of the kind. The *Suramgamma Sutra* – maybe. That's different. And there's a lot of classic shit in that too. Fortunately I had some bourbon in the hermitage.

August 4, 1967

Fortunately I have got over that particular bout of nonsense and feel much better. I guess, however, it is understandable. Light is thrown on the situation by an article Sister Luke sent (review of [Irving] Goffman's *Asylum* [Chicago, 1961] by Sister Aloysius – a student of Marcel's) – the question of the *total institution*. I am undoubtedly feeling the effects of twenty-five–twenty-six years of "total isolation" – in which I have been freer than most but in which, because of my masochism and insecurity, I tend to bog down in self-pity and self-defeat. And Dom James is a case any way. – The thing that was really irritating me was the fact that Cardinal Koenig is coming to this country, and had invited me to meet with him, Norman Cousins and some others in the East to discuss the business of his commissions and the Archbishop urged me to go – and Dom James refuses. The refusal is not absolutely definitive yet but might as well be. I know he has a bad conscience about it because he was rattled and almost incoherent, besides telling a few lies, or rather getting across a few deceptive insinuations. The problem is partly that I cannot believe him or really respect him. But so what? For my own part I know I do not need to be present at a meeting with Cardinal K. and it is just as well I don't get involved in something that might lead to a "career" of sorts – and this is what Dom J. wants to prevent above all: my having any kind of importance in the Church. Honestly – I am not sorry about that!

Anyway, last night Dom Ignace gave a talk with lantern slides about Hong Kong. Curious! The idea of the Abbot General who goes around making everybody happy some way or other! I appreciate his well-meant kindness. One feels he is at least trying. I enjoyed some of the pictures of Hong Kong at night – and some of the sampans, beautifully built boats, even though half-ruined. Came up home thinking of the difference between the way a sampan is built and the way an American car is built. The sampan is beautiful because it is built to be what it is according to traditional design that embodies experience and is practical. The car may or may not be beautiful, depending on the year but the design is self-conscious and the purpose is to "sell" beauty. Hence the project is essentially meretricious. There are indeed lovely whores – both here and in China. But the whore's society should not become a standard of truth, a measure of the human. When it does . . . With us it has. And I can see where in certain areas and periods of Chinese culture it did too.

Yesterday I had to see Dr. Mitchell about a bad knee now. Arthritis, or more especially some long word I can't remember – so I can't kneel. "Old soccer injuries" he keeps saying. (What I played was rugby.) Around the U. of L. – struck above all by the overcompensating efforts at friendliness on the part of some Negroes. One of them in a very loud rather comic conversation with a girl student about an exam. The Negro girl in the cafeteria calling a white cracker type girl "honey." Well, it was good. I don't think most Negroes are too happy about the summer's violence and they don't want to get themselves feeling separate and excluded.

The U. of L. library is a great mess because they are in the midst of changing their cataloguing system and moving all the books around. I couldn't find anything I was looking for. But I did manage to find a few things I was not looking for – [Bertolt] Brecht's *[Die] Hauspostille*, something of Giordano Bruno – [James] Mooney – on *The Ghost Dance [Religion* (Seattle, 1965)] and two volumes of *Man* with good articles. Particularly now I see I have to read Claude Lévi-Strauss.

August 5, 1967. F[east] of Our Lady of Lourdes
Said Mass at hermitage and fasted. A beautiful day. At noon, instead of sitting around feeling hungry, I went for a walk over to see Fr. Hilarion's new hermitage, the trailer which has been installed over on Linton's. The door was not locked (it would not shut properly) so I got in and looked around. It is fairly roomy for a trailer but still looked as if a good sneeze would blow it over and as far as I am concerned I don't think I would like it. But my three-room cinder block cottage is luxurious in comparison, and very nice now, full of books and supplies, venetian blinds, curtains etc.

Fasting was not too hard, even on a 24-hour stretch. And it slows you down, which perhaps in my case is a good thing. Took some pictures – roots again, this time with a Roleflex which I like very much. I need to get something that might serve as a cover for "Edifying Cables." Typed a couple of new poems from the big longhand book and can't say I am sure about them. Yet they sound good on tape, at least to me.

Yesterday I went to Dom Ignace for my official turnout at the scrutiny – he took careful notes, and when I happened in passing to refer to René Char (who after all has family near Aiguebelle) Dom Ig. had never heard of him. He carefully wrote down in my report "René Char." Also he had not heard of the Detroit riots. I told him of them but he did not write them down!

August 9, 1967

Hot night. Woods alive with insects and tree frogs. Steamy. My glasses got steamed up when I put them on. There was a heavy four- or five-hour storm this morning during which lightning hit the utility pole next to the hermitage and blew out some bulbs. A great whack! I thought all the lights were gone. Read with a kerosene lamp when it appeared that all my front room lights were useless. Glad I had finished Mass (though I would say Mass with candles only and do, after the Sanctus).

The regular visitation closed. I had to interpret for Dom Ignace in chapter every evening and tonight read the Vis[itation] card. Nothing very special on it. But I think the visitation was a good one, all things considered. It was peaceful and he is a nice, reassuring, well-meaning person, obviously not looking for opportunities to prove himself the boss etc., but content to keep people tranquil and things in order. So nothing much is done, but perhaps in this situation it is best simply to stay quiet and find our situation tolerable – I won't say hopeful.

Reading Carl Amery's excellent book on the German Church. *Capitulation* [New York, 1967]. Instructive for everybody. A lot of what is said applies here too. Very much so!

The Church of the monastery is nearly finished, finally – after nearly 16 months of work. I find it looks pretty good inside, and is still recognizable as the Church of Gethsemani, though the apse windows are gone (which I don't necessarily regret). The stalls are in a different place and so is the altar, but it is improved all around. Since I am glad it is basically the same, after all those years of sweat and patience and exultation in the old one. I don't expect to be in this one much except occasionally for concelebration. There are fewer stalls than there were before and a great void between the stalls and the sanctuary.

So many memories of the old Church – the energy and agony I had to put into just *getting through* some of the ceremonies – and yet I remember all with a kind of joy, because of the graces, especially of the first days here. And being Hebdomadary, singing the Mass, was a joy, too, though I was often so painfully nervous about it.

I'll always remember the temporary third-floor chapel too – standing in the sacristy there on Sundays looking out over the starlit fields and St. Joseph's hills and the distant hills behind Athertonville, and praying for M. (especially last year!). What a crazy life this has been!

This afternoon wrote out some answers to an interview from a Marxist magazine in Chile *(Punto Final)*.

August 11, 1967

Finished Carl Amery's *Capitulation.* One of the best things I had read on modern Catholicism as it *is* – in its identification with bourgeois material establishment, its inclination to favor the bomb and war (against Communism), to frown on pacifists and radicals, but at the same time to triumphally present "progressive" images of itself – Mercedes-Benz churches – streamlined liturgy conducted by boy Sergeants etc. And (as in Germany) its serene capacity to eat its cake and have it: to celebrate in the same breath [Franz] von Papen, who lined the Church up with Nazism, and the [indecipherable] resistance fighters – all five or six of them, who were destroyed by the Nazis while abandoned and excluded by their fellow Catholics ([Fr. Alfred] Delp, [Fr. Max Josef] Metzger, [Franz] Jägerstätter etc. Even unknown to fellow Catholics).

The book reinforces my conclusion that there is *nothing* to be looked for from Church officialdom. Any good that I will ever do for the people of my time will be done, if at all, *in spite* of my Superiors rather than with their help. This is certainly true of my writing: Dom Frederic actively encouraged it (but probably would not have done so if he had known where it would lead). Dom James has tolerated what he could no longer prevent –

because it was too successful and he would look like a reactionary. He confines himself to hints about writing "only spiritual things." His prohibition on any going out, and contacts at semi-official conferences etc. (like the Koenig affair) is really all to the good. It keeps me from getting involved in the ambiguities of official dialogue and image making for the Post Conciliar Church. Good!

August 14, 1967. *Vigil of the Assumption*

Said Mass quietly at the hermitage and fasted in the morning. (In the evening made too much rice and creole and am weighted down with it. No matter!)

Yesterday I went to concelebrate, under the impression that it might be the last Sunday Mass to be concelebrated in the 3rd-floor temporary Chapel. But after the Mass Fr. David, questioned by signs, said that no it would be a month or so yet before we moved into the renovated Church.

At the concelebration I was tense and depressed. I don't exactly know why, except that I wished I were not there.

Tonight, I realize that I have too much let myself be influenced by people who are bad for me, and Dom James is one of them. There are plenty of others, perhaps worse, but he is the one who has the most decisively bad effect in some ways. Yes, it is probably counteracted and compensated for by the grace of the visitation. But he is a depressing and deadening force in my life, sickening, negative, sterile. I suppose I can still adapt to it and neutralize it. Rosemary Ruether says the most Christian thing I could do with Dom James would be to tell him to go to hell. She means I should leave. And yet I really have no desire to leave. Nor anywhere else I really want to go – except I think I would gain by getting out of this atmosphere and going somewhere to get a new perspective and maybe learn a few things I need to know. To get out of this stagnation.

But my own feeling about it is that I can be more really solitary here, and more careful about the things, people and ideas I open myself to here. The point of solitude is to preserve myself from a certain type of mental contagion. And of course I know a lot of the people I have been seeing are also not good for me either. On the other hand I do seem to be able to give them something. I don't know. The whole thing is very deceptive.

August 15, 1967

Expressed myself poorly in yesterday's notes. "Let myself be influenced . . ." I have always resisted any real influence from Dom James and reacted against it. But I let my life be controlled by him – as my vows in any case demand – but in so doing I am submitting to a dead and sterile conception of the Church and of monasticism. He is in "good faith" and is a "good administrator" but the situation is corrupting. One cannot avoid being harmed by it – and I am vulnerable anyway. Yet now I see I *can't* leave here. And I don't take credit for this as virtue. I have invested too much of myself in this place for better or for worse. And there is perhaps really nowhere else to go – to Ernesto Cardenal perhaps, but I am not for the Tropics at this stage of the game, with my vulnerable intestine, am close enough to dysentery here at times.

It is a bad situation but I am sure the way out is in the life of prayer and contemplation themselves. Not in sleep but in awakening. Not in death but in resurrection.

More notes from Dom Leclercq on his trip to Vietnam, Indonesia etc. Utterly frank and uncompromising observations on the corruption of the Church, of monasticism etc. – and all of it intensified by the Vietnam war and the American presence there. Sense that the Vietcong will win, and the results will be brutal, and that the people are simply and mindlessly making the best of the American glut while it lasts. And they are rotting in consequence.

But hope in the young, there as everywhere.

A young Redemptorist student read a statement on "poverty" which included the following:

"*Surtout au Vietnam les religieux catholiques sont regardés par tout le monde chrétien ou non-chrétien comme une classe de bourgeois de villes . . . conservateurs et étrangers du monde actuel. Alors au lieu d'être dans le monde sans être du monde, l'église, ou plutot nous, nous sommes du monde sans être dans le monde?*" ["Especially in Vietnam the Catholic religious are regarded by everybody, Christian and non-Christian, as a class of bourgeois of the towns . . . conservators and strangers of the present world. Instead of living in the world without being of the world, the church, or more particularly, we ourselves, are of the world without being in the world?"]

Pretty well put!

Hence the vow of poverty is no longer a sign of anything. "*Le signe n'est plus un signe puisqu'il ne dit plus rien.*" ["The sign is no longer a sign since it no longer says anything."]

August 16, 1967

Faulkner's judgment of the writer who continues to do only what he knows he can do well . . .

August 20, 1967

Andy Boone says that if you watch the wild turkeys flying South and see them in formation spelling out W-A-R – it means etc. . . . Fortunately there are no more wild turkeys. Or if there are, they seldom get together in large enough numbers to fly in formation.

Letter from Fr. Timothy. Because he was one of whose who protested against the air-conditioning in the new Church, he has been relegated to a couple more years in Rome – to study moral theology.

The Church will be reoccupied in two weeks, Sept. 3. The archbishop will bless the altar then.

Finished a piece on Auschwitz for *Peace News*. Deeply disturbing and depressing. Everything has been depressing lately. Perhaps also I haven't been getting out enough. Yesterday was a grey afternoon, and rain threatened, but anyway I went out for a walk – after getting a haircut at the monastery and picked up my laundry bag (all the laundry bags have been renewed). Went out past the cowbarns to the lake at St. Bernard's field. Everything lovely, silent, peaceful. I watched the green-brown water, rippled by steady wind, the red Virginia creeper on an old tree, listened to the quiet. Then walked back through the field saying Vigils for the Feast of St. Bernard. Felt a lot better. Deeper sense of prayer returned. On target again. I have been worrying too much about the "unhealthy situation" here. And of course it *is* unhealthy and my reaction to it is also unhealthy. The thing to do is find the slow, patient, delicate way of extrication which leads again to interior liberty, true liberty. I have that, but I realize I am far from being as free as I should be. There is a mental contagion here, to which I have been too much exposed and so I am sick, or let's say allergic. My reaction to things is really an allergic one – a sweat and snot and life-stinging, breaking out, itching sort of reaction – especially to Dom James. Every time I see him now – and I have to see him once a week – ! – I come away with this psychic allergy. I have absolutely nothing to say to him – except formalities. Yet some talk is made and I feel we are not talking to each other but to people who aren't there. We talk to our own obsessions. It is miserable. Thursday – with his usual beating around the bush – he talked at some length about some Indian bishop who was here. Wanted to see me. "Oh you know! Can't I see Thomas Merton? Just curiosity etc. etc." That I didn't see him hardly mattered. The point of it all apparently was to get in a dig about celibacy. The B. had said the Hindus respected the Catholic clergy for their *celibacy*. Get it? He's a year late, however. I was rather amused.

Later.

On my way down to concelebration went to the cloister round through the ravaged cemetery and the new almost finished Church. Stood in the empty nave (why two organs for God's sake?) and it was beautiful. Quiet, calm, neat, simple, tall, airy, the old beams looking good, the sanctuary OK, mysterious with its window, but I suppose artificial light will do away with that. It is a good Church and what is good about it is due mostly to William Schickel and Br. Giles. I am glad it is finished. Some things I dislike: black granite ambo too aggressive, etc.

Then up to 3rd floor for concelebration, trying to resist the inner feeling of alienation, rebellion etc. Not very successful. But at least ashamed and knowing I was wrong. No point in all this self-pitying complaining stuff – only add more poison to the spiritual climate, which in fact is so much better than before the Council even here. Everything was much more human and relaxed. It was OK. What is there to be moody about? "Judge not," I tell myself, "judge not, judge not!" But that is the trouble with capital "R" Religion: the juices of the medicine men get acting. There are shamanic secretions that do not accord well with the Eucharist. Even mine perhaps, but certainly some others. And one feels all this being used for power, drama, "feeling," "impact." It upsets my stomach.

Evening.

Going down for conference. I looked again at the new altar in the evening light, close at hand. It is monstrous. A perfect Aztec altar for the sacrifice of the heart. Or a block for Druidical immolations. Black, squat, large, "tragic," grim, black. No unbloody sacrificial meals here! This is for the real thing! And the throne – narrow, rigid, terse, fierce, for a presbyter with his fists on the two arms ready to spring up and grab the knife and rush at the victim. For a judge ready to bound up with a yell and pronounce sentence. Strangely it revives all the old grim and implacable spirit of the former Chapter Room throne – that of Dom Edmond and probably the other bloodthirsty ones before him. It makes me shiver.

Tonight I find myself half voluntarily wondering – and very uneasily – if perhaps I should not take thought in case – just in case – it might become suddenly necessary for me to leave here in a big hurry one of these days! A strange and dreadful thought in a way and yet it may not be altogether beyond the bounds of reason. There is a strange kind of madness in the air . . . or is it only my madness? Somehow I feel more lucid than usual, but that may be the ultimate deception.

August 21, 1967

What I wrote last evening was really crazy. But no matter. I wrote it and it needed to come out. Though I sat up late wondering about the idea, I don't think it was serious, except as another indication of my inability to really fully identify with this place as an institution – and a realization that it is perhaps in some way slowly destroying me. Perhaps that is exaggerated. But I can see the day coming when I will probably be a semi-idiot in the infirmary, frustrated, stupefied, taking refuge from it all in a kind of defensive torpor, with occasional bouts of futile and hopeless arrogance.

On top of all that, today comes a letter from Rome – from the Abbot of Frattocchie [Dom Francis Decroix] who has just had lunch with Pope Paul at Castel Gandolfo, with one of his monks who has been a friend of the Pope's in Milan. The Pope spoke of me – and that was very nice, sent a cordial message etc. etc. All very nice. Then the Pope spoke of the contemplative life, how much he expects of the contemplative orders, and now he wants a message from the contemplatives to the world. Some men in our Order are working on it and I was asked to contribute my ideas. On first reading I misunderstood: thought the Pope was going to send the message to contemplatives. Oh no! Contemplatives are going to send a message to the world for we are "the aviators of the spirit" (his phrase!!). Then the whole thing began to dawn on me! Such a nice idea of the dear Holy Father! But in what relation to reality? What am *I* doing in this mess? Let some Abbots get together and piously urge everyone to pray, fine. The interior life is a wonderful thing. Certainly contemplatives should teach the rest of the Church the ways of interior prayer. But the illusion that we are somehow specialists, know "secrets of the interior life," and can easily formulate them in a document that will make sense – and be "safe" at the same time. A dreadful predicament. Not knowing what to do and having to answer fast, I put down the first things that came into my head, probably absurd and totally non-acceptable, a kind of Christian existentialist mishmash which will please no one and which they probably won't even understand. Tomorrow maybe I'll get down some notes on prayer.

August 22, 1967

A beautiful day. F[east] of the Immaculate Heart. Early Mass at hermitage. Reading on "Bantu Prophets," i.e. the Nativistic Church split-offs in S. Africa. But above all Faulkner's *As I Lay Dying* – certainly his finest work, far and away – a great work of art, on the highest level, perfectly put together, and with immensely important implications. To my mind one of the great works of all literature, comparable to the best in any field. Today I read the central part, the crossing of the river, and the chapter on Addie, which gives the key to everything, and was simply floored by it. I don't remember when I have read anything with such admiration – it is so full of insight, irony and a whole view of language and reality that is so exact and pertinent to our time that it is breathtaking. And the roots of myth, the solemnity of it. Then the following chapter, the contrast, the little wordy minister hurrying to her death . . . The most completely damning pages on Southern Christianity in all Faulkner, not excepting Hightower and the other Church people in *Light in August*. This is so sharp, so exact, so final! This is a book I must study to write about. I have never seen anything written on it that came anywhere near being an adequate appreciation.

Toward the middle of the morning Bro. Maurice brought up drinking water. Then I went off to the other end of the field to see what is coming off with that bizarre construction of Bro. Odilo's. (I can see the roof among the trees from my place and consider it an intrusion.) I suppose the best thing is to let the woods grow back and take over the top of that field so it will be hidden eventually.

In the afternoon after writing a couple of necessary letters, went for a walk halfway up Vineyard Knob. Read a little on Poverty in Sufism. The woods are pleasant but this year there are many gnats: they fly into your ears and nostrils and your eyes too if you don't keep glasses on.

Anyway, today I am much less depressed, and had a peaceful meditation in the evening looking out over the valley from the field outside my gate where, apart from the road up, the weeds are in some places higher than I am.

"The man who has his mind set on enlightenment . . . "

Such a one does not need to worry about Abbots, commissars, etc. etc.

August 28, 1967

Last Thursday a letter came from Rome that in reality *I* was supposed to write the "message of contemplatives."[17] I should have finished it long ago I suppose, but I have had a bad attack of flu and spent most of yesterday in bed. A miserable weekend. Managed to write about half the "message" on Saturday. Then a Belgian Dominican, P. Walgrave, came and I talked with him a bit on Sunday, but was feeling quite ill. Monday it was very hard to get down to the Abbey and back, and when I got back to the hermitage I just went to bed. After I had slept a bit I made some tea, but was mostly unable to read – or think – or do anything except lie around and cough. A dry cough that simply shook my bones without breaking up any of the congestion in my lungs. Looked at a little book of pictures of Japanese tea ceremony bowls etc. sent from Asia House and was very moved by them – so I was still capable of human feeling. At that point things began to get better. Went to sleep again around six, and slept on and off for eleven hours, sweating constantly, and having some interesting dreams. (I was in Harlem – looking for a Subway to get back downtown and scared of being beaten up – but visit interesting places – a church – a white girl who was afraid of me when I asked the way to the subway – etc. Before that a curious "party" where the highball glasses were all on long chains so they could not be stolen! I am trying to fix a highball for a Negro friend with whom I went to Harlem eventually etc.) Very curious, vivid dreams.

Evening. It is quiet and cool. Sounds of locusts in the dark and voices of children playing over at Boones'. It is their bed time and mine.

This afternoon I finished the "Message" – and very early. I was surprised that it went so smoothly. I had been very anxious about it, especially since getting sick. Now, relieved, I feel much better.

[17] Merton wrote two letters in response to Dom Decroix's request: one on August 21 and another on August 22, 1967. See Thomas Merton, *The Hidden Ground of Love*, edited by William H. Shannon (New York: Farrar, Straus & Giroux, 1985), 154–59.

I sit here and drink Linden tea before bed. It is still one of the best things I know of for flu, and I am glad I still have some left. Something I need always to have around!

The sickness has taught me something: first that I am perhaps too obsessed with reading and work – and I know the pressure of letter writing is too heavy. This morning, saying Mass later than I usually do, when the sun was up, I realize I have been losing – in a way – some of the best of the day with my nose in a book.

August 30, 1967

It has been a serious day.

The Church now being finished there is no more noise of machines from the monastery. The woods are once again beautifully quiet. Last night I slept badly for some reason. Perhaps the pressure of working on that "message" and my own conflict about it. Today I read [George] Orwell's fine essay *Politics and the English Language* [Evansville, IN, 1947]. How much the same trouble is found in my "message"! Semi-officialese.

I am more and more oppressed by the mail that comes in. So much of it is fakery or manipulation. People trying to get something on me or use me for something, even with the most "religious" of intentions (like Joel Orent and his insistent badgering about "fellowship"). So much of the mail shows the kind of moral brutality that is everywhere latent – and comes out so clearly in Vietnam.

Then there are the people who simply tell me to get my pants on and *leave* this place. Dungarees today. Clayton Eshleman. In a word I am bombarded by beggars, fakers, con-men, business men, and operators and good enough people who want to talk me into something I am absolutely not interested in.

Today I came to the conclusion that I am thoroughly sick of all of it. I am not going to let myself be opened to all that by any playing around in the general games. Once again – I feel the falsity of the statements, reflexes, reactions I have foolishly given out in the last few weeks. Certainly glad Martin Marty *(NCR)* changed his mind about my ideas on the race situation. (He said this summer's riots and the whole reaction proved I had been right after all in "Letters to a White Liberal.") Still was it necessary for me to reply? Maybe so. But perhaps in the future I'll do a lot less of that. It would be better.

Then Dan W[alsh] came back from Toronto from a Theology Conference for everybody, with lots of Bishops etc. giving bad talks and being hooted. Not surprising, and yet I don't find it very inspiring either. There is too much spite, envy, pettiness, savagery, and again too much of a brutal and arrogant spirit in this so-called Catholic renewal: too much conceit and hubris, and in the end the same old authoritarian and intolerant ways in a new form. I don't especially like it and I don't want to get mixed up in it.

According to Dan (who must always be taken with a grain of salt) people at the conference were down on Pope Paul VI, fed up with him, calling him all kinds of names, saying he was "psychotic or at least neurotic" etc. and passing around a lot of denigration. And Dan with stories – apparently straight from [Bernard] Häring – about Carmelite cloistered nuns now having to go out and teach or something. Again – wait and see. You know Dan's tales!!

But the whole blessed thing adds up to a climate that is not healthy, smells bad. The air is gassy and polluted. I prefer the air of the woods.

I feel with the greatest seriousness that we are in for difficult times, for violence, confusion, nastiness, mess, blood, destructive maneuvers everywhere, in everything – in the Church and outside it (I don't say people will kill each other in the Church!!). And I feel that there is nothing I can do by talking about it, or trying to intervene in it. I have said what I know how to say and it wasn't much. Now I see no point in trying to cope with piles of mixed up and unconnected information and opinion or to keep up with what "everybody is thinking." It is exhausting and pointless and totally *unreal* as far as I am concerned. Better to stay out of it, not be used, do what I am really *supposed* to do and live the life that has been given me to live. That is the important thing – if I can *do* it. I'll have plenty to do writing poetry, meditations, criticism, and the thing I hope to do on "Cargo," for instance. Or Camus.

September 2, 1967

Great serious days continue – bright sun, bright sky. I am not on retreat but might as well be. I have put work aside and am taking long walks and praying in the woods. Had to write some necessary letters. I keep away from the monastery as much as possible, though today I had to go to the shoe shop, since the heel was falling off my right shoe.

Fasted today – this is always good not only because of the "penance" but because of the change of tempo and perspective. Instead of dinner – being out in the woods, seeing everything in the light and silence of noon – in the universal quiet – all machines stopped. Walked barefoot in a mossy spot under oaks and pines reading a new book of which a review copy came today – *Two Leggings* [edited by Peter Nabokov, New York, 1967] about a Crow Indian, his fasts, his efforts at acquiring vision and "medicine." I could use a little medicine myself!

Inner problem, deep problem about the validity of staying here under someone like Dom James. Is it really a defeat, a defection, a *failure* of my vocation to stay rather than to leave? No way of really answering. If I had anything else definite to do … But one does not just leave for the sake of leaving, and the hermitage, as far as I am concerned, is fine. Even though he has obviously intended it as a way to make sure I am kept from encounter and participation – in monastic renewal. For instance, I was invited last week by Fr. Aelred to come to Christ of the Desert in New Mexico – though I would like to go: not a hope, the way things are now. But no: isn't that wrong? Isn't it wrong for me to go on accepting it? I wish I knew. I don't think it's clearly wrong. I wish I were sure it was right, and not an evasion.

Obviously, all you can do is choose, on the basis of what you know. So I choose to continue in the hermitage, under conditions that are from a certain viewpoint political, fraudulent (i.e. on the part of authority). Something like Pasternak in his dacha. He did not repudiate communism, or rather Russia, as many would have liked him to do.

Began Claude Lévi-Strauss *Mythologiques I* yesterday. Very exacting. Real new and stimulating beginning after my morning reading had more or less bogged down.

Lord Northbourne wrote the other day about Garabandal, which he too has discovered. Dan Berrigan is teaching at Cornell. Haven't heard form Sy or Slate in a long time. Suzanne B. was distressed over Brian Epstein's death and asked me to say a Mass for him. Picture before me, of Louise Gosho's two entrancing little girls, Japanese and Western faces, very lovely. *Mystics and Zen Masters* to be in Japanese – at least the part on Asian stuff. – This the first request for translation rights. I'm glad. Martin Marty's "Apology" in *NCR* [August 30, 1967]. (My reply next week.)

September 7, 1967

I found the first ceremonies in the Church last Sunday beautiful but trying. Got there late for the consecration of the high altar and watched from the side as the five little heaps of incense flamed on the big black stone. That was pretty.

During the Mass I was strained and depressed. But I am glad the Church is finished and that it looks nice.

I have been praying a lot over the problem of this place.

Then suddenly today Dom James told me he had reached his decision about what he wanted to do: he is planning to *resign* and live in a hermitage over in Edelin's place. I was surprised, and respect him for the decision! In fact I envy him the little place Clement has planned for him, out on a high spur – and it will be much more solitary there than here. (Now I hear the roaring of the motorcycle on the road, 1/4 mile away. Houses are going up on monks' road everywhere – and soon I suppose I might as well be at the edge of a small town!) But there may be a dam at Howardstown, and lake water may back up to Edelin's hollows – so there will be motor boats out there. Solitude may be much more rare in ten years' time – if I am still alive.

I wanted to collect my thoughts but had to work in the afternoon finishing a re-reading of the *Journal of My Escape from the Nazis*, which I want to get copied, and submit for publication after all these years. (It reads well, for the most part.) After supper, with a gut full of Kasha, I walked on the brow of my hill and looked out over the valley and mused on everything. Certainly it is better for Dom J. to retire. He has been abbot there for nineteen years. It will be a relief to get someone younger. But who? Fr. Anastasius is rigid and uncooperative. Fr. Eudes unpredictable and too many don't like him. Fr. Matthew enthusiastic but maybe not emotionally stable enough. Fr. B. has no brains, and is too wavering. Fr. Callistus is practical and good hearted but perhaps not yet experienced enough. Who else? For my part I certainly would not accept the job of Abbot. Fr. Flavian might be the best in many ways: but he is a hermit, and would they vote for him now?

September 10, 1967

"I don't need any paper. I know who I am," says a sailor in [B.] Traven (sudden big fuss about Traven – again fabrication – publisher's gag – *Ramparts* collaborating). Still, in terms of book providence, I can learn. It comes at a time of special absurdity: a tension of varying absurdities and questions that are probably useless, and yet raise themselves now. About the monastery, myself, my life, what is happening, the country, people I know, the Church etc. All the patterns fuller of clash and shock: that, anyway, is certain.

My more constant depression, disillusionment, realization that there are no structures and no projects worth hoping in, not within reach.

Ad Reinhardt's death.

Ed Rice – the collapse of *Jubilee*, the awful dirty deal he got from the Herder people.

The monastery – its problems and its future (if any).

The misguided questions of mine.

And now yesterday the very negative, almost hostile bearing of Thompson Willett of all people! No explanation, nothing I can think of, perhaps I caught him at a wrong moment; in the midst of a personal crisis of some sort, but got a very cold reception and was for all intents and purposes thrown out. This is a new experience, in recent years! Don't remember anything like that since college days! Anyway his whole bearing was (within the limits of his indelible surface politeness) implicitly insulting. As if I'd tried to rape one of his daughters or something. (Suppose someone had invented some crazy story and he'd believed it!) The only thing I can think of – Fr. U. (who has been out of the order for several years now – no one can get along with him, he causes trouble everywhere he goes) is a friend and classmate and was visiting there recently. U. detests me from way back – ever since the novitiate, with the cold, self-righteous neurotic hate of a deeply frustrated being. And maybe he took occasion to express some ideas about me and what I have been doing! I can imagine from the patterns of the past! He would do a thorough job of discrediting me.

So anyway, I don't know and there is no way of guessing.

Wounded and perplexed – telling myself "I know how niggers feel."

And above all realizing the stupidity and inner contradiction involved in my going there at all! It is only another product of confusion and conflict in myself and I don't even know what I am looking for. So that made the humiliation complete.

This morning I am able to laugh at it, though several times during the night I woke up thinking about it.

In the end – it just seems I've reached a corner I've got to turn, and there is a whole suburb that has to be left behind and never revisited. I am heading for some other city and had better *get going!*

After meditation – a good one in an anguished way – went to the Bible needing comfort (am reading Isaiah again – seem to read it over and over) and my pericope for today was Isaiah 44:21–22. None would have been better. *Deo gratias* [Thanks be to God].

———

"How terrible for life to force deceptions upon an honest man," says Judy Shine in the *Ramparts* article on Traven. Well, that is no consolation. We "honest men" are not so much made deceivers by life: it is that in the end (with everyone else collaborating) we prefer to let the deceit in us come out and we come to terms with it in one way or another so that we can deceive acceptably and not get too badly caught. And some of us, in despair, have to act this out in a self-defeating rather than self-justifying way. Do we want to get caught, for the sake of having some kind of company? Or just for the sake of an official state of "isolation."

Oh well. There is a magazine called *Reality* which offers to tell you (among other things) all about the sex-life of J. Edgar Hoover.

Talking all around it: but the one thing that has to be said, and I don't quite know how to say it. A feeling of great violence is in the air everywhere. We are really on the verge of a blow-up. And this time it is the real blow-up. No one yet quite knows what it will be, because there is no fantasy to prepare us for it. Bolshevism, Fascism, Nuclear War, Civil War, these are all inadequate or misleading. One year, two years . . . Something unparalleled and unspeakable is getting ready for birth. Life is not going to be comfortable for anyone, but least of all for dissident writers, mavericks, non-conformists, people who look and act different. Different from who, from what? All depends where you happen to find yourself at the moment when people are throwing things, shooting, parading, coming down in helicopters, racing about in fast armored cars . . .

Everywhere you go you meet the eyes of truculent people and eyes say "You are one of the bastards we'll be shooting tomorrow." (Beam in his Bardstown store! Probably thought I was thinking the same of him.)

September 11, 1967
The last couple of days have been extremely painful and difficult.

But now I am on top of it and I can see the whole thing has been good – the kind of good anguish that squeezes and sweats a lot of nonsense out of you. But at one point I wondered if I were going to go crazy. Except: what would be the point of cracking up? What would it get you? There comes a time when one simply has to stand firm and face the fact of mistakes and wrongness and madness. I have felt a kind of anguished despair at the *hopelessness* of trying to make real sense out of anything. No matter where you turn you run into the blank, rocklike absurdity (this whole situation of T. Willett and Fr. U. and all that!) – the absurdity of social life. For instance – ever since last December T.W. has been urging us to come over there, asking why I did not come, offering to come and drive me over, etc. I have consistently been conservative and cool about it – and even then have felt it was far too much and it was. Now, I presume, Fr. U. told him what was the letter of the law here, the old business of stealthy egress and sin: and knowing Fr. U. I am sure he laid it on as thick as he could and persuaded T. I was committing a mortal sin by going over there. So then I ran into this implacable, angry man, ready to defend his whiskey with his life rather than give me a drop of it etc.

Of course, the truth is that I had no business going there: not that it is a sin but it simply is none of my business and not part of my vocation. By yesterday's concelebration I had come to my conclusions on that: no more visiting. You can't trust people; and in any case I don't want it or need it, it is only a distraction. Part of the trouble comes from taking the new-think too seriously and being "open to the world" and all that: it can be pure nonsense. I see the whole pointlessness of it – and that adds to the absurdity.

More absurdity. For a couple of weeks I could hear the pounding of McGruder's well-rig over at Fr. Flavian's. Finally after 125 feet they gave up. No water. This morning, bright and early, he was banging away at Fr. Hilarion's I was ready to double up with laughter – but I didn't have that much real laughter in me, I'm afraid.

The main thing: yesterday afternoon – day of recollection – thinking very seriously about everything: one other absurdity was that Dom James proposed I take up a hermitage on the next ridge to him over at Edelin's. I can think of nothing worse! Having him watching everything I do, or just being in the same acreage. It would drive me crazy. Possibly one reason: his intentions are secret, still, and if I were going there he would explain the activity by saying a place was being set up for *me*.

Yesterday afternoon I decided to submit an alternative proposal. A request to be allowed to go and be a hermit at La Dehesa in Chile. This brings up the old South American idea of 10 years ago which I had practically given up (though I asked if I could go to Chile, perfunctorily, last year, and was instantly brushed off!).

Reasons –

1. Real solitude, wild mountains, another country.
2. Desire to serve God in South America.
3. Desire to get out of the U.S., be in a country that does not have the Bomb, to renounce U.S. citizenship and stop being part of the world's richest society.
4. Desire to get out of the essentially unhealthy and sterile situation here, and find at least a slightly better milieu – with more breadth and less obsessiveness.

I wrote this in a note – usual way to present such things – and will discuss it with him tomorrow probably.

Tonight, after some work, a walk in the sun, a supper of rice, chop suey and Chinese tea, I am feeling much better. Not that I don't like this hermitage – but it would be a good sacrifice to leave it too. In any case I am ready to go, and feel perfectly free one way or the other. I do not intend to put pressure on him, but I do want a real answer, not just a brush off and it may take a little work.

In my opinion, Dom James will probably try to engineer things to be sure that *his* candidate is the next abbot – and will keep him under control from a distance. That candidate is probably Fr. Baldwin.

There is a chance that Dom J. may see some point in my going to Chile, only to get me out of here before the elections. In this I agree and I shall make a point of it – I'd like to be as far from here as possible when the voting takes place!

September 14, 1967. *Exaltation of the Holy Cross*

I always like this feast – beginning of the monastic "winter."

Of course Dom James refused permission to go to Chile. Told me to stay here and convert warlike Americans from within. That so many in the community were edified by my presence. That so many people felt this was where I belonged. That it was just not God's will etc. I could have told him that the exact same line of reasoning could have been advanced against his becoming hermit (as it was in the past against *my* becoming a hermit). But why bother? I really don't think Chile is any special kind of answer. I don't think there *are* any real answers. Except to live here and meditate and take advantage of the silence of the woods, which have been very peaceful and quiet these last days.

This afternoon Joe Carroll came up and cut the grass, cleaned out behind the woodpiles and I enjoyed walking out there after supper. (He cuts with big tractor.)

Mary Ann Schmidt, who has been doing some typing for me – and I sent her my first tape for typing the other day – suddenly sent me a scarf she had knitted for me. Very sweet of her. It is rather heavily scented, however, and this is a sort of feminine invasion of the hermitage. I don't mind. But I come around the corner and run bang into it and start laughing. Absurd. Absurd! Yet somehow a whole picture of someone's sufferings and confusions is involved, and I think of her with fondness.

Tommie O'Callaghan had a baby boy on Wednesday – and Dan is going to baptize him.

Ed Rice sent a long obituary of Ad Reinhardt from the *Times*. Poor Ad. I wonder if any of our bunch will live much beyond sixty. I don't have much confidence in Slate or Freedgood doing so after the way they looked (tired, overworked, overwrought) this year.

I expect I'll die just tired of sheer silliness at about 56 or 57. 4 or 5 years.

Today I finished that Easter Homily for the Argus recording.[18] It had been hanging over me for several weeks. Did a poor job on the first draft but may be I can improve it before sending it to be typed. Guilty about not getting my work done on Camus, but there's time for that. Illtud Evans wrote about my contributing to the new theology supplement in the revamped *Our Sunday Visitor*. Yzermans taking over. I just can't get into that. It would be stupid for me to do so. I'll write to tell him. Refused permission for *Catholic Digest* to reprint "Day of a Stranger" from the *Hudson Rev[iew]*.

Bob Shepherd sent a couple of Traven books and I read two stories during the evening. I enjoyed them. Traven is a good story-teller anyway. But the real discovery of these last days has been David Jones. Rich, exciting, resonant, witty, Catholic poetry: the only really good Catholic poet writing in English that I know of except Peter Levi. Ping sent the D. Jones issue of *Agenda*. The verse and art, beautiful, and I enjoy the critical articles.

---

[18] This was published as *He Is Risen!* (Niles, IL: Argus Communication, 1975).

September 18, 1967

The weekend has been good. Fasting on Saturday is a very helpful thing, at least when the days are fine and instead of eating I can wander in the woods. This time, finished *Two Leggings* – a rather sad, futile sort of book. With all his striving for powerful visions and strong medicine he never got to be chief. Fought the Sioux on the side of the whites – and the whites took away the Crows' land anyway.

In the end a white officer gave him a five-dollar gold piece. Sunday was great. Discovery of the Zapotecan city of Monte Alban in new book edited by J. Paddock. Re-reading Mosley on the Mayas. Sacred cities in center of sparsely populated rural areas. Cult centers without army and without King. An ideal, peaceful civilization. No one knows why it finally folded up. Same all through Mexico in the "Classic" period. Zapotecs, Mayas, Toltecs. Violence came with decadence. Aztecs were the last end of it. The final corruption.

I am very tired of the Sunday evening talks. Still on Sufism. But uninspired.

I really need the quiet, the silence, the peace of the hermitage and have been very foolish to create so much destruction for myself. Especially this idiot running around, when I am in town or away from the monastery for an hour or two. I do not remember any of it with pleasure. I used to have fewer visits. This month has been good – it always is – because the guest house is full of the diocesan clergy.

September 20, 1967. Ember Wednesday

Hot weather again. The Bishop came up to the hermitage yesterday (at my invitation and we had a talk and today he had me talk to the OMI [Oblate of Mary Immaculate] who is preaching the clergy retreat. Both were worried about the fact that so many priests "don't like retreats," "don't like silence" and whatnot. And seemed to expect support from me. For my part I have no idea what the priests want or don't want, and I don't particularly care. I think they should be able to choose to make whatever kind of retreat they feel would really benefit them. Probably their objection (when it exists) is pretty much the same as that of the monks, a refusal to be herded into a room and lectured – to be dosed with official medicine instead of being allowed to choose something of their own. Personally, I am not attracted by what they seemingly do want – guitars, endless dialogue.

The retreat master gave me a copy of an article which I think explains the trouble – at least from the side of the bishops, Retreat masters, etc. They feel they are no longer able to sell the idea of a retreat. This is a disaster. If they can't sell retreats, God himself must be letting them down. There's something the matter somewhere!

But the Bishop is a good sort, and I guess life is not easy for Bishops these days!

Blue night-groups of lighted helicopters going back and forth in the dark, blat-blat-blat, an awful racket, making the place look like town and noises with their traffic and illuminations. Now I suppose *that* will go on every night for six months, until they find another game to play. Lately too there have been some sonic booms – three or four a day. I suppose we'll get more. These are not very close. I'd hate to have them right over the house.

– More damn choppers!

September 22, 1967

John Slate is dead. He died of a heart attack Tuesday (19th) in St. Francis Hospital, Roslyn, L.I. I knew he had a bad heart. That was, in fact, what led indirectly to my getting in touch with him again after all these years – his fuming piece in the *Atlantic Monthly* about his hospitalization. I wrote to him about it. Then got a card from Oxford (this was last summer). Then this year I wrote to him about helping me draw up my will and that was how he came down this Spring. We had a good hot argument about Vietnam, in Louisville. And he was talking with the Franciscans at their Residence at Bellarmine! . . .

A brilliant day – warm, bright, early fall day, trees have not yet begun to change, grass still green, the lake at St. Bernard's field was deep blue. Walked out there fasting and it was there I read the news of Slate's death, around noon, and walked up and down in the sun trying to comprehend it. I know I too must go soon and must get things in order. Making a will is not enough, and getting manuscripts in order is not enough. These fast days seem to be the most lucid and helpful. Skipping dinner at noon and eating only once in the day, about 4:30 p.m. (a little coffee to keep awake at 4 a.m.), this makes for an easy, leisurely, alert day when you don't have to be any-where or get anywhere on time. A big chunk of meditation in the fields about noon, instead of dinner, seems very effective. Above all the change is stimulating.

Maybe I can get Julian Cornell, Ezra Pound's lawyer, to take over my will after all. J. Laughlin had first suggested him. I have been trying for three years to get something done on this, but nothing ever seems to happen. That is what comes of being so far away from everything.

September 23, 1967

Evening. A good day in Louisville. Went in for a back X-ray and for my knee also. Both are tolerably good. Had lunch with Jim Wygal at Cunningham's as is our custom. He was depressed at first but after a while we both cheered up. Talked of many things – who will be abbot (Baldwin?), the future of Gethsemani, whether I should stay on. We both agreed that I really was in the best situation I could expect at the moment. I was happy about it.

Leo Denoncourt and his wife and a Glenmary sister dropped in to our booth to say hello. I called Pat Welsh (of the M[erton] Room at Bellarmine) and we went to her house for a couple of drinks and some conversation.

Pat got married when she was in Ireland this summer and is now Mrs. Oliver. I am happy about that, and she seems very happy. On the way to her house we stopped at St. Joseph's Infirmary and saw Fr. John Loftus, who has just been operated on for a cervical disc. Was lying in bed very hoarse after the beating his neck took. (Dr. Mitchell told me about this when I was in his office.)

The day was bright and cloudless from morning to night.

It was good to get back to the monastery and hermitage. Calves lowing in the dark and many crickets.

I was going to call J. Laughlin about the lawyer business but forgot.

September 29, 1967

Joyous feast of Archangels, and now at dawn in the South under Sirius appears there a great smooth ancient hogback mountain of cloud – as if it had been there for a million years.

Heavy rain for two days, now it is clearing and cold. Yesterday was quiet and lonely in the hermitage with rain batting down interminably and a fire on the hearth (partly for burning of papers). Once again I am trying to get things in order. But the avalanche of paper goes on. I have got to get some new system of active resistance. Throwing stuff away down in the monastery before even bringing it up here. Simply not answering letters. (Yet as soon as you say that something more heart breaking than ever comes in and you have to acknowledge it – or some business presents itself and I am sold on it.)

The other day Barry Garfunkel in Slate's office called and says he can set up a Trust for my writings. I hope he can get to see J. about it and something can finally be got on paper. I called J. myself on Sunday about the possibility of getting a lawyer down here (John Ford maybe). We'll see about it. Meanwhile Pat Oliver and Martha Schumann came out Wednesday and we went over some papers – sitting in the car under the first downpour of the long rain. They got away with some photos of mine that had just come back from Griffin's (I am getting Gregory Griffin to develop and print up some of my new root pictures).

Though Dom James has tried to keep it quiet, the news of his resignation is all over the house. He is leaving Monday (Oct. 2) for a tour of the daughter houses and then the meeting of the American Abbots.

September 30, 1967

A fine clear silent night. During meditation – listening to the vast silent coldness and sleep of woods and awakeness of stars.

Last night I had a strange dream about starting on a journey somewhere with Dom James – but I was having trouble finding clothes to travel in!

I am beginning to get acquainted with G[aston] Bachelard (discovered him through David Kilburn at Birmingham U.). Tried his *Psychanalyse de Feu* [*The Psychoanalysis of Fire*, Paris, 1938] and found it rather obvious so I am dropping it and taking up *La Poétique de l'espace* [*The Poetics of Space*, Paris, 1948] which is quite another thing again! Very good material – phenomenology of poetic experience. And he is not afraid of ontology either. I suppose now that the Catholics are abandoning ontology the secular thinkers they claim to be imitating will rediscover it.

Bachelard's phenomenology of poetry is of course first of all a phenomenology of language – and an anthropology of man as "*un être parlant* [a speaking being]." I wonder if there is any connection with Parain. I keep wondering back to this.

Yesterday sent the Cain song from *Lograire* to *Hudson Review*.

"*Quel charme l'imagination poétique trouve – se jouer des censures!*" ["What charm the poetic imagination finds in making light of censures!"] *Bachelard*

October 2, 1967. F[east] of Guardian Angels

I love this feast. Hope my angel is not mad at me. Are you?

The Indian emphasis on encounter with one's "vision person" and obeying him thereafter. Beautiful and very real.

This morning I read Ruth Benedict's essay on the Pueblo Indians as an Apollonian culture surrounded by Dionysians. Extremely comical, for the insight it gives into Ruth Benedict surrounded by imagined rapists. And the trouble she gets into, her efforts to justify breakthroughs of the Dionysian even in her favored area – above all the business of ritual shit-eating and piss-drinking. I am afraid she doesn't win. Oh, all the poor dear lady anthropologists – and Margaret Mead is another.

More seriously: Bachelard's intuitions are most fruitful psychologically. In his study on houses, rooms etc., *"demeures,"* he suddenly opened up a whole set of obvious questions for me.

The hermitage – OK.

But the *Merton Room* – to which I have a silver key, and where I never go, but where the public go – where strangers are and will be.

A bloody cuckoo's nest.

This becomes a *typical* image of my own stupid lifelong homelessness, rootlessness.

Ambiguities at work here: the pretended "roots" at Gethsemani, where I am alien and where most everyone else is alien too. Yet paradoxically to many people I am completely identified with this strange place I can't firmly believe in. Where all these people with vows of stability are so obviously on the point of taking flight (and don't know it) or else simply staying by force of repression. Even the ones who are at home here remain alien though they don't realize it. Dom James. Br. Clement. Fr. Anastasius. Certainly their deep personal investment in the place is so complete that they are inseparable from it. And all the dead whom no one remembers.

I am here to a great extent because of the guilt and force exercised by Dom James. He knows it and I know it. Yet there is nowhere else I want to go. Also I have a kind of legal, factual separation from the common roof and board, here in the woods. The hermitage is a more personal reality of some sort – however ambiguous.

But the *Merton Room*.

A place where I store away endless papers, in which a paper-self builds its nest to be visited by strangers in a strange land of unreal intimacy.

Knowing Pat Oliver and Martha Schumann who take care of it, this is a good thing. It becomes a recognizable kind of enterprise, a form of communication. A "demeure" (demur? demure? De-mural. With and without walls. Glass walls looking over to the madhouse!!).

The *Merton Room* is a kind of escape from Gethsemani, a protest against their messing up, destroying, losing, frittering away, dispersing, rotting, canning, feeding to mice everything I have put my heart into.

The anxiety I have felt lately is due probably to the surfacing awareness that all this is futile – a non-survival, more alien to me even than Gethsemani to some extent. A last despairing childish effort at love for some unknown people in some unknown future. But this is Rilkean. Hell, it is Peter Pan. It is no good. All right if they do like what I have written – or don't – if they understand or don't – this is only a kind of non-communication in the end. It is not what I am so desperate for (and what I am supposed to have forgotten).

Part of the trouble is the questioning of the whole traditional concept of monasticism. The liberation that *has to be there* (or else the whole thing is a lie). But *is it?*

Is it really there? Does "willing it" make the difference?

The only issue, in reflexion, is by dialectic maybe.

But really there are situations that are only *lived:* they do not exist in reflexion.

My living seems so haphazard, so open to unpredictable swings and veering, such risky emotion: I see how easily I could go the way of Fr. H., poor guy, who has not stayed at the parish in California and is on the run again. Poor, poor guy. And in some ways one of the best, who put so much into the big illusion here, in his years with that incredible houseful of brother novices. Of course all that was madness. Part of Dom J.'s madness – and mine, with the book!

Merton Room again – ambiguity of an open door that is closed. Of a cell where I don't really live. Where my papers live. Where my papers are more than I am. I myself am open and closed. When I reveal most I hide most. There is still something I have not said: but what it is I don't know, and maybe I have to say it by not saying. Word play won't do it. Or *will* do it = *Geography of Lograire.* Writing this is most fun for me now, because in it I think I have finally got away from self-consciousness and introversion. It may be my final liberation from all diaries. Maybe that is my one remaining task.

Importance of the fact that Thompson Willett is on the M. Room committee, and that the break between us – for no real reason – the other day is in
reality a deep break between me and the fans. Their illusion of me is seen to
be completely out of touch. They have trusted me in building something
like a house I myself once built and then destroyed. I frighten them! Maybe
I frighten myself! But there is no question that my world and the world of
Thompson Willett have *nothing* in common. And neither of us wants to
pretend.

Deeper problem – to avoid a stupid and unnecessary consistency. I don't
have to frighten them all away just to recover my sense of identity. It is not
like that!

October 3, 1967. St. Therese

Good as he is, subtle, fascinating, Bachelard does not go deep enough. The
spaces and houses, the attics and garrets, the cellars and homes, are those of
reverie and not of meditation. Centers of intimacy for the incubation of passion and poetry. And that is all right.

But it is also all wrong if there is not a deeper discussion, beyond reverie
and poetry. A mere space for reverie, a phenomenological solitude, a house
of imagination, will eventually get corrupt. That is the trouble with Rilke,
again! (Yet I respect his love for the house where most of the *Elegies* were
written. The garden of that solitude had in it the rose that poisoned him.)
There *has to be* a deeper meditation, beyond dreams, beyond imagination,
beyond biography and beyond psychology.

Hence the danger of forgetting the "interior man" and living only in phenomenology and the experienced self. The madness of wanting to integrate
and unify man by reducing him entirely to his exterior self. His true unity
comes from the discovery of a non-experienced self, an invisible, non-
phenomenal, non-volitional, non-acting self, a self of liberty, a dwelling "in
God" who has no house. Eckhart's castle where even the Divine Persons
don't enter – only the Godhead. I don't know if I can agree with that – it
seems to misunderstand the very root of theology! – but anyway this No-
house with no-walls, the Abyss, not "where," not "which," but the Abyss
(purely) is – God and self in one. Beyond (metaphysical) *Atman* [Hindu
name for the individual, eternal spirit or soul].

Yesterday I heard from Catherine Meyer (of *Harper's*) that Sy Freedgood
was in the hospital with an inflamed heart.

October 7, 1967. F[east] of the Holy Rosary

Dreams which I can't fully remember – voyage – woman: a dark girl and I (M. and I, I guess) decide to wear kilts. I will put on MacGregor Tartan and thus identify with my "true" ancestors. But the red seems startling, unfamiliar. Islands. Journey. Bull. Horse. All sorts of images. She releases the bull but we are safe . . . etc.

Glad to have finally got some work done. Wrote on *Two Leggings*, the Crow Warrior and his fasting for vision. Then Preface to Japanese translation of *New Man*.[19] Then yesterday afternoon the piece for Msgr. Fox's Spanish Harlem photo book. It is perhaps unreasonable to undertake all these things but each is also an act of love and communion – Indians – Japan – Puerto Ricans.

I am really most excited by the sophistication, versatility, scope, horizons of Lévi-Strauss. In *Le Cru et le cuit [The Raw and the Cooked]* one tends to get snowed under by the sheer mass of material, concentrated in Brazil. But *La Pensée sauvage [The Savage Mind]* is more universal and gives a clearer exposition of his understanding of the epistemology and logic based on the idea of species. Real cosmic and "contemplative" quality – aesthetic and scientific at the same time – yet with a sophistication that excludes romance and reminds us we are moderns, not neolithics – but that neolithic thought is more relevant than we think – more sophisticated and complex than some modern "scientific" common-sense categorizing.

October 8, 1967

Best thing about Lévi-Strauss: he makes you work. There is no nonsense about it and if you want to keep up with him you have to run. No idling along, no clichés, no rehashing of familiar material: *masses* of new stuff, organized in an extremely wide and complex way, with multiple intersections you have to remember. Only if you move fast (and sometimes know where to begin skipping) do you get the whole view. But once you have caught sight of where you are going, you *have to* work. Because you know you are really coming out somewhere with someone who has extraordinary views and is ahead of everyone (even though he may be "wrong"). It is not just a question of getting a "right answer" to a problem but a whole view of *many* problems together which are basic to man. Problems of thought, knowledge, culture,

[19] The preface appears in *"Honorable Reader,"* 127–36.

man's relation to nature, to himself, intercultural relations, science, art, etc. etc. "Paradigmatic relationships" and "syntactical chains." Bachelard too has tried this "bricolage" but he is not as energetic as Lévi-Strauss and he deals in aesthetic trifles. Compared with L.-S., Bachelard is flaccid and uninteresting, except for occasional intuitions. Lévi-Strauss is much deeper because he deals in the *basic substance* of experience and discourse in *primitive* society – the raw matter and the primitive luxuriance of forms. Bachelard gets at it only in indifferent and recent poetry where the matter has gone thin and everything has long since been worked out of it.

But see the magnificent concrete poem – mobile, visual and conceptual of Lévi-S. on p. 201 of *La Pensée sauvage*. And this as a mere model of a great cosmic poem based simply on the duality species-individual. (Imagine it with 2 million species working and an almost infinite number of possible individuals: primitive thought really grappled with the *world!*)

A Midsummer Diary for M.

June 1966

I will never really understand on earth what relation this love has to my solitude. I cannot help placing it at the very heart of my aloneness, and not just on the periphery somewhere.

June 21, 1966

jhs

Or the account of how I once again became untouchable. Yet it is impossible for me to be what I was before I met M. The old life is a habit which no longer exists. Habit of isolation, of worry, of intent preoccupation with I no longer remember precisely what. A kind of poetic religiosity and an intention to be interiorly honest. And above all the insistence on being different from other people.

I no longer know what these things mean, or what their opposites might mean. I am not passing from this to something that stands against it. I am not going anywhere. I exist because I have the habit of existing. Perhaps I will in due time put other habits on top of this one, but they had better be more fruitful than, for instance, sitting around drinking Christian Brothers' brandy out of an old marmalade jar big enough to get ice cubes in and not as big as a whole glass.

The abjection of the hermit life. The what of *what?*

Yet that is their trouble: acute anxiety about meeting up to prearranged definitions. So they have defined a lot of new ones for me to meet now. "You will not try to contact her in any way whatever, anywhere, either by phone, by letter, etc. etc. You will never go to that hospital again."

Concelebrated Mass for the Feast of the Sacred Heart. They are ending Lauds in the temporary third-floor chapel and I stand at the sacristy window looking at the beautiful wide valley and the fields in the early morning sun. So peaceful, so convincing: they seem to say I have a place in the world, my place. That everything is OK. The comforting, sad, pure melody of the Benedictus antiphon. The words say that Christ is not consoled. Probably no one is thinking much about the words or about who is consoled and who is not. (Except each one of us individually realizes he is not consoled. Maybe that is why Christ is not consoled.)

At Communion, as I approached the altar to take the chalice, they sang the antiphon: "There was no one to comfort me." The absolute aloneness of Christ. I happened to look up and there in front of me the Brother who reported my phone calls was receiving the host. A plain, simple, honest guy, obviously the best intentions in the world. Am I supposed to say "I forgive him"? But am I even mad at him in the first place? It would be like getting mad at a tree. It would be absurd to even think of forgiving him. I forgive the main road because it does not take me to Louisville today to see M. Right thing? Wrong thing? He did what he thought he had to do. The Abbot did (joyfully) all the negating he thought he had to do. All the joyful depriving, all the assurances that he knows what I suffer. What I suffer? They all tell me that I suffer, that I am half dead, that I am all covered with blood, that I have been nearly ruined, that I am in terrible shape etc. etc. What do they think about *her* suffering? It does not enter their heads. Hence I cannot take seriously what they pretend to say about my suffering. It is just they themselves are anxious.

The total loneliness of Christ. I don't claim that my loneliness is His. Still less that I understand anything about His. Only it is TOTAL.

Furthermore they all tell me what I suffer and they don't know half the story. They can't even imagine all the joy that was in it. They know nothing, really, only enough to quiet a few credible scandals for themselves in their own heads.

After Mass I got out of there and went over to the other chapel where I usually say my own Mass. On the way I meet the Abbot's secretary who gives me the guilty embarrassed smile of one who knows too much for his own little good. And of course wants to be brotherly about it all, and yet at the same time make like he knows nothing. He probably helped the Abbot to decide where your letter came from – the one the Abbot destroyed.

Up in the quiet chapel, dear, you came to me insisting on being present and most real. It was as if your voice itself was speaking with the urgency of a love that cannot be defeated or frustrated, that demands absolutely to be attended to, no matter what. They insist that loving you and loving Christ are different as day and night. To me they are the same, on this level at least, because it is in Him that I truly find you. It is at Communion that we are most one in our love. It is true that all our love has not been completely unequivocal, but I no longer know where one draws lines. Except I do know where lines have been firmly drawn, [. . .]

I am reading Camus on absurdity and suicide: *The Myth of Sisyphus*. I had tried it before and was not ready for it because I was too afraid of the destructive forces in myself. Now I can read it, because I no longer fear them, as I no longer fear the ardent and loving forces in myself. If they all turn against me I don't care, but I think for some strange reason they are all for me. As to suicide: I would be delighted to drop dead, but killing myself would be just too much trouble.

All the love and all the death in me are at the moment wound up in Joan Baez's song "Silver Dagger." I can't get it out of my head, day or night. I am obsessed with it. My whole being is saturated with it. The song is myself – and yourself for me, in a way. Dear, I have a terrible desire for fidelity to what has been far greater than either of us. And not a choice of fidelities to this or that, love or vows. But a fidelity beyond and above that to both of them in one, to God. To the Christ who is absolutely alone and not apart from us but is the dreadful deep hole in the midst of us, waiting for no explanation. Sacred Heart? Well, they made that one out of plaster so as to really exorcise and forgo the loneliness: so as to console themselves. But when the consolation is taken away there is this hole that goes deeper than hell and you have to go all the way down into it before you find heaven.

Fr. L., the young cantor who just left for Rome, talked to me before he left. He said he thought the songs of Joan Baez had "sensuality in them." My eye. I told him that he was hearing the deep archetypal symbols and resonances that come from the love and death planted deep in our hearts: things the monks would rather not hear. Better to calm it all, exorcise the potential worry of it. Just say that Christ is not consoled and then be consoled yourself. It is always safer. It is neutral. To be a monk is to be forever neutral. At least with respect to certain incidentals like life, love, despair, anguish. (But of course we have our home-made anguish too. It keeps us out of mischief. That is the plan for me: return to the habit of a neutral anguish, a life lived by quiet custom, according to precise specifications.)

The specifications are all very precise. There is no sensuality in them. There are no archetypes in them either. Maybe there is a kind of death in them, and maybe even a life comes out of them. I don't question that there is probably something behind it all. I am still the guy who obeyed in *The Sign of Jonas*, and still riding in the whale's belly.

No one can ever prevent us from thinking of each other and from loving each other. No one can change the fact that we belong to each other. That we have been through experiences of an incomparable love upon which no human being is entitled to pass the slightest judgment. No one can prevent me from remembering all these things [. . .]

But they can and do prevent us from knowing what our thoughts are now (though from our deep experience of each other we can still truly *know*). They prevent us from following, from day to day, our feelings, our hopes, our acts, our conflicts, our encounters with life. We cannot encounter each other directly and thus we are prevented from that which lovers ordinarily can do: orienting our lives by each other's thoughts and feelings. They have taken away love's compass and instruments, except the rare and secret ones in our hearts, of which we can never be deprived.

Do you wonder what I am thinking at a given moment? Think of the deep and lasting essence of our love: it is the root of all my thoughts. What is passing on the surface I could write in a letter but by the time the letter reached you it would all be changed. The essence remains the same.

What is my life? My solitude? The determination to be lucid and quiet and to wait, and to nourish the unspeakable hope of deep love which is beyond analysis and is so far down it has no voice left. Down there we are one voice: the voice of your womanness blends with the man I am, and we are one being, completing each other, though we no longer can express it by taking each other in our arms. How deeply can we believe this? I think our capacity to believe it is inexhaustible and if it is, we win.

Last night when I was more restless and desperate, for something to do I picked up an article on Russian women by Olga Carlisle, who is a friend of J.'s [James Laughlin]. Someone sent it [to] me on that account. What do I want with Russian women? What I was looking for desperately was *you*. Any womanness ends up by being for me some indication, some pointer, to the womanness of you. I skipped through the article and the pictures, avoiding the gross and massive women with faces like trains and medals on their stone breasts, looking for something of you in the pretty ones, but there was nothing really, only in one picture one girl was looking with love at her lover, seriously, sincerely. I caught a faint glimmer of your love, our love. But we can no longer look for it outside ourselves.

"The absurd has meaning only in so far as it is not agreed to" (Camus). That is the real point and irony of my life. They think that I have agreed with them, when I have only obeyed them. To obey with perfect honesty is to express the absurd and at the same time to reject it, to be free from it. Only by this obedience can I attain to complete freedom from the absurdity that is imposed by *every* form of institutional life. To escape the absurdity here with some implication that life outside would make sense, would be to succumb to the greater absurdity. This is central in my vision of things.

Faith begins here. I have nothing to do with a faith which claims to show the absurd really makes sense. My faith is that the absurd is ridiculous and to keep faith with God is to refuse to believe that He is the kind of Joker that would want you to believe that the senseless makes sense. When you are thereby made free by truth, you can begin with God's grace to make your own sense out of it all. This is a difficult business and it is the life of the desert, which is what I am involved in. Because I am you are too. Don't ask me to explain. I don't have any idea whether you will experience it with me. It does not matter that much, as long as you live in me by love. No further explanations are needed.

One thing I must admit: a failure of lucidity in regard to love. It is so easy to assume that love is somehow a solution to a problem. Like: life is a problem which is impossible until someone comes along that you can love. Or man is himself a problem, solved by love. Love is a key to a hidden answer in us. And so on. But is this true? Or is it only what everybody *wants to be true?* Supposing it is not true, does it make any difference? Maybe love, like everything else, is in large measure absurd. I don't declare this, but just admit it is a distinct possibility. Does love too *have to* make perfect sense? In what way does it have to?

The sense that love makes, and I think the only sense it makes, is the beloved. The discovery, the revelation of the *absolute value* of the one loved. This is not so much a discovery of meaning as a discovery of goodness. To think of love as an answer or a "solution" is to evade the stark directness of this discovery. The fact that you are you is something of absolute value to me. But if I love in a certain way this becomes covered over and hidden with all the operations of love and what happens then is that love takes the place of the beloved. Then love instead of being a solution (which it is not supposed to be) becomes a problem for which there is no solution. For then love stands in the way between the lovers. It veils the goodness of the beloved. It dresses (or undresses) the beloved as desirable object. Which is all right too, except that one loves desire instead of the beloved.

The fact that you *are:* that you *are you.* This is all I have left. But it is the whole of love. And nothing can change it.

And you have me your absurd man (in the sense of Camus), your poet, your patient, who has been completely taken out of your hands and whom you can still secretly heal with the power of your love. I *am.* By that fact I need your love and by that fact I have it.

This afternoon was brilliant, cool, beautiful. I went out to the place where we had the picnic on Derby day. Everything was totally empty. The woods empty of everything except air, light and flies. Not a sound, until some character started with a chain saw on the knob behind the lake. What for? Anyway, I began carefully reading the wonderful poems of Eugenio Montale: dry wine, arid landscape, splendor of Dantesque and austere sincerity. The modern Italian poets: I have a special liking for them, Ungaretti, Quasimodo, and now Montale, the best. Perfection. Yet I still think there is more sap in Quasimodo, I won't say more fire because there is controlled fire in Montale too. More. I have just read "Mount Amiata." An inexhaustible poem, that justifies [Robert] Lowell's rendering. Better than anything by Quasimodo. Maybe better than anything by anybody.

If Zen is absolute affirmation, how can I hope to think in Zen terms? One does not think in Zen terms, one *is*. It is the thinking that blocks the absolute affirmation. But I think too much, and try to decide too much, because I think there are so many things I have to decide. And in a way there are. I am bound to decisions, and that is the trouble. But the whole life I am living is a life filled with total uncertainty and I have to be constantly re-deciding, because I refuse the fake certainty of conforming and allowing everything to be decided beforehand by others.

What is she thinking? How is she bearing this awful business? I think of the fatal brutality of it. Worse for her than for me. I had surrendered long ago because I surrender easy. She had had a struggle about revealing her whole self, and then did so completely: then what? The building fell in. We are separated. We cannot talk, we cannot help each other, we can do nothing. Desire. Baffling, inarticulate desire. Hopeless. This is something we cope with in entirely different ways, because I automatically say "no" to it, and she is built for "yes." But it gets into me with a force that can destroy me utterly. Her too. The sense of disaster and helplessness. And one must say it is all right? It is absurd. There is no clear answer to it. The point is not to decide between this and that crazy answer when all the answers are crazy. There is no clear answer. Her fatal propensity is to need an answer. I can do without. Poor sweet kid, if only it were given me just to be the answer. But there is no clear answer, least of all me. I am nobody's answer, not even my own.

Several times today your presence has come to me suddenly like the cry of someone badly hurt. And I read an Italian poet. But what else can I do?

She has no one to talk to. Neither have I, although everybody here who knows about it, confessors and all the other boyscouts available on the premises, think they are there for me to talk to. I remember my black silence with the Abbot the first time we talked. I refused to say anything except what had to be said. The second time I was more buoyant to show there was "hope" (of what?). But still said nothing, except to take the conditions that were imposed, but taking them if possible in a less absolute sense and then getting out before things got any worse. She has no one to talk to. Or perhaps she has at least some friend, and is better off than I. All I talk to about anything tell me I am ruined.

Nobody seems to think that this involves two people. And that these two people have a right to decide a few things for themselves. No. That is impossible. This is what comes of signing away all your rights in advance by a vow of chastity. The only answer of course is that I should never have written that first (love) letter, but what else could I do? It was only the truth, and I thought we could handle it with ease.

All this torment comes from the contradictions I have allowed in myself by being open. By not closing all the gates and doors and carefully locking them and then winding myself up in a blanket and going to sleep. All the things a hermit should not do I have done. Should a hermit like Bob Dylan? He means at least as much to me as some of the new liturgy, perhaps in some ways more. I want to know the guy. I want him to come here, and I want him to see one of my poems, he might even use it. I have not closed the right doors. I should be writing the new English version of some hymn nobody is ever going to sing.

Necessarily, there are always new questions when you have not decided all the answers in advance. This is what they want me to do, and if I won't do it, then they are determined to do it for me. And the trouble is that my position is so ambiguous that they can still do this and I have to put up with it, hoping that God will open one after another all the doors they have closed. But He will probably not open all of them.

Night is falling on an impossibly beautiful day without you. We will probably never spend this kind of day together again. I have given up trying to understand it. When we began, we knew it could not be understood. As we went along we wanted it to be understandable, and it never was. There is nothing *understandable* in love: just joy and then sorrow and then if you are lucky, more joy.

(June 18, 1966)

The bitter and lucid joys of solitude. The real desert is this: to face the real limitations of one's own existence and knowledge and not try to manipulate them or disguise them. Not to embellish them with possibilities. To simply set aside all possibilities other than those that are actually present and real, here and now. And then to choose or not, as one wishes, knowing that no choice is a solution to anything but merely a step further into a slightly changed context of other, very few, very limited, very meaningless concrete possibilities. To realize that one's whole life, everybody's life, is really like that. In society the possibilities seem infinitely extended. One is in contact with other people, other liberties, other choices and who knows what the others may suddenly all choose? Who knows but that someone may come up and give me a check for a million dollars? But has this ever happened? It always *might*.

In society, in the middle of other people, one can always imagine he will break through into other liberties and other frames of reference. Other worlds. But today everyone realizes that this is illusory to a great extent. The solitude of the other is like my own: there is no real way of deciphering it. Except to get down to the same radical desert perspective: what are our possibilities here and now, what do they mean, where do they lead? Nowhere except into another small, slight pattern of other very limited possibilities. But we have trained ourselves to think that we live at every moment amid *unlimited hopes*. There is nothing we cannot have if we try hard enough, or look in the right place for it.

But in solitude when accurate limitations are seen and accepted, they then vanish, and a new dimension opens up. The present is in fact, in itself, *unlimited*. The only way to grasp it in its unlimitedness is to remove the limitations we place on it by future expectations and hopes and plans, or surmises, or regrets about the past, or attempts to explain something we have experienced (and the revived, warmed-up experience) in order to be able to continue living with it. Live with it? To live with something past is to put a limitation on the present. And yet the past does enter into the present: as the limitation against which we must assert our liability. How?

It is all right to tell myself this. But *her*. Do I owe it to her to choose solitude only in terms that accord with her own loneliness? This is a false question. She thinks that when I accept being alone in the above sense, I am rejecting her, I am thrusting her out of my solitude. This implies the illusion that I can reject her. But that is impossible. I cannot put her out of my mind and see no reason for even trying to. That is another unreal possibility. The idea of a perfect, empty solitude in which there is only "mind" is preposterous. The only solitude is the solitude of the frail, mortal, limited, distressed, rebellious human person, made of his loves and fears, facing his own true present. What is my own true present? A present without her, in which she is loved as absent, as needed, as trusted, as remembered. As a value and a reality of great mystery and preciousness that can never be changed. She asks of my solitude that it have in it a place for her in which she is always known, reverenced, loved, valued, prized for herself as she is in her actuality. I will never refuse her this: it is the root of my commitment and my fidelity to give her this anchor in my own sea of loneliness. Forever.

"To take up the marvelous, heart-rending wager of the absurd" (Camus). Yet I am not sure I agree with the stoic limitations the hero of the absurd must impose upon himself. He must not "leap" (into the unknown). But Camus is perhaps deluded with his own supposed lucidity. To assume the known is only absurd seems to me not much different from leaping into the unknown, trusting it will be coherent. It generally turns out to be so. This too is a form of the absurd. Luck is absurd. We have a lot of luck.

Here is the real problem: what is the root nature of solitude? The whole predicament I am in is the result of conflicting ideas of solitude. In giving me permission to live alone, they gave me only the permission to restrict myself to *their* idea of what a man is when he is alone. They gave me permission to live alone in such a way that it would *justify them*, not save my own soul.

M. is caught in the middle, desperately rebelling against their idea, not sure that she accepts and understands mine, and in the end saying that I should leave it all behind and settle for love. But at this stage of the game, to face the absurdity of life in this other form is much too complicated for me. I have lost any ability to hope in that kind of happiness, because as soon as love gets fixed, stabilized (as society wants it to be), then it commands its own battery of fictions and illusions. One would have to pretend something else, something more complicated even than what I try to avoid pretending now.

Their idea of solitude is fundamentally this: the hermit is a man who out of spite has made himself completely unavailable. He can do this with complete assurance and deadly complacency because he has on his side an unavailable God who is in fact secretly and magically available only to him. The solitary is then in a position of unassailable spiritual comfort. He lives for and with God alone. He is the totally consoled, by a consolation that he wills to accept by a blind leap into the decision to be consoled. To be able to achieve this autistic feat is the sign of a hermit vocation. Or, I might add, of paranoia.

What I am fighting for is the idea that the solitary is also available to everyone in a certain kind of way. Paradox, because one must preserve the authentic reality of aloneness, that is the true sense of the absurd in Camus' terms (and more than in his terms, which exclude any faith). To drink every day the bitter wine of the absurd, and to revolt (solitude is a revolt and an acceptance of the absurd: acceptance of the necessity to revolt, to protest). To abandon solitude and then to sink into what is imagined to be the warm comfort and forgetfulness of social occupation would be, for me, the denial of my own life, my own need for lucidity which resembles that of Camus – and is totally different because of faith. Availability in love, in compassion, in understanding. The solitary must be open to the hearts of those he loves.

The great question, the baffling one now, is in what way my solitude is still "open" and "available" to M. When of course the whole idea is to close it off, make me totally unavailable, make love impossible. They are insisting on their own definition of solitude. I am not allowed to quarrel with it, for if I do so openly I shall have no solitude at all. The answer is in Camus' principle: that the absurd man is without (human at least) hope. His hope-lessness isolates him in the pure present. And makes him "available" in the present. They have done me the favor of blocking off all avenues to a certain kind of hope, which in fact would have implied restriction. The unful-fillment of the solitary life is necessary if the solitary is to be available. But how? I don't know, I am not supposed to know everything. I accept what I don't know as unknown (like Camus) and I do not contaminate the accep-tance by inserting into it imaginary hopes. I differ from Camus in the im-mense, unknown hope that is my own aspect of the "absurd" – and comes not under knowledge and stoicism but under faith. Faith and revolt are in-separable. Faith is the fundamental revolt. But of course to many Christians this is the most unbearable of the Gospel truths and it has had to be swept under the rug a long time ago.

If God has brought her into my life and if God has willed our love, then it is more His affair than ours. My task consists in not forcing my love into a mold that pleases and reassures me (or both of us), but in leaving everything "open" – and not trying to predetermine the future.

Today Victor Hammer and Carolyn came over from Lexington. They are two of my oldest and best friends in this area: he is one of the finest craftsmen living. A hand printer, type designer and painter, an old Aus-trian. We had a picnic and I took them out to the place where we were Derby Day: on the flat ground, among the dry leaves, under all the tall straight trees. It was cool and nice – and I could think of M. better. In fact I told them about the situation, and they understood perhaps better than anyone except J. and Nicanor [Parra]. But like everyone else, in the end, they said it could not get anywhere. That we had reached a dead end, and the only thing to do was to accept the fact. Even Carolyn, who is not Catholic and is normally in favor of the runaway monk in novels, was saying: "but you have given up everything on entering here." Everybody knows this, and it is a most inexorable fact. There is no getting around it even though, as she suggested, there would be a lot of (non-Catholic) people who would be very sympathetic.

They brought a few copies of the *New Yorker*. I flipped over the pages to read the cartoons (before settling down to a long report on China) and the sight of the ads just turned me inside out. I was in complete revolt against them and all that they imply, the attitude, the values, the suppositions, the axioms so to speak behind them. This is a realm that I cannot take, I cannot be part of. I am ashamed of feeling that way, I hate myself in a way for feeling it, but my entire being says *no*. I am not as open as I thought. Whatever it may mean, I simply cannot go back to the kind of society where that is accepted as normal – and that is after all not bad. There is a certain taste, a sophistication, a refinement even, which I am attracted to (the ads in some other magazines would just revolt me period, without any attraction at all). I am ashamed of myself, but I am set in this. I belong in the woods. There is no other way left for me. Except perhaps that impossible island.

Then suddenly today I realized that there is no longer any problem about our love. It is no longer a problem, just an impossibility, on one level: and a pure fact on another. On the level of impossibility: we cannot see each other, we cannot meet, we cannot hold each other, we cannot bring our lips together and cling to each other warmly, helplessly, in a long embrace. That is all over. On the level of pure fact: we love each other as we have never loved anyone else, and the love remains. Neither of us will do anything to destroy or falsify it. It will live as long as we live, and we will live forever. Your presence in me is pure and quiet and secure, the more so as I myself am free, attuned to the reality and absurdity of my own life, and obedient to God. Now that it is practically impossible for us to be together physically, we remain together spiritually without difficulty: or at least so it seems to me. It is true that all this will one day be less intense, less a matter of obsessed consciousness (it is no longer an obsession anyway, just a pure fact, a presence, like one's own being). And it will be just love without need and without name. We will no longer need to identify it and to name it. We will be part of each other always.

When I told Victor and Carolyn of the poems I had written about our love, immediately they wanted to print them. We discussed the various problems. Of course there would have to be an assumed name. The identity of the poet would have to be carefully concealed, unsuspected by anyone. Can this be done? Nobody knows. But we discussed the thing as a possibility. It would certainly be a very elegantly printed, strictly limited edition: a real work of art. Not more than fifty or sixty copies in all. They are very eager to do it, and I am very eager to have it done: but can it be done? Let's hope so. Few people will have had such a memorial to their living love. They will write to J. for copies of the poems. Then we will see. J. may have ideas about it.

A touching letter came today from Nora Chadwick – this is one I really love, though I never actually met her. She is an old retired Cambridge professor in her eighties and an authority on Celtic monasticism. She is busy writing still, and another old friend, Eleanor Duckett, a prof from Smith, is there with her writing too. All about the old monks. She writes that she is delighted that I am living the same kind of life as the old guys she writes about: that there actually should be something of the sort in the world of today. This is important to me. For she knows what monasticism is, and she respects the *reality* of monastic solitude (not just the ersatz and the institutionalized forms that have survived today). That there should be men willing to live in real solitude . . . Seeing it through her eyes, I am deeply moved by the meaning of this strange life. Here I am in the middle of it. I know I have not been truly faithful to it in many ways. I have evaded it. Yet who can say what its real demands are other than the one who must meet them? And who knows what were the failures and problems of those forgotten people who actually lived as solitaries in the past? How many of them were lonely, and in love? The stories of the Desert Fathers are full of material about all that!

All I know is that here I am, and the valley is very quiet, the sun is going down, there is no human being around, and as darkness falls I could easily be a completely forgotten person, as if I did not exist for the world at all. (Though there is one who remembers and whom I remember.) The day could easily come when I would be just as invisible as if I never existed, and still be living here on this hill . . . And I know I would be perfectly content to be so.

Who knows anything at all about solitude if he has not been in love, and in love *in his solitude?* Love and solitude must test each other in the man who means to live alone: they must become one and the same thing in him, or he will only be half a person. Unless I have you with me always, in some very quiet and perfect way, I will never be able to live fruitfully alone. See how necessary you have become to me! I cannot even be a hermit without you!

Another letter, and an important one, came: a message from a Moslem Shaikh (Spiritual Master) – actually a European, but formed by one of the great Moslem saints and mystics of the age (Ahmad al'Alawi). That I can be accepted in a personal and confidential relationship, not exactly as a disciple but at any rate as one of those who are entitled to consult him directly and personally. This is a matter of great importance to me, because in the light of their traditional ideas it puts me in contact with the spirit and teaching of Ahmad al'Alawi in a way that is inaccessible just to the scholar or the student. It means I have a living place in a living and secret tradition. It can have tremendous effects. I see that already. Here again, the Shaikh attaches considerable importance to my life in solitude.

So for you too: I am of no value to you except in so far as I am this absurd man all alone on a wooded hill, with the darkness falling all around him, the stars coming out over his head, a man difficult for anyone to really approve of, a friend of Zen monks and mixed up with a secret Moslem sect, a man in trouble with his Abbot and somehow inexplicable to his community, a man who has no clear ideas about God but just hangs around waiting to be struck by God as if by lightning . . . That is what you have chosen to love, my darling, and that is the strange being who will love you forever, even when the lightning strikes: and there is something fierce about the One with whom no other is to be compared, the Moslem vision of Allah the One God. Don't worry, I am not practicing a lot of Moslem disciplines on top of everything else: but there is this spirit of stark adoration and blinding desert fury which is another aspect of the absurd and the absolute . . . Who is like unto Him? Who knows anything remotely like unto Him? Who can dare to be the kind of fool that gets up and talks about Him?

Saturday – Late (June 18, 1966)

I went to bed like a good little monk at eight o'clock. But could not sleep. Arm hurting, back hurting, heart empty and desolate. Lay there thinking. And thinking some more. Obsessed with the idea that M. might conceivably find her way out here though she has never seen the place and could not possibly find it in the dark etc. If only there were a soft knock on the door, and I opened it, and it was she standing on the porch. Finally I couldn't stand it any more and got up, put my clothes on and started wandering around. For a moment I had a strong desire to start down to the monastery and sneak into the office again and make another phone call. But I don't even know where she is. In Louisville, or where. Perhaps she has gone home for the weekend. I no longer have any idea what she is doing and no way of finding out.

So I went out on the porch. Nothing. Silence. Vast silence of the woods full of fireflies. The stars. Down in the south, the huge sign of the Scorpion. The red eye of Regulus. Just stars. Not a light from any house or farm. Only fireflies and stars and silence. A car racing by on the road, then more silence. Nothing. Nothing.

When a car goes by you can feel the alien frenzy of it. Someone madly going somewhere for no reason. I am a complete prisoner under these stars. With nothing. Or perhaps everything.

I sit on the porch and deliberately refuse to rationalize anything, to explain anything or to comment on anything. Only what is there. I am there. Fireflies, stars, darkness, the massive shadows of the woods, the vague dark valley. And nothing, nothing, nothing.

Is she thinking of me? Loving me? Is her heart calling to mine in the dark? I don't know. I can't honestly say that I know. I can't honestly say I know anything except that it is late, I can't sleep, there are fireflies all over the place, and there is not the remotest possibility of making any poetic statement of this. You don't write poems about nothing.

And yet.

Somehow this nothing seems to be *everything*. I look at the south sky and for some ungodly reason for which there is no reason, everything is complete. I think of going back to bed, in peace without knowing why, a peace that cannot be justified by anything, any reason, any proof, any argument. Any supposition. There are no suppositions left. Only fireflies.

I kneel down by the bed and look up at the icon of the nativity. The soft shaded light plays over the shelves of Buddhist books in the silent bedroom. I want to tell you something, and I don't know how to begin to say it. I am afraid that if I start talking and writing I will confuse everything. Nothing needs to be said. If I try to say what I want to say, not knowing what you yourself are going through (God knows you may be in a completely different situation – you may be in anguish, or you may have forgotten me, who knows?), it may only upset you or confuse you. Or irritate you. Like the letter I tried to write (and yet you got it after all – the one about everything being *right there*).

The hard thing is to write it without adding any rationalization, any explanation, any words about God. It is disastrous to speak of God. Yet not to speak of God means that nothing can be said. I mean about this thing. To know that under all these stars which He made (and that is in a way suddenly irrelevant) He is as small as myself and as present as myself and we are both nothing and both lonely. That both God and I are lost. And that this is the beginning of everything. And that I want you in on it. Be lost with the lost stars and fireflies. Maybe you are. Maybe somehow your love has brought this lostness upon us, me and God. Maybe it has all risen out of your own loneliness. Or maybe you have just forgotten us both. How can I say? I have no way of knowing. But I know that there really exists in the world such a thing as freedom, and dear, I want you to have it with me. I want so badly for you to have it with me.

(June 19, 1966)

I finished *Sisyphus* in a hurry, bored with its systematic aridity. It is inconclusive even in the thought of Camus himself, an essay, a note, a way station, and all that he proclaims in the middle of it about the "ethic of quantity" (finding meaning in the repetition of meaningless acts) is highly ambiguous because what he finds is precisely a hidden *quality*. Well, that's that. I turn to something else.

To what? In the sweetness of the mild morning I am reached again by the insistence, the pathos, the loveliness of your love. Something I cannot describe or explain, that seeks me out, that reaches me with its gentle appeal. The message that comes saying "I need you, I love you." How explain it and how doubt it? What is the use of an ethic and an aridity when this sweetness breaks through everything with another kind of victory? I love you as I always have, and perhaps more than ever in this inexpressible freedom and peace and certainty, on this level where no human force can get between us and no one can prevent us loving one another, not for anything we get out of it but purely because love is love and has been given us by God. And they cannot stop it. God made love, not death. Love is stronger than death. Our love is stronger than their denial of it. It always will be.

It is a strange thing: now that I cannot plan anything, or try anything, or seek in any way to contact you, your presence is more clear, more quiet, more constant, more assured. You are just "here," as if God were saying: "You don't need phones and letters any more – you are both dwelling in each others' hearts, you are present to each other, you can speak without words, just by the mute movement of longing and of love." You are present to me in a quiet, gentle pathos that is reassuring, appealing, comforting and mysterious all at the same time. That says "I *do* love you, I am loving you now, I am thinking of you now, I need you now." And perhaps in your own heart I am present in the same way. That is where I want to be. If I am there, perhaps it explains the peace and the sort of empty, untroubled quiet that surrounds me here, where I seek nothing else, and am in need of nothing but God, and your nearness to me in Him. This solitude is now a thousand times more precious to me. In the monastery I would have to be busy with a dozen trivial and distracting things, acts, gestures, rites that might simply disturb and unsettle my emotions. And for nothing. Here, it is quiet, I am alone, we are alone together. The secret that we have needed has been granted to us, and it is very precious. I hope we will never lose it.

For some reason today I am no longer mad at the *New Yorker* ads (I have finished the first installment on China and don't have the second). There was a real good double-spread long poem about a crazy house and it contained these touching lines:

> Everyone has left me
> except my muse
> *that good nurse*.
> She stays in my hand
> Like a wild white mouse.

And the italics are in the original too. Dear, never leave me. Have you perhaps found out the art of being that mouse in the hermitage after all? You have been so close all morning, so quiet, so sweet, so gentle and so patient. How could I ever be without you?

I am tired. I only got about four hours sleep last night after all. Too tired to be mad at anything, resentful of anything, or to complain. I will just go down and say Mass, quietly, alone, not concelebrating, for us, for our needs, for our love, for our future, that we may always in some ineffable way be together merely by wanting to be. Perhaps if we are a little patient and stubborn about this magic it will work forever, until we meet in heaven and no more magic will be needed.

This evening in my conference (on the technological culture) I read a bit about some characters who, supported by two foundations, were bugging the last grizzly bears in the west with radios to find out about their love-making habits. When I had read this sardonic material I thought I saw some funny looks and some amusement: perhaps more people know my story than I realize. The smiles were in general sympathetic.

A long, silent afternoon, clouds, planes, trees, sun. Then I went down to give my conference, had supper, came back. I have no interest in being down there now that I can no longer use the phone. Wanted several times to call anyway but I knew it would be suicidal. Where is she? What is she thinking? It is terrible not to know what is going on. But apart from that – I don't care about anything else. I am lonely for her, but that is only a partial loneliness and it does not alter the fact that it is part of a general loneliness that I have chosen. Or that has chosen itself for me. I can never be anything else than solitary. My loneliness is my ordinary climate. That I was allowed to have so many moments of complete accord and harmony and love with another person, with her, was simply extraordinary. I like people, but usually I am tired of being with others after about an hour. That I could be with her for hours and hours and not be tired for an instant of her – it was a miracle, but it did not mean that I was not essentially solitary.

Sunday Evening – Late

Same thing again. Can't sleep. It makes no difference. I love the aloneness of the night. I have been lying thinking of you. In a way I cannot be without you: you are part of my life itself, and of my very loneliness. I know we are together in our hearts, have been for hours perhaps. Tonight my thoughts and loneliness have been tranquil, not dry and abstract like last night. Just as free, more free. To be alone in a solitude that is with you, though without your bodily presence, is certainly a special kind of freedom: as though we were even free of time and space, and could be together at will in our love, in all its simplicity. As though for me to be, even in lostness and isolation, were necessarily to be with you. I know we are very loved by God. This is a sign of it, really, that he lets us have this strange freedom that is so seemingly natural (because it is pure gift). Yet on the other hand (this was disturbing me last night when I was more tormented at first and more obsessed with your body) I honestly think that we were in a fair way to a kind of relationship in which we could have destroyed each other, if it had gone on without obstacle. Perhaps we still have to be careful of that – being overconfident is not a help. But I know – and have experienced it from the beginning: as long as we take this entirely on His terms and do not try to force our own conditions through, we will never break our hearts. We will be protected and guided. It seems awfully strange to love like this, in this way in which we do not really have much to say about how it will go (though maybe you have got me out of bed just by calling to me in the night) but it is sweet and wonderful, and it is worthy of everything that has happened to us since the beginning. I believe in it, though. It is the only way. It is absolutely free of all care, at least for me. I don't have to figure anything. (Though for a moment I was walking on the porch and heard cars over there on the road, and thought wildly of going off and getting a ride to town . . . Then what? But that is in me, too, the instinct to suddenly go and not know where or why I am going. But it has been a long time since I have been able to really live like that. The evening at the airport was an exception, a throwback to my natural self, the guy that used to vanish into the heart of France or Germany and just wander.)

You know, don't you, that the Abbot will never again let me be hospitalized in St. Joe's (Louisville)? Partly because he does not like to pay. But now he has the perfect excuse: danger of a woman. I doubt if he will ever let me go to a hospital in Louisville again, though maybe St. Anthony's is still open, but he would then extract a solemn promise that I would not let you know etc. In my opinion, all my future hospital days will be in Lexington. Or God knows where. If you ever got a job in Bardstown and he knew it, it would be a disaster.

(June 20, 1966)

Finally got five hours of sleep or so. At the end I was dreaming that I was being hazed by Jesuits, as though in a sort of initiation into a fraternity into which I had no desire to be initiated. I can't remember details of the dream, only that I seemed to be mixed up with a lot of people with whom I had nothing in common, that they resented me, and that they were trying to ridicule and discredit me. And I was thinking, "How did I get mixed up in all this?"

Solitude as act: the reason no one really understands solitude, or bothers to try to understand it, is that it appears to be nothing but a condition. Something one elects to undergo, like standing under a cold shower. Actually, solitude is a realization, an actualization, even a kind of creation, as well as a liberation of active forces within us, forces that are more than our own, and yet more ours than what appears to be "ours." As a mere condition, solitude can be passive, inert, and basically unreal: a kind of permanent coma. One has to work at it to keep out of this condition. One has to work actively at solitude, not by putting fences around oneself but by destroying all the fences and throwing away all the disguises and getting down to the naked root of one's inmost desire, which is the desire of liberty-reality. To be free from the illusion that reality creates when one is out of right relation to it, and to be real in the freedom which reality gives when one is rightly related to it.

Hence the need for discipline, for some kind of technique of integration that keeps body and soul together, harmonizes their powers, brings them into one deep resonance, orients the whole being toward the root of being. The need for a "way." Presence, invocation, *mantram*, concentration, emptiness. All these are aspects of a realized solitude. Mere *being alone* is nothing. Or at least it is only a potential. Sooner or later he who is merely alone either rots or escapes.

The "active life" can in fact be that which is most passive: one is simply driven, carried, batted around, moved. The most desperate illusion and the most common one is just to fling oneself into the mass that is in movement and be carried along with it: to be part of the stream of traffic going nowhere but with a great sense of phony purpose. It is against this that I revolt. Because I revolt, my life at first must take on an aspect of total meaninglessness: the revenge of the social superego. The perception of the absurd. Freedom begins with the full acceptance of the absurd: the willingness to *realize* and experience one's life as totally absurd – in relation to the apparent meaning which has been thrown over life by society, by illusion. But the experience of this absurdity is again only a potential. A starting point for a deeper realization: the realization of that root reality in myself and in all life *which I do not know and cannot know*. This implies the capacity to see that *realizing* and *knowing* are not the same. In realization, the reality one grasps, or by which one is grasped, is actualized in oneself and one becomes what one realizes, one is what he realizes. Knowing is just a matter of registering that something is objectively verifiable – whether one bothers to verify it or not. Realization is not verification but isness. For this, solitude is necessary, and solitude itself is the fullness of realization. In solitude I become *fully able to realize what I cannot know*.

It is for this that I have to give up everything else, have long ago given up everything else. If I could have both solitude and M. (it might be theoretically possible), then I would certainly take both. But as in concrete fact the issue becomes a choice: then I choose both in another form. She will be my love but in this absurd and special way: as part of the "realization" which is solitude. In a funny way this will, I think, give her own life a sort of new reality which it would not otherwise have, even though her way will be different from mine. Yet I think she will remain with me in this strange life of being alone – while grappling with her own strange aloneness in the midst of people. (An aloneness which she fights desperately and in vain.)

What does the lonely and absurd man have to teach others? Simply that being alone and absurd are not things to be feared. But these are precisely the two things that everybody fears: they spend all their time reassuring themselves that they make sense, that they are not ridiculous, that they are acceptable, desirable, valuable and that they will never have to regard themselves as really alone: in other words they plunge into the reassuring stream of illusions which is created by all the other people like themselves. A great common work, a liturgy, in which everyone agrees publicly to say that in these terms everything is real and makes sense. But the terms are not satisfactory. Everybody remains secretly absurd and alone. Only no one dares face the fact. Yet facing this fact is the absolutely essential requirement for beginning to live freely.

My apostolate: to realize that my life is absurd and not to care, to teach others that they do not have to care. But this has not been clear, for in fact I have spent too much time and effort in convincing others and even myself that all this makes sense. My work is in fact invalid in so far as it seems to make sense and in so far as it seems to say that solitude is something to be desired. Of course one has to make some kind of sense: I do not deny that I want to write coherently, in accord with a basic realization. But merely to spell out a logical message, or worse still a sales pitch for something spiritual, something religious, something "interior," or worse still "monastic". . . what a total waste. More than half my life and work have been wasted in this kind of thing.

Camus does not go far enough: he is both too western, too French and too post-Christian. He sets up absurdity as something to be faced with stoic bravery. Hence by implication something fearful. It is not fearful, it is just the ordinary stuff of life. And the life of Sisyphus is not that tragic (as Camus admits, "let us assume that Sisyphus is happy"), but there is still too much lip-smacking over the bitterness and futility of it. Futile? Life is not futile if you simply live it. It remains futile, however, as long as you keep watching yourself live it. And that is the old syndrome: keeping a constant eye on oneself and on one's life, to make sure that the absurd is not showing, that one has company, that one is justified by the presence and support of all the others.

Note a false solitude can simply stand this on its head: to make sense by proclaiming oneself absurd (a more sophisticated way of evading absurdity) and to be willing to do without the presence of others, provided that one's solitude is somehow admirable to a select few. These are the subterfuges of the idiot and the charlatan. I hope I am not doing this, but obviously to some extent I am. I will perhaps learn not to.

For all these reasons I am glad of my love for M., which adds a special note of absurdity and therefore of reality to my professed "solitude." It is in many ways the best thing that could have happened. But I do not value our love for that: what a betrayal that would be! I value it because of her. Her own solitude and uniqueness, in a sense her helpless appeal to my own solitude, and her intuitive acceptance of my absurdity as a value because it is mine: as something of inexhaustible meaning for her. This is the victory over death – and we must keep this alive in each other. Flawed though we are, we are also authentic enough and wounded enough to be intent on this, intent enough to keep it up in the depths of our being. And to learn from this, in a hard way, that infidelity cannot be excused by appeals to the "absurd," because you can't have it both ways.

The great joke is this: having a self that is to be taken seriously, that is to be proved free, right, logical, consistent, beautiful, successful and in a word "not absurd." Yet this self is by definition isolated from other selves, it affirms itself by its egohood, by being "not the others" and by being alone.

At this point the beauty of the dilemma and of the joke begins to appear. To be "not the others" is to be "not like the others" and to be unlike the others is to be absurd. But to be like the others is impossible because concealing at all costs one's aloneness in order not to appear absurd. What then? Do I save my soul by learning to affirm it courageously in the midst of absurdity? By determining to "be alone" in the sense of "standing alone" on the acceptance of my own absurdity? This is not it, only a potential.

One only ceases to be absurd when he ceases to take seriously the affirmation of the self that is unique (even though it is in its own way unique). The uniqueness is not to be taken seriously. To take oneself with unique seriousness is to be absurd. But this is original sin: it cannot be avoided. Salvation becomes then a bitter joke, a gamble with the absurdity of a pure

contradiction: rescuing and making sense out of what is not really insecure, as provisional, and as absurd. Try to make what is essentially absurd
and provisional, absolute and final, totally unique and serious. What do
you get? The pure absurdity of hell. One only ceases then to be absurd
when, realizing that everything is absurd when seen in isolation from
everything else, meaning and value are sought only in *wholeness*. The solitary who merely stands apart trying to make sense out of himself is still
lost, perhaps worse than the others. The solitary must therefore return to
the heart of life and oneness, losing himself not in the massive illusion but
simply in the root reality. Where does he encounter this? In the heart of
his own absurdity, but only by plunging through the center of his own
nothingness and coming out in the All which is the Void and which is if
you like the Love of God.

Therefore one cannot cease to be absurd by dint of metaphysics, or concentration, or meditation, or study, or knowledge: only by experiencing the
fact that there is no wall between ourselves and others, in other words by
accepting the absurdity of our own life in terms of the suffering of others:
not separating "my" pain, suffering, limitation, lostness, etc. from that of
others. As long as a single person is lost I am lost. To try to save myself by
getting free from the mass of the damned *(massa damnata)* and becoming
good by myself, is to be both damned and absurd – as well as antichrist.
Christ descended into hell to show that He willed to be lost with the lost, in
a certain sense, emptied so that they might be filled and saved, in the realization that now their lostness was not theirs but His. Hence the way one
begins to make sense out of life is taking upon oneself the lostness of everyone – and then realizing not that one has done something, or "made sense"
but that he has simply entered into the stream of realization. The rest will
work out by itself, and we do not know what that might mean.

Where does one find this? I notice that someone like Bob Dylan has a better intuitive realization of it than the bishops and the clergy. "There is something happening here and you don't know what it is. Do you, Mister Jones?"

But of course he has rejected the sin of being Mister Jones. Even Bob
Dylan is not perfect. The imperfection is right, provisionally. What is said
about Mister J. always has to be said since the problem of Mister J. is that he
is not absurd. We go round in the circle. It makes no difference, once you
know it is a circle.

To affirm the self by fulfilling desire: desire conditioned by the illusions
of what people consider a fulfilled desire: turns out to be unfulfillable:

hence absurdity: and one tries to hide the absurdity by fulfilling another desire. The beginning is to recognize the radical absurdity of desire.

So far so good. It is a familiar pattern. But it is only a sketch, a beginning. Because the desire to be without desire is equally absurd and unfulfillable. Camus thinks the answer is to be like Sisyphus, and accept the absurdity, roll the rock with immense effort to the top of the hill and let it roll down again, then start over: just keep at it. For no reason. To admit one has no reason for keeping at it is to be free. The glad acceptance of hell. "Let us suppose Sisyphus is happy." But this is just as bourgeois as contenting oneself with the clichés: "Well, at least we *tried*."

The other way is difficult: it means getting free, by realization, from total enslavement to an absurd self that has to be constantly reaffirmed *against* others but *in their own terms*. One must be accepted and not-accepted. Recognized with envy. Loved and hated. The proof that one has succeeded and has overcome absurdity. This is the ultimate absurdity. But to ignore this and go one's own way is not enough. It is better than nothing. One needs to be against nothing, and one needs to take little or no account of the terms in which self-affirmation is considered possible or important. Then absurdity does not matter and one no longer has to care about it. There is a whole new frame of reference: *compassion*.

Basic: the struggle for lucidity, out of which compassion can at last arise. Then you are free. That is, you are lost: there is no self to save. You simply love. Free of desire for oneself, desiring only lucidity for oneself and others.

Monday evening

Lucidity does not prevent anguish. In spite of all these stoical considerations I am missing her tremendously today. The worst thing is to be unable to call, to hear her voice even. Several times I have wanted to get to a phone but it would be absurdly useless and would make things far worse. There is no question of the depth of my attachment to her. It is very deep, and the real depth of it is only just beginning to appear. How far down does it go? It is certainly deeper and stronger than anything I ever got into before. I need her love in the deepest possible way, and I know she needs mine. And there is now nothing we can do about it. I underestimated the power of this love, and was wrong in thinking that we could just keep it on the level of a friendly sort of affection, something rather detached and pleasant, not too involved. This was certainly not possible, and now I know it, and a strong physical desire is part of it. There is enough power involved in it for it to be ruinous for both of us. I am sure we will get through it because the circumstances, brutal as they are, will make it almost impossible for anything to go too far wrong. But we may have to suffer far more than we expected, or at any rate far more than I did, with my rather naive ideas about it all. It is of course easy enough to look back and say that "here" or "there" I should have turned another corner and got off the road. But is was not possible to get off that road. I was on it before I knew it, and going fast. At one point she saw the danger far more clearly than I did – and I talked her out of it. Or rather she saw how good my intentions were, and the basic innocence of it . . . The most intolerable thing of all is not to know what she feels, whether or not she needs my help, whether or not I can do something for her. Perhaps after all the most helpful thing is that we are kept apart in spite of ourselves.

There is a loud pump in the valley (irrigating). I have been drinking. Good thing they do not know I have the stuff here. It won't last long at the present rate. Especially if that pump keeps me awake tonight. I fell and bumped my back. My arm hurts, my leg hurts, everything hurts. But I am not sorry for myself. There is no point in it. If only I can keep from thinking about her body maybe I can sleep . . . "Let us suppose Sisyphus is happy!"

(June 21, 1966)

The most shattering thing of all for both of us is the fact that a real and deep love has been blocked and prevented: was perhaps socially impossible anyway. Not just that we were compatible in so many ways, but we were open to each other in our deepest and most intimate need for full acceptance and understanding. We were: we *are*. But all communication is now blocked. Yet I think we are so open to each other that even when we cannot communicate, we remain somehow in contact, sharing our lives on a hidden level too far down for expression. We had been together so little, yet in the intense intimacy of the hours we did spend together we were fast learning every aspect, every inch of each other, not in the usual sort of collision of objects that love turns out to be, but in the need to give and surrender without disguise and without pretense, in our complexities and in our obsessions, in our deepest need for love, for comprehension. We are very different from each other in many ways, and for that reason very drawn to each other. I felt that if we had only had a chance, we could have grown magnificently together into a beautiful dual organism of love: we could have slowly healed and strengthened each other, brought out all that was waiting to develop, that was blocked, that was held back by society. But also there was a sort of double desperation about it: the sense that time was against us, that life itself would not let us fully live, because we could never live together. That soon it would all be stopped and we would fall back into our solitudes.

This torments me. I say we are different, and where we are most different is perhaps also where we are most the same. In our solitude, our aloneness. She is such a complete waif. That is perhaps what I most love in her – and it is what she wanted me to love, I think. I am too a waif. But for me that is a bit more complex because I am a man and men are not supposed to be waifs. There was, however, one point where I sensed that she fully knew and accepted and loved precisely this in me, and I had a great secret joy in it. I was very glad of that particular, small, symbolic surrender. But getting back to our aloneness: where we differ is that I accept it and I suppose both of us end up with most unsatisfactory solutions. Both of us wanted to pool our lonelinesses and make one reality out of two voids and because we saw that it was really possible, an immense hope was beginning to rise up in our hearts: perhaps especially hers, for she is not as resigned as I. Now the hope has apparently been shattered. I hope we can still go on with it in spite of everything.

Dear, we must not forget the reality of our love and the reality of the sharing, the penetration into our mutual secrets. We have really done this and done it much more than lovers ordinarily do. We are really in possession of one another's secrets, the inmost self of the other, in its glory and its abandonment. To have seen this in each other as we have seen it is a great gift of love, a great creative joy, one of the greatest and most awesome gifts of life: let us never forget this. Let us cherish the secrets that we have exchanged, more beautiful than any ring or any symbol of union, secrets that are unspeakable and cannot be explained to anyone for we alone will ever know them: we and God.

Yet behind all this is the fact that I could not say I was entitled to any of it. Or was I? I have ended up deciding for my vow and clinging to it, and yet I will never really understand on earth what relation this love has to my solitude. I cannot help placing it at the very heart of my aloneness, and not just on the periphery somewhere. But that is against all "reason" and all the Church believes. But don't let me bring in the Church. Everyone would say that it is the Church that separates us. The Church in fact is blamed for everything. Is it really the Church? The Church is blamed for burning St. Joan of Arc, too.

(June 22, 1966) Wednesday

I dreamt in several different ways of trying to contact M. I cannot remember what the dreams were, only that the last one, before I woke up, was that I was sending a child to the hospital to tell her that I loved her. I realized this was most unsatisfactory but there was nothing else I could do. (I was aware that the child would just go in and say "He told me today he loves you" in an embarrassed sort of way and walk out again.)

I almost never dream of M. as she is, but of someone who, I instinctively know, represents her. Yet this girl is "different" from M. How does one explain this? Still, just when I wake up, the archetypal M. and the reality merge together: the M. I love in the depths of my heart is not symbolic and not just the everyday M. either, but the deep, mysterious, personal, unique potential that is in her: the M. that is trying to become free in my love and is clinging to me for love and help. Yet not that either, because it is the insecure and unreal self in each of us that clings so hard to the other. Even that has to be qualified, however. It was basically right that she should want me to make love to her fully, and there is no question that I wanted to do this in my heart. And yet now, because for me somehow the situation was all wrong, psychologically and spiritually, yet it did not matter. It seems to me now that with her, our love (at least as I see it) was and is so much the important thing that the details do not make any difference. But precisely at this point everything was cut short, bombed out, gutted. What should naturally have turned into a long warm, slow-growing, sweet love expressed in all its depth, has been amputated just when it was about to begin. And I have no right to complain because I have committed myself to another kind of life. As for her, at least I told her over and over what was coming. But the result is cruel for us both, and I am only just beginning to discover how cruel it really is.

I cannot regard this as "just an episode." It is a profound event in my life and one which will have entered deeply into my heart to alter and transform my whole climate of thought and experience: for in her I now realize I had found something, someone, that I had been looking for all my life. I know too that she feels the same about me. No matter what happens I think we will both always feel that this was and is something too deep and too real to be essentially changed. What we have found in each other will

not be lost: yet it will not be truly possessed either. Hence the awful loneliness, deprivation, desolation of being without each other, even though in
our hearts we continue to love each other deeply. Yet we are going to have
to face the fact that we now go separate ways, and that is what I think neither of us is quite willing to face. *Can we* really go separate ways? In a sense,
no. We have to travel together in our hearts as long as we live. She says she
can never love anyone else. That moves me deeply and breaks my heart,
yet I know that she must someday love another, because it would be inhuman to expect such a deprivation in anyone's life. As for me, I am supposed
to be lonely and live alone and sleep alone, so I have no problem and no
complaint. It is merely what I have chosen and the choice is ratified over
and over each day. Even though I so vividly remember her body and long
for her love.

Yesterday Fr. Joe Watt suddenly came (ex-monk, now in California) with
John G. (former novice now a med. student in Louisville). Incredible number of people have been leaving, especially from the California monastery.
This is certainly due to the deep ambiguities in the life of the Order, especially those kept in existence by people like Dom James. One senses the
awful power of the resentment he has generated against everything he believes in and represents, so that what he considers the true "contemplative
life" becomes hateful, nauseating to the people he is trying to influence.
They get themselves finally in a position where they have to rebel against it.
Those who do not rebel remain either as semi-comical and self-satisfied idiots, or else bitter and withdrawn individualists who keep to themselves and
live their lives in their own way, salvaging what they can from the wreckage.
That is my lot, I suppose. It implies rebellion as well as a certain exterior
resignation. I am not proud of my resignation, but I think it is dictated by
circumstances and by God's will – I still don't know what the future will
bring. Perhaps some strange redress: or just the healing reactive work of literal creation. In any case, one senses the basically destructive and desperate
nature of Dom J.'s brand of fervor. It poses an immense problem. But since
I am now little concerned about the survival of monasticism (it will take
care of itself, and the new small monasteries will continue as signs and
sources of hope), I will not waste time worrying about it. He is a providential affliction, a kind of skin disease that I have to live with in patience. I
loathe everything he stands for. And yet I can see that basically he is a man
of good desires: but they have been twisted and corroded and he is now,
without knowing it, a most inhuman person: even though there is so much

potential warmth and concern. Under it all is a deep contempt for man, for love, and for the persons of his monks.

I wrote her a letter, a short one, for Joe W. to take out. It was a very poor letter, written in haste, when I could not think straight, and with all kinds of questions in my mind about it, since I have been strictly forbidden to write and therefore have to wonder about the necessity of any exception (I believe that exceptions can be made, but when they are strictly necessary only). Perhaps it was a useless letter but I wanted at least to give her a sign of life, and some reassurance, because I feel intensely at times that she suffers from our separation, and I can almost register physically the impact of love and longing and suffering that come to me through the evening and the night from Louisville. She must feel the same coming from me.

Last night about twelve-thirty I woke up convinced that someone was knocking softly on the door of the hermitage.

Last evening when Joe and John G. were leaving, I said jokingly, "Why not take me into Louisville with you?" But I was not really joking. I would certainly have gone if they had taken it seriously. But the whole thing was so futile, and so desperately silly. I know now that though I am drawn to this, it is not what I should do. I am no longer the unknown kid that can do things like that. I do have a responsibility. It is not just that I care about being found out here – and losing all the liberty and leeway I have in the her-mitage – but it is a question of a deeper responsibility. Vocation is more than just a matter of being in a certain place and wearing a certain kind of costume. There are too many people in the world who rely on the fact that I am serious about deepening an inner dimension of experience that they desire and that is closed to them. And it is not closed to me. This is a gift that has been given me not for myself but for everyone, even including M. I cannot let it be squandered and dissipated foolishly. It would be criminal to do so. In the end I would ruin her along with myself.

It is a cool brilliant morning. The birds sing. The valley is full of sunlit mist. The tall fiery day lilies are opening to the June sun. I know I am where I belong. The books and papers are on the table and work is waiting. I know the poets I must read (yesterday for the first time really got into Louis Zukofsky, who is certainly one of the great classic poets of our time. Great mastery and richness and structure).

I know I have to read, and understand, and think, and grasp, and experi-ence. And this is easy and delightful to me. I have a rich life, but built on the central cost of cruel deprivation. That cruelty burns into my heart at times like a brand. But I know that I am not in a position to choose another kind of richness: that of love and living with M. I can have her love in a deep and lasting, very fruitful form, as long as it is part of my solitude. If I try to take it on other terms, the wall will crumble. She has desperately refused to believe this, and has in her own silent and womanly way challenged me on it, and tried to force the issue. The issue cannot be forced.

There is a lovely doe in the woods behind the hermitage. At times dogs come and chase her. Yesterday I saw her and them: she leapt into the open without seeing me, looked around in distress, then bounded off into another thicket. The dogs came presently and I fired at them with the twenty-two (that has be-bes in the shells). Stung one of them good, and perhaps hit the other (but he was still in the bushes – I fired twice) and they went away. I felt it had been worth while. These were different dogs from the ones I stung up the other day. (The two black ones.)

Back to the question of M. "challenging" me. There is perhaps an undercurrent of implicit argument – or there was at one point, like June 11 – between us. As if she wanted to prove in some way that erotic love had to win over everything else, that it had to affirm its priority, its deeper reality. I do not question its natural priority, its deeper reality and all that – especially when it comes to a confrontation between authentic love as *experienced* and an abstract, formal concept of the vows. On the other hand, my vocation is not a formality that I can evade or set aside with a mental operation. On the contrary, it is built more deeply into my experience than anything else in the world, and I am now completely identified with it. To test it is to test my own identity. Yet secretly I am glad that she thinks there is something else in me besides the monk and the priest, although she knows I am a priest perhaps better than I do (I have always had trouble really believing it, but at the moment the argument has been closed for us by fate – or whatever you want to call it).

What is it that I have tried to evoke in her? I do not really know. I have no conscious project in that regard, and I never talk to her of spirituality, God and so on. It is her true self, her essential inner self that I seek, and it is this that has responded to me so beautifully. Yet at the same time I think her empirical and outer self has resisted this. She wants to stay on the comfortable plane of habit and anxiety that she is familiar with, and perhaps she feels that I am a threat to that. Actually, I think I was wrong to write all the long involved letters I wrote to her before we were stopped. I wrote too much about the wrong things, and these notes too will disturb her in many ways.

They are about the wrong things – for her. But they are the things that come to my mind, and so they cannot be completely irrelevant. There is still something here for both of us.

But I know that analyzing and rationalizing are of very little help. With me this can easily be a vice.

Erotic love and the sleep of nature: the contentment of the body. Being drawn back into the general satisfaction of all nature, of society: but it is also a trap: to be deluded with all the self-justifying illusions with which society surrounds itself by means of sex. Uses sex to justify its hold over everyone. But ironically enough it uses chastity in the same way (in religious life). Both eros and agape are invoked in favor of various slaveries. Hence the agony and unquiet life of the deprived and alone man, necessary to keep alive creative discontent.

There has to be a real fear by which one orients his life. What you fear is an indication of what you seek. Usually there is a double fear and a double seeking. You fear to seek the wrong thing: therefore what you fear, you also seek. You fear to lose the right thing. Therefore seeking the right implies a fear of loss. Right and wrong here are not defined in terms of external norms, but in terms of one's inmost need and calling. What do I fear most? Forgetting and ignorance of the inmost truth of my being. To forget who I am, to be lost in what I am not, to fail my own inner truth, to get carried away in what is not true to me, what is outside me, what imposes itself on me from the outside. But what is this? It can take manifold forms. I must fear and distrust them all. Yet I cannot help being to some extent influenced by what is outside me and hence I must accept that influence to some extent. But always in such a way that it increases my awareness, my remembrance, my understanding, instead of diminishing these.

Fear of ignorance in the sense of *avidya:* the ignorance that is based on the acceptance of an illusion about myself. The ignorance that comes from the decision to regard my ego as my full, complete, real self, and to *work to maintain* this illusion *against* the call of secret truth that rises up within me, that is evoked within me by others, by love, by vocation, by providence, by suffering, by God. The ignorance that hardens the shell, that makes the inner core of selfhood determined to resist the call of truth that would dissolve it. The ignorance that hardens in desire and willfulness, or in conformity, or in hate, or in various refusals of other people, various determinations to be "right at any price" (the Vietnam war is a clear example of the American people's insistence on refusing to see human truth). Fear of ignorance that comes from clinging to a stupid ideal. Fear of ignorance that comes from submersion in the body, in surrender to the need for comfort and consolation. Yet at the same time, one must not fear the possibility of relative lucidity in all these things, provided they are understood. There is a *little* lucidity in love, a little lucidity in alcohol, a little lucidity in religion, but there is also the danger of being engulfed more or less easily in all this. The great fear is then the fear of surrendering to sham lucidity and to the "one source" theory of lucidity – clinging to one kind of affirmation and excluding everything else – which means sinking back into ignorance and superstition. One of the worst sources of delusion is of course an exclusive attachment to supposed "logic" and to reason. Worse still when the logic and reason are centered on what claims to be a religious truth. This can be as deep a source of blindness as any in the world, sex included. One always has to distinguish and go beyond: one has to question reason in order to get to the deeper awareness of reality that is built into life itself. What I fear is living in such a way that life becomes opaque and one-sided, centered on one thing only, the illusion of the self. Everything else has to be defined in relation to this kind of ignorance. Once this is understood you can understand what makes me run – not only run in the sense of escape but run in the sense of tick. What runs and what ticks is, however, no longer important. What is important is that life itself should be lucid in "me" (whoever I am). I am nothing but the lucidity that is "in me." To be opaque and dense with opinion, with passion, with need, with hate, with power, is to be not there, to be absent, to non-exist. The labor of convincing myself that this non-existing is a real presence: this is the source of all falsity and suffering. This is hell on earth and hell in hell. This is the hell I have to keep out of. The price of keeping out of it is that the moment I give in to any of it, I feel the anguish of falsity. But to extinguish the feeling of anguish, in any way whatever short of straight lucidity, is to favor ignorance and non-existence. This is my central fear and it defines my task in life.

Wednesday Afternoon

It is hot. I have been uneasy and depressed, especially since after my Mass, when it seemed to me that my blunt and hasty letter of yesterday must have hurt M. unnecessarily (she must have received it at about that time). It was a carelessly written, almost thoughtless letter, done in a hurry in order to get something on paper to send her, and in the midst of worry about whether I could legitimately send it. In the end it was probably more of a shock than a consolation to her. It was intended to comfort her. To tell her that I love her. All it told her was that I was worried and mixed up and that it was very likely that we would never really be able to see each other again except perhaps for a brief moment – and that would perhaps only be to say good-bye. She has perhaps not realized this, though it has been plaguing me for the last week. It is simply awful to think that something so good, so rewarding, so helpful, has to "end" as far as its outward expression goes. And it is awful, too, to think of the risk that in trying to accept this we may hurt each other more. One thing is sure: that I will never stop loving her, and that our love in that sense cannot have an "end" even though we may not be able to meet, or to embrace or even to call on the phone, or exchange letters (except perhaps very rarely and surreptitiously). It is awful that it has to be like this, but once again it cannot change our hearts, or the love that is in them, if we do not let it.

Still, the whole thing has got me feeling miserable about everything. About myself, my life, everything. It seems to me that I have made a mess out of everything. I have not been either a good monk or a good lover. I have been nothing. I have tried to be things that were incompatible and have ended up only hurting her and leaving her sorrowful, confused, pained. In getting the pieces of my own life together, I have really done little that can help her: except I honestly feel that in being myself I can help her best. But what will she make out of all these notes, assuming I can give them to her somehow? Will they just make things worse? This is one of those wretched afternoons when everything seems wrong, in fact seems completely ruined. Part of this is due to the fact that I have not heard from her, have not been able to, and do not know what she feels or thinks (I am sure she loves me, but still it is nice to be *told* so) or what is going on in her heart. Yet this is going to be our usual condition from now on, for long periods. But I do think we are entitled at least to hear a little from each other from time to time, to exchange a few words at least, to say we have not forgotten each other.

All this shows, once again, that you cannot love without getting hurt. But if I start complaining about getting hurt, then does it mean that I regret loving? No. In the first place it does not worry me that I am hurt, but that I may be hurting her. And in the second place, we both know enough to anticipate that we would be badly mangled in this inevitable separation and we went toward it with our eyes open. The days we had together in May especially, and early June too, were the reward for taking that risk. They were

days of perfect love. Now we have to be mangled a bit. If we can only remember what that love meant, we can see that the fact that we are a bit torn
by this brutal separation need not mean too much. We can survive it and
our love is stronger than the hurt. It will continue, and will even grow, if we
only let it. But the trouble is that I am weak and insecure and let myself get
shaken: and then let her see that I am shaken, and this may perhaps unnerve
her and make her start blaming herself – as if there were anything to blame
herself for. We both went into all that we did with our eyes wide open. We
knew what it meant and what it might cost, and I think we have accepted it
realistically. But it still hurts, and we are still shaken, and confused, and in
pain. Poor darling, don't let me hurt you by my stupidity and uncertainty. I
do love you and will never stop loving you, and I believe in your love too.
The pain will change nothing, and we can stand it because in our hearts we
are not separated, we are suffering it together.

(Wednesday Evening)

Well, I did some work (preparing conferences) and then went out to empty
my mind and do a little Zen for a change and get limbered up. Got my
mind good and free (what mind?) when suddenly a couple of hawks came
along and did a little sharp ballet overhead, slicing here and there through
the quiet sky. It was very pretty. After that I was thinking of what some old
Zen joker said about "until you know the mind is no mind you do not understand it" and of course he is right: all the worried thoughts I have had
today are not "my mind" and the thinking that goes on when I am like that
is not "my mind." Whatever it is, it is not I. And then I realized how free
one can really be. All these worries and anxieties have nothing to do with
love either. I can bog down in them if I want to, but when I do I need not
kid myself that this is "love." On the contrary, love is quite free and unconditional. It loves without seeking to explain itself even to itself. It does not,
in other words, look for conditions under which it is reasonable to love, or
right to love, it simply loves. And that is how I really love M. I love her un-
conditionally, straight, and always will. Because I will not be looking for
conditions that will change it. True, externally we are hindered, but that
does nothing to the essence of a love which is unconditional, for I do not
say I will stop loving when I cannot see her or hold her close to me. I simply love. And all these worries about it are silly. Of course, there remain my
vows. They are certainly a condition. But external, and they too do not
need to affect the heart of my love for her. There is nothing in my vows

that says I cannot love her in my heart, for her own happiness and salvation in God.

June 23, 1966

What will I be without her? What will she be without me?

First of all, we cannot really be without each other any more. There is something completely permanent and irrevocable in our lives: the love that we have known in each other, that has changed us, that will remain with us in a hidden and transfigured – transfiguring – presence. "Derby Day is always beautiful." The beautiful "day" of our love, love's creation in our lives, will remain as the day in which we most deeply live and walk together. I will never be without the mysterious, transcendent presence of her essential self that began to speak to me so stirringly and so beautifully those early mornings in May between sleeping and waking. She will always be to me her soft voice speaking out of the depths of my own heart saying that the central reality of all is found in our love that no one can touch and no one can alter.

Hence no one can say that our love has nothing to do with the truth of our lives – as if it were something like an attack of flu or an unfortunate accident. That is the logic behind the prohibitions that have been inflicted on me. (I do not deny there is a certain logic in separating us, but why can't we sometimes write to each other, or talk to each other on the phone? If things were not so unreasonable here, we would have gone less far, for we would have been visiting nicely like everyone else within view of the gatehouse and talking properly like good children. It could have gone on a long time and no damage to anyone.)

I have needed this love, and being without it is something I cannot yet grasp – that is, being without the chance to see her at all. Frankly, if things were not what they were, I can see that it would be terribly right and important for me to change everything and live the rest of my life with her. From a certain point of view, that is what *should have* been. But that was impossible. Hence all the ambiguities that follow. To be without her is to be without the fulfillment of the deepest love I ever experienced. It is in a sense to be deprived of a central meaning in my life. It is to remain incomplete and to some extent maimed. But also I probably could not have coped fully with the problems that would have arisen from our social situation. Anyway, what is, is.

Being without her, on the other hand, puts me in a state of permanent trial, facing the question whether or not the whole religious life and all it implies is not a big illusion. Whether or not I have simply missed all the boats there were to miss. From a certain point of view it can be put this way: "You had your last chance to get with reality. You found what few people manage to find, someone made for you, for whom you were made. You should have had the courage to throw everything overboard and simply go and live with her. You should have gambled on love, and you would have won. As it is, you are stuck with a futile and absurd existence in which besides *knowing* your failure and your ambiguities, you will now spend the rest of your life manufacturing alibis." If that is true, then I am really up a creek. And if the temptation is to manufacture alibis, then I had better not start arguing about it, or I will manufacture alibis.

All I can say is that I don't honestly feel in my heart that I have either missed a boat or got on one. To me, frankly, the possibility of going and living with her – marriage being more or less impossible by Catholic standards – remained a pure abstraction, mere theory. It would be simply impossible for me in fact. It would destroy me completely. If I experience this so deeply, then it is at least a fact to be taken into account. (Alibi?) I experience it, and I feel guilt about it, as if I should have been above all contingencies: as if life expected me to somehow jump over all the barriers, sweep everything aside, etc. Well, I didn't.

In the quiet morning air I hear a woodpecker drumming on a tree. Once again the sun is rising on this misty valley. Is this right or wrong? The question turns out to be completely stupid. I hear a crow down the valley. A car passing on the road. Good or bad? I live a life that ought to train me not to ask such questions at all.

So too in love: I think it is the nature of love in our society today to raise a lot of irrelevant questions. As if from the moment one kissed someone there were ultimate problems to be solved: the whole question of life and death and the universe, heaven and hell, Christ and antichrist. It comes from the feeling that one risks his life in loving another. He puts his life in the scale with love. He sticks out his neck. This is true, but mostly on the level of social illusions. (An illusion is a fact after all, even though it remains an illusion.) The problems of love arise out of a certain popular mythology about love: the "they lived happily ever after" myth, or the more modern one about sexual fulfillment, etc. We can't help thinking in those terms, we are conditioned that way. In my own life such thinking is supremely misleading, because I have chosen a different way, a different dimension. You can't judge by five standards at once.

Hence for me a supposed choice between a religious ideal and an ideal of marriage is a mere mental game. I am caught in fact between two unsatisfactory legal conditions neither of which offers me any real fulfillment: and what I really have to do is the same thing I have always had to do: to find my own way, without a map, taking neither this nor that except in so far as I have to, and working it out as I go along. As I understand it, this means in fact living as an absurd kind of hermit when I am really not a hermit. Living as a writer when I am not sure I want to write any more, or *what* I want to write, living as someone who is identified as a typical monk when I have the most serious reservations about everything that is going on in the monastic life, etc. etc. What is this? It is only my usual condition. What is important is that, in this condition, I have been to some extent accepted, understood and truly loved by another person who lives in other contradictions, and who is capable of understanding what I go through. If we can continue to share this understanding, life will be easier and the way plainer for both of us.

The tyranny of diagnosis: the diagnostic compulsion which makes us think of everything in terms of cause and effect, *pathological* cause and effect. Not only do we always uselessly ask questions about good and bad, right and wrong, but we immediately look for the reason, the cause, the source of "what is wrong." Maybe there is nothing wrong. Maybe the guy is just trying to live and grow and to come to terms with his own inner truth. But we substitute an artificial, mythological norm for our own inner truth, and when it blocks our growth and happiness, we look for mythological reasons. We diagnose in terms of myth, to justify the myth at our own expense. Science, or society, has to be right. Or what we have told ourselves about ourselves has to be right. We depend on the myths we fabricate (with the help of others) and block our lives by resorting to them. To diagnose is to "decide" arbitrarily that such and such is wrong, and for such and such a reason. Once one has "decided" one conducts himself accordingly – in such a way as to make it plain that one decided right. Thus one destroys himself. And perhaps there was nothing whatever wrong, from the very beginning. (Note: "wrong" does not mean necessarily "morally wrong"; one can live by a rigid and doctrinaire myth of amorality and pseudo-psychology. There are even more compulsions in a society where ethics have become vague and indistinct. Compulsions that are more elementary, more crude, more haunting, more rooted in the body, more gripping, more destructive and above all more convincing. It is in terms of these compulsions that we diagnose everything.)

I hope I have not given the impression that I am always trying to find out "what is wrong" with myself – or with her. I don't think that really there is a great deal "wrong" with either of us. It is just that we are hurt and broken up inside and are trying to get ourselves together without getting a great deal of help from anyone, and often doing the job badly for ourselves. Inevitably, when one is lacking in wholeness he tries to pull himself together in such a way that he keeps himself broken (because he sees only a part of himself and thinks this is the whole. Trying to consolidate a part in itself, means breaking it off from the rest which one does not apprehend or realize in himself). We could have helped each other a great deal by the *realization* that our love had given us, of the wholeness of the other (not by any means the ability to diagnose and analyze). We could have brought about that wholeness by simply loving – though it is always possible that we could have used love to consolidate partial aspects of our own selves, and this would have been useless and destructive. Were we beginning to do this? I don't know. It is still possible for our love to fulfill something of this function: helping each other to be "whole" and "complete" in some way. But much more difficult without contact, without talking, without communication. Perhaps not really possible.

"Possible." "Not possible." Why do I keep struggling with these two ideas? The one thing that is not possible, for me, for both of us, is *turning back*. There is absolutely no going back to the old self, the old habits, the old anxieties. *There is no going back to the time when I did not love her.* All these other considerations are foolish. They seem to show that I hesitate on this point. As if there were some need to turn back, as if I had to turn back, and had to find some way of making it livable for myself. This is out of the question. I cannot turn back and even if I tried I could not live with it. There is only one way to go and that is forward, even though I have no notion where it will go and who it will involve. Everybody else says "turn back," as if there were some norm in the past that I had to recover. That is what is impossible, there is no "back to normal." The normal is now, on the way to the unthinkable. To what I cannot know because it has not even begun to develop. I beg God that it may develop in us both together and that we may somehow share it, and that it will be only one thing: love.

(Thursday Evening)

It has been a hot afternoon. Stuffy, stupefying. I have forced myself to get some letters out at least: letters to De Martino (authority on Zen asking me to write for Suzuki's new magazine – or revived magazine), to a Benedictine Prior in the Congo, to a French girl who was writing to me for direction when she was at Mount Holyoke and has now gone back to France (a friend of Daniélou's) and so on. Had to force myself to write the letters. Everything has been going into letters to M. or poems, or things like this journal. Doesn't matter. But there are other people in the world too. Then said the office of St. John the Baptist with joy, though God knows if he would recognize me as anything but a sinner needing the whip. Went down for supper, raided the kitchen for peanuts and potato chips and then discovered that I had some chips left over from Ascension day (our marvelous picnic in the woods). I have a few cans of beer so since it is a hot night . . .

I have been rereading these pages. Badly written, incoherent, but there is still something there. Or perhaps I only think that because I am feeling mellow and uncritical. Anyway, I think I have said what was going on in me, but not all, and not the deepest. Just the worried, self-searching part of it. I suppose I have been trying to find myself again without her, to recognize myself as entirely and unequivocally solitary. Not an easy job.

So I go and get another beer. The supply is already running out. I only had five cans. It is a hot night. Where will I be when the dark falls and the dragons come and there is no more beer?

Darling, at this point I could easily get garrulous. A kind of shame prevents me. I don't want the beer to do all the talking. You know, always with us it has been someone else doing a great deal of the talking. I mean we have not talked much at all. Perhaps we ought to have said more. But yet our love said everything. Or did it? In a way it did, and yet you can't trust affection to tell the whole story. It would have been good if we could also have just sat around and *talked*. Yet it was so wonderful to hold you, and I knew it would not last. Each time might be the last time. Yet that put a wrong perspective on it, or at least a distorted one.

Why can that beast Raymond have all these people coming out to see him every day? And not I? It comes of this crazy racket of being a hermit. There are people in the house who are hoping to be hermits one day (wait till they find out) and they have all their hopes pinned on me. There is a "hermit movement" (God help us) in the monastic orders and I am supposed to be a shining example. Here I am crazy mad with love and sitting around the hermitage drinking beer like a damn fool. (Running out though.) Thus I have to be a model, I am a pilot project. If they want to go on the rocks, just let them follow me.

This is silly. I don't mean it that way.

It has been a long time since I just sat and drank beer. Years in fact. It takes me back to the time when . . . (Oh God, there we go again) . . . I was a kid on Long Island and so on.

There is no point wasting time and paper on that kind of stuff. It seems to me very likely, dear, that if we had got married you would have found yourself hooked to an alcoholic ex-priest. That would have been very unpleasant. It is better if I continue to be a bit exalted. If I live in woods and seek stimulation from Sufism or something. More entertaining and less destructive. And doesn't do any harm to other people.

The fact that I have not discarded the last page is positive proof of my heroic trust in you. That is absolutely the worst writing I have ever done in my life: as bad as the song I wrote. (Why?) There is no question that there is a flaw a mile wide in me somewhere. But there is no point in a prolonged self-examination on that point now.

They have now got an irrigation pump going on the other side of my place, nearer and louder. This is going to be an interesting night.

I can now see with absolute clarity how easy it would be, living alone, to become a completely non-existent thing, a non-person. All you need to do is take yourself seriously. And try to exist. *Will* it. Get God to back you up in your insane project.

Why do I live alone? I don't know. The whole question of my love for M. has got me backed up to the wall on this particular choice. As if there were a choice. Actually there is not even a choice, really. I have to lead this absurd existence. In some mysterious way I am condemned to it. Not as to something wonderful and mysterious, but as though to a vice. I cannot have enough of the hours of silence when nothing happens. When the clouds go by. When the trees say nothing. When the birds sing. I am completely addicted to the realization that just being there is enough, and to add something else is to mess it all up. It would be so much more wonderful to be all tied up in someone, to work for someone, to come home and love her, to have a child, and I know inexorably that this is not for me. It is a kind of life from which I am absolutely excluded. I can't desire it. I can only desire this absurd business of trees that say nothing, of birds that sing, of a field in which nothing ever happens (except perhaps that a fox comes and plays, or a deer passes by). This is crazy. It is lamentable. I am flawed, I am nuts. I can't help it. Here I am, now, sweated up, in a misty foul summer evening when all is loused up to the neck, happy as a coot. The whole business of saying I am flawed is a lie. I am happy. I cannot explain it. I cannot justify it by pretending I am guilty. I love you darling, I love you in this mad life that I lead. I miss you, I wish I could see you, I wish I could hold you and love you, but I cannot be tied to any living being. I just cannot be tied. And I cannot let myself be tied. I am a wild animal, and I know you know it, and I know you don't mind. I know in fact that you love me for it, and that it is the deepest thing you love in me. And I am happy about it, even though you may not be able fully to admit it to yourself. You are in love with a fox, or a deer, or a squirrel. Freedom, darling. That is what the woods mean to me. I am free, free, a wild being, and that is all that I ever can really be. I am dedicated to it, addicted to it, sworn to it, and sold to it. It is the freedom in me that loves you. If only you were wild in the woods with me. If only we were never trapped in any way. But we cannot be free and wild together, because I am afraid of it. I am afraid I would be held and imprisoned. Darling if only you lived in the woods near me, and I could come and seek you out when I liked, and when I was not compelled, and when there were no demands, and when we were like little kids. When we did not know what we were doing. As soon as I know what is happening, I am lost. I am no longer free.

Darling, I am telling you: this life in the woods is IT. It is the only way. It is the way everybody has lost. They have all lost their way and ended up in Coney Island, with the distorting mirrors and the clowns with cattle prods that sting them up the tail and make them run to their shame. Here from morning to night nobody tells me what to do, nobody tells me what to think, nobody tells me what to eat. If I want to I can starve to death. I can die of the nonsense. I can go crazy with illusions, and who cares? There are no laws in the woods except you have to watch what the hell you do when you are around hornets and things like that. It is life, this thing in the woods. I do not claim it is real. All I say is that it is the life that has chosen itself for me.

(June 24, 1966 – Friday)
The night did not turn out to be as hot as I feared. I slept more or less (began waking up around one). Dreamt a series of dreams that were more or less about the community. For instance: I am at the hermitage and down in the valley are some people (monks) who are trying to signal to me by semaphore, wig-wagging and whatnot. I do not know how to read the message. I make helpless gestures about not knowing "the rules." I really don't care that much, I just want to show I would like to be in communication

with them if it were possible. Later I dream of the Abbot and Fr. Flavian (my confessor), we are walking around more or less friendly and open to each other, talking pleasantly about the hermit life and its possibilities.

Got up, and during my meditation (having killed an enormous centipede on the wall of the front room – would not like that to crawl down my neck while I was sleeping) thought about the letter from Urs Von Balthasar yesterday. His complaint of being theologically isolated from the people in fashion ([Karl] Rahner, [Hans] Küng, etc.). Realized to what extent my own theology goes along with that of Balthasar, and I should read him more deeply. (I now have his *Herrlichkeit [The Glory of the Lord]* in French, so I can handle it.) He has been very friendly, is writing a preface to the German selection of my poems, is happy about Bro. A.'s translation of his article on vows etc.

Looking back at the pages of this journal I wrote last night: curious the way I hit that bump in page 26 [Thursday evening]. A real crash. I wonder what happened. For a moment all spontaneity was impossible. Self-conscious, tongue tied, paralyzed, and trying to break out of it with a diagnosis (well, I am diagnosing now but it is different). I don't know what the matter was, but the way I feel about it now is that I was starting to tell lies. The lies begin after I mention "that beast Raymond" – who in fact has all the visitors he wants apparently, though I know he has a bad time with mail too. It is not a lie that I am regarded as sort of "pilot project" in monastic eremitism. But that whole concept is to me phony and absurd. Was I buying it for a moment? I don't know. It is nevertheless a fact that people *think* in those terms, and this has to be taken into account. I think where I was lying was when I pretended to be guilty about a) being in love and b) drinking beer. Actually I do not really feel guilty about either, deep down. I know that neither of these fits anyone's standard idea of what a hermit ought to be, and if I take such an idea seriously I am bound to feel confused, guilty, embarrassed, whatnot. But I don't think that in loving or in drinking beer I am at all untrue to myself and to what God wills for me – except in details. Because I can see too that I don't *need* for instance to drink beer, or five cans of beer at one sitting, while being here. I am really not all that lonely. I am certainly not unhappy. I do not have to drink to be happy. I think probably what I was really doing was slipping back into an act I had given up long ago, "when I was a kid on Long Island," playing a very old role that was so phony that even I could detect it.

The real wrong is playing these roles and taking them seriously. I do not think I take any role too seriously, but still, one has to play roles in order to communicate with the rest of the world. The beauty of the solitary life (this business of trees that say nothing and skies that are neutral) is that you can throw away all the masks and forget them until you return among people.

The mask I was putting on at that moment was the very old, worn out, dilapidated one of my Columbia days: I am the guy who finds his happiness in drinking and in love. But I am not. I have never been able to convince myself that either of these *produced* happiness. They just go along with it. When they do, they are fine. As soon as you try to use them to produce happiness, to make yourself happy, it becomes a lie and the whole thing breaks down. Maybe that is what I was doing. I don't know.

Since the thing that is most important to me is the deepening and the exploration of consciousness, then obviously if I catch myself lying about *that* I will be deeply embarrassed. Perhaps that was part of the bump too. Pretending that sitting here drinking beer was actually a sort of enrichment of an unhappy solitude. Nuts. Or, conversely, that it was a reverse enrichment by dilapidation: the modern poet pitch, the deepest experience is that of going to the dogs. It would be ridiculous to pretend that I am going to the dogs, or on the rocks, or whatever else. It would take more than five cans of beer, at any rate. When I take the beer cans to the dump this morning I will also take the following masks: the monastic failure; the *poète maudit*; the ex-priest alcoholic driven to drink by M.; the loner misunderstood by everyone; and I might as well add the wild faun bit while I am at it.

So I went out on that mission and have returned. It was a beautiful walk. Seven o'clock. Sun high, but yet not high enough to overtop the tall, majestic trees of the wood at the top of the long field. Mist everywhere: it is going to be hot and foul today. Wet grass. I walk thinking of you, darling, and with you (you are just going to work). With that simple presence of you that has become a living part of my own psyche, and is such a precious gift to me. The thing is that we did not play any part, we did not wear any mask – except perhaps the very unconscious ones that went with our deepest compulsions. But on the whole we were very clean and straight with each other, and that was one of the most wonderful things about it. It was what made it possible for us to be present to each other in that direct and deep psychic presence. I hope we will never lose this. We know each other well, and we love each other as we know each other, without conditions and without pretenses: and there is nothing better on the face of the earth. Perhaps things would have got too complex for us to handle in this simple way. I don't know. There is no point in surmising. But at the point where we are now, we can go on forever with the love that is ours and I don't think we will ever be able to go wrong with it or destroy it. It will remain a real force in our lives. I am so happy about that. In this sense, your love has really made me happier and I count on it to continue doing so. I also want my love to always make you happy in this way, or to enable you to bring forth out of yourself the happiness that is in you, in your essential self: there is a great spring of happiness and joy there, dear, and I hope it will always be available to you and to those you love with a true love.

(Later)

In the last analysis what I am looking for in solitude is not happiness or fulfillment but salvation. Not "my own" salvation, but the salvation of everybody. And here is where the game gets serious. I have used the word "revolt" in connection with solitude. Revolt against what? Against a notion of salvation that gets people lost. A notion of a salvation that is entirely legal and extrinsic and can be achieved no matter how false, no matter how shriveled and fruitless one's inner life really is. This is the worst ambiguity: the impression that one can be grossly unfaithful to life, to experience, to love, to other people, to one's own deepest self, and yet be "saved" by an act of stubborn conformity, by the will to be correct. In the end, this seems to me to be fatally like the very act by which one is lost: the determination to be "right" at all costs, by dint of hardening one's core around an arbitrary choice of a fixed position. To close in on one's central wrongness with the refusal to admit that it might be wrong. That is one of the reasons why solitude is a dangerous thing: one may use it for that purpose. I don't think I can. I am not that stubborn. I am here for one thing: to be open, to be not "closed in" on any one choice to the exclusion of all others: to be open to God's will and freedom, to His love which comes to save me from all in myself that resists Him and says no to Him. This I must do not to justify myself, not to be right, not to be good, but because the whole world of lost people needs this opening by which salvation can get into it through me.

I have been talking up a good fight about solitude, but the fact remains that I do not know how on earth I am going to live without ever seeing you, talking to you, being with you, loving you warmly and directly, pressing you to myself and kissing you. It will have to be, but I do not know how it is going to be, or how I am going to stand it: you too, I know. I suppose a lot of the abstract thinking in these pages has just been a ruse to quiet my anguish about this: when I stop thinking, the naked anguish comes back to the surface. Then I think, once again, maybe I was wrong, maybe I ought to have made some more drastic choice . . . Yet I do not believe, cannot believe such a thing either. But I want you to know how I really feel. Do not think that because I keep saying I can make it in solitude and even be happy, because I know it is what I am supposed to do, that I am not lonely for you. I am terribly lonely, in a deep anguish of loneliness and desolation without you. I need your love and your presence as I need light and air. How can I live without all that? Yet I have to, and you have to. God alone can give us the strength to do it.

(Friday Evening)

Since it is a feast day (St. John Baptist) I went for a walk in the afternoon. It was like walking in a furnace. I tried several places, and most of them were airless, burned, baked dry. Finally I ended up again at the place where we had the picnic Derby Day: it was relatively cool and all quiet, empty, lonely, with nothing going on at all except a wood thrush singing perfectly in the tall trees. Somehow I feel at peace in that place, and closer to you, and closer to myself, without too many cares.

On the way back, thinking about the last lines I must write on these pages before I come to town tomorrow, I wondered if there were some things I had to say. For instance, that though I will always love you, I want you to know you are free as far as my love is concerned. I do not want to hold you or possess you for myself. I cannot demand that your heart belong only to me. I know you will always have a special love for me, but though you have told me not to say this, I will say it anyway because I have to: I cannot possibly consider you committed in any way solely to me. That would really be an injustice and an absurdity. I want only your happiness and if that happiness means marrying and loving another, it is just what I want for you. Only one thing I ask: that all our life we consider each other most faithful, most loving and most special friends, united by a deep and unique bond that was made by God rather than by ourselves. It is on this level that I will always love you, always think of you, always want to know how you are and how things are going with you, always be ready to help you if I can and if they will let me. I do hope we will never drift apart even though our communication may be rare and unpredictable. I don't say I want to get sick or have operations all the time, but I certainly hope God will bring me once again into a hospital where you are. And perhaps in the future the superiors will ease up a bit and let me see you and receive letters from you again. I hope so. It would only be fair. Don't lets get out of touch if we can help it.

And now for my own part, I do have to get down to my job of solitude. Though when you look at it too close it gets confusing, and there are no real blueprints for it. Still I have a feeling that I should measure up more to the traditional demands. God knows, I am *solitary* enough. Who knows what it means to be so utterly alone before God with decisions and choices that no one else agrees with or approves of, yet which conscience dictates. That is a much more frightening desert than one of rocks and sand where one is living an "approved" monastic life. But there is no use my talking about it. Even you do not agree with me on this, I guess. Nobody quite does. I have to find my own way, and it really is *lonely*. I can imagine how much more so it will be now, without you. But since it is what I have chosen and since it is the way in which I know I must travel, I don't ask anyone to pity me or feel sorry for me. I don't feel sorry for myself. I just hope I can make it safely without too much folly. God will help. Pray for me darling. Your prayers will keep you with me.

It is usually a joy to finish a book. I am not able to finish this one and am not going to. Anyway, who says this is the end of it? I don't. And if I make a point of "finishing" this – which does not need to be finished – it will look too much like good-bye. I don't want it even to look like that. I do not even want to think of that. Let us just say that our friendship and or love have gone into a new phase . . .

I find myself back at the beginning. It is exactly three months since the operation. (Tomorrow is the 25th and the operation was on the 25th of March.) I will never forget that morning of March 31st. I will never forget that Wednesday in Holy Week, that rainy night when you came in before going to Chicago, and when we were too tongue tied to say what we almost knew. And the night after that when I lay awake and realized that I loved you. And that Good Friday when I decided to leave a note for you to write to me. (How glad I am that I did that.) And your first letter, with its "opening." And my letter, impulsive and "intense" that began everything. How glad I am that all these things took place. How glad I am that they led to such wonderful days together. Such beautiful letters from you. And all the phone calls that finally got me in trouble, as I expected. What about the future? Who knows? But I cling to one hope: that future morning in heaven which the morning of March 31st "prefigured." That is the beautiful day I live for. The rest is nothing but time to pass until the real morning comes. I am not patient. I don't expect you will be either. Meanwhile, we have to both make it there. That is the important thing. And by the mercy of God we will.

Between now and then I will obey my nurse as best I can. I have got some barrels of fresh water here (there has been no rain, and this water is actually *clean*). The hermitage is relatively sanitary. I killed a wasp in the bedroom and sprayed it all with a bug bomb.

And I washed my feet good, and cut my toenails – straight.

Some Personal Notes

January 1966–March 1966

Beauty and necessity (for me) of solitary life—apparent in the sparks of truth, small, recurring flashes of a reality that is *beyond doubt*, momentarily appearing, leading me further on my way. . . . They lead further and further in that direction that has been shown me, and to which I am called.

March 6, 1966

[*Editor's Note:* Merton wrote on the right page of this small spiral notebook, occasionally adding quotations or notes on the opposite page. These quotations and notes are indented below and precede the entries they may elaborate.]

    7 words:[1] Death
                 Theology
                 Divine
                 World
                 Ethics
                 Purity
                 War

Work. January 1966.[2]
    /   Text for Gethsemani picture book. [checked off and crossed out]
        "Descent" for *Der Xt in der Welt [The Christian in the World].*
               for *Katallagete* [checked off and crossed out]
        Directory for Cardenal.
        Monastic Spirituality for Hermits [checked off and crossed out]
        Monchanin [checked off and crossed out]
        Eremitism for *Mon[astic] Studies*
        7 words for N. O'Gorman by May 1 [circled]
        Preface for Cardenal [checked off and crossed out]
   (?) Conscience, Church and World
               for C[atholic] P[eace] Fellowship

---

[1] List of topics for "Seven Words." Two essays, "Purity" and "Death," were published in *Prophetic Voices: Ideas and Words on Revolution,* edited by Ned O'Gorman (New York: Random House, 1969). Merton's reflections on all seven words are published in *Love and Living,* edited by Naomi Burton Stone and Brother Patrick Hart (New York: Farrar, Straus & Giroux, 1979).

[2] This "to do" list is marked in several ways – some items are crossed out, some are marked with a slash in the left margin, still others are checked off on the left. Finally the whole list is crossed off.

Revise Peace and Protest for *Continuum*. [checked off and
  crossed out]
Notes on Rilke (summer perhaps)
Preface for [John C. H.] Wu.
/ Preface for [William] Johnston.
(Notes on Myst[icism] – Eck[hart] for R.B.S.
/ Franciscan Eremitism for *Cord*
/ Pref[ace] Jap[anese] Trans[lation] of *Thoughts in Sol[itude]*
  [checked off]
/ Christianity and Humanism – for *Journal do Brasil*
  by August 1.
  (send July 15.)

A retreat is a kind of "cramp" in time – a paralysis induced by arbitrary
and sterile reflection, a concentration on "yes" and "no" without motive,
but with greater deliberation and insistence. An act of force! Not this.

Perhaps the real function of a retreat is to help one *appreciate time differently* – by removing routine, but not seeking to replace it with some
other special set of experiences.

i.e. not trying to experience oneself as making a "very good use of time"
– that is by eliminating certain contradictions, or a *feeling* of contradiction, of being contradicted, of contradicting oneself.

Artificiality of retreat – special "awareness" of time created. The beginning – the middle days – the final day – and "what we are doing." This is
a help in so far as it creates tension (then relaxation). But tension for
what? Merely for relaxation?

Retreat begins today January 18.
I do not have to go to conferences etc.
Hope to read more, reflect more, do no writing, certainly not letters
anyway!
Perhaps change afternoon schedule – take a couple of afternoons off in
the forest.
Perhaps reflect on some Spanish-American material – Nishida – Isaac of
Stella – Desert Fathers (already too much, *or* and not *and*).

Time is measured by the awareness of something else, not just by a supposed "self-awareness of (the self in) time." Time is *quality* not *quantity*.

Time in the affluent society: the instant is when one is real, realized by a pleasure, by a "taking possession." (Neurotics become upset by this instant, and if they can't possess themselves by "taking possession" – if it no longer means "reality" – they panic. For they see the void.) Art of living – art of moving from pleasure to pleasure, from intense moment to intense moment (dexterously using the *gaps* in between to keep the right momentum).

Is time-consciousness the product of our self-awareness *at work*? (Nishida). We take stock of ourselves as "formed" and "forming," as "makers," as changing our environment and ourselves. Our time sense is related to our *work* and where we are in it.

Value of retreat – realizing how much one "escapes" from "time" by activity. How much our work can be simply a desperate expedience for reassuring ourselves that we are "using time" well; "giving a good account" of ourselves etc. "Value" (?) of time is not in time but in clarity of thought: the moments when we see through time and everything else, and see our way "*through*" everything. Time is valuable only for the moments that cut across and through it vertically.

Yet these moments must not be sought and exploited only to reinforce a sense of absolute validity in our own ego-self. (For then they are not authentic.) They are to be moments of obedience to Him who wills to love in us (not separate from us but identified with us).

This means regarding poetry as more essentially my *work* (instead of an accidental pastime) in working. Poetry – includes Journal and poetic prose – records of poetic (creative) instants.

Modern man becomes aware of himself as "timed" and so working. To increase his self-awareness he systematizes his work – and complicates it too and multiplies activities which can be timed. His infinite ways of watching himself in movement (Slow motion movies, tape-recorder, etc.).

Yesterday p.m. (January 19) realized importance of a definite relationship of response to my Latin American friends, poets etc. Whether I ever go to Solentiname[3] is accidental.

---

[3] The community in Nicaragua established by Ernesto Cardenal.

1. Answer letters. – Answer more letters *in Spanish*.
2. Read the books that are sent. Read many of them entirely, cover to cover.
3. Read important articles.
4. Use the dictionary for precision – don't just get the general drift of the more universal language. (Yesterday – in good poems of Enrique Sanchez.)

To really know Latin American lit[erature] – poetry, history etc. in reparation for the incomprehension, one-sidedness of U.S. relations with L.A. I do know something of it – not nearly enough.

5. Purity of motives. (esp[ecially] as concerns imagination).

Another conviction: great importance of poetry in my life now. My "attention" must be total on the level of meditation, but also must be free for poetic awareness outside time of meditation: that is, less *preaching*, less editorializing.

Note *where* God revealed Himself and *when*.

After man had been a million years on earth or more.

After millennia of relatively peaceful, agricultural existence, village existence.

After the growth of the big valley cultures and the beginning of cities.

Where empires began to face each other in competition to dominate their "world" (Assyria – Babylonia – Egypt – Persia).

At the point where the clashing empires would often meet.

At the time of their clashing.

The word of God came to the people of Israel who were conscious of being drawn *out of* Ur and *out of* Egypt, speaking to them in terms of wars and cataclysms that were really not their affair, in which they were not to be actively involved . . .

Saying that it was the time of the end, the time of reckoning, conclusions.

God reveals Himself in the middle of conflict and contradiction – and we want to find Him *outside* all contradiction.

Too suspicious of poetry all along because of the narcissistic, romantic image of the poet having "special experiences" –

Translating can be helpful here I guess. Not simply trying to respond more fully to life etc. (which is good) but also technically deepening awareness of the capacity of words, speech, "idioma" to be real (Octavio Paz). This not only in English but in French, German and Spanish. Particularly Spanish.

(January 20)

"The world where innumerable individuals, negating each other, are united, is one simple world which, negating itself, expresses itself in innumerable ways," Nishida *[The Unity of Opposites]*. Importance of contradiction: the contradiction *essential* to my existence is the expression of the world's present: it is my contribution to the whole. My contradiction and my conflict are my part in the whole. They are my "place." It is in my insight and acceptance that the world creates itself anew in and through my liberty – I permit God to act in and through me, making His world (in which we are all judged and redeemed). I am thrown into contradiction: to realize it is mercy, to accept it is love, to help others do the same is compassion. All this seems like nothing, but it is creation. The contradiction is precisely that we cannot "be creative" in some other way we would prefer (in which there would be no contradiction).

Here N[ishida] is talking only of our historical self in the world of action – history ("from the formed to the forming").

    not – our physical being

        biological self. (no creative freedom, no action – intuition).

    "The individual is individual only in so far as it participates in the forming of the world." *191*

    "*Intuition separated from action is either a merely abstract idea, or mere illusion.*" *208*

    But the acceptance means also *work*.

    (Poiesis – artistic creative intuition)

"Our true self is there where our consciousness negates and unites [the singular acts]." *Nishida*

Yet the consciousness is *not* the whole self or the true self. The point is that the True Self neither is the conscious "I" nor is it the "not-I." But it is not elsewhere than the "I" (which would make it "not-I"). The true self is, acts, is expressed in the meeting of "I" and "not-I." But the "I" seeks to be the True Self by being, acting, expressing itself where there is no "not-I."

Yet where there is no "not-I," there is no "I" for the "I" is aware of itself by negation as well as by position.

Frank acceptance of negation (nothingness out of which I am "created" – so that I "am" nothing in so far as I am only "I").

I need the "not-I." I need to *reject* the "not-I" in order to have distance from it, to "be."

I need to eliminate this distance, in view of fruitful polarity.

This polarity is a work entrusted to me, which in many ways seems fruitless and irrelevant.

Hence I try to dispense with it altogether – but this means pure nothingness and is impossible (i.e. a nothingness "outside" and utterly "apart from" any reality).

It is the "nothing" in my being that must be accepted.

The acceptance – in God's love – becomes pure creativity, insight, etc.

"action"

Obviously a duty of charity to help with the *Collectanea*, to give the weekly conferences asked of me in the community – but this is not really "work" and can be done in stride.

Mail – I can give preference to Latin American mail where possible, though more difficult.

Professio te eremitam devotio faciet evangelistam. [Your profession will make you a hermit, and your devotion, a spreader of the Gospel.]

– *Peter [the] Ven[erable] to Gilbert.* PL *189. 98.*

What was said about L.A. poets, poetry, etc. above was *too active*, too busy. Certainly I will maintain friendly contacts and do some reading, keep informed. This human side of my life is important.

A hermit is essentially a man who has renounced an earthly future and plans – projects. Even Solentiname is no plan of mine and I think seldom and little of it.

January 29

Useless to simply substitute the "experience" of oneself as hermit for the "experience" of oneself as active, as a "monk," as a "writer" etc. The same error is repeated in a new way. In reality the hermit life does imply a certain attrition of one's identity. In context a word that implies "loss of" identity. This must also be resisted, one does not live alone in order to become a vegetable. Yet the resistance does not take the form of asserting a social and evident identity of one who is going somewhere or doing something special. A curious kind of identity, then: "In God."

Note – the letter of Eshleman chiding me for identifying with the Latin Americans and too lightly dismissing U.S. poets, while right in its context (my loose statement in *Harper's*), does not alter the fact that I am identified with the Latin Americans more than with the U.S. poets. Certainly I am not clear enough about the motives myself.

Distraction – from the illusory expectation of some fulfillment, which in the end is only a human loneliness.

> *Warst du nicht immer*
> *noch* von Erwartung zerstreut, *als kündigte alles*
> *[eine] Geliebte dir an?*
> [Were you not forever
> *distracted by expectation*, as if everything were announcing
> to you some (coming) beloved?]

Distracted that is from the solemn *Auftrag* – [a commission entrusted to one by another] the [indecipherable] suddenly "giving itself" etc.

Rilke (1st [Duino] Elegy)

Merely living alone, but continuing to engage in a lot of projects, is not yet an authentic hermit life. The projects must go. – Solitude demands an emptiness, an aimlessness, a going nowhere, a certain "having nothing to do," especially nothing that involves the growth and assertion of one's "image" and one's "career."

This writer really must die down a bit. I am aghast at the things I have left to do. *Must* take care not to get more commitments – except the really unavoidable ones! This has to be a *real retirement*, everything depends on it. The spontaneous writing that arises out of such freedom is eminently desirable. Not "slower" projects – the bricks without straw kind – (except really essential services).

February 3

A basic conviction grows more and more clear to me. That I am called into solitude by God's will in order to be *healed* and purified. That there are deep wounds in me which would cause me despair if I saw them all at once – but I see them gradually and retrospectively. (I see a danger when I have somehow been taken past it by the mercy of God, and what a danger it was!) Hence I cannot play with this vocation. I must gradually learn to hear and obey Him directly in everything.

There is an immense amount of nonsense in me, but He is wise and tolerates it for the time being. I must trust Him, and trust more perfectly, more completely, more wholly as I go on. The useless and the false preoccupations will gradually be liquidated by His action in my life.

February 4

To be healed of mendacious activity – the lying acts by which, in homage to an imaginary self (self-idol) man manipulates and falsifies reality. Depth and significance of this activity characteristically human, and fallen, "creative" yes and in some ways also demonic (*dai*-monic), Faustian. Ambivalence of this activity. The sickness of it in fact. Analyzing, "knowing," retreating further and further into the abstract – and the conviction, arrogant, brutal conviction that this *has to be* the "real" – resulting in conflict, barbarity, the awesome fact of this struggle. It comes clear to me in this silence, at dawn. The substitution of mechanical images for the creative silence of God, of the Logos . . . The hard impulsion to "do this" (in order to set up the idol over and over again).

Let the idol fall on its face in the presence of the hidden Child. (Yeah, but beware!!)

Acceptance of the "*Auftrag*" in sense of R[ilke]'s 1st Elegy – the central thing.

And of course, critically important, is the question of the purity of my own faith – my willingness to risk compromises perhaps with other doctrines? This must be faced. But I can say here I have no hesitation in firmly desiring and intending to *be a Catholic* and to hold with all my heart to the true faith of the living God manifested in Christ and in his Church. And no monkeying! Amen. Whatever I seek in other traditions is only the truth of Christ expressed in other terms, rejecting all that is *really* contrary to His Truth. (Not what is irresponsibly and hastily *said* to *be* contrary to it.)

Today I realized very clearly what I am doing with Rilke and why, though I see so many flaws in him – and such greatness too – I must go on with this study. It is my own case that is under judgment. Specifically, the possibility of the same flaw in my own solitude. I can confidently face it, I think, because I see solitude is for me, anyways, flaw or no flaw. And indeed it is given me precisely to *see* this flaw and take care of it as a Christian and as a monk – not with a beautiful and clever aesthetic confabulation. (Yet *is* R.'s answer a confabulation? Is it not much more authentic, though flawed with error?) Anyway, it is a central problem for me and for this age and I might as well cope with it as best I can, without illusions and without pretense – in other words humbly, doggedly, patiently, faithfully. This too is *Auftrag*.

Septuagesima Sunday
February 6

Have been living completely in the hermitage about 6 months – this corresponds to the slight crisis that I noticed many novices would get after about that length of time. A corner is to be turned and my vocation must develop. That is – proper of *conversatio* – penance – true conversion of my entire life. Not easy!! Plenty of opportunities to make mistakes and misjudgments.

Whole purpose of the solitary life is really "*Nepsis*" [sobriety], alertness, awakeness, attention. All the *ascesis* of the life centers on this – or is a waste of time. What do I know of it? Real "awakenness" is rare, yet thank God there are in each day three or four fairly long moments of it, sometimes extending over an hour. In the community I was lucky to have a minute of such "attention" here and there. Exercises simply moved it under.

February 12

Tired as a result of the long cold spell, rather intense study and writing under pressure to finish the article for *Katallagete* – very aware of my incompetence to say what needs to be said, not knowing where to begin. I ended with an ambiguous sort of letter that took great labor and much rewriting and I am still not at all satisfied, but there is no point in fooling with it any more.

It has brought me close to a nervous crisis – tension yesterday, and last night, interrupted sleep, nightmares, etc. All to the good. I have to sweat it all out and try to find my way forward. Perhaps I can keep Lent free of writing and see how that works (except purely monastic notes, under no pressure, for E.C. [Ernesto Cardenal].

Real need for the *quies [contemplationis]* [quietude or inner repose] of the solitary life. By my anxiety to keep going, I am perpetuating useless movement, action and tension. I can see there is a real fear in me of stopping altogether – fear of vanishing, of *really* facing my own nothingness! To be realistic, I know that writing has been a help to do this, up to a point. Sooner or later I must do without it – but I can see I cannot get to that all at once. It has to be gradual.

Qui autem cellulam perpetuus incolit, ad stabilitatis praeconium de toto corpore linguam facit. [Whoever dwells in his cell for life makes of his whole body one tongue to proclaim the praise of stability.]

St. P.[eter] Damian. Opusc[ulum] XV. c 28.

In my own case this is complicated by the fact that I have caused literally thousands of people to have, for me, the illusory expectations I have of myself: expectation of something to be *manifested* in and through me – a deep new truth of some sort, a fundamental hope, a solution. Even though I know enough to tell myself that I will never find "a Solution," yet secretly my nature insists on this project!

Mary ever Virgin, Mother of God our Savior, I entrust myself entirely to your loving intercession and care because you are my Mother and I am your dear child, full of trouble, conflict, error, confusion and prone to sin. Because my whole life must change and because I can do nothing to change it by my own power, I entrust it with all my needs and cares to you. Present me with pure hands to your Divine Son, pray that I may gladly accept all that is needed to strip me of myself and become His true disciple, forgetting myself and loving His Kingdom, His truth and all He came to save by His Holy Cross, Amen.

(Intention of my Mass today, February 12. Saturday)

February 15

Solitary life and struggle with illusion: not with objectified exterior devils but with the devils which are illusions about self.

Pattern of thought – *the expectation of something happening:* basically, an habitual attitude of mind is an orientation toward "something good happening to me, in me, as a result of my disposing my life in view of such a happening." In monastic life – "attaining" to an experience of fulfillment, union, etc. By ascetic and other preparations. To illumination. To possession of the truth. To be fixated in this pattern means that when it is not simply and rapidly brought into effect, one becomes anxious and the "pattern" works itself out in illusory and unpleasant ways.

These are a *good.* They show how, and to what extent, the pattern itself is illusory, arbitrary, even self-willed.

True theological hope must be substituted for this arbitrary pattern of achievement and expectation. But this hope is a *deep mystery* – and it goes with self-forgetfulness and love of others (not wanting a special fulfillment for oneself and giving to others what one can here and now, without demanding that it be a "rewarding experience").

Si vous avez le sentiment de l'espérance à vous reservée, vous serez délivrés de toutes les passions dommageables et vous mettrez dans vos âmes l'image de l'amour des hommes. [If you have a sense of the hope in store for you, you will be delivered from all hurtful passions and you will put in your souls the image of (God's) love for man.]

Jean le Solitaire (5–6 cent[ury]), Dialogue on Love and Passions

Ash Wednesday. February 23.

From the *Paradise of the Fathers* –

Fasting is the subjugation of the body

Prayer is converse with God

Vigil is a war against Satan

abstinence is the being weaned from meats

humility is the state of the first man

kneeling is the inclining of the body before the Judge

tears are the remembrance of sins

nakedness is our captivity which is caused by the transgression of the command

and service is constant supplication to and praise of God II. 548. p. 263.

Il y a dans la lectio divina une grâce quasi-sacramentelle. Comme l'Eucharistie, comme la prière, comme la solitude et le silence, comme les divers renoncements inscrits dans la tradition apostolique; elle transforme insensiblement l'être tout entier et le divinise progressivement, amenant peu à peu l'ermite à l'état parfait de fils de Dieu, faisant passer et grandir en lui la vie de l'Esprit. [Lectio divina possesses a kind of sacramental grace. Like the Eucharist, like prayer, like solitude and silence, like the various renunciations prescribed by apostolic tradition, *lectio* imperceptibly transforms one's whole being and divinizes it progressively, little by little bringing the hermit to the perfect state of being a son of God, making the life of the Spirit enter into him and grow within him.] *Dom J[acques] Winandy*

It is not for me to be disturbed particularly by *some* of the developments in the community. I know by now that, for various reasons, there is *nothing* I can do directly to affect anything that happens there. Yet how strange that I am still required to give a weekly conference (in which as much as possible I avoid anything directly concerned with new policies etc.). My aim in these conferences is simply to try, with those who come (attendance is entirely spontaneous) to "seek wisdom" in various ways not usually explored.

My part in the renewal of religious life is simply to be in my cell or in my woods, seeking in silence to follow where the Spirit leads, into depth, purification, humility, hope. And to have less and less to say about it.

The writing of letters is simply a torment. All I can do about that is to make sure that those I write *are required* by the needs of the situation or the person. And not fear to let the others go. It is the division and uncertainty that increases the anxiety connected with them.

Dom J.'s letters from Rome (February 66), no matter what anyone says, there is certainly a trend to centralization – the "unity of the community" is being used by him consciously or otherwise as simply a means to get everybody in choir under strict obligation – under the abbot's eye. He admits theoretically the principle of "diversity in unity" but one can see his mind. The (former) brothers who stay out of choir are, in his eyes and those of the other American abbots, to be regarded and treated as an extinct species, and the old ones will be tolerated while they are dying out. No sense of the real meaning of the relative freedom of the brothers' vocation – quasi-eremitical in its original spirit.

Yet nevertheless – a different matter – importance of a true *sensus ecclesiae* [sense of the Church]. *Respect* for preoccupations and for the needs they express – without taking them obsessively. Still less imagining that they are in some sense "saving events," matters of life and death. They are simply occasions for *decision:* many decisions remain possible including the decision to be wide open – rather than the decision to be "in fashion."
"La verité de la foi n'est pas solidaire des contextes idéologiques qui la présentent et peut-être la favorisent sur le moment." ["The truth of faith is not a part and parcel of the ideological contexts that convey it and perhaps even foster it for the moment."] *[M. D.] Chenu*

The "spiritual preoccupations" of this time – post-conciliar years. (An imaginary era we have thought up for ourselves – *divertissement* [diversion]!) I need perhaps to be *less* preoccupied with them, to show that one can be *free* of them and go one's own way in peace. But there is inculcated such a *fear* of being out of everything, out of touch, left behind . . . This fear is a form of tyranny, a *law* – and one is faced with a choice between this law and true grace, hidden, paradoxical, but free.

An unformulated "preoccupation" of our time – the conviction that it is precisely in these (collective) *preoccupations* that the Holy Spirit is at work. To be "preoccupied with the current preoccupations" is then the best – if not the only – way to be open to the Spirit.
Hence one must know what everybody is saying, read what everybody is reading, keep up with everything or be left behind by the Holy Spirit. Is this a perversion of the idea of the Church – a distortion of perspective due to the Church's situation in the world of mass-communications? I wonder if this anxiety to keep up is not in fact an obstacle to the H[oly] Spirit!

February 24

Excipientes verbum in tribulatione multa cum gaudio Spiritus Sancti . . . [Welcoming the word among many trials with the joy of the Holy Spirit . . .] *I Thess. 1:6*

At the same time I have realized in a moment of bitter conflict that the whole thing is *not* simple, as I owe it to God to preserve a certain personal integrity and inner freedom which *precludes* masochistic submission. And there are human motives in his [Dom James's] actions which are to be taken into account, though they are not decisive. Hence, genuine obedience and *not* subservience to false ideas and principles especially in regard to writing.

Historical point – ordination of monks to priesthood became very common in 11th–12th centuries precisely in view of hermit life. Priest-hermit considered his Mass primarily as the perfect means of uniting his sacrifice – passion with the Passion of Christ.

February 26

Evening. February 24. Thurs[day] after Ash Wed[nesday]
Si consurrexistis cum Xto . . . [If you have risen with Christ . . .]
Before one can rise with Christ, one must die with Him. My central problem comes back to this: my passionate resistance against being "put to death" in a way I do not like and do not understand – a way that seems to me brutal and irrational.

No question that certain policies of my Abbot in my regard amount to an execution and a putting to death of myself as a public figure and as any kind of influence in the Order by personal presence and contact. (i.e. I am sure there will never be any question of my being one of the *periti* [experts] to be summoned to help G[eneral] Chapters or Abbots' Committee meetings in Europe or even America. I know I am wanted by some others and Dom J. will never permit it.) This is precisely what I must accept. Not that I really want to go, and if it were up to me, I would probably refuse anyway. If I thought I *could*. But this business of simply *having no choice* . . . not even being spoken to (as he did not even discuss the question of the meeting of the editorial board of the *Collectanea*). The question of being put to death morally is real. I see aspects of his motives which he probably does not see. I do not agree with a sado-masochistic spirituality. I think he is simply *wrong* and even in some sense perverse. Yet I have to accept all this without evasion and without retaliation. Only the Grace of Christ can help me!

They are to me a source of strength by their goodness and simplicity, also I am sure by their prayers.

The community

There is little use in my thinking of my own conflicts and burdens and trying to reason them out. I do not consciously try to analyze and understand everything that goes on in myself, but try to accept the conflict and bear with it intelligently, ready to give up anything I am in myself that is an obstacle to humility and truth. However, more and more I think of the burdens and conflicts of monks down in the community – young monks I know well because I had them as novices or students.

I can see that there is a fruitful and happy obligation on my part to love them here [in the hermitage] and pray for them, and to share their burdens in solitude (*alter alterius* [*onera portate*. Bear one another's burdens] . . . the capitulum of Sext.), to believe that I can be for them a source of healing and strength by prayer. Not to waste time with my own conflicts but to bring others help in theirs. Also to pray for any I may have offended or scandalized, and not merely worry about whether or not they were hurt by something I said or did.

(February 28)

After the abandonment of the Norway foundation Dom J. may be likely to try a hermitage for several – or a group of hermits in other words – in Edelin's Valley. In so far as this would imply a community, organization etc., I would be against it. Better individual hermits depending directly on the main community.

March 1

Why not do real *theological* work in the afternoons, especially this Lent, now that there is less pressure to finally finish off the things I had unwisely promised to write? Real work of theological reflection and construction?

Once again – there is no question that *all* my conflicts and problems can be traced in the end to lack of faith. That is also to say that they are all intended as means of purifying my faith by driving me to it as to the last and unique resort. Solitude makes this particularly clear. I must live in and by *THE* Truth, not merely by this or that truth, this or that "explanation," this or that ideal, or system. Hence importance of the Bible and the Eucharist above all!

March 2

At least a flash of sanity: the momentary realization that there is *no need* to come to certain conclusions about persons, events, conflicts, trends, even trends toward evil and disaster, as if from day to day and even from moment to moment I had to know and *declare* (at least to myself): This is so and so, this is good, this is bad; we are heading for a "new era" or we are heading for destruction. What do such judgments mean? Little or nothing. Things are as they are, in an immense whole of which I am a part, and which I cannot pretend to grasp. To say I grasp it is immediately to put myself in a false position, as if I were "outside" it. Whereas to be *in* it is to seek truth in my own life and action, by moving where movement is possible and keeping still when movement is unnecessary, realizing that things will continue to define themselves and that the judgments and mercies of God will clarify themselves – and will be more clear to me if I am silent and attentive, obedient to His will, rather than constantly formulating statements in this age which is *smothered* in language, in meaningless and inconclusive debate, and in which, in the last analysis, nobody listens to anything except what agrees with his own prejudices.

End of February – Marie Tadié started acting up again. Even though it has been arranged that she deal directly with publishers or w[ith] abbot, she is still trying to get through to me and bombard me with her interminable complaints and accusations. The best solution is to take her as a further reason for cutting down on publication – at least of books etc. that require to be translated in Europe. Rather – continue writing in freedom and peace, without a view to immediate publication

 – discreet dissemination of work

 – publication in magazines and out of the way places, perhaps limited editions

 – an *infrequent* full-length book for Doubleday. *One in five years* would be plenty!!

against the καρδία σκληρά [hardened heart]

 – to have τὸν ἔλεγχον ἐν τῇ καρδία.

 Μνήσθητι ὅτι δεῖ σε τῷ θεῷ ἀπαντῆσαι. . .

 καὶ τί θέλω ἐγὼ μετὰ ἄνθρωπον;

 [– to have disgrace in the heart.

 Remember that you must meet God . . .

 and what do I want with humankind?]

Not popular, but exactly right for me!
Fear of man and fear of God cannot coexist in one heart!

"The wise follow the path of non-assertion and teach without words."

Lao Tzu.

March 6

Beauty and *necessity* (for me) of solitary life – apparent in the sparks of truth, small, recurring flashes of a reality that is *beyond doubt*, momentarily appearing, leading me further on my way. Things that need no explanation and perhaps have none, but which say: "Here! This way!" And with final authority!

It is for them that I will be held responsible. Nothing but immense gratitude! They cancel out all my mistakes, weaknesses, evasions, falsifications.

They lead further and further in that direction that has been shown me, and to which I am called.

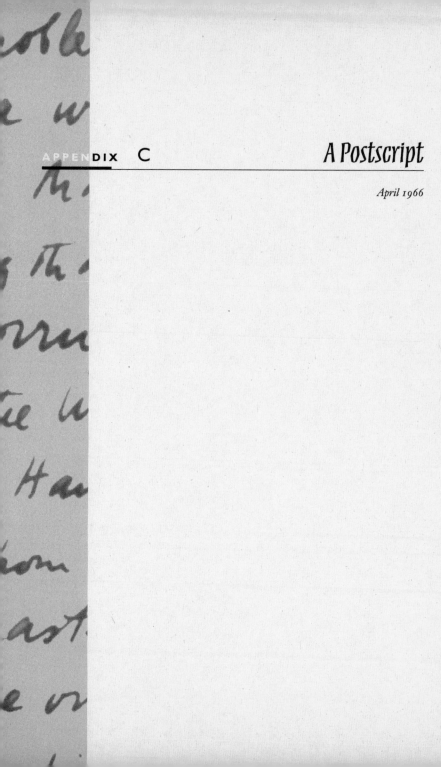

A Postscript

April 1966

The work of writing can be for me, or very close to, the simple job of *being*: by creative reflection and awareness to help life itself live in me, to give its *esse* an existant, or to find place, rather, in *esse* by action, intelligence and love. For to write is love: it is to inquire and to praise, or to confess, or to appeal. This testimony of love remains necessary. Not to reassure myself that I am ("I write therefore I am"), but simply to pay my debt to life, to the world, to other men. To speak out with an open heart and say what seems to me to have meaning. The bad writing I have done has all been authoritarian, the declaration of musts, and the announcement of punishments. Bad because it implies a lack of love, good insofar as there may yet have been some love in it. The best stuff has been more straight confession and witness.

April 14, 1966 [1]

[1] This note appears in Notebook CI, 1966 March–April–May–June–July (The George Arents Research Library, Syracuse University, Syracuse, New York).

Index